Approaches to Teaching Teresa of Ávila and the Spanish Mystics

Approaches to Teaching World Literature

Joseph Gibaldi, series editor

For a complete listing of titles,
see the last pages of this book.

Approaches to Teaching Teresa of Ávila and the Spanish Mystics

Edited by

Alison Weber

The Modern Language Association of America
New York   2009

MLA and the MODERN LANGUAGE ASSOCIATION are trademarks
owned by the Modern Language Association of America.
For information about obtaining permission to reprint material from
MLA book publications, send your request by mail (see address below),
e-mail (permissions@mla.org), or fax (646 458-0030).

Library of Congress Cataloging-in-Publication Data

Approaches to teaching Teresa of Avila and the Spanish mystics /
edited by Alison Weber.
p. cm. — (Approaches to teaching world literature)
Includes bibliographical references and index.
ISBN 978-1-60329-022-7 (alk. paper)
ISBN 978-1-60329-023-4 (pbk. : alk. paper)
1. Teresa, of Avila, Saint, 1515–1582—Study and teaching.
2. Religious literature, Spanish—Study and teaching.
3. Mysticism in literature—Study and teaching.
I. Weber, Alison, 1947–
PQ6437.T3Z55 2009
860.9'424822—dc22   2009002117

Approaches to Teaching World Literature 109
ISSN 1059-1133

Cover illustration of the paperback edition: *Teresa of Avila's Vision of a Dove*. Peter Paul Rubens,
c. 1614. Oil on panel. © Fitzwilliam Museum, University of Cambridge,
United Kingdom / The Bridgeman Art Library.

Published by The Modern Language Association of America
26 Broadway, New York, New York 10004-1789
www.mla.org

CONTENTS

PREFACE TO THE SERIES

In *The Art of Teaching* Gilbert Highet wrote, "Bad teaching wastes a great deal of effort, and spoils many lives which might have been full of energy and happiness." All too many teachers have failed in their work, Highet argued, simply "because they have not thought about it." We hope that the Approaches to Teaching World Literature series, sponsored by the Modern Language Association's Publications Committee, will not only improve the craft—as well as the art—of teaching but also encourage serious and continuing discussion of the aims and methods of teaching literature.

The principal objective of the series is to collect within each volume different points of view on teaching a specific literary work, a literary tradition, or a writer widely taught at the undergraduate level. The preparation of each volume begins with a wide-ranging survey of instructors, thus enabling us to include in the volume the philosophies and approaches, thoughts and methods of scores of experienced teachers. The result is a sourcebook of material, information, and ideas on teaching the subject of the volume to undergraduates.

The series is intended to serve nonspecialists as well as specialists, inexperienced as well as experienced teachers, graduate students who wish to learn effective ways of teaching as well as senior professors who wish to compare their own approaches with the approaches of colleagues in other schools. Of course, no volume in the series can ever substitute for erudition, intelligence, creativity, and sensitivity in teaching. We hope merely that each book will point readers in useful directions; at most each will offer only a first step in the long journey to successful teaching.

Joseph Gibaldi
Series Editor

ACKNOWLEDGMENTS

In the course of preparing this work, I have been fortunate to receive support from many quarters. My thanks go first to Joseph Gibaldi, who proposed a volume on the Spanish mystics for the Approaches to Teaching series and who enthusiastically supported the project until his retirement as general editor of the series in 2007. Carole Slade offered wise counsel, and Margaret Greer and Laura Bass shared their valuable experience as editors of *Approaches to Teaching Early Modern Spanish Drama*. For meticulous and cheerful editorial assistance during their summer vacations from college, I am grateful to my multilingual godchildren, Nicolás Pellón and Sofía Pellón. The fathers of the Order of Carmelites and the Order of Discalced Carmelites generously opened their libraries to me in Washington, DC, and in Rome. Patricia O'Callaghan, the libararian of the Carmelitana Collection, was a gracious host and bibliographic guide during my visits to Whitefriars Hall in Washington, DC. My profound thanks also go to the contributors, whose creativity and commitment to teaching are truly admirable.

Introduction

First, a Note on Names

The daughter born to Alonso Sánchez de Cepeda and Beatriz de Ahumada in 1515 was known throughout her childhood and early adulthood as Teresa de Ahumada. It is understandable that she should have adopted her mother's surname. Before her birth her paternal grandfather and father, suspected of secret Judaizing, had been penanced by the Inquisition. At the age of forty-seven, as an act of humility consonant with her ideals of monastic reform, Teresa de Ahumada took Teresa de Jesús as her name in religion. Today in the English-speaking world she is better known as Saint Teresa of Ávila, although she also appears as Teresa of Jesus in some scholarly writing. Similarly, Teresa's collaborator in the Discalced Carmelite Reform, baptized as Juan de Yepes in 1542, took the name of Juan de la Cruz when he joined Teresa's cause in 1568. English speakers know him as Saint John of the Cross. Hispanists, even when writing in English, often prefer the abbreviated forms Santa Teresa and San Juan. With an eye to an English-speaking readership, however, I have asked contributors to use the anglicized form of their names at first reference for Teresa of Ávila, John of the Cross, and Ignatius of Loyola. Scholars, whether secular or religious, often omit the honorific "saint" and refer to these canonized saints—without any disrespect—by their first names. We follow this practice in this volume. To insist on anglicized names throughout, however, would have given jarring results. It is unusual to see the brilliant Augustinian poet and biblical scholar referred to as Friar Louis of León; in this collection he bears the name Luis de León (as he does in the catalog of the Library of Congress), and, following a long-standing tradition among Hispanists, he will also be referred to in brief as Fray Luis. Since lesser-known figures from this period most often appear in scholarly literature under their Spanish names, we follow this practice; hence, María de San José rather than Mary of Saint Joseph and Ana de Jesús rather than Anne of Jesus. For this volume, the honorific "saint" is reserved for contexts in which the postmortem reputation for sanctity is relevant.

Why the Mystics?

The works of the two most famous Spanish mystics and saints, Teresa of Ávila (1515–82) and John of the Cross (1542–91), might well never have been published. In 1575, the Spanish Inquisition collected all manuscripts of the Carmelite nun's spiritual autobiography, which had been denounced for containing heretical errors. Although the inquisitorial censor found no evidence of heresy, he recommended that the work be kept in secret archives in perpetuity, on the grounds that it was not fitting for a woman to presume to teach religious doctrine. Accusations of heresy continued even after Teresa's works were published in 1588. Like Teresa, John of the Cross did not dare publish his poems and mystical treatises during his life. His works first appeared in print in 1618, twenty-seven years after his death. In 1622, copies of this edition were found among the papers of Alumbrados (Illuminists) imprisoned by the Inquisition in Seville. As a consequence, one inquisitor energetically campaigned to have the work banned, alleging that it contained fifty heretical errors. The Inquisition failed to take action, but lingering suspicions regarding John's orthodoxy held up the movement for his beatification for fifty-three more years.

Just a few years ago, most students would probably have been perplexed about why these accounts of intimate religious experience elicited such passions. But in a post–9/11 world, it is acutely evident that religious beliefs and experiences can have far-reaching consequences: they can liberate or subjugate individuals, stimulate or constrain creative expression, inspire altruism or provoke horrendous acts of cruelty, and bind societies together or tear them apart. The life and works of the Spanish mystics provide a fruitful starting point for exploring religion's potential as a liberating or repressive force, and they have much to reveal about the negotiations necessary to marshal religion's power as a dissident discourse. Although it is not necessary to appeal to contemporary world events to justify teaching the works of extraordinarily powerful writers like Teresa, John, Luis de Léon, and others, as teachers we recognize that teaching with an eye to the present is not necessarily a bad thing. Reading authors from an earlier age requires patience and concentration, and our students may be more willing to expend this mental energy if they suspect that the past holds some insights into the enigmas of the present. If current circumstances cannot let us forget that we live in a world rent by seemingly incompatible religious beliefs, this is surely a propitious moment for engaging students in a dialogue with personalities and ideas that, not long ago, might have seemed arcane, archaic, or simply bizarre.

Teaching across the Disciplines

Responses to the MLA survey conducted in 2004 suggest that many instructors have already begun to take advantage of what our profession refers to as a teachable moment. As one instructor wrote:

> In the past, my students had become dismissive of religious themes and were especially uninterested in theological issues, preferring texts addressing physical drives and presenting social satire, such as *Celestina* and *Lazarillo de Tormes*. For a time I dropped mysticism from the syllabus, restoring it about ten years ago when I sensed a renewal of interest. In recent years, John of the Cross is again regularly the favorite of some stu-

dents and the least favorite of none. His works are chosen frequently for research papers.

It is not surprising that most respondents were teachers of Spanish, since Teresa of Ávila, John of the Cross, and Luis de León have long been considered canonical authors of the Spanish Golden Age. However, the survey revealed that the Spanish mystics form a challenging part of the curriculum in a variety of disciplines; they are taught in world literature and Western civilization courses, in specialized courses on early modern Spain, in courses on autobiography and on the history of women in the West, and in art history and religious studies departments. Responses also indicated a growing interest in lesser-known religious figures and in themes of spiritual crisis and conversion in secular writers.

The principal themes and issues that arise when teaching the Spanish mystics vary considerably, as might be expected, from one discipline to another. Instructors in introductory literature classes tend to focus on close stylistic analyses of mystical poetry. "La noche oscura" ("The Dark Night"), by John of the Cross, was often mentioned as an ideal text for introducing the concepts of symbol, allegory, and paradox and for illustrating poetic techniques such as alliteration, internal rhyme, oxymoron, and chiasmus. Instructors in advanced undergraduate courses were more likely to place the mystics in a broader literary context, tracing the lines of contact between the mystics' language and other traditions of lyrical poetry, such as the cancionero poetry of the late Middle Ages and the Petrarchan lyric of the early Renaissance. At this level, greater attention is paid as well to the sociohistorical context; instructors have found it important to draw attention to the precarious position of mystics—especially those who were conversos (converts to Christianity and their descendants)—during a time of religious schism and ethnic suspicion. Many expressed the opinion that students must understand the uncertain status of the mystics in their society in order to appreciate their rhetorical strategies and their tendency to express themselves through paradox and indirection.

Given the difficulties Teresa's unconventional language often presents, it is initially surprising to discover that Teresa is taught in an intermediate-level language course. One instructor described how she has incorporated selected passages from Teresa into a conversation course in a community college. Teresa's determination in the face of opposition, this respondent observed, is a powerful model for students who have experienced difficulty in identifying and pursuing their goals.

Although the canonical mystics continue to retain a secure position in the syllabi of traditional literary surveys, they are also taught in Spanish culture and civilization classes. The survey indicates that some departments have chosen to replace or supplement the civilization requirement—traditionally a panorama of masterpieces of art, music, and architecture—with courses focused on social and cultural history. In these courses, the mystics provide the opportunity to explore how and why Spain rejected its multicultural heritage in the fifteenth and sixteenth centuries. Here, the mystics are studied not only as poets but also as religious reformers, dissidents, and ambivalent symbols of national identity.

Another development in Spanish departments is the incorporation of courses on Spanish women writers into the curriculum. In decades past Teresa of Ávila might have been the only woman writer students encountered in medieval and Golden Age courses. Today, her works are taught in the context of her literary foremothers—late medieval and early Renaissance female mystics—and of her literary daughters, religious and secular. Some courses take a transatlantic perspective: Teresa of Ávila is read alongside Sor Juana Inés de la Cruz, for example. In each case, responses reflect a desire to teach Teresa not as an anomaly but as part of a continuous literary and cultural tradition.

Issues

Whether the texts of female mystics are taught in courses focusing on women's writing, in culture and civilization courses, or in history courses, respondents reported that these texts invite investigation into the interrelation of power, gender, and authority. Since women's spiritual autobiographies were written (at least ostensibly) at the command of their male confessors, these life narratives are, to a great extent, conditioned by the expectations of their addressees. While reading these mandated autobiographies, students can be asked to ponder the extent and limits of women's freedom to speak with their own voice. For historians, especially those teaching women's history courses, Teresa's texts provide the occasion for discussing the constitution of the early modern family; notions of honor, gender roles, female reading and literacy; and the changing politico-religious climate in sixteenth-century Spain.

Instructors from several disciplines commented on the importance of discussing the mystics' representations of the body. One response deserves to be quoted at length:

> If students don't understand the boldness of these writings, it is easy for them to be turned off by what they perceive as their conventional religious content and their commitment to a spirituality bound to Catholic doctrine. I think . . . it is important to emphasize how daring they are, how radical the formulations they achieve are, in the representation of the body and sexuality. . . . Students need to understand that the mystics were anything but naïve where the role of the body in their spiritual experience is concerned. This is a crucial stumbling block, since many students associate intense religious devotion—especially if it is Catholic devotion—with the denial of the body.

Others prefer to address this topic in a larger chronological and geographic framework. One instructor recommended teaching the sixteenth-century Spanish mystics in conjunction with medieval mystics (such as Catherine of Siena and Angela of Foligno) and mystics from the seventeenth and eighteenth century (such as María de San José, a nun from New Spain, or María de Ágreda, a nun who acted as a spiritual adviser to King Philip IV) in order to appreciate the continuities and changes in attitudes toward penitential practices, charismatic powers, and notions of holiness. Another respondent observed:

> As a historian, I believe it is very important to read Saint Teresa in the context of lesser mystics, who are perhaps more representative of the culture of female spirituality in early modern Spain than their more famous sisters. . . . It is also crucial to bring in a comparative study between Spain and other Catholic countries.

Several respondents reported that they found it stimulating to teach "successful mystics" (those who were eventually beatified or canonized) in comparison with "failed mystics" (those who were punished as heretics or who simply faded from history). Although students may not come up with a definitive answer to the question of why some mystics fail to become saints while others succeed, framing the question in this way prompts them to think about a variety of topics: the influence of canonized models on subject formation and the impact of class, gender, location, and individual skills of persuasion on the historical perception of holiness.

Pedagogical Challenges

When asked about the difficulties they have encountered in teaching the mystics, Spanish instructors commented on students' frustration over reading texts written in premodern Spanish. Although sixteenth-century Spanish is closer to modern Spanish than Shakespearean English is to contemporary usage, there are still significant lexical and syntactic differences. If the poetry of John of the Cross challenges students with unfamiliar vocabulary, Teresa's unconventional, digressing syntax constitutes an even more serious stumbling block. Ways of coping with these difficulties include leading close readings in class, using colored markers to tease out the different lines of argument, providing students with heavily annotated passages and glossaries, and in general limiting the reading assignments to a manageable length. Once the linguistic barriers are lowered, students can respond to "the freshness of Teresa's voice" and "the simple elegance of San Juan's verse."

Instructors across the disciplines reported that the greatest difficulty is presented by the students' lack of historical and religious background. "Some of my students have never heard of the Protestant Reformation, let alone the Catholic Counter-Reformation," wrote one professor. A teacher from a small Catholic women's college was surprised to find that "Catholic women do not seem to have encountered a history of women in their church." Another instructor similarly bemoaned that "even those who claim to be militant Christians are often ignorant of the biblical intertexts or the theological problems associated with them." American students also have a very different experience of the role of religion in public life than did people in early modern Europe, as the following response explains:

> I find it is very difficult for students in the United States, where religious affiliation is a matter of family background and personal choice, to understand what it means for an entire society to see its collective identity and historical destiny bound up with a specific religious tradition. Even for Catholic students the role of the church in early modern Spain is something altogether different from what they have experienced. The pervasiveness of religion in early modern Spain needs to be explained to them and clearly differentiated from what we today might perceive as "fanaticism."

The survey asked if instructors found that the religious affiliation of their students presented any particular pedagogical challenges. No one described overt hostility to the material, although some respondents reported initial wariness or confusion. One instructor wrote:

> In the overwhelmingly Protestant South religious affiliation does present a challenge. Students can't figure out why Teresa doesn't simply realize she has been forgiven for her sins. Why does Teresa pray to the Virgin Mary or Saint Joseph when she could be praying directly to God? How does becoming a nun and praying for people all the time really help people? Why all this suffering?

A professor who teaches at a university with a strong (non-Catholic) religious affiliation observed, "The most difficult part is that most students have never thought that sexual vocabulary and imagery have anything to do with representing the divine." And a teacher from a Catholic college remarked:

> Students have expressed shock when they find out that the "love" poems or narratives that they are reading are not the expression of profane love but the mystics' declaration of their spiritual union with God. At first some students reject this intimacy and view it as sacrilege. After a discussion that explores the conventions of human love that are used to present sacred matters, they become engaged.

A number of respondents expressed the need to establish ground rules for frank but respectful discussions. The following statement is representative:

> I believe that above all else students need to understand the worldview of the author they are reading. In order to achieve this, it is useful to begin

with an uncensored discussion of the range of reactions students have to the material.

Some teachers prefer to shift the focus from the religious content to aesthetic or historical issues: "[I explain that] we are not studying these texts to believe or not believe in them, but to understand the aesthetic paradigm that informed the authors." Another reported:

> The challenge I've faced is that my students want to read these texts only as religious texts. Since many of our undergraduates are quite religious, they often want to share their own conversion stories. I try to work with this interest, since it ultimately motivates them to read the texts, while drawing their attention to linguistic and sociohistorical issues.

Classroom Activities and Evaluation

The survey revealed that instructors use a wide variety of classroom activities in addition to lecturing. Oral presentations and weekly journal assignments proved to be very popular. Although some Spanish teachers discourage students from consulting English versions of their readings, others have incorporated translation exercises successfully into their classroom activities: "Rather than curse translators as traitors, I invite my students to try to do better themselves." Comparing different translations of the same poem was also described as a fruitful exercise.

Instructors also noted that many teachers take advantage of electronic mailing lists and class Web sites to supplement classroom discussion. Programs such as *Blackboard* allow students to post reactions or questions on a single site and read and respond to one another before and after class. One respondent has students e-mail her an initial response to each reading:

> As we move through our discussions, I read to the class samples of their initial ideas (anonymously) and spend some time letting the class critique or correct these initial ideas. This exercise has proved to be very successful and has allowed the class to react critically, and many times humorously, to some of their earlier erroneous ideas.

Instructors were less enthusiastic about using the Internet in place of print materials. As one respondent put it:

> It can be frustrating to direct students to Web sites that are available one moment and then suddenly are inaccessible. You always have to check that a Web site is still functional just before you ask the students to consult it.

However, one respondent encouraged eager students to use sites such as *Biblioteca Virtual Miguel de Cervantes* or Fred Jehle's *Antología de poesía española* (http://users.ipfw.edu/jehle/poesia.html) to read more works by the authors studied in class. The ability to search texts electronically also allows students easily to create a glossary of key terms or to brainstorm for paper topics.

Technological advances have made it more convenient, however, for instructors to supplement texts with art, music, and film. For example, one teacher shows clips from *Sister Act* (in which Whoopie Goldberg, disguised as a nun, adds religious lyrics to a familiar Motown song) to explain the continuing interaction of profane and sacred love poetry. Screening scenes from biographic films was also recommended as an effective way to familiarize students with an unfamiliar historical and religious context.

Instructors of courses at all levels recounted success in incorporating images into their lectures and discussions. One wrote:

> I have used El Greco's paintings, especially the ones that illustrate scenes from Revelations, to complement the writings of the mystics. The eccentricity of his representation system is immediately apparent to the eye, and it sensitizes students to the extraordinary meanings that are made to attach to rather ordinary kinds of imagery in the mystics' writings.

Another instructor shows students paintings by El Greco, Diego Rivera, Bartolomé Esteban Murillo, and Diego Rodríguez de Silva Velázquez to convey the nature of early modern piety. Not surprisingly, Gian Lorenzo Bernini's famous statue of Saint Teresa in ecstasy figures prominently in the list of visual sources. It is often discussed in conjunction with Teresa's description of the transverberation and Jacques Lacan's interpretation of it. Another writes that Bernini's statue invites a discussion on the characteristics of the baroque from an art historical as well as a literary perspective. A historian introduces her lectures on Teresa by showing Teresa's portrait, painted by Juan de la Miseria, photographs of Ávila, and maps of Teresa's journeys as she made her foundations. Finally, some instructors use religious iconography to explore the cultural construction of sainthood.

Answers to a question on methods of evaluation indicate a similar mix of traditional and innovative techniques. In addition to short reaction papers, research papers, midterms, and comprehensive finals, instructors reported more novel assignments such as asking students to compose a love poem and explain it "a lo divino" ("as a religious allegory"), to create a visual representation (such as a drawing or painting, a sculpture, collage, video, or performance) based on a particular text, or to write a final exam for a hypothetical undergraduate course on the same topic.

The problems most often noted in teaching the Spanish mystics—students' lack of familiarity with the linguistic, historical, and religious history of early modern Spain—are obviously related. The teachers who participated in the survey, as we have seen, have tried to overcome these lacunae by placing the Spanish mystics in the context of Catholic theology, by tracing the traditions of mystical language, and by explaining the special circumstances of mystics in Counter-Reformation Spain. Yet mastering and synthesizing these materials for students is enormously time consuming. As one respondent remarked, "I have spent countless hours preparing reading guides." When faced with voluminous bibliographies on these topics, teachers approaching the mystics for the first time may find it difficult to know where to begin.

Part 1 of this volume, "Materials," is designed to help teachers select readings and use their preparation time efficiently. "The Instructor's Library" offers suggestions on editions and translations, reference resources, historical and critical studies, and philosophical and theological responses to the Spanish mystics. My aim has been to select works in English or Spanish that, for the most part, will be accessible to nonspecialists. Works that are especially well suited for undergraduates are noted as well. The essay by Amanda Powell discusses the qualities of various translations of Teresa of Ávila; she reminds teachers that selecting an appropriate translation will depend on the purpose of their course and their sense of audience. Emily E. Scida's contribution will give teachers a keener appreciation of Teresa's idiolect; it describes the most salient archaic features of Old Spanish that Teresa retained in her writing and explains the differences between sixteenth-century and contemporary Spanish.

Part 2, "Approaches," begins with "Historical Perspectives," which is similarly designed to offer teachers a survey of the scholarship on the historical context of the mystics and guidance for further readings. Elizabeth Rhodes describes how orthodox Spanish mysticism emerged from the matrix of political and religious unification at the end of the fifteenth century. Her essay will help instructors appreciate why some mystics were considered subversive and others became powerful national symbols of Spain's religious identity. William Childers traces the controversies over whether Sufi mysticism exerted significant influence on the Spanish mystics. Whether or not the striking parallels between the language and symbols of Islamic and Christian mystics can be traced to direct, conscious influence, Childers suggests that they may well point to a greater degree of cultural interaction during the final crisis of Hispano Arabic culture than previously imagined.

It is often remarked that Teresa of Ávila had at least two strikes against her as a mystic: she was a conversa (the daughter and granddaughter of converted Jews) and a woman living at a time when women's roles in the church were seriously circumscribed. Was Teresa influenced by her Jewish heritage? Did she accept or challenge the gender ideology of her society? How was she able to assume a role as a spiritual teacher? Three complementary essays in this section address these issues. Michael McGaha surveys the scholarship on the relation between Jewish mysticism and sixteenth-century Spanish Christian mysticism before discussing the debates over the significance of social prejudice against conversos in shaping the life and works of Teresa of Ávila. In "Was Teresa of Ávila a Feminist?," Bárbara Mujica addresses the question of Teresa's feminism while reviewing the notions of womanhood found in the theological, medical, and legal texts of her day. Finally, Cordula van Wyhe calls attention to the artistic, literary, and theological works produced or inspired by the second generation of Discalced Carmelites. These works constitute a rich but little-studied source for teaching the history of seventeenth-century Catholic Europe.

Although this section is intended primarily to provide teachers with a survey of historical perspectives as they prepare to teach the Spanish mystics, these essays also raise pedagogical issues. For these contributors, the background to the mystics is an unfolding object of inquiry, and they provide suggestions for how to engage students in ongoing scholarship. Childers recommends passages from Islamic mystics for students to compare with those of the Spanish mystics, so that they can ask themselves, How can we decide the question of influence? and What difference does it make now? Mujica uses the question of whether Teresa was really a feminist to encourage students to define terms precisely with an eye to historical circumstances. Wyhe, an art historian, outlines how analyzing a religious painting such as Peter Paul Rubens's *Saint Teresa's Vision of the Holy Dove* can illuminate theological debates, such as the legitimacy of an intensely visual christocentric mysticism.

The next section, "Theoretical Perspectives," provides ample evidence that the Spanish mystics are taught in a broad range of disciplines and contexts. The first two essays describe how their writings can elucidate contemporary theories of language and sexual difference, subjectivity, and epistemology. Linda Belau teaches Teresa's autobiography as a case study for examining the theories of Jacques Derrida and Jacques Lacan. Belau describes how she uses students' frustration over understanding Teresa as a point of departure for discussions of the Derridian theory of abyssal language and the failure of the signifier. Similarly, she leads students to see connections between, on the one hand, Teresa's desire for an unmediated enjoyment of the divinity and, on the other, Lacan's theory of the paternal prohibition of the desire for maternal jouissance.

In the second essay, Sherry Velasco describes teaching life writing written by women in convents in reference to theories of autobiography and gender, disability studies, confessional discourse, and diary writing. Velasco argues that convent life narratives, which were most often written at the behest of a confessor over a period of many years, require a much broader conception of the autobiographical genre if we are to appreciate the often fragmentary, reiterative, and relational features of these texts. A third theoretical perspective is offered by Barbara Simerka, who explores the parallels between Teresa's achievement in defining gender-specific modes of cognition and present-day feminist theories of epistemology and pedagogy. Understanding how Teresa's writings and reform activities were designed to promote and shelter women's ways of spiritual knowing, teaching, and learning, she argues, can encourage students to evaluate their own learning experiences and formulate their own pedagogical philosophy.

Opening the following section, "Specific Course Contexts," Lisa Vollendorf explores the challenges of teaching mysticism in the undergraduate classroom and points out that linguistic and conceptual difficulties can be offset through concrete pedagogical strategies, such as choosing texts carefully (and avoiding the temptation to assign too much), placing the mystics in the historical context of Counter-Reformation Spain, and incorporating exercises using English translations. The essay also provides suggested background readings for instructors, a guide to frequently used anthologies, and tips on using Internet resources.

It is widely accepted that Augustine's *Confessions*—his narrative of sin, conversion, and return to God—became a model for self-presentation in Western life writing, religious and secular. Indeed, in her autobiography Teresa describes her conversion as in part a response to reading the *Confessions*. Nevertheless, Teresa's conversion experience, her conception of her sinfulness, and her models of holiness did not conform to Augustine's. In the next essay, Carole Slade describes the advantages of comparing Teresa's *Life* with the *Confessions* in an advanced comparative literature course on autobiography in the Western tradition. Such juxtaposition, Slade argues, illustrates how Christian narratives of salvation are gender inflected. Furthermore, Teresa's efforts to adapt the Augustinian paradigm to her own spiritual experience illuminates Teresa's specifically feminine piety.

In a large survey course in women's history, Marta V. Vicente teaches Teresa alongside her less fortunate sisters, those "failed saints" whose spiritual claims were repudiated. What led some women to be declared holy while others were denounced as frauds? Vicente argues that this comparative perspective leads students to consider how the agency and authority of individual women were shaped by such diverse factors as class, community, and national or local politics.

Like Vicente, María del Pilar Ryan teaches the Spanish mystics in the context of their ambivalent reception by the Spanish church. In her history courses at West Point, she compares Ignatius of Loyola and Teresa of Ávila as mystics and reformers who, at various points in their lives, both challenged and bowed to institutional religious authority. Framing the mystics in terms of defiance and obedience, Ryan reports, has been particularly effective in engaging cadets who might otherwise consider religious history alien and irrelevant.

As Kathleen Ann Myers observes in her essay, after the publication of Teresa's works and her canonization in 1622, the Spanish saint became a crucial point of reference for nuns and aspiring holy women in the New World. Myers describes a unit in a colonial Latin American literature course in which she explores the impact of the Teresian model of sanctity and authorship on three women: America's first saint, Rose of Lima; the Mexican mystic Madre María de San José; and the celebrated poet Sor Juana Inés de la Cruz.

My own essay outlines a senior seminar on Spanish women writers from the late Middle Ages to the Enlightenment. I argue that placing Teresa between her literary forebears and daughters helps students identify recurrent themes and tensions in women's literary tradition and in the historical development of feminist consciousness. My goal in the course is to lead students to understand the Carmelite nun in the context of her historical moment and religious heritage and yet also to see the connections between that heritage and the movements that made modern feminism possible.

Beginning in the 1990s, texts by mystical writers began to appear on syllabi in the religious studies department at the University of Kansas—a large, secular state university. Ralph Keen describes curricular changes he has witnessed in his discipline over the last decade and the pedagogical approaches he has developed for teaching texts by Ignatius of Loyola, Teresa of Ávila, and John of the Cross. Their writings, he observes, are ideally suited to exploring such issues as the relation of experience and emotion to thought and the limitations of language when depicting the ineffable. He also remarks on the particular reflexivity and self-restraint that teaching subjective religious experience demands, especially in the context of a secular institution.

In contrast to the secular setting Keen describes, Gillian T. W. Ahlgren teaches in a Jesuit university, where faith and learning are inseparable. Because Teresa's writings are intensely personal, Ahlgren explains, their theological dimensions can be overlooked. She describes a method of teaching *The Interior Castle* that helps students recognize how Teresa's theological statements are embedded in metaphors, scriptural allusions, and narratives of personal experience.

Like Vollendorf, Dona M. Kercher describes the challenges of making mysticism accessible to undergraduates. Noting the mystics' emphasis on experience as a complement to book learning, Kercher details how she has successfully integrated field trips to monasteries, castlelike monuments, and art museums into her syllabus. Through films on the mystics, she guides students to appreciate how contemporary attitudes and concerns affect the representation of mysticism. Kercher also describes the experience of self-censorship—a lay teacher's apprehensions when teaching mysticism at a conservative Catholic college.

What makes a saint is a major theme in Christopher C. Wilson's essay. In his courses on Spanish Renaissance and baroque art, Wilson explores the seventeenth-century iconography of John of the Cross and Teresa of Ávila to show students how images not only reflect a society's values but also play a role in shaping them. His courses contrast images of the two Carmelites so that students can appreciate the role of gender expectations in the construction of sainthood.

The last section is devoted to essays on teaching specific texts. As the survey indicated, "Noche oscura," by John of the Cross, is an enormously popular text among teachers of Spanish literature courses at all levels. Howard Mancing adopts an approach to the issue of sexuality in John's poetry that is at once direct and devious. He initially leads students in a historically naive reading of "Noche oscura" as an erotic poem; he then provides them with the missing cues—the author's name and the poem's rubric—that signal an implicit allegory. Mancing encourages his students to consider a variety of explanations—historical, neurological, and evolutionary—for the coincidence of spiritual and sexual imagery.

What would a conversation between Ignatius and Teresa have sounded like? As Darcy Donahue points out, although these two powerful icons never met, they had much in common. Both experienced a conversion that brought about an intense inner spirituality, struggled with illness and censure, collaborated with members of the opposite sex, and in their mature years became active reformers. Yet there are also salient differences in the ways they carried out their goals and represented their spiritual trajectories. Donahue suggests that teaching their autobiographies in juxtaposition helps students appreciate how the contours of agency and self-perception were shaped by complex gender ideologies.

When teaching Teresa's *Castillo interior* (*Interior Castle*), Joan Cammarata focuses on the fact that Teresa was a teacher herself, in her role as prioress and reformer. Teresa intended her third major work to be a guidebook for her nuns, one that would show them how to lead a simultaneously active and contemplative spiritual life. This essay suggests ways to help students see that the characteristic features of this work—its colloquial style, rhetoric of humility, multiple comparisons from the natural world, and architectural allegory—were part of a spiritual pedagogy.

Helen H. Reed, like Donahue, finds that the question of women's agency is a fruitful approach to teaching Teresa's *Libro de las fundaciones* (*Book of Foundations*). She recounts successfully including in an undergraduate survey course chapters from Teresa's engaging but unfairly neglected chronicle of her reform. Teresa's pragmatic cleverness as a woman of action, the ironic humor of her narration, and her intimate portraits of female followers and patrons, Reed has discovered, help stretch the historical imagination of her students. Through comparison with male-authored texts, students are encouraged to consider what heroism meant for early modern men and women and what opportunities they had to realize it.

The last three essays in the volume are devoted to works by Luis de León, the Augustinian friar who is sometimes denied the title of mystic because his poetry describes the yearning for, rather than the realization of, union with the Godhead. Dana Bultman guides potential instructors through a comparison between Fray Luis's "Noche serena" and John's "La noche oscura," two poems that illustrate the commonalities and differences between mystical and humanist approaches to knowledge of God. She also shows that the Augustinian and the Carmelite shared a belief in the compatibility of the sensual language and spiritual knowledge encoded in the Song of Songs and that in distinct ways they made a radical departure from the medieval tradition of allegorical exegesis. Whether or not one describes Fray Luis as a mystic (a distinction that depends on whether one chooses to emphasize the experience of union over the desire for an intimate encounter with God), Bultman makes a strong case for the pedagogical value of teaching Fray Luis in the context of the mystical tradition.

David H. Darst's point of departure is the clarity of León's thought and style. Darst leads students to see that a recurrent theme in Léon's poetry, as in the works of Teresa and John, is the ascending journey from the material world to a heavenly abode where the soul finds itself in the presence of God. In his under-graduate and graduate courses on the Renaissance and baroque poetry of Spain, Darst acquaints students with the key aspects of the intellectual traditions of the period—Augustinian, Thomistic, and Ptolemaic—so that they can appreciate the elegant clarity of Fray Luis's vision.

In the final essay in the volume, Mario A. Ortiz, a musicologist and liter-ary scholar, approaches teaching the poetry of Fray Luis through a different intellectual paradigm: the Renaissance fascination with rediscovering the lost knowledge of the music of the spheres. Ortiz reconstructs with his students the story of how Francisco Salinas, a renowned Renaissance musician and human-ist, abandoned the Aristotelian quest for a sentient music of the spheres and de-veloped a new aesthetic paradigm of musical harmony. Ortiz follows with a close reading of Fray Luis's "Oda a Salinas" as an encounter with a harmony so sweet that it leaves the poet in ecstasy. Whether or not students have any religious inclinations, they can appreciate how in León's poem harmony is a metaphor for beauty and perfection and for the human desire to become one with harmony.

Whether the context is aesthetic or theological, secular or religious, histori-cal or theoretical, the contributors to this volume and the respondents to the survey give abundant evidence of their creativity in eliciting students' curiosity, empathy, and appreciation for writers who may have initially seemed to come from a distant past and alien culture.

Part One

MATERIALS

Editions

Anthologies in Spanish

Instructors surveyed in 2004 who taught texts by mystics used a wide variety of materials including anthologies, print editions, and assembled course packets of selected works. For lower-division Spanish courses, the most widely used anthology was *Aproximaciones al estudio de la literatura hispánica*, edited by Carmelo Virgillo, Edward Friedman, and Teresa Valdivieso, recommended for its organization by genre and lucid introductions. *Voces de España: Antología literaria*, edited by Francisca Paredes Méndez, Mark Harprint, and José Ballesteros, was also recommended. It includes "Vida retirada" and "Noche serena," by Fray Luis de León; selections from *Libro de la vida* (*The Book of Her Life*), by Teresa of Ávila; and three poems by John of the Cross. David William Foster's *De los orígenes hasta 1700*, the first volume of *Literatura española: Una antología*, provides the broadest selection of mystical writing from Teresa, John, and Fray Luis, but some instructors felt that the absence of notes or glosses on vocabulary limited its usefulness for undergraduates.

Bárbara Mujica has edited several anthologies for different levels of instruction. *Milenio: Mil años de literatura española*, a third-year anthology, was praised for "extensive introductory essays [that] ground the literature in the historical background and provide a theoretical framework with analysis in current theory and critical trends." *Milenio* includes chapter 11 from Teresa's *Life*, four poems by John of the Cross, one poem by Luis de León, and a selection from Fray Luis's *La perfecta casada* (*The Perfect Wife*). *Milenio* also provides questions on comprehension and topics for literary analysis. Mujica's *Antología de la literatura española: Renacimiento y Siglo de Oro*, designed for advanced undergraduates and beginning graduate students, offers extensive selections of prose and poetry by Teresa, John, Fray Luis, as well as the lesser-known mystics Malón de Chaide and Miguel de Molinos. Although it is currently out of print, a reprint edition is forthcoming from the publisher Wipf and Stock. Instructors interested in longer selections from Teresa's works may prefer *Representative Spanish Authors*, edited by Walter T. Pattison and Donald W. Bleznick. Volume 1 provides an introduction to mysticism in English; chapters 10, 38, 40 from Teresa's *Libro de la vida*; chapters 18, 19, 40 from *Libro de las fundaciones* (*The Book of Foundations*); and several poems by John of the Cross. (Vollendorf's essay in this volume describes selections from these anthologies in greater detail.) The most comprehensive selection of works by the Spanish and Spanish American mystics can be found in *Los místicos de la edad de oro en España y América: Antología*, edited by Melquíades Andrés Martín.

Elias Rivers's *Renaissance and Baroque Poetry of Spain*, which provides generous selections from the poetry of John of the Cross and Luis de León with English prose translations in footnotes, is widely used in advanced undergraduate and graduate poetry courses, although some instructors prefer the Spanish edition, *Poesía lírica del Siglo de Oro*, without the English translations.

There are now several anthologies appropriate for women-writers courses in Spanish: Amy Kaminsky's bilingual anthology *Water Lilies / Flores del agua*, Mujica's *Women Writers of Early Modern Spain: Sophia's Daughters*, and a forthcoming revised edition of the groundbreaking bilingual anthology *Untold Sisters*, edited by Electa Arenal and Stacey Schlau. *Water Lilies* has the broadest chronological range and includes writers from the late Middle Ages to the nineteenth century. *Untold Sisters* offers writings by nuns—excluding Teresa—from early modern Spain and the New World. *Women Writers* includes extensive selections from Teresa's *Libro de la vida* (although not the autobiographical chapters) and *Castillo interior* (*The Interior Castle*), writings by María de San José Salazar, Cecilia del Nacimiento, María de San Alberto, and Marcela de San Félix, as well as selections from secular women writers. The texts are accompanied by introductions to individual authors and discussion topics.

Editions in Spanish

The complete works of Teresa of Ávila are available in several excellent scholarly editions. *Obras completas: Edición manual*, edited by Efrén de la Madre de Dios and Otger Steggink, includes Teresa's spiritual writings and her letters in one volume. *Obras completas de Santa Teresa de Jesús*, edited by the foremost Teresian textual scholar, Tomás Álvarez, does not include the letters. Also recommended is *Obras completas*, edited by Alberto Barrientos and his colleagues. Teresa's letters have been edited and placed in chronological order by Luis Rodríguez Martínez and Teófanes Egido (*Epistolario*); in Alvarez's edition (*Cartas*), they are grouped according to addressee.

Two paperback editions of *Libro de la vida*, one edited by Steggink, and one by Dámaso Chicharro, were popular choices, praised for their excellent historical introductions and bibliographies. Antonio Comas's *La vida / Las moradas*, which includes both the *Vida* and *Castillo interior*, is another option in paperback, although its critical apparatus is minimal. It is more difficult to find good paperback editions of *Libro de las fundaciones* (*The Book of Foundations*). The edition by Víctor García de la Concha, with an excellent historical introduction, is at present out of print. For John of the Cross three editions were highly recommended: *Cántico espiritual y poesía completa*, edited by Paola Elia and María Jesús Mancho; *Obra completa*, edited by Luce López Baralt and Eulogio Pacho; and *Poesía*, edited by Domingo Ynduráin.

The works of Luis de León in Spanish have been edited by eminent scholars: José Manuel Blecua, Cristóbal Cuervas, Oreste Macrí, and Juan Francisco Alcina. Blecua's *Poesía completa*, Macrí's *La poesía de fray Luis de León*, and Alcina's *Poesía*, all with extensive critical apparatus, are available in affordable paperback editions. The preferred scholarly edition for the works of Ignatius of Loyola in Spanish is *Obras completas*, edited by Ignacio Iparraguirre and

Cándido de Dalmases. There are numerous inexpensive paperback options for individual works.

Bilingual Editions and Translations

As Amanda Powell explains in her essay in this volume, no single translation will reach all readers or serve all purposes. One respondent lamented that the available translations of Teresa were too reverent and formal and longed for a translation that would better render the "homely, down-to-earth allusions" that transmit Teresa's egalitarian values. When the *Life* in English is a required text, many instructors assign the translation by J. M. Cohen, because it is widely available in an inexpensive paperback. Kieran Kavanaugh and Otilio Rodríguez's three-volume *The Collected Works* provides a contemporary American translation that adheres closely to the original Spanish; it can be purchased directly from the Institute of Carmelite Studies (www.icspublications.org). Their translation of the *Life* is in paperback from Hacket, with a new introduction by Jodi Bilinkoff. Kavanaugh has also published the letters of Teresa in paperback *(Collected Letters)*. Some readers prefer Edgar Allison Peers's graceful, British-inflected translations. His *The Complete Works of Saint Teresa of Jesus,* first published in 1946, is now available in a paperback reprint under the title *The Complete Works of St. Teresa of Avila*. Neither edition includes the letters, which are published separately in the two-volume *Letters of Saint Teresa of Jesus*. Peers is adept at capturing Teresa's sense of playful irony, which is particularly evident in his translations and notes to the letters. Mirabai Starr's recent translation of *The Interior Castle,* as Powell notes, seeks to convey Teresa's thought in a contemporary ecumenical language.

Teachers of comparative literature are fortunate because they can count on several bilingual editions of the poetry of John of the Cross with translations by noted poets: Willis Barnstone, Roy Campbell, and John Frederick Nims. As with Teresa, readers are faced with a choice between Peers's British-inflected translation in *The Complete Works* and the contemporary American rendering of Kavanaugh and Rodríguez in *The Collected Works,* which is enhanced by a biographical essay, a glossary of terms, and an index of key words. Jane Ackerman has ably translated the two versions of *The Living Flame of Love,* John's prose gloss on his poem "Llama de amor viva," widely considered to be a prose poem in itself. For specialized courses on John of the Cross, instructors may wish to consider *The Collected Works of St. John of the Cross: A Digital Library*. This CD-ROM includes the translations by Kavanaugh and Rodríguez and by Peers, the Spanish text edited by Eulogio Pacho and Luce López Baralt, and the Douay Rheims Bible (an English translation of the Latin Vulgate). It is computer searchable and can be ordered online (www.icspublications.org).

The poems of Fray Luis are available in fluid translations by Willis Barnstone. *The Names of Christ,* Fray Luis's most famous prose work, has been translated by Manuel Durán and William Kluback. His conduct book for women,

La perfecta casada (*The Perfect Wife*), is available in a bilingual translation (*Bilingual Edition*). There are numerous options for the writings of Ignatius of Loyola. Especially recommended is The Spiritual Exercises *and Selected Works*, edited by George E. Ganss and a team of Jesuit historians, which includes selections from the *Spiritual Diary* and excerpts from Ignatius's little-known letters. An extensive introduction traces the development of Ignatius's spirituality. Works by three important precursors of the Carmelite mystics are available in English. *Of Prayer and Meditation*, a 1582 recusant translation of Luis de Granada's enormously influential *Libro de la oración y meditación*, was reprinted in 1971. Modern translations of Francisco de Osuna's *Third Spiritual Alphabet* (*Tercer abecedario espiritual*) and John of Ávila's *Audi, filia*, with extensive introductions, appear from the Paulist press.

The Instructor's Library

Reference Works

Instructors and students approaching the Spanish mystics for the first time will want to familiarize themselves with a number of reference works that will provide key definitions, historical surveys, and bibliographies for further research. The *HarperCollins Encyclopedia of Catholicism*, edited by Richard P. McBrien, Harold W. Attridge, and others, is an excellent starting place for students, who will find brief entries on many aspects of Catholic history, theology, and iconography. The *New Dictionary of Catholic Spirituality*, edited by Michael Downey, would be a valuable addition to the instructor's personal library. Essays of approximately two to four pages in length, written for the most part by Catholic theologians, treat topics such as enthusiasm, the discernment of spirits, and the negative way. The six-volume *Encyclopedia of the Renaissance* (ed. Grendler) includes essays of approximately 500 words in length on individual mystics as well as on more general topics such as the Catholic Reformation and mysticism. The essays in the *Oxford Encyclopedia of the Reformation* (ed. Hillerbrand), averaging 1,200 words in length, are followed by selected bibliographies. With entries on Roman Catholicism, the Council of Trent, religious orders, Illuminism, mysticism, popular religion, among others, this is a valuable resource for nonspecialists in the early modern period. More detailed still are the articles in the *New Catholic Encyclopedia*, a standard reference on Catholic doctrine and history.

Two relatively new reference books will be of particular interest to those teaching specialized courses on Teresa of Ávila or John of the Cross. *Diccionario de San Juan de la Cruz*, edited by Eulogio Pacho, and *Diccionario de Santa Teresa: Doctrina e historia*, edited by Tomás Álvarez, include brief entries on the personalities associated with the Discalced Carmelite reform and longer essays on key concepts in their writings. Edgar Allison Peers's *Handbook to the Life and Times of St. Teresa and St. John of the Cross*, though somewhat outdated, is still a handy guide to the personalities and politics of the Discalced reform. Although long out of print, it is often available from used book dealers. *Bibliographia Internationalis Spiritualitatis*, published yearly since 1966, provides an impressively comprehensive bibliography of studies on world spirituality. The *Bibliographia Carmelitana Annualis*, an annual bibliography of works on Christian spirituality with a special emphasis on the Carmelite school, is another valuable and often overlooked reference source. *San Juan de la Cruz: Bibliografía sistemática*, compiled by Manuel Diego Sánchez and published in 2000, lists 6,328 citations to biographical, textual, literary, and theological studies, arranged by topic. Since 1955 the *Archivum Bibliographicum Carmelitanum* has published a yearly bibliography on the works of Teresa of Ávila. The *Diccionario Histórico de la Compañía de Jesús*, edited by Charles O'Neill and Joaquín María Domínguez, is an indispensable source for Jesuit topics; it provides brief biographical and thematic essays with selected bibliography.

Historical and Literary Studies

For a concise overview of the cultural and religious history of early modern Spain, suitable for undergraduates, two inexpensive paperbacks are recommended: Teófilo Ruiz's *Spanish Society, 1400–1600* and Helen Rawlings's *Church, Religion and Society in Early Modern Spain*. Good choices for more advanced courses include John A. Crow's *Spain: The Root and the Flower*, John H. Elliott's *Imperial Spain, 1469–1716*, and Henry Kamen's *Spain, 1469–1714: A Society of Conflict*.

Historians praised two books, William A. Christian, Jr.'s *Local Religion in Sixteenth-Century Spain* and Sara T. Nalle's *God in La Mancha*, as excellent studies on popular attitudes toward religion. John W. O'Malley's *The First Jesuits* provides a masterful account of how the early members of the Society of Jesus sought to make interior spirituality compatible with an active ministry. Enrique Llamas Martínez presents a concise synthesis of John's and Teresa's encounters with the Inquisition in "Teresa de Jesús y Juan de la Cruz ante la Inquisición"; his *Santa Teresa de Jesús y la Inquisición española*, which includes transcriptions from primary sources, remains the most comprehensive study on this topic. In English, the most thorough treatment of the subject is to be found in Gillian T. W. Ahlgren's *Teresa of Ávila and the Politics of Sanctity*. Indispensable primary sources for the study of Teresa's and John's canonization are *Procesos de beatificación y canonización de Santa Teresa de Jesús* (ed. Silverio de Santa Teresa) and *Proceso Apostólico de Jaén . . . San Juan de la Cruz. Informaciones de 1616* (ed. María Dolores Verdejo López). Instructors can also consult Melquíades Andrés Martín's *Historia de la mística de la edad de oro en España* for an exhaustive survey of the Golden Age mystics, with extensive bibliographies of primary and secondary sources. Edgar Allison Peers's three-volume *Studies of the Spanish Mystics* is still the most comprehensive source of information in English on the lesser-known figures such as Luis de Granada, Francisco de Osuna, and Jerónimo Gracián.

For the topics of pseudomysticism and the construction of sanctity, José Luis Sánchez Lora's *Mujeres, conventos y formas de la religiosidad barroca*, Stephen Haliczer's *Between Exaltation and Infamy*, Kathleen Anne Myers's *Neither Saints nor Sinners*, Kathryn McKnight's *The Mystic of Tunja*, and Andrew Keitt's *Inventing the Sacred: Imposture, Inquisition, and the Boundaries of the Supernatural in Golden Age Spain* were highly recommended. Ahlgren's recent translation of the inquisitorial trial of Francisca de los Apóstoles—a contemporary of Saint Teresa's—is ideally suited for a comparative analysis of a failed and a successful mystic (*Inquisition*). Alastair Hamilton's *Heresy and Mysticism in Sixteenth-Century Spain: The Alumbrados*, offers a lucid exposition of the heretical movements that coincided with the flowering of Spanish mysticism.

Those interested in the relation among Jewish, Islamic, and Christian mysticism will want to consult Catherine Swietlicki's *Spanish Christian Cabala*, Deirdre Green's *Gold in the Crucible: Teresa of Ávila and the Western Mystical Tradition*, and the many studies by Luce López Baralt cited in this volume in William Childers's essay. A shorter introduction to López Baralt's scholarship is her "Simbología mística islámica en San Juan de la Cruz y en Santa Teresa de Jesús." Michael McGaha provides an introduction to the question of Teresa's converso heritage in his essay in this volume.

In courses on early modern women's history, Merry E. Wiesner's *Women and Gender in Early Modern Europe* was favored as a basic text, along with the following supplemental readings: Gerda Lerner's *The Creation of Feminist Consciousness from the Middle Ages to Eighteen-Seventy* (especially chapters 4 and 5), Mary Elizabeth Perry's *Gender and Disorder in Early Modern Seville*, Sherry Velasco's *Demons, Nausea, and Resistance in the Autobiography of Isabel de Jesús (1611–1682)*, and the essays in *Women in the Inquisition*, edited by Mary Giles. Instructors will find vivid portraits of women from various strata—lay and religious—in Lisa Vollendorf's *The Lives of Women: A New History of Inquisitional Spain*. The collection of essays edited by Susan E. Dinan and Debra Meyers, *Women and Religion in Old and New Worlds*, similarly provides a transatlantic perspective on lay and monastic women. Two recent books, Elizabeth Lehfeldt's *Religious Women in Golden Age Spain* and Jodi Bilinkoff's *Related Lives: Confessors, Female Penitents, and Catholic Culture*, are great choices for history or culture courses with an emphasis on female monasticism. Excellent overviews in Spanish, with suggested bibliography, are provided by José Luis Sánchez Lora's "Mujeres en religión" and Asunción Lavrin's "Las Esposas de Cristo en Hispanoamérica."

In undergraduate literature survey courses in Spanish, most instructors do not assign secondary readings. One respondent reported, however, that he directs curious students to E. W. Trueman Dicken's *The Crucible of Love: A Study of the Mysticism of St. Teresa of Jesus and St. John of the Cross* or to Margaret Wilson's *San Juan de la Cruz: Poems*, described as "short and sweet and unmatched." Elias Rivers's *Fray Luis de León: The Original Poems* was similarly praised as a concise, accessible introduction to the poet and to the genres of Renaissance lyric poetry. Undergraduates may also be interested in comparing selections from Cathleen Medwick's recent biography, *Teresa of Ávila: The Progress of a Soul* (now translated into Spanish), with chapters from Teresa's *Life*. Rosa Rossi's brief biographies of Teresa and John are also available in Spanish. The most comprehensive biography of Teresa is *Tiempo y vida de Santa Teresa*, by Efrén de la Madre de Dios and Otger Steggink.

Instructors teaching Teresa for the first time can find no better place to start than *Introducción a la lectura de Santa Teresa*, edited by Alberto Barrientos and other Carmelite scholars. It comprises a chronology; an extensive bibliography; and essays on the historical context of Teresa's life, Teresian theology, language and rhetorical strategies, and individual works of the Carmelite founder. For the historical context of Teresa's life, respondents enthusiastically endorsed Bilinkoff's *The Ávila of Saint Teresa* and Ahlgren's *Teresa of Ávila and the Politics of Sanctity*. For courses with a literary emphasis, Víctor García de la Concha's *El arte literario de Santa Teresa*, Alison Weber's *Teresa of Ávila and the Rhetoric of Femininity*, and Carole Slade's *St. Teresa of Ávila: Author of a Heroic Life* are often included in course syllabi. A provocative recent study, Juan Marcos's *Mística y subversiva*, approaches the question of the subversiveness of Teresa's theology from the perspective of pragmatic linguistics. After much neglect, Teresa's correspondence is beginning to receive some critical attention. Peers's "Saint Teresa in Her Letters" provides a good introduction to the Carmelite's unconventional epistolary style. Weber ("'Dear Daughter'") describes how Teresa provided spiritual and practical advice for her nuns through her letters, and Slade ("Relationship") examines Teresa's political strategies in her letters to Philip II.

In advanced literature courses with an emphasis on poetry, the classic studies on John of the Cross by Jorge Guillén, Dámaso Alonso (*Poesía de San Juan* and *Poesía española*), and Leo Spitzer ("Three Poems on Ecstasy") enjoy continued popularity. Willis Barnstone's "Mystico-Erotic Love in 'O Living Flame of Love,'" and Ian MacPherson's "'Rompe la tela de este dulce encuentro': San Juan's 'Llama de amor viva' and the Courtly Context" offer sensitive readings of one of John's most famous poems. Colin P. Thompson's *St. John of the Cross: Songs in the Night* explores the connections between John's theology and his works in prose and verse. Chapter 2 provides a concise, up-to-date biographical essay. *Introducción a la lectura de San Juan de la Cruz*, edited by Salvador Ros García and his colleagues, will be particularly useful for courses with a focus on John of the Cross. It includes an extensive bibliography; a chronology of John's life; and historical, literary, and theological essays prepared by a team of Carmelite scholars; part two comprises essays on individual works. Another valuable collection, *San Juan de la Cruz and Fray Luis de León: A Commemorative International Symposium*, edited by Mary Malcolm Gaylord and Francisco Márquez Villanueva, includes stylistic, philological, and biographical essays by eminent scholars from the United States and Europe. Thompson's *The Strife of Tongues: Fray Luis de León and the Golden Age of Spain* remains the most comprehensive study in English on the Augustinian poet and biblical scholar.

There is a substantial and growing body of work on life writing by monastic women. James S. Amelang gives a good overview of the field and bibliography for further reading in "Autobiografías femeninas." Key readings on nuns as writers include Electa Arenal and Stacey Schlau's introduction to *Untold Sisters*, Darcy Donahue's "Writing Lives," Isabelle Poutrin's *Le voile et la plume*, Sonja Herpoel's *A la zaga de Santa Teresa: Autobiografías por mandato*, Myers and Powell's "Gender, Tradition, and Autobiographical Spiritual Writings," and Myers's "Crossing Boundaries: Defining the Field of Female Religious Writing in Colonial Latin America." The introduction and essays on Teresa, her forebears, and literary daughters collected in *Recovering Spain's Feminist Tradition*, edited by Vollendorf, are ideally suited for courses on women writers. Velasco and Slade offer guides to important theoretical studies of autobiography as genre in their essays in the present volume.

Instructors of graduate classes in theory reported teaching works by mystics in conjunction with texts that have now become classics of postmodern theory: Michel de Certeau's *The Mystic Fable* (*La fable mystique*), Jacques Lacan's *The Four Fundamental Concepts of Psycho-analysis*, Luce Irigaray's "La mystérique," and Julia Kristeva's *Revolution in Poetic Language*. Paul Julian Smith ("Visions of Teresa: Lacan, Irigaray, Kristeva") and Swietlicki ("Writing 'Femystic' Space: In the Margins of Saint Teresa's *Castillo interior*") apply these theories with more specificity to Teresa's texts. In her epilogue to *St. Teresa of Ávila*, Slade offers a cogent overview of these theories, pointing out the pitfalls of ahistoricism.

Religious and Theological Studies

Some students, as a number of respondents remarked, have little familiarity with Catholic doctrine, let alone mystical theology. Absolute beginners can be directed to *Catholicism for Dummies,* by John Trigilio and Kenneth Brighenti. Breezy in style, it nevertheless provides clear explanations of fundamental Catholic practices and beliefs. A more advanced option is Alister E. McGrath's *Christian Spirituality: An Introduction,* which offers an overview of theological issues and terms, along with short extracts from the classics of Christian spirituality, suggestions for further reading, a bibliography of Internet resources, and a glossary of terms. *Reformation Theologians: An Introduction to Theology in the*

Early Modern Period, edited by Carter Lindberg, includes concise, illuminating articles on Teresa of Ávila by Ahlgren and on Ignatius of Loyola by O'Malley ("Teresa"; "Ignatius"), as well as essays by other contemporary Catholic and Protestant theologians. More challenging but still accessible are the essays by the eminent scholar of mysticism, Bernard McGinn: his general introduction to *The Foundations of Mysticism*, "The Language of Love in Christian and Jewish Mysticism," and "Love, Knowledge, and *Unio mystica* in the Western Christian Tradition." The forthcoming *Cambridge Companion to Christian Mysticism*, edited by Amy Hollywood and Patricia Beckman, which will include essays on apophasis and cataphasis, sexuality, gender and mysticism, *unitas*, among other topics, will be a welcome addition to the instructor's library. Suggestions for readings on theological issues directly related to the Spanish mystics include J. Mary Luti's *Teresa of Ávila's Way*, Rowan Williams's *Teresa of Ávila*, Edward Howells's *John of the Cross and Teresa of Ávila*, and Ahlgren's *Entering Teresa of Ávila's* Interior Castle. The essays by O'Malley ("Early Jesuit Spirituality") and Kieran Kavanaugh ("Spanish Sixteenth Century") in Louis Dupré and Don E. Saliers's *Christian Spirituality* place theological questions in the historical context of the Catholic Counter-Reformation and also provide bibliographies for further reading.

In courses with an emphasis on feminine spirituality, Ursula King's *Women and Spirituality*, the essays in *The Feminist Mystic* (edited by Mary Giles), Elizabeth Petroff's *Body and Soul*, Prudence Allen's "Soul, Body and Transcendence in Teresa of Ávila," and Patricia Ranft's *Women and Spiritual Equality* figured prominently. Carole Slade's "Saint Teresa's *Meditaciones sobre los Cantares*" is a suggestive article on Teresa's gendered approach to hermeneutics. Readings for students in advanced theology courses included Grace Jantzen's *Power, Gender, and Christian Mysticism*, Amy Hollywood's *Sensible Ecstasy*, Steven Payne's *John of the Cross and the Cognitive Value of Mysticism*, Sarah Coakley's *Powers and Submissions*, and Mary Frohlich's *The Intersubjectivity of the Mystic*.

Aids to Teaching

Music

Instructors who wish to bring musical interpretations of mystical poetry into their classroom have several choices. RTVE-Música has recently released *Coloquio de amor*, a recording of poems by Teresa of Ávila, John of the Cross, and Ana de San Bartolomé, sung to sixteenth-century melodies and accompanied by the vihuela. In *La sonora soledad de Juan de Yepes*, a music video, renditions of John's poems are played against a background of Spanish landscapes. *¡Iberia!: Spanish and Portuguese Music of the Golden Age*, performed by the Waverly

Consort, will introduce students to *romances*, the popular ballads that were sung—adapted with religious lyrics—during the recreation periods in Teresian convents. The lyrics for ballads written by early Carmelite nuns have been collected in *Libro de romances y coplas del Carmelo de Valladolid*, edited by Víctor García de la Concha and María Álvarez Pellitero. Students might be encouraged to adapt period music or compose new music for these verses. Students will also be interested in contemporary musical interpretations of mystical poetry. John Michael Talbot performs poems by John of the Cross and Thomas Merton on his compact disk *The Lover and the Beloved*. John's "Cántico espiritual" is beautifully adapted by the Spanish guitarist and folksinger Amancio Prada. The popular Canadian folksinger Loreena McKennit sets John's "The Dark Night of the Soul" to music on *The Mask and the Mirror*. And Joan Osborne interprets Teresian mysticism in the songs "One of Us" and "Saint Teresa" on her album *Relish*.

Internet Resources

Although some respondents expressed misgivings about the Internet, it is clear that the Internet is becoming an increasingly important tool for teaching and research. Clearly, students need guidance in searching for, evaluating, and documenting Internet materials, skills that will be valuable for the rest of their lives. The accessibility of texts and translations on the Internet is a particular boon for teachers of the Spanish mystics, making it possible to assign materials that are out of print or prohibitively expensive. Instructors can easily annotate difficult texts or assign groups of students to prepare their own annotated editions. The complete works of Teresa of Ávila and John of the Cross are available in Spanish at the Web site sponsored by the Congregation for the Clergy of the Holy See. (At www.clerus.org, it is necessary to select Spanish and then click on "biblioteca." At this point, individual works or authors can be searched using the advanced search option. Note that it is necessary to use diacritics for a successful search.) Teresa's complete works in Spanish (alphabetized under "Jesús, Santa Teresa de"), the poetry of Luis de León, and Luis de Granada's influential *Vita Cristi* can also be found at the *Biblioteca electrónica cristiana* (www.multimedios.org). The Web site maintained by the Discalced Carmelite Order has links to *Teresian Carmel: Pages of History* by Ildefonso Moriones de la Visitación (www.ocd.pcn.net/histo_l.htm) and "Juan de la Cruz: Bibliografía fundamental" by Manuel Diego (www.ocd.pcn.net/gvcrux.html). On its home page *Catholic First* provides links to texts for *Canticle of a Soul, Ascent of Mt. Carmel,* and *Dark Night of the Soul* by John of the Cross, translated by David Lewis and the *Complete Works of Teresa of Ávila*, translated by Peers (www.catholicfirst.com). Another useful source is the Christian Classics Ethereal Library (www.ccel.org), a large online library that includes works by Teresa, John, Ignatius of Loyola, Miguel de Molinos, and other European mystics such as Julian of Norwich, Catherine of

Siena, and Johannes Eckhart in English translation. Students can use the site's search engine to create a glossary of key terms or to brainstorm for paper topics. The Web site of La Compañía de Jesús, España (www.jesuitas.es) displays a brief biography, bibliography, and the texts of Ignatius's *Autobiography* and *Spiritual Exercises* in Spanish. The *Spiritual Exercises*, translated by Elder Mullan and essays on Jesuit spirituality and history are accessible at www.jesuit.org, the site sponsored by the Society of Jesus USA (select "home," then "Ignatian Spirituality," then "Spiritual Exercises"). *Biblioteca Virtual Miguel de Cervantes* maintains an extensive catalog of information on the life and works of numerous Spanish authors, including Teresa, John, and Luis de León (www.cervantesvirtual .com). Fred Jehle's *Antología de poesía española* offers selected poems by these authors, with notes on meter and rhyme (http://users.ipfw.edu/jehle/poesia .html). Instructors of women's writing courses will find Dorothy Disse's *Other Women's Voices: Translations of Women's Writing before 1700* especially valuable. Available here are passages in English translation and bibliographies for 125 women writers who lived before 1700. The Spanish writers include Teresa de Cartagena, Teresa of Ávila, María de San José Salazar, and Juana Inés de la Cruz. Anyone reading the mystics in Spanish will want to bookmark the Web site for the *Diccionario de la Real Academia Española* (www.rae.es). Students can be encouraged to consult this dictionary for archaic meanings of words they will come across in their readings.

Illustrated Books

As noted in the introduction, instructors at all levels reported that supplementing readings with images was an effective way to engage students with unfamiliar historical and religious subjects. An Internet search will easily produce hundreds of images of the religious art and architecture of early modern Spain. Illustrated books and exhibition catalogs, whose images are often of higher resolution than those found on Web sites, can also be brought into the classroom or placed on reserve. Recommended illustrated surveys of Golden Age art include Jonathan Brown's *Painting in Spain: 1500–1700* and Janis Tomlinson's *From Greco to Goya: Painting in Spain, 1561–1828*. The exhibition catalog *Monjas coronadas: Vida conventual femenina* reproduces twenty-two exquisite portraits of nuns from colonial Latin America. *The Jesuits and the Arts: 1540–1773*, edited by O'Malley and Gauvin Alexander Bailey, is illustrated with 476 full-color images of Jesuit buildings, paintings, sculpture, and theatrical sets from Europe, Asia, and the Americas.

Images can also help students visualize daily life in early modern Spain. *God Speaks in the Night*, edited by Federico Ruiz and others, is a lavishly illustrated collection of biographical essays by a team of Carmelite historians that incorporates maps, iconographic images, reproductions of John's manuscripts, and photographs of the geography and architecture of Castile. *Teresa de Jesús y el siglo XVI*, an exhibition catalog, compiled by José Ignacio Piera Delgado, offers an equally rich trove of images of sixteenth-century material culture—*chapines* (ladies' platform shoes), amulets, reliquaries, an ink well, a nun's habit, a ceramic cooking pot, a spindle—all objects mentioned in Teresa's writings. Anyone teaching Teresa's *Book of Foundations* will want to consult *Spanish Cities of the Golden Age*, edited by Richard L. Kagan, which reproduces the panoramic views of Spanish cities drawn by Anton van den Wyngaerde between 1561 and 1571. Exquisite pen-and-ink renderings of Ávila, Alba de Tormes, Salamanca, Medina del Campo, Valladolid, Seville, and Burgos make it possible for students to reconstruct a visual tour of the towns and cities where Teresa made her foundations.

As the art historians Christopher Wilson and Cordula van Wyhe point out in their essays in this volume, representations of potential and canonized saints can reveal how their images were shaped to promote their cults, defend or reinterpret their teachings, and enforce contemporary notions of gender-appropriate holiness. Sources for iconographic images of Teresa and John include Laura Gutiérrez Rueda's "Iconografía de Santa Teresa," Irving Lavin's *Bernini and the Unity of the Visual Arts,* and two essays by Christopher Wilson, "Masculinity Restored: The Visual Shaping of St. John of the Cross" and "Saint Teresa of Ávila's Martyrdom: Images of Her Transverberation in Mexican Colonial Painting." Reproductions of 101 emblems from *The Idea Vitæ Teresianæ*, an emblem book published in Antwerp around 1686, are appended to Santiago Sebastián López's "Mística Teresiana." An essay by Heinz Pfeiffer, "The Iconography of the Society of Jesus," describes sources for Jesuit iconography.

Films

Films are an effective way to engage student interest and fill in gaps in historical background. *La Máquina del estado*, produced by RTVE, the Spanish equivalent to American public television, explores the relation between church and state during the reign of Philip II, with segments on the Spanish Inquisition and Spain's response to the Protestant Reformation. *Fray Luis de León: Un intelectual comprometido*, another RTVE production, chronicles the life of the friar and his inquisitorial trial and imprisonment. Readings from his written works, including his biblical commentary, *De los nombres de Cristo* (*The Names of Christ*), and his conduct book for married women, *La perfecta casada* (*The Perfect* Wife), are enhanced with images of his manuscripts and first editions. *La noche oscura*, directed by Carlos Saura, one of Spain's most notable directors, dramatizes John's imprisonment by the Calced Carmelites, a period during which he is believed to have composed his most famous poems. The eight-hour miniseries *Teresa de Jesús*, produced for Spanish television and directed by Josefina Molina, was recommended for its historical accuracy, excellent acting, and confessional restraint. A new film, *Teresa: El cuerpo de Cristo* ("Teresa:

The Body of Christ"), directed by Ray Loriga, has evoked considerable controversy in Catholic circles for its eroticism and its portrayal of the Carmelite as
a feminist. *Thérèse*, a film based on the life of the nineteenth-century French
Carmelite and future saint Thérèse de Lisieux, unflinchingly depicts the nun's
exercises in self-mortification. As Dona Kercher indicates in her essay in this
volume, these and similar films are not simply more or less accurate portraits of
historical figures but rather aesthetic interpretations shaped by contemporary
political, social, and religious attitudes. Her essay offers further suggestions for
teaching the aesthetic dimensions and ideological implications of such films.

Teresa in English Translation

Amanda Powell

Of the hundreds of "Englishings" of Teresa that have appeared beginning soon after her seventeenth-century canonization and continuing to the present, each one has criteria that shape the resulting translation. Some are devotional and inspirational, others scholarly, while still others aim to present a highly readable classic of world literature for general readers. Of course, such categories do not remain strictly separate in translation, just as they will not be separate in the various encounters with spiritual texts that we may have as students, researchers, and instructors. In many academic settings where Teresa is read and taught in English, instructors will emphasize the literary qualities of Teresian texts, as represented by her translators, or will focus on such matters as historical contexts, convent life, or comparative interpretations of mystical experience. In other classrooms where explicitly religious or devotional approaches are appropriate, for instance where there is interest in present-day applications of Teresian spirituality, instructors will seek books compiled as manuals guiding English-language readers in Teresa's methods of prayer. Whether approached with literary, scholarly, or devotional perspectives, or some combination, a given translation demonstrates implicitly in its linguistic choices, as well as explicitly in its general textual apparatus (introduction, annotations, etc.), the sense of audience and purpose that commissioned and informed it.

My comments focus on the key recent English translations of Teresa's *The Book of Her Life* and *The Interior Castle* that are more apt and readily available for general scholarly and classroom use. However, instructors are encouraged to browse libraries, interlibrary loan, *Books in Print*, and other resources for equally profitable but out-of-the-way versions. Scholars of history and theology will be interested in seventeenth-century translations that reveal earlier, shifting attitudes in the Anglo-American world to Catholicism generally or to Carmelite spirituality specifically. Over time, numerous translations have offered guides for the practice of Teresian methods of prayer. Some are more conservative and others (especially in the latter twentieth century to now) are freer in applying the content of Teresa's counsels to renewed spiritual criteria; according to its approach, a given translation will hew closer to or move further away from a representation of Teresa's sixteenth-century, Roman Catholic, Discalced Carmelite heritage and context. My comments focus not on manuals of spiritual praxis per se but on translations that represent the rich literary textures and historical contexts of Teresa's works; such renderings demonstrate that, in addition to being a practical guide to otherworldly matters, the works form a vital literary and cultural contribution to European history.

A translation recognizes the "literariness" of Teresa's work by conveying characteristics (treated in detail elsewhere in this volume) that include elaborate language displaying a range of registers from colloquiality to biblical resonance;

an alternate copia and spareness; a wealth of rhetorical strategies such as the well-known Teresian similitude; clear choices shaping her utterance as evident self-deprecation and subtle self-defense; and, not least, wit. A translator's job, then, is to bring across both the originating consciousness of the author, as traced in her text, and the ways the text bodies forth its originating contexts (social, cultural, literary, spiritual, ideological, political) in myriad dimensions. Further, to convey the power and the (mixed) conventionalities and originalities of her text, a translator seeks to convey the effects it produces in the original for a capable reader of Spanish.

For succinct illustrations of some of these qualities of Teresian language, we can look briefly at a passage from Teresa's *Life*. The section heading to chapter 13 of that book pointedly designates its examples of demonic temptations and advice for dealing with these as "muy provechoso" (*Vida* 64), which is given variously as "profitable" by Peers (1: 94), "helpful" by Kavanaugh and Rodríguez (1: 123), and "useful" by Cohen (88).[1] Since teaching was almost entirely off-limits for women of her period, and doctrinal disputation entirely so, Teresa in this chapter characteristically presents her understandings of and methods for spiritual practice as nothing more than handy tips based on direct experience and tossed off in passing. However, her observations here as elsewhere in fact constitute theologically learned and rhetorically expressive as well as pedagogically astute instruction. Her deft and often humorous approach to what Alison Weber famously designates the "double bind" facing women writers on spiritual matters appears clearly in the carefully maintained, apparently offhand tone that does much to construct the Teresian "rhetoric of humility" (Weber, *Teresa of Ávila* 42–76). Thus in one passage Teresa uses the biblical resonance "Y ansí será ello *si se anda en justicia* y vamos *asidos a virtud*" but then quickly modulates to the deflating colloquiality of "mas es paso de gallina" (*Vida* 66; emphasis added). E. Allison Peers's translation gives this as "[w]e shall get along all right if we walk in righteousness and hold fast to virtue, but it will mean advancing at the pace of a hen . . ." (75–76). We might note that Teresa's wording implicitly makes male readers part of her intended audience—and therefore among those who might learn from her instruction—with the gender-inclusive "asidos a virtud" (the feminine "asidas" would have designated females only, limiting her implicit readership to the convent), thus subtly indicating the pervasive ambition and scope of her project. The J. M. Cohen translation of this passage reads, "We shall do all right if we walk in righteousness and cling to virtue, but we shall advance at a snail's pace" (90). Although it successfully translates a Spanish idiomatic expression ("es paso de gallina") into an analogously colloquial and proverbial English one ("at a snail's pace"), this rendering loses the lightly humorous gendering of "hen" that works at many levels. In Teresa's wording, both male and female spiritual aspirants are reminded that without such useful instruction as she offers, they may be no more effective than a clucking barnyard fowl. This example demonstrates the rhetorically nimble way that Teresian prose employs a range of registers and fields of citation. Her translators face the challenge of capturing these nuances of style and meaning, which draw richly on her era's familiarity with biblical and proverbial expression from both oral and elite traditions, and then carrying them over for our very different cultural and historical context.

It is widely observed that, although some wear better than others, in general translations fare badly with the passage of time; they become dated as original texts do not. The term "original" itself, however, cries for quotation marks, since any text is marked and directed by intertexts. Teresa would be the first to disavow her importance as an "original" author. Whatever twenty-first-century academic readers make of her faithful attribution of authorship to divine sources, however, our critical inquiry sees her work as achieving a lasting place in the literary canon. That is, readers in subsequent eras continue to read back across time and cultural difference to (re)discover in her works what their present age terms literary excellence.

With Teresa's writings, we are in the presence of delightfully, or frustratingly, complex texts that insist that they proceed from God; their ascribed supernatural sources, however, are conveyed in earthy and pragmatic imagery, with an intricately crafted presentation of apparently colloquial or "artless" language (we might recall that hen). Teresa's prose is poetic not in being flowery but in wedding rhythmic sound to sense: she charges her language with spirit by using pithy, sometimes clipped everyday expressions, omitting what an alert speaker of sixteenth-century Castilian would not need iterated. The challenges to translation are thus remarkable. Any translation must make interpretive decisions about utterances in the target (or receiving) language that correspond in richness of tone and imagery to what is expressed in the source language. The translator seeks to find or invent or impose linguistic and conceptual synonymy.

There are two principal translations of Teresa's writings that current scholars work with that demonstrate the deep knowledge of her life, language, and period and are supported by the research apparatus that scholarship requires. Both are learned and useful; others also merit consideration, as noted below. For mid-twentieth-century readers of English, the central translation of Teresa was the magisterial version by Peers, in *The Complete Works of Saint Teresa of Jesus* (found in many libraries and available in a reprint edition). Peers states the priority that his translation gives to conveying the "intensity" of Teresa's personality (1: xiv): "it would be nothing short of a tragedy if [the translator] turned her into a writer of text-books" (xvii); instead, she is "vivid, disjointed, elliptical, paradoxical and gaily ungrammatical" (xviii). When necessary, Peers opts for expansion of phrases that might otherwise be unclear by reading through Teresa's clipped elisions. His versions are lively; in their British idiom that harks back to the nineteenth century they often sound quaint (for example, in the use of "thee" and "thou"), positioning Teresa in a world somewhat remote from ours, as I show below.

Continuing from the late twentieth into the twenty-first century, Kieran Kavanaugh and Otilio Rodríguez are rendering their American English version in the volumes of *The Collected Works of St. Teresa of Ávila* (Kavanaugh's translation of Teresa's letters is now complete). Kavanaugh and Rodríguez, in contrast to Peers, give their goal as "above all fidelity to Teresa's thought; in addition . . . to capture something of her style, while at the same time rendering her in the language we use today" (1: 49). Their version pays great attention to theological consistency as well as linguistic accuracy. It is sometimes less lively than Peers's, however, and in paralleling Teresa's syntactic structures the English can become choppy. More literal, it is less literary: less entertaining in its rhythms, dialogues, or intercalations (examples follow below). Nonetheless, for present-day readers the transparency of the Kavanaugh-Rodríguez translation with regard to Teresa's Spanish usefully conveys the content of her spiritual thought and identifies the persons, events, and settings that form her world.

Teresa's account of her life is certainly her most accessible and appealing text for the general reader. A translation of this work by Cohen, *The Life of Saint Teresa of Ávila by Herself*, fluently presents this "literary masterpiece that is, after *Don Quixote*, the most widely read prose classic of Spain" (11). In the nineteenth- and early-twentieth-century belles-lettres tradition, this version evinces the translator's capacious general knowledge of period language and mores, without detailing the Carmelite or Counter-Reformation context. As was standard to critical views of Teresa in the mid–twentieth century, Cohen views her *Life* as "candid self-revelation, written in the liveliest and most unforced conversational prose" by a spontaneous talent whose "thoughts seem naturally to clothe themselves in simple, direct, and picturesque language"; Teresa's utterances are "homely," "simple," and "clear" (11). In other words, the translator as reader-interpreter seemingly accepts at face value Teresa's in fact complexly multivalenced self-description as an untutored, but unwittingly effective, writing "mujercilla" ("little woman"). Given this assessment of her means and achievement, the translation accordingly reads smoothly, often eloquently, with untroubled syntax. Unlike Peers's version, this one does not distance Teresa with archaic pronouns (we have "you" and "your" rather than "thee and thine"); nor, however, are we treated to as many flashes of humor. Again, examples follow below. Overall, the Cohen translation is well suited to classes prioritizing Teresa's literary qualities and paying less attention to historical or religious groundings (the text succinctly notes the identity of most important persons and places, without the meticulous annotations of Peers or Kavanaugh and Rodríguez).

A few passages chosen almost at random give a basis for comparing the vibrant urbanity of Peers's Teresa; the solemn, sometimes stiffer tone of the version by Kavanaugh and Rodríguez; and the capable, literate, but occasionally slightly bland Cohen translation. In her *Life*, at the opening of chapter 13, Teresa observes, "Hame parecido decir algunas tentaciones que he visto que se tienen a los principios, y algunas tenido yo. . . ." Evidently following the criterion of supplying to the reader of English what would be understood by the reader of Spanish, Peers holds true to the playfulness and rhetorical acuity of Teresa's text: "It has seemed to me appropriate to speak of certain temptations which, as I have observed, often attack beginners—I have had some of them myself . . ." (1: 75). He thus makes explicit the elision, available to Spanish readers, of the understood "conveniente" or "oportuno" in the opening phrase "Hame parecido," by adding "appropriate." Further on, a reader of English might appreciate the vividness of temptations that "often attack" beginners, for "se tienen"; the figurative usage is artful, as Teresa tends to be. On the other hand, the active verb might seem an intrusion that is added to the leaner original sentence.

Kavanaugh and Rodríguez translate the same phrase more neutrally: "It has occurred to me to speak about some temptations I have observed in beginners—I myself have had some— . . ." (1: 123). While accurate, this rendering may seem flat compared with the passage in Spanish. The explicit rendering of Teresa's shortened and colloquial phrase that the Peers version supplies to readers is left out in the Kavanaugh and Rodríguez translation, just as it is in the original; this strict concordance may be seen as more respectful of the text for some readers. For others, Peers's addition may appear more apt and thoughtful in conveying to readers the larger or the colloquial sense of the original.

In turn, Cohen presents information evenly and clearly: "I think it right to speak of certain temptations that I have observed, which occur at the beginning—I have experienced some of them myself— . . ." (88). The supplementation of "right" deftly clarifies this ellipsis, without making much of an addition to the economy of the original. The use of "beginning" rather than "beginners" is accurate to the Spanish, but we lose the implied presence of living readers who are new to the practice of mental prayer, an audience Teresa repeatedly addresses. Here, as elsewhere, then, Cohen's prose becomes slightly more abstract than Peers's, although it is generally smoother than Kavanaugh and Rodríguez's text.

In the same chapter, where Teresa lauds "un no estimar honra," Peers translates this as "no regard for honour" (1: 75); Kavanaugh and Rodríguez, perhaps awkwardly though with semantic parallel, as "disesteem of honor" (1: 125). Thus we see the earlier version more thoroughly pulling the phrase into English idiomatic expression. In the other, a stricter regard for following the cognate and syntax ("no estimar") produces the permissible but inelegant "disesteem of honor." Highly Latinate, this stilted phrase does not evoke Teresa. Finally, Cohen opts for an ennobling phrase, "to despise honours" (89), that, while accurate, does not convey the "conversational" tone he has claimed to hear in her writing.

As a third example, Teresa soon after this passage declares her disdain for bodily comfort, "Si el descanso, no he menester descanso, sino cruz." In context, the brusqueness of this highly elliptical statement conveys her no-nonsense contempt for the wiles of the devil, who lures a lazy body to forsake the good of the soul by tempting it with the prospect of rest rather than of effort or self-mortification. Peers again makes use of expansion to deal with the extreme compression but connotative resonance of Teresa's statement. Adding dialogue and a conversational mode that is true to the general spirit and to many particular sites in her text, he fleshes out this spareness: "'Rest, indeed!' I would say. 'I need no rest; what I need is crosses'" (1: 76). Peers thus works to keep an animated style before us, with the rhythms of a lively speaker; as with the exclamatory "indeed!" here, he boldly fills in apparently disjointed expressions and could be faulted for a high level of intervention against the brevity of the original.

With their version, ". . . or at the thought of rest, I answered: I no longer need rest, but the cross" (1: 126), Kavanaugh and Rodríguez too see the need in English to elaborate Teresa's intrinsically Spanish ellipsis; they add "at the thought of" and "I answered." However, they hold closer to Teresa's syntactic structure by keeping the full statement in one sentence, rather than dividing the remark into briefer exclamations. Kavanaugh and Rodríguez, choosing fidelity to the precise movement of Teresa's thought here in Spanish, come across more woodenly in English; "the thought of" lacks the vivacity of "indeed!"

In this passage, Cohen takes an approach similar to Peers (with whose translation he was familiar) but more succinct: "I would answer . . . 'Rest! I don't need rest but the Cross'" (90). He makes the dialogue explicit, but less fleshed out than in Peers. Syntactically smoother than Kavanaugh and Rodríguez, the phrasing does not have the rhythmic energy of Peers; while Cohen's introduction praises Teresa's "conversational" liveliness, his translation often reads more like competent writing than a brilliant melding of various registers of oral and literary currents. To summarize, all three versions of the *Life* are masterful in conveying the content of Teresa's experience, vision, and expertise; they vary more widely, as described here, in rendering the particularities of her literary style.

Similarly, three translations of *The Interior Castle* are relevant here; a more recent version joins the Peers and Kavanaugh and Rodríguez renderings. Mirabai Starr provides a new translation and introduction. Culturally, Starr's translation emphasizes present-day spiritual values from an ecumenical or noninstitutional perspective over faithfulness to the criteria of Teresa's Catholicism. Linguistically, it favors a contemporary American English idiom. The translator observes:

> I confess that I took the liberty . . . to soften some of [Teresa's] more loaded religious vocabulary. . . . I opted to minimize references to the inherent wickedness of human beings and replace such terms as "sin" and "evil" with "missing the mark," "imperfection," "unconsciousness," "limitations," and "negativity." "Mortal sin" is "grave error." I call "hell" "the underworld" and the "devil" the "spirit of evil." . . . (18)

Again, this translator makes choices that diverge from others because she is faithful to particular aspects of the original rather than inattentive or outright unfaithful to it. Starr's priority is to render the content of spiritual writings rather than their generating context. Starr conveys a Teresa who speaks to spiritual seekers in any of various faith traditions rather than to scholars or students in an academic setting (or to traditional Catholics). Within this framework, the translation demonstrates insight into the structures of Teresa's method of prayer and contemplation and provides a fresh, untrammeled representation of her complex texts for twenty-first-century, United States readers. Some points of comparison and contrast between this and the other two standard translations will further illuminate the qualities of each.

In the prologue to *The Interior Castle*, Teresa begins her customary dismissals of any literary talent on her own part. At face value, her statements claim an automatism rather than expertise to her act of writing. In fact, as Weber and other critics have emphasized, her disavowal of ability functions in complex ways as it works to underscore the divine authorship, and thus authority, that lies behind her supposedly "unskilled" utterances. Further, this claim subtly suggests her cautious and gendered propriety in following rather than interpreting "the letter of the law": "porque ansí como los pájaros que enseñan a hablar . . . soy yo al pie de la letra" (*Vida* 272). Peers, in keeping with his already cited method of bringing Teresa's utterances into a straightforward English idiomatic expression, gives "for I write as mechanically as birds taught to speak" (2: 199). The adverb "mechanically" aptly brings to mind the untutored production that Teresa indicates. However, it lacks the additional sense of conformity and obeisance suggested in her description of herself as writing, or indeed being, "al pie de la letra." Kavanaugh and Rodríguez, on the other hand, find a word that more precisely suggests these qualities: "I'm, literally, just like the parrots that are taught to speak" (2: 281). In a neat example of the impossibility of complete synonymy (and thus the inevitable frustration of the translator's task), this choice loses one sense of "al pie de la letra" while it gains another. It deftly indicates her "literalness" (that is, a faithful carrying out of all and only what she has been taught) in writing. However, it lacks the meaning that Peers's version captures: not only that she herself "is" but also that she "writes" by the letter of the law. Additionally, Kavanaugh and Rodríguez's choice is choppily phrased in English, whereas Teresa's Spanish is smoothly colloquial.

In a third comparison, Starr's version of this phrase comes not only smoothly but perhaps blandly into today's American English: "I feel like one of those birds they teach to speak . . ." (30). In keeping with current rather than early modern cultural values, emphasis is on the speaker's self-conscious, emotionally framed experience ("I feel like") rather than on a responsibility to place herself with respect to authority. The advantage here is that readers are not stopped by the English phrasing on their way to the central message of the passage.

In *The Interior Castle*, dwelling 7, chapter 3, Teresa moves toward the conclusion of her description of souls who have progressed from the lofty state of spiritual betrothal to the "great effects" of spiritual marriage. Her elevated topic does not prevent her from using down-to-earth language to represent the advanced soul's continuing desire to suffer for God, although the soul wishes above all that God's will should be accomplished in it. Therefore, Teresa observes, even if God does not ordain that such a soul should be gratified by being allowed to suffer for God, "no se mata como solía." In Peers's translation, "she [the soul], does not worry herself to death as she did before" (2: 339).[2] Characteristically, Peers again maintains the figurative resonance of Teresa's Spanish (which uses the verb *matarse*, literally, to kill oneself). At the same time, he finds a (British) idiomatic expression that communicates the homely, direct sense of the original phrase. *Matarse* as Teresa uses it means precisely "to wear oneself out with worry," to fret a matter to death. Peers's choice has the advantage of rendering the spontaneous tone, dramatically figurative verb, and understood meaning of the original.

Kavanaugh and Rodríguez, also characteristically, follow literally the construction of the original: "it doesn't kill itself as it used to" (2: 277). Rather than personify the soul with a gendered pronoun, they choose the neutral "it"— probably closer to a modern English speaker's sense of the term, but coldly abstract. Their handling of the verb in English has the possible advantage of suggesting, without overdetermining, the idiomatic meaning that Peers makes explicit; however, if the English reader misses this connotation, there is an inapt sense of suicide.

Finally, Starr boldly carries the phrase over into a present-day, pop-psychology American English idiom: "she won't launch into the self-destructive behavior she used to engage in" (277). On the one hand, this would seem radically to misrepresent the often positive valence of self-mortification in Teresa's early modern Catholic world. On the other, and setting aside its talk-show resonance, the phrase in fact rather precisely conveys Teresa's critique of misplaced or willful attempts at holiness by some nuns, overly enthusiastic practitioners of self-mortification.

Curiously, the sticking points in a translation may serve as awkwardly eloquent pointers toward key meanings in the original. Theorists repeatedly draw attention to literature's making of complex meanings precisely where facile or surface meaning is disturbed. Michael Riffaterre identifies significant "ungrammaticalities" that presciently open out the deeper meanings and reaches of a text. Walter Benjamin similarly describes these useful disruptions, for instance, as vestigial fractures that richly mar a translator-archaeologist's reconstruction, from language shards, of an ancient vessel. In Benjamin's view (aptly mystical, for discussions of Teresa), an original work with its translations together suggests an eloquent and unflawed ideal text, unattainable except as evoked by their interaction. Thus translation, far from betraying, works to complete the original. In the first example from *The Interior Castle* cited above, Peers's odd, oblique suggestion of the author as a wind-up toy bird is one such moment; Kavanaugh and Rodríguez's stuttering "I'm, literally, just like" is another. The seemingly uncontrolled metaphor of the first example or infelicity of the second can draw our attention, in translation, to something key that lies buried in the text's layered meanings—for instance, Teresa's complex, hampered, gendered relation to the act of writing. Here, in fact, the smoothest version,

Starr's, least calls our attention to this difficulty, central for Teresa as she writes. The translators discussed here do not work automatically or "parrot" a meaning of which they are unaware. Their careful and informed deliberations show through each translated text; for instructors bringing Teresa to their classes in English, the criteria directing one or another translation will determine which best suits the curriculum.

NOTES

[1] Throughout this essay, citations to Teresa correspond to the following works under her name in the works-cited list: *The Complete Works*, translated by Peers; *The Collected Works*, translated by Kavanaugh and Rodríguez; the *Life*, translated by Cohen; and *Vida*, edited by Comas.

[2] In Spanish, the referent for the reflexive pronoun "se" is "alma" ("soul").

The Language of Teresa of Ávila

Emily E. Scida

The linguistic characteristics of Teresa of Ávila's writing are in many respects representative of sixteenth-century Spanish and other Golden Age authors. In this essay I describe the most salient features of sixteenth-century Spanish found in Teresa that may cause problems for readers primarily accustomed to modern literature, focusing my discussion on orthography, morphosyntax, and vocabulary, with examples taken from *Libro de la vida* (*The Book of Her Life*). In teaching Teresa, it is essential to know how and why her language differs from modern Spanish to guide students in a thorough understanding of her work.

Orthography

Although many have commented that Teresa wrote spontaneously and improvised without attention to style or cultured written norms, linguists consider her orthography to be systematic rather than haphazard or primitive (e.g., Menéndez Pidal; Ruiz de Loizaga). Teresa's orthographic system is phonetic and reflects the speech and pronunciation of her time, giving us insight into those sound changes completed or in progress in the sixteenth-century Spanish of Old Castile. Even though editors of her manuscripts altered some of her spelling to conform to the written standards of the time, we can observe many orthographic features unique to her writing even in these revised versions.

Teresa's writing shows an alternation between the letters *b* and *v* for the sound /b/. This spelling alternation might represent the loss of the *b-v* distinction or perhaps a change in progress. In most cases, we find the change from an etymological *b* to *v*, but not normally from *v* to *b*. This can be explained by the fact that the medieval stop /b/ had undergone fricativization, and the letter used at that time to represent the fricative was *v* (Ruiz de Loizaga 274). Examples of this spelling alternation are numerous and include: "havía" 'there were' (17), "cavello" 'hair' (18), "travajos" 'troubles' (21), "escriva" 'writes' (16).[1]

Another orthographic feature in Teresa's prose is the simplification of consonant groups in words like "estiende" 'extends' (26), "estremo" 'extreme' (18), "escusarían" 'would excuse' (20), "perfeción" 'perfection' (37), "descrición" 'description' (30). There are also examples of metathesis, a change in the order of one or more sounds in a word: "ternían" 'they would have' (34), "hiproquesía" 'hypocrisy' (31), "primitir" 'to permit' (36). We also find the occasional substitution of the letter *l* for *r* and vice versa, as in "milaglo" 'miracle' or "naturar" 'natural' (Ruiz de Loizaga 277). In a few cases, Teresa uses the letter *s* to represent the modern Spanish velar fricative /x/: "relisión" 'religion' (20), "relisiosos" 'religious' (32), and "colesio" 'college' (172).

As for the vowel system, there is much variation in Teresa's spelling of unstressed vowels. For example, Teresa frequently uses the letter *i* for unstressed *e* and vice versa: "mijor" 'better' (16), "sigún" 'according to' (18), "cerimonias" 'ceremonies' (30), "destraída" 'distracted' (89). There are doublets where the same word is spelled with either vowel, such as "afleción/afición" 'affection' (26–27). Her writing also shows an alternation between unstressed *a* and *e*, as in "ascondida" 'hidden' (18), "piadad" 'piety' (17), and "monesterio" 'monastery' (32), as well as an alternation between unstressed *o* and *u*, in "mormuración" 'murmuring' (29) and "puniendo" 'putting' (17). Teresa consistently spells the conjunction or as *u*: "seis u siete años" 'six or seven years' (17).

In Teresa's original manuscripts, the following orthographic features are of interest (Sánchez Moguel; Ruiz de Loizaga; Menéndez Pidal). Teresa uses the letters *c* or *ç* where in Modern Spanish we would expect *c* or *z*: *conoçer* "to know," *raçones* "reasons," *deçir* "to say." This convention is different from medieval orthographic distinctions of voiced and voiceless sibilants (Ruiz de Loizaga 268). Teresa uses the letter *n* instead of *m* in syllable-final position before a bilabial stop: *inporta* ("it matters"), *tienpo* ("time"; Sánchez Moguel 66). Generally, Teresa omits an initial letter *h* where we expect to see it in modern Spanish: *aver* ("to have"), *ombre* ("man"), *uyr* ("to flee"). This also seems to indicate that the pronunciation of initial /h/ from an original Latin /f/ was already lost in the language of Old Castile. These texts also show a use of the letter *g* for /g/ in *gerra* ("war"), *agila* ("eagle"); the use of *j* for /x/ in words like *jente* ("people"); the use of the combinations *qua-* and *que-* where modern Spanish has *c* as in *quan* ("how"), *quenta* ("account"); and the use of *y* for /i/ in word-initial or word-final position and in diphthongs, in words like *yr* ("to go"), *sy* ("yes"), *reyna* ("queen"; Sánchez Moguel 60–61, 69–73).

Morphosyntax

Teresa's writing exhibits many characteristics typical of the noun and verb systems and sentence structure of sixteenth-century Spanish. Although one could address an endless number of developments in this regard, my description here will focus on those features of the morphological and syntactic structures that may be problematic for a reader unfamiliar with the language of medieval and Golden Age texts.

A characteristic of other Golden Age authors as well, Teresa's prose contains occasional examples of incorrect subject-verb agreement (Lapesa 408): "el daño y destraimiento que después entendí era semejantes tratos" 'the harm and distraction which I found would be the case later' (33). In other cases, certain verbs that continue into modern Spanish are used differently in Golden Age texts. For example, *ser* and *estar*, both "to be," have a different distribution in Teresa's writing (Criado de Val; Lapesa 400–01). While in modern Spanish *estar* is used to express location, Teresa uses *ser* especially when referring to the existence of God: "El espiritu santo sea sienpre con v.m." 'May the Holy Spirit be always with you' (Pountain 158; my trans.). In another instance, Teresa uses *estar* where we would expect *ser* to identify a characteristic: "Dormía una monja con las que estávamos seglares" 'There was a nun who slept with those of us who were seculars' (20). In her writing, we sometimes see *estar* used instead of *haber* with existential meaning: "Estava una persona de la iglesia que risidía en aquel lugar" 'There was a person from the church who resided in that place' (25).

In Teresa's work, the verbs *haber* and *tener* are used both with the meaning "to have" and with the periphrastic perfect tenses (Lapesa 399). Where we might expect *tener*, we find examples such as "yo he lástima" 'I have pity' (17) and "han miedo" 'they have fear' (39), showing the use of *haber* to mean "to have" with an abstract direct object. Although modern Spanish uses the auxiliary verb *haber* in the compound perfect tenses, Teresa occasionally uses *tener* instead: "parece tenéis determinado que me salve" 'it seems that you have determined to save me' (18). And finally, *haber* and not *hacer* is used in time expressions, as in the following examples: "me hallo buena ocho años ha" 'I have been well for eight years' (34) and "havía casi siete años que estava en muy peligroso estado" 'For nearly seven years he had been in a dangerous state' (26).

Verb forms in Teresa's prose are usually identical or similar to those in modern Spanish, but there are some interesting differences. For example, metathesis of *l* or *r* can occur in some command forms or in the irregular forms of the future and conditional. In second person plural affirmative commands, we sometimes find that the *l* of the object pronoun and the *d* of the verb form have been interchanged: "Daldes a entender" 'Give them to understand' (85). Metathesis also occurs in the future and conditional in forms like "ternían" 'they would have' (34), "porná" 'she will put' (66). In her writing, the future and conditional generally appear as one-word synthetic forms (as they are in modern Spanish), but Teresa at times uses the older analytic construction composed of the infinitive plus the form of *haber*, written as two words: "escrivirlo he todo lo mijor que pueda" 'I will write it the best I can' (45). We also find this older construction in "nos lo tornará a tomar y quedarnos hemos muy más pobres" 'he will take it back from us, and we will be much poorer' (44). And finally, Teresa's writing shows the use of older forms of the second person plural of the preterite and of the imperfect tenses. These preterite forms do not display the diphthong present in the modern Spanish *vosotros* forms: "quisistes" 'you wanted' (23), "dejastes" 'you left' (31). The imperfect forms retain the original intervocalic *d* in the second-person plural: "llamávades" 'you called' (31), "estávades" 'you were' (33).

Another interesting feature of Teresa's language is the use of the future subjunctive, a verb tense common in Old Spanish but largely formulaic in Modern Spanish. The future subjunctive can appear in relative clauses: "Sólo pido . . . que lo pruebe quien no me creyere" 'I only ask that whoever does not believe me try it' (30). Conditional sentences can also use the future subjunctive: "si Su Majestad nos quisiere subir a ser de los de su cámara y secreto, ir de buena gana" 'If His Majesty wants to promote us to be among those of his chamber and privy council, we must go with him willingly' (91). In addition, hypothetical conditional sentences in Golden Age Spanish can use the imperfect subjunctive in both clauses: "Si leyera toda la Pasión, no llorara una lágrima" 'If I read the whole Passion, I would not shed a tear' (20).

In the compound perfect tenses, Teresa's prose frequently shows the ellipsis of the auxiliary verb *haber* when its use is understood from the context of the sentence (M. Alonso; Pountain). In the following sentence, the second *havía* is suppressed but understood: "pues tantas veces me havía tornado a Sí y yo dejádole" 'since He had so often brought me back to Himself and I had left Him' (40). In another example, we see the ellipsis of the auxiliary *he* in the second verb: "de lo que el Señor me ha enseñado por espiriencia, y después tratádolo yo con grandes letrados" 'about which the Lord has taught me by experience, and afterward I have discussed with men of great learning' (45). According to Pountain (157), ellipsis is more common in the spoken language, but what is most interesting here is the omission of *haber* even when there is a change of subject.

As we have seen in these examples, the position of object pronouns in the sixteenth century differs from Modern Spanish use. In general, pronoun position is less restricted in older texts. In Old Spanish a pronoun is prohibited in the initial position of a sentence or clause, unless other words or phrases precede the verb (Pountain 264). Since a pronoun cannot occur at the beginning of a sentence, in this example the pronoun *me* appears attached to the end of the verb: "Acuérdome que cuando murió mi madre" 'I remember that when my mother died' (17). Compare this with a sentence where the verb is preceded by the subject: "el Señor me favorecía" 'the Lord favored me' (16). As seen in the previous paragraph, the object pronoun can occur before *haber* or can be attached to the past participle in the compound perfect tenses. With commands, infinitives, and gerunds, the object pronoun can precede or follow (Lapesa 407): "para no la perder del todo" 'to not lose it altogether' (19), "para no perderme del todo" 'to not lose myself altogether' (19).

Another common feature of Teresa's style and of sixteenth-century prose is the omission of the complementizer *que* between two clauses. Examples of this abound in Teresa's writing, so I provide only a few: "mas todavía deseava no fuese monja" 'but I still wished not to be a nun' (21), "me decían no iva contra Dios" 'they told me that I was not offending God' (20). In many cases there is an alternation between the use and the omission of *que*, which occurs here after the verb *parecer*: "parecíame no era malo" 'it seemed to me that it was not bad' (18), "Paréceme que comenzó a hacerme mucho daño" 'it seems to me that it began to do me great harm' (18).

Outside the verb system, there are many noteworthy features in Teresa's writing with respect to the nominal system, modifiers, and prepositions. Repeatedly mentioned as unique to Teresa's style is her frequent use of diminutives and superlatives. Many have claimed that the use of diminutives is characteristic of informal, spontaneous language or that it is particular to female speech (e.g., Menéndez Pidal; Lapesa). More current studies hold that the percentage of diminutive forms in relation to total words is not high in any of Teresa's works (Carpi, Saba, and Sassi) and that diminutives used in her writing express affect and irony intended for a specific, more intimate, audience and are not a quality of feminine language (Weber, "Teresa's 'Delicious' Diminutives"). Diminutive and superlative suffixes tend to occur most frequently with the same words in Teresa's prose, for example, *pobrecito, poquito, grandísimo*.

Scholars have noted a lack of gender agreement between some nouns and their articles in Teresa's writing (Sánchez Moguel 81; Bastons Vivanco 238). This supposed change of gender is really a remnant of the Old Spanish use of the masculine articles *el* and *un* with nouns that begin with /a/ and other vowels (Lapesa 391): "el aldea" 'the town' (23), "aquel agonía" 'that agony' (65), "el amistad" 'friendship' (36), but "la amistad" (33). We know that the noun has not changed gender if we look at the adjective that modifies it: "un alma sola" 'a soul alone' (36). In Teresa's works we also notice an inconsistent use of the contractions *al* (*a* + *el*) and *del* (*de* + *el*); in the same paragraph she writes "a el infierno" and then "al infierno" 'to hell' (32). Another feature common in Teresa but largely absent from standard Modern Spanish is the use of *cuán* before an adjective or adverb to express the notion of "how": "cuán bien hablava de Dios" 'how well she spoke of God' (20), "cuán merecido tenía el infierno" 'how deserved I had hell' (33). Teresa also uses *muy* in comparative phrases, such as "muy muchas veces" 'very many times' (41) and "muy más pobres" 'much more poor' (44).

The use of personal pronouns for the second-person singular and plural had undergone significant changes since Latin, and in the sixteenth century the second person plural *vos* was used with reference to both singular and plural. In *Libro de las fundaciones* (*The Book of Foundations*), a nun addresses Teresa using *vos*: "Díjome: Madre, estoy pensando, si ahora me muriese yo aquí, ¿qué haríais vos sola?" 'She said to me: Mother, I am thinking, if I should die here now, what would you do alone?' (549). In the same work, Teresa uses the plural *vos* to address her fellow nuns: "Ya habéis visto, hijas" 'You have already seen, daughters' (577). Teresa addresses God with *vos*, and he responds using the pronoun *tú*: "respondístesme Señor: 'Sírveme tú a Mí y no te metas en eso'" 'You responded to me Lord: "Serve thou me and don't meddle in that"' (75). To express formality or deference in Golden Age Spanish, various phrases were used along with the third-person forms of the verb—*Vuestra Merced, Vuestra Señoría*, and so forth. Teresa uses *Vuestra Merced* (sometimes abbreviated *v.m.*) when addressing her confessor: "Pues dice vuestra merced que me quiere" 'you say that you love me' (66).

Vocabulary

The language of Teresa contains some lexical items that have been lost in Modern Spanish along with others that have continued but either with different forms or with different meanings (Sánchez Moguel 51–55). Of the first category of vocabulary uncommon or lost in the modern language, we can include words like *ruin* ("bad"), *estotro* ("this other"), *menester* ("necessary"), *mas* ("but"), *acaecer* ("to occur"), *cuantimás* ("much more").

Other lexical items in Teresa exhibit older forms that had not yet undergone the linguistic changes they would make in Modern Spanish. Some of these words include *priesa* (mod. *prisa*; "hurry"), *naide* (mod. *nadie*; "no one"), *ansí* (mod. *así*; "so"), *mesmo* (mod. *mismo*; "self"). In other cases, Teresa's writing shows forms or stems similar to Modern Spanish but with the addition of a prefix or the use of a different prefix than that expected in Modern Spanish: *encomenzar* for *comenzar* ("to begin"), *deprender* for *aprender* ("to learn"), *abajar* for *bajar* ("to go down"), *enjemplo* for *ejemplo* ("example").

Other lexical items in Teresa's work exist in Modern Spanish but with different meanings or uses. A very common feature of Teresa's language is the use of *harto* with the meaning of "very" or "much": "harto entendimiento" 'much understanding' (17), "harto mijorada" 'much bettered' (21). The word *cabe* is used in the sense of "near," in "vi cabe mí" 'I saw near me' (106). The adverb *luego* is used with the meaning of "right away; at that moment": "muérame yo luego" 'I die at that moment' (Lapesa 406). And finally, Teresa uses various phrases to refer to God, such as *Su Majestad* "Your Majesty," *Criador mío* "my Creator," *Señor mío* "my Lord," *Rey mío* "my King."

In teaching Teresa, we must not forget that her strategies of language use contribute to the overall meaning of her work. An awareness of the orthographic, morphological, syntactic, and lexical features found in Teresa that are distinct from Modern Spanish conventions will certainly facilitate the reading of her prose and enhance one's interpretation of her work. For example, readers with a familiarity of sixteenth-century Spanish will correctly interpret the analytic construction of the infinitive plus *haber* (*escrivirlo he*) as the future tense and will recognize a verb with a postposed object pronoun (*paréceme*) as equivalent to Modern Spanish *me parece*. An understanding of the prominent features of sixteenth-century Spanish will contribute to a more thorough reading and appreciation of the meaning and content of Teresa's work.

NOTE

[1] All citations to Teresa's work are from *Obras completas* (ed. Efrén de la Madre de Dios and Steggink). Translations are my own.

Part Two

APPROACHES

Mysticism in History:
The Case of Spain's Golden Age

Elizabeth Rhodes

The nature of mysticism, as traditionally defined, discourages us from exploring the relation between mysticism and history, from ferreting out the circumstances that make the direct human experience of God possible, meaningful, and understandable. As inherited wisdom has it, mysticism happens when the divinity makes the (presumably) executive decision to erupt directly into human affairs through a human being; the human passivity recognized as a hallmark of the mystical way suggests that people have relatively little to do with how or when that actually transpires. However, although transhistorical, mysticism is deeply rooted in a historical context, and Spain's Golden Age provides a particularly compelling example of how God works in and through human history.[1]

Teresa of Ávila and John of the Cross are by far the best known mystics of Golden Age Spain and are universally recognized as among the most compelling voices of Catholic mysticism of all time. Indeed, so famous are they that their words eclipse other equally important individuals of mystical expertise who lived during the same period. Most famous mystics are famous not so much because they were mystics but because they were exceptionally able writers, capable of persuading audiences of the intensity, authenticity, and legitimacy of their mystical experience. By all accounts, the direct experience of God cannot be captured by human language with anything close to high fidelity. The mystic who rises to the surface of history is not only able to attain and endure contact with the ultimate power and presence but is also able to pick up a pen and articulate that amazing and excruciating experience in a way that moves readers.

Less esteemed as mystics by posterity are those who are less able writers, even if expert at experiencing God, and those who wrote instructional manuals about how to be a mystic rather than first-person accounts of their own experiences.

By the time Teresa was finding her way to God, a path in that direction had been well paved by her precursors and specific historical events of the late fifteenth and early sixteenth centuries. The marriage of Ferdinand of Aragon and Isabel of Castile in 1469 formally united their two kingdoms into what we now call Spain, in a tentative political embrace that was plagued with transitional difficulties. The rest of the regions eventually ruled under their crowns were in flux and formation for most of the sixteenth century.[2] Having spent from 711 until 1492 at war with the Moors in Iberia, the Christians who eventually triumphed were well versed in the rhetoric of state religion and the justification of conquest in the name of God, the practice of holy war normalized on the Iberian Peninsula by the Arabs. To put it somewhat bluntly, Isabel and Ferdinand's God—at least the God whose voice was given a public forum—was decidedly interested in occupying the Iberian Peninsula (and later the New World) geographically, politically, and socially as well as spiritually. The successful mystic of this period, then, was the individual able to find and represent a god supportive of aggressive, action-based piety. The silent ecstasies in the dark that John of the Cross describes in his poetry would probably not have made literary and religious history had they been written during this age.

The year 1492 is key to understanding the wave of mystical manifestations in the kingdoms of Ferdinand and Isabel as well as those that followed. It was obviously a banner twelve months: Columbus set off on his first voyage in search of a waterway to the Indies; Antonio Nebrija's *Gramática de la lengua castellana* was published, the first grammar of a vulgar (versus classical) language, which signaled the Castilian hegemony that was to last through 1650; the kingdom of Granada, the last Moorish stronghold in Iberia, fell to the Catholic kings; the Jews were expelled, as a contemporary account recalls, "from Castile, Catalonia, Aragon, Galicia, Majorca, Minorca, the Basque provinces, the islands of Sardinia and Sicily, and the kingdom of Valencia" (the same account recalls that Isabel had expelled them from Andalusia in 1483).[3] Clearly, many boundaries were being renegotiated with particular force. During a period in which two or more faiths are contesting geographic occupation of the same space, the need to prove that God is "with" each party becomes especially acute, and, given that the story of the victors is the one that endures, early modern Spanish mysticism is a recognizable flower of this expansionist age: the beata visionary María de Ajofrín died in 1489; Beatriz de Silva Meneses, whose visions of the Immaculate Conception had important theological and political consequences, died in 1490; Juana de la Cruz's locutions were recorded in 1508–09; María de Santo Domingo's *Book of Prayer* was first printed in 1518 under the patronage of Archbishop Francisco Ximénez de Cisneros himself.[4]

Women's prominence in this context is to be expected; heroic standards of masculinity in Castile and Aragon, meaning the behavioral models deemed imitable by the dominant group, were centered on war values. Cisneros (1436–1517), an Observant Franciscan, was appointed archbishop of Toledo in 1495 and had been ueen Isabel's confessor since 1492. Cisneros exemplifies the heroic male religious of this pugnacious age: a powerful reformer of his order, he was also deeply involved in intellectual pursuits that served Catholicism, as well as the violent pursuits of its goals. In 1509, he personally led a crusade to Oran (Algeria).

The demands of masculinity away from contemplative, passive, and ecstatic prayer during Spain's formative years are on record as frustrating the mystical ambitions of several important men. John of Ávila, as reformist as Cisneros but not at all politically inclined, laments repeatedly in his letters that his active apostolate denied him the time and attention necessary to sustain the intimate relationship with God for which he longed. In his famous letter of 1544 to Luis de Granada, "To a preacher," he advised his friend, "Reveal your private secrets about your communication with God to none of your confessants nor anyone else, for you will learn by experience that they are so unable to keep it secret that you would be unable to believe it did you not try it yourself"(*Epistolario* 23; my trans.).[5] John of Ávila wrote prescriptive treatises for others rather than descriptions of his own experience; he is famous not for being the mystic he surely was but for his extraordinary apostolic public life, which, even though informed by humility and poverty, nonetheless touched the lives of the rich and famous as well as innumerable lesser individuals and made possible his visibility to future generations. Only when the violence and activism inherent in the cultural construct of the heroic Spanish male subsided did a publicly sanctioned paradigm for the male mystic make a successful appearance. This shift allowed male mystics not to exist, for they had always existed, but to be public figures as mystics and thereby to become visible to posterity as such, supported by the dominant group whose sanction was necessary for that visibility.

The physical stasis, responsive spirit, and exercise of contemplative prayer necessary for mysticism, by contrast, were celebrated as the virtues of the heroic woman of the period, features that intensified as gender models became increasingly patriarchal as the century progressed. During the reign of Isabel of Castile (1474–1504), religious women throughout Europe were imitating ecstatic visionary female figures of thirteenth- and fourteenth-century Catholicism, particularly Angela of Foligno (1248–1309) and Catherine of Siena (1347–80), whose works, translated into Spanish, were among the first books published by the newly invented printing press. Dominant society's understanding of women as inherently receptive, passive, weak, and inferior to men not only made it possible for them to represent their mystical experiences in first person but eventually required that they do so, as part of their superiors' discernment of their spiritual experiences.[6] Late medieval mystics and the early modern women who imitated them cemented female Catholic mysticism into parameters that were quickly assimilated by women religious.

Throughout these years, during which the praxis and expression of mystical experience were being explored and defined, the political efficacy of the Spanish mystic continued to intensify along gendered lines. Archbishop Cisneros's transformation of Sor María de Santo Domingo from an illiterate peasant into a famous holy woman speaks to the dichotomies inherent in the male and female heroic models for this period. It is no coincidence that God also spoke to her in favor of the Inquisition and against the recently expelled Jews. According to dominant gender constructs, the ideal woman, whose expertise was surrender, was raised from her naturally low state by the hand of God. This never transpired as a consequence of her own merit, the lack of which her gender amply testified to; divine elevation enabled the female mystic to serve men as the mouthpiece of God. Fray Antonio de la Peña's 1511 translation of Raymond of Capua's *Life of Catherine of Siena* represents this justification well:

> And what is truly remarkable and in my opinion quite noteworthy is how these days God seems to work this abundance of grace most singularly in the weak lineage of women; and perhaps He does so to confound men's arrogance, particularly of those who, puffed up with their own reputations, have no shame in calling themselves wise, when it is true that they know nothing, nor do they truly taste the sweetness of God.
>
> (prol., n.pag.; my trans.)[7]

History makes it clear that when God spoke in Spain, that voice was heard only after careful editing; the determination of when God's articulations were allowed to be disseminated, or who believed it was God speaking in the first place, was a matter of interpretation and power.[8] During the period in question, mystical bodies and texts abounded in ongoing waves of reformist groups whose members rejected the formalistic facets of a time-weary Catholic cult and put the worshipper back into direct contact with God: the *recogidos*, Spain's native mystical movement; the Illuminists, eventually determined to be heretical; Protestants, exiled from Spain for political as well as religious reasons; and, eventually, the Catholic mystics themselves, *recogimiento*'s progeny and the product of centuries of ethnic and religious cleansing on the part of Spanish political and ecclesiastical institutions.[9]

Anyone claiming to be speaking with God, particularly a woman, was subjected to rigorous scrutiny by ecclesiastical authorities to determine whether it was God or a malign spirit at work in the individual, clearly a highly vexed determination. Women were examined systematically, whereas men were not because men were understood to possess the intellectual capacity to discern their own experiences. As the case studies in *Women in the Inquisition*, edited by Mary Giles, reveal, what remain today are the voices of those found to be orthodox. Inquisitorial records, in which the words of the silenced speak through the muffling and slanted filter of an inquisitorial scribe, provide hard and fast, if problematic, evidence of how monotone the official, published voices extant for posterity really are in comparison with the polyphony that surged forth from the spiritual energy generated by the proud people whose young country was about to take the world by storm.

The Golden Age of Spanish mysticism has its roots in the Catholic reform that began, according to some, as early as the fourteenth century; this was the same restless, reformist Catholicism that produced the Protestant Reformation itself. As European society shifted from a theocentric understanding of life to the anthropocentric worldview typical of the Renaissance, medieval Christianity was reassessed. It was found to lack engagement with the world and social problems and was seen as excessively formulaic, overburdened with ritual, and unproductively emphatic on the distance between God and humanity rather than celebratory of the relationship between human beings and the divinity. By the time Cisneros was appointed archbishop of Toledo in 1495, the Catholic reform had become integrated into the religious life of Spain. This reform, in which Teresa of Ávila was a leader, normalized self-examination and corrective behaviors designed to reconcile one's beliefs with one's actual practice of living. The self-discipline and purification implicit in self-examination is the first step in the mystical way, and thus the historical coincidence of the Catholic reform with Spain's energy and particularly fervent religious conviction institutionalized the reflective processes that make mysticism possible.

Desiderius Erasmus (1446–1536), the Dutch reformist author and famous Christian humanist, held great appeal for Spanish Catholics anxious to prove the superiority of their religion over the systems of belief with which the Castilians and Aragonese were constantly in conflict, particularly New World natives, Moors, Jews, and Protestants.[10] The influence of Erasmus, magisterially imprinted on Spanish historiography by the French scholar Marcel Bataillon, indicates the readiness of the young state to flex its intellectual and cultural muscles in harmony with a renewed Catholic spirit. The conscientious practice of inner virtue, in contrast with prescribed formulas of traditional Catholic prescriptions, and the exercise of the human spirit whose praises were sung by the Christian humanists of the early sixteenth century, deepened the intimacy of spiritual discourse in Spain. This, in turn, allowed Teresa's teachers, and Teresa herself, to speak of the workings of the soul in specific, calculated terms that sprang from a morphology of prayer conducive to union and sustained intimacy with God. Humanism provided mysticism with a landscape it had not had before, making it possible for Spanish Catholics, energized by the age of exploration they dominated, fearlessly to seek out new frontiers of the human interior.

The genius of Ignatius of Loyola (1491–1556), whose *Spiritual Exercises* transformed the praxis of vocational discernment and self-reflection in the Catholic tradition, has proved without parallel in its impact on the history of mysticism and on Spain's status as premier authority on the nature of how God works through human beings. The *Exercises* formalized the role of the spiritual guide who serves a novice, different from the confessor-confessant relationship more typical of earlier Catholicism. Ignatius introduced intimate human contact and instruction that was based on the sharing of a common experience of God as the great facilitator in the realization of one's spirit, making the enterprise of knowing oneself as a means to knowing God more a human responsibility than the sometimes arbitrary privilege with which it had been represented under the medieval, theocentric rubric. Perfectly balanced between contemplation and action, the exercises are a method, not a text; living words, they were designed to be *made*, not read, and only under the guidance of a superior.[11] This balance between knowing oneself and God intimately and accomplishing with others the work in the world that God needed done, is deeply imprinted on the *Exercises* and became a hallmark of Spanish Catholic mysticism. The question of whether Ignatius himself can be considered a mystic, which perplexes to this day, derives from the absence of a first-person account of his spiritual life or any other kind of text written by him that would assure readers today of the answer.[12]

It is difficult to overestimate the importance of the Protestant Reformation on the spiritual and institutional history of Spain. Martin Luther (1483–1546) and John Calvin (1509–64) generated not only different systems of Christian belief but forced political rupture on the Holy Roman Empire, whose emperor, Charles V, was also King Charles I of Spain (ruled 1516–56). The bitter conflicts between Protestants and Catholics, inseparable from the developing national identities of the sixteenth century, intensified Catholic spirituality and fomented a passionate longing to hear God speak directly to Catholic believers. There is a political logic to the fact that Spain's most famous mystics lived during the very period in which Catholicism was formulating its response to Protestantism and redefining itself against the Protestant enemy. That saints and other members of the Catholic celestial hierarchy, such as orders of angels, figure with increasing prominence in the mystical writings of the Counter-Reformation speaks to the fact that one of the features believed to distinguish Catholics from Protestants was the Catholics' belief in precisely those saints and celestial figures.

The legitimacy of Catholic mysticism was bolstered even more by the eloquent, widely read writings of the Dominican preacher Fray Luis de Granada (1505–88), Ignatius's contemporary. Fray Luis shares with his friend John of Ávila the difficult status of the male mystic who lived before the Council of Trent: Spain was not ready to support fully and publicly the male mystic during the years when Granada was writing his amazing books for delighted readers. Those books manifest all the positive, optimistic energy of the Catholic reform before the conservative response to the Protestant threat had become embedded in Catholic ideology. Naive, sincere, exquisitely educated, and exuberant, Fray Luis proposed to accomplish nothing less than to make a mystic of every single Catholic, and he wrote the books to achieve that. The Spanish public's overwhelmingly positive response to his instructions manifests the deep enthusiasm for and commitment to living faith and understanding of God as accessible to all that had permeated Spanish Catholicism by 1560.

The first broadly popular self-help manual for would-be mystics, Luis de Granada's *Libro de la oración y meditación* (*Book of Prayer and Meditation*), first published in 1558, is the premier primer of Spanish mysticism, or *recogimiento*.[13] *Recogimiento* differs from the other heterodox movements in Spain—Illuminism

(first censored in 1512–25), Erasmism (1516–59), and Protestantism (1517–63)—
in its emphasis on sacramentals (rites and material artifacts such as holy images)
as legitimate tools of devotion; its respect for Catholic ceremony and tradition;
its understanding of suffering as a virtue to be willingly sought, embraced, and
overcome; and its monastic discipline, which focused the individual on self-denial
and discipline as the necessary first step in any knowledge of self, then of God.
The piety of the empire, *recogimiento* resulted from the happy union of the
medieval Catholic mystical tradition and the fifteenth-century Catholic reform,
charged with the electrifying energy of humanism and the political and material
prosperity of sixteenth-century Spain.

By the time the inquisitor general Fernando Valdés published his 1559 *Index
of Prohibited Books*, on which the *Book of Prayer and Meditation* appeared
(with works by other famous Protestant and Catholic reformers), the tide
against the Catholic reform had turned and began to ebb quickly. From this
time forward, it was difficult for any Catholic to support unconditionally the
experience of unmediated contact with God, which threatened the existence of
the church itself. Mysticism became dangerous in the climate of retrenchment
characteristic of Spain after the years of the Council of Trent (1545–63). Previously esteemed Catholic reformers and intellectuals, such as the Dominican
archbishop Bartolomé Carranza de Miranda (1502–76) and the future general
of the Society of Jesus—and saint—Francis Borgia (1510–72), found themselves censored in Spain, whereas ten years earlier their liberal piety and generous ideas about Christian contact with God had been frankly celebrated by the
highest religious and political figures. The Catholic Church and state were on
the defensive, and the nature of mystical experience took a radical turn to the
right after the Council of Trent.[14]

Ironically, as if liberated by the chains in which it was bound, the indomi-
table spirit of the Catholic God in Spain began to act in mysterious ways, most
famously in the soul of a gravely ill young woman from Ávila, who found solace
from the excruciating pain and limitations of her illnesses in the exercise of her
spirit.[15] Healing her body along with her soul, holding God ever tightly by the
hand, Teresa of Ávila soared to previously unknown heights not of mystical experience but of its expression, in the several energetic and exuberant treatises
she composed to satisfy the vigilant skepticism of her superiors and to satisfy
the hunger of her nuns and other supporters for the same kind of experience.
Teresa's first-person voice brightly illuminated the mystical way, endowing mystical experience with an intimacy never before seen through her frank admission of how difficult and long her road to God was and through her careful
balancing of the agonies of self-knowledge and discipline with the ecstasies of
knowing God to the core of one's being.

Ideologically, Teresa sits astride the Catholic reform, during whose years she
grew up, and the conservative period of the Counter-Reformation, in whose
reality she accomplished her reformist mission in the world. Although decried
as a gadabout by her critics, Teresa prescribed strict enclosure and poverty for

her nuns and for women religious in general. Similarly, although her ideas about women's spiritual independence seem liberating and liberal to this day, her belief in the importance of prayer as the foundation of nuns' social contribution to the world outside its walls did little to advance what today would be called a feminist cause. Ultimately, Teresa was a mystic, and as such her primary concern was the spiritual well-being of all, and that spiritual well-being depended absolutely on her having an intimate relationship with God, which Teresa, like Luis de Granada before her, advocated for everyone. Her activism as a monastic reformer and founder was political, however, in the sense that she attempted to break with traditions that had tied religious vocation and patronage to the dynastic agendas of the elites.

Teresa's companion, John of the Cross, inscribed the mystical experience in poetry with an intensity and eroticism made possible by humanism, with its forthright celebration of the human being as God's most exalted creation, and by the various textual traditions with which John was familiar (Sufi mysticism, the popular Spanish lyric, and the elegant verse forms recently imported from Italy, for example). Teresa and John flourished during the period after the Council of Trent, whose mandates they were careful to step around quietly or overtly support. Both satisfied the political exigencies of the Catholic Church in crisis, which found in Teresa an eloquent and rhetorically humble woman whose intimacy with God was ultimately determined to be beyond question.

For his part, John of the Cross embodies the softened male hero whose disposition to serve God in spirit as well as in flesh captures perfectly the shift in Spain's male heroic paradigm that came about during the Counter-Reformation. As Spain's political dominion began to crack (the failure of the Spanish Armada in 1588 is telling) and as the nation's economic and social energy began to wane, one can observe in Spanish literary and plastic arts of the end of the sixteenth century a moment of stepping back and taking stock. No longer a warrior, the new man was expected to function as a courtier, to be physically tempered, able as a poet and an intellectual, reflective yet still authoritative, and unwavering in his understanding of his own rights and position in the world. Although it may seem remarkable that John's poetic voice is so often female, in fact it is not remarkable at all: the ideal man could not yet engage in such sensual, transgressive behavior, certainly not with another male (the divinity is consistently masculine during this period), and still be heroic. Were John of the Cross's poetic voice male, it would have been remarkable indeed; as it is, his ventriloquism of the heated, highly emotional, and desiring voice of the soul, cast as a woman seeking the evasive and powerful if also desiring beloved, fully satisfied the exigencies of hegemonic gender constructs during this period.

After the turn of the seventeenth century, Spain's baroque age ushered in a period of artistic splendor, during which mysticism figures consistently and profusely. Like the terminology of psychology today, mystical referents were normalized, systematized, and disseminated into public discourse at large, a context in which they lost impact and precision as they gained popularity. The writings of virtually all female mystics—and there were dozens—of the seventeenth century are informed by those of Teresa of Ávila, whose lightning-quick beatification (1614) and canonization (1622) made her a safe and reassuring model to imitate. The Spanish king's support of Teresa assured her entry into the pantheon of saints, and that support speaks once more to the political efficacy of a woman who proved that God was with Spain, especially when the realities of social, political, and economic failures in which the country was increasingly mired seemed to suggest otherwise. John of the Cross, whose mystical poetry is "pure" (that is, not explicitly allegorical) and less persistently reformist and political in its prescriptions of behavior than Teresa's writings, was not canonized until 1726.

By the seventeenth century, the edge of Spanish mysticism had softened, in that mystical texts represented the intensification, not innovation, of the contemplative process so ably defined by Teresa, whose works were first published in 1588. Remarkable, however, is the extent to which Spanish culture in general has been informed by the country's mystical voices and founded on its fervent quest for God within. In baroque Spain, religion was intensely and perhaps uniquely present in culture of all types and that presence itself speaks to a belief in a rightly intimate relationship between God and humanity. This presence may have problematized the country's passage into the capitalistic economy that bristled with energy in Protestant countries during the sixteenth century, and it may have complicated Spain's experience of the Enlightenment. But it was, after all, a consequence of one of the most vivid flowerings of humanity's relationship with the divinity in all of history.

NOTES

[1] Anyone writing about mysticism faces the choice of either representing the experience from within the perspective of belief ("God did this and this") or from outside it ("God was believed to have done this and this"). My intention here is to respect the belief without claiming it as my own.

[2] Elliott; Kamen (*Spain* and *The Spanish Inquisition*); and Lynch are good sources for the historical background of Spain's imperial age.

[3] See the account of the expulsion composed in Hebrew by an anonymous Italian Jew in April or May of 1495 ("Jewish History").

[4] On Beatriz de Silva Meneses, see Mayberry. Surtz studies María de Ajofín, particularly her commitment to the reform of the Toledan church (*Writing Women*). His *Guitar of God* provides a study of Juana de la Cruz. María de Santo Domingo's text has been translated and studied by Giles (*Book of Prayer*); on this figure, see also Bilinkoff, "Peasant Visionary."

[5] Teresa of Ávila requested that John of Ávila evaluate an early manuscript of her "book," now considered her autobiography, in which she describes her own mystical experiences. He concluded, "The book is not ready to be in the hands of many . . . for the individual things by which God carries some along are not to be shared" (*Epistolario*

573; my trans.). Coleman considers Juan de Ávila's commitment to moral reform in the face of political inconvenience.

6 Tuana provides ample evidence of Western society's construct of woman.

7 "Y avn lo que mas es de marauillar: y a mi ver muy de notar: que en estos dias parece obrar mas singularmente esta abundancia de gracias en el linaje mas flaco de las mugeres: y por ventura lo faze para confundir la sobervia de los varones: mayormente de aquellos: que de su propia reputacion hinchados: no han verguença de llamarse sabios: como sea verdad que nada sepan: ni con sabor guesten de la dulçura de dios."

8 On the politics of mysticism during this period, see Weber, "Between Ecstasy." Sánchez Lora proposes to avoid the difficulties inherent in the terms *orthodox* and *heretical* mystical manifestations by using chronological standards that distinguish mystical texts by period (*Mujeres*). I suggest that the texts that survived the period, and certainly those celebrated as representative of it today, were inevitably subjected to that problematic distinction, whether we point to it today or not.

9 Andrés Martín's book is the most complete account of *recogimiento* (*recogidos*); for further distinctions between Spain's several reform movements, see Rhodes, *Unrecognized Precursors* 50–89. That Teresa of Ávila's grandfather was a convicted Judaizer is one of the wonderful ironies of history. Whether she was aware of this or not remains unknown; that Madeline Albright (United States Secretary of State from 1997 to 2001) was raised Catholic and completely unaware of her own Jewish blood makes the question particularly compelling.

10 Perhaps because their demons and scapegoats had other faces, Spaniards were not as obsessed with witches as other European groups. Spanish inquisitors tended to interpret accusations of witchcraft as manifestations of ignorance. On the Spanish Inquisition, see both Rawlings and Kamen, whose books are titled *The Spanish Inquisition*.

11 The first written version of the *Exercises* dates from 1541 and was transcribed by a Roman copyist long after Ignatius had been teaching it to his disciples and an astounded, enthralled public whose membership was largely women (Rhodes, "Join").

12 Ignatius's description of his life, *El peregrino* (*The Pilgrim*), was written to inspire new Jesuits to action and focuses on events leading to the foundation of the Society of Jesus.

13 Huerga's biography of Luis de Granada is the most complete; on the popularity of Granada's *Book of Prayer*, see Rhodes, "Spain's Misfired Canon."

14 Some mystics were able to accommodate themselves to this transformed climate. For example, Luis de Granada's *Book of Prayer,* which appeared on the *Index* in 1559, was republished with inquisitorial approval in an expanded and emended version that appeared in 1566. By the end of the seventeenth century, there were over one hundred Spanish editions of this guide to prayer.

15 Weber's now classic *Teresa of Ávila* considers Teresa's writings in their historical context.

Spanish Mysticism and the Islamic Tradition

William Childers

In this time of conflict, we can respond to students' desire for relevance by placing before them the tantalizing question of whether Spanish Christian mysticism reflects the influence of Islamic mysticism (Sufism). The pioneering Spanish Arabist Miguel Asín Palacios devoted considerable energy to this topic, subsequently explored by other scholars, most notably Luce López Baralt. The striking similarities between the symbols, visual imagery, and poetic language of Spanish mystics and Sufis such as Muhyi'ddīn Ibn-'Arabi, Maulana Jalāl al-Dīn Rūmī, and others leave little doubt that Islamic mysticism played some role in the genesis of the Spanish mystical tradition. Moreover, the elements that appear to have entered the Spanish tradition through Sufism are precisely the ones that most powerfully distinguish Iberian mystics from those of other European nations.

Nonetheless, recognizing this link raises more questions than it answers. The issue of the means of transmission is an extremely thorny one, given that the sixteenth century was a time of intense religious intolerance in Spain, during which Sufi texts would have been difficult, though perhaps not impossible, to come by. We may never know whether Teresa of Ávila and John of the Cross were aware of the provenance of much of the imagery they used in their writings. They lived and wrote during the final crisis of Hispano Arabic culture, which ultimately led to the expulsion of the Morisco minority and the elimination of Islam from the Iberian Peninsula.[1] Only recently, with new immigration from North Africa, have large numbers of Muslims begun to live once more in Spain. To suggest that the great Christian mystics of Spain took their inspiration, knowingly or not, from Muslim sources thus situates their work in the broad historical context of a millennial competition between two rival religions of Spain.

The best way to introduce students to this topic is through concrete examples that give an idea of the kinds of parallels scholars have established. This prepares them to take up the challenging question of transmission. Finally, we can ask them to consider what this connection meant historically, as well as what meaning it holds for us today, given the current atmosphere of conflict between Christendom and the Muslim world. In the following pages, I take up each of these stages in turn, beginning with several specific examples of the purported Sufi influence on Spanish mysticism.

Examples

The most commented-on instance of Sufi influence in Teresa's writings is the image of the soul as a transparent castle with many rooms in *Las moradas* (*The Interior Castle*); this image, described in dwelling 1, chapter 1, provides the conceptual axis for the work:

Estando hoy suplicando a Nuestro Señor hablase por mí, porque yo no atinaba a cosa que decir ni cómo comenzar a cumplir esta obediencia, se me ofreció lo que ahora diré, para comenzar con algún fundamento: que es, considerar nuestra alma como un castillo todo de diamante u muy claro cristal, adonde hay muchos aposentos, ansí como en el cielo hay muchas moradas.

(*Moradas* 5)

Today while beseeching our Lord to speak for me because I wasn't able to think of anything to say nor did I know how to begin to carry out this obedience, there came to my mind what I shall now speak about, that which will provide us with a basis to begin with. It is that we consider our soul to be like a castle made entirely out of a diamond or of very clear crystal, in which there are many rooms, just as in heaven there are many dwelling places.

(*Collected Works* 2: 283)[2]

While many Christian allegories represent the soul as a fortress that must be vigilantly defended against temptation, those castles have no internal divisions. No known Christian source before Teresa interprets this "interior castle" as a series of *moradas* ("dwellings"), each inside the other, leading to the inner sanctum, where the soul enjoys mystical union with God. Yet in the Sufi tradition this metaphor constitutes a key concept, since "dwelling place" (*maqam*) is the term used to refer to the stages of spiritual growth. Already in the ninth century, a leading Baghdad Sufi, Abū'l-Husayn an-Nūrī, composed a treatise titled *Maqamat al-qulub* ("The Mansions of the Heart" [Schimmel, *Mystical Dimensions* 60–61]). Nuri's text is now available in a Spanish translation by López Baralt, titled *Moradas de los corazones*. Like Teresa's, Nuri's castle is organized concentrically in seven dwellings, one inside another. As one moves toward the center, the materials become more valuable: clay, iron, silver, gold, and so forth. The innermost dwelling, made of gemstone of near-diamantine hardness, stands for mystical union with God. Nuri's text marks the beginning of a tradition that became so widespread it constituted a veritable cliché in Sufi writings (López Baralt, *Huellas* 83–86). Without claiming Nuri as a direct antecedent, we can plausibly assume that Teresa's figure of the interior castle comes from the same Sufi tradition as his allegory.

Teresa's use of the cocoon of the silkworm as a symbol of the transformative power of contemplation provides another instance of striking parallels between her unusual imagery and the Sufi tradition. In *The Interior Castle*, fifth dwelling place, chapter 2, Teresa exhorts her readers to get to work weaving the silkworm's cocoon, thus "quitando nuestro amor propio y nuestra voluntad, el estar asidas a ninguna cosa de la tierra" 'getting rid of our self-love and self-will, our attachment to any earthly thing' (94; *Collected Works* 2: 343), so as to become butterflies, transcending the lowly worm who must die within the cocoon. According to López Baralt, "the silkworm was employed as a mystical symbol in Islam in exactly the same sense as St. Teresa's," by, among others, the great thirteenth-century Persian poet Rūmī (*Sufi Trobar Clus* 74–75). She points in particular to the following lines from Rūmī's poem *Divan-e-kabir* ("Great Work"): "When the worm eats leaves the leaf becomes silk / we are the worms of love, for we are without the / leaves (provision of sorrows, *barg*) of this world" (qtd. in Schimmel, *Triumphal Sun* 111).

To conclude with Teresa, let us consider the most celebrated passage in all of her writings: her erotic vision of an angel who pierces her heart with an arrow tipped with fire, producing a pleasurable sort of pain, or a painful kind of pleasure, "Es un requiebro tan suave que pasa entre el alma y Dios, que suplico yo a su bondad lo dé a gustar a quien pensare que miento" 'a loving exchange . . . between the soul and God . . . so sweet that I beg Him in His goodness to give a taste of this love to anyone who thinks I am lying' (*Libro de la vida* [ed. Chicharro] 353; *Collected Works* 1: 252). For J. A. Carpenter and Come Carpenter, the conjoining of the mystical and erotic in this passage goes beyond anything found previously in the Christian tradition, which in their view tends to separate asceticism and sensuality. They insist that in Sufism sexual or quasi-sexual encounters with angels and other spiritual beings are commonplace. Though the penetration of eroticism into mystical experience is far from uncommon in the Christian tradition, it does indeed appear that Islam is less concerned to restrict its reach to the purely metaphoric. The Carpenters list examples from Rumi and Ibn-'Arabi, along with an especially suggestive passage from the most famous of the early Sufi masters, al-Husayn ibn Mansur al-Hallaj, in his *Kitab at-tawasin* ("Book of Unity"), where he describes the heart as the target of the fiery arrows of divine love. They conclude that Teresa's angelic vision has its roots in "the terrain of Helleno-Arabic faith" (169–72).

The writings of John of the Cross offer innumerable examples of the supposed Sufi element, so much so that he often seems more at home in a Semitic context than a strictly European one. For brevity's sake, I concentrate here on three of the most important and striking: his concept of poetic language, the famous image of the "dark night of the soul" 'noche oscura del alma,' and a curious conceit in which he compares the mystic's soul in search of God to a solitary bird.

Much of López Baralt's monumental study *San Juan de la Cruz y el Islam* deals with his "poetics of delirium," a continually shifting language of symbols transforming themselves one into another, producing a dizzying effect that, rather than describing mystical ecstasy, enacts it. As López Baralt points out, despite the rhetorical gesture of bringing clarity that prose commentaries make, in John's case their effect is just the opposite, producing an even more "delirious" use of language. Thus in John's commentary on his poem "Llama de amor vivo" ("Flame of Living Love"), "fire" is miraculously transformed into "water" and then back to "fire" repeatedly, dismantling the referential function of language in favor of a mirroring of the ineffable mystical experience (López Baralt, *San Juan* 56–85). After insisting that no such conception of language was available in Spanish, López Baralt goes on to describe the existence of a series of Arabic language poets who share a similar approach, forming a "consistent literary tradition" in which John would be more at home than in the Christian one (201). She illustrates this tradition, among other examples, by means of Ibn-'Arabi's *Tarjumán al-ashwáq* (*Interpreter of Desires*), a mystical-erotic poem by one of the most influential Sufis of all time (199–211). Ibn-'Arabi, inspired by his visit to Mecca in 1215, wrote of his mystical ecstasy in terms that sounded to contemporaries rather too much like a celebration of sensual pleasure. Like John nearly four hundred years after him, Ibn-'Arabi found himself compelled to offer an elucidation of the symbolic meanings of his text. In *Tarjumán*, then, as in *Cántico espiritual* (*Spiritual Canticle*), we have an apparently erotic poem accompanied by a prose commentary written by the poet himself, in which the scandal of the poem's sensuality is overcome by a pious allegory. Yet, as in John's commentaries, Ibn-'Arabi so multiplies the meanings attached to any one term (for example, there are at least fifteen equivalences for *camel*) that the relation between the poem and its commentary, far from clarifying and fixing the meaning once and for all, renders it hopelessly indeterminate. This is necessary, since, in Ibn-'Arabi's words, "gnostics . . . cannot explain their feelings to other men; they can only indicate them symbolically to those who have begun to experience the like" (Ibn-'Arabi 68). In his prologue to *Cántico espiritual*, addressed to Ana de Jesús, John acknowledged the same limitation:

> Cierto, nadie lo puede [expresar el 'fervor de amor de Dios' con palabras]; cierto, ni ellas mesmas por quien pasa lo pueden; porque ésta es la causa por que con figuras, comparaciones y semejanzas, antes rebosan algo de lo que sienten, y de la abundancia de el espíritu vierten secretos y misterios, que con razones lo declaran.   (Cántico espiritual 257)

> The truth is, no one can [put the fervor of divine love into words], not even the souls who have the experience. And so this is the reason that, by means of figures, comparisons, and similitudes, they rather let something of what they feel overflow, allowing mysteries and secrets to pour forth out of abundance of spirit, than declare it with rational discourse.
>   (my trans.)

One of John's most celebrated figures is the "dark night of the soul" 'noche oscura del alma.' A phase of unknowing preceding divine revelation is common in Christian mysticism, but what sets John apart and links him to the Sufis is the paradoxical presentation of this night as a stage of both anxious suffering and joyous celebration. Miguel Asín Palacios shows that the Andalusian Sufis known as Sadilies, who flourished in fifteenth-century Spain, sought privations and discomforts to cause mental suffering and thus to facilitate the renunciation that leads to mystical union. He points out that they expressed this alternation in terms of a tightening (*qabd*) followed by an opening (*bast*), which is in line with John's distinction between *apretura* and *anchura*, and that they symbolized

the two states by means of the contrast between night and day ("Un precursor" 259–61). In the Sufi tradition, there are two primary ways this paradox is
expressed. One is the division of the night into separate phases, so that the stage
immediately preceding the dawn comes to stand for the positive dimension of
the mystic's confused state. An example of this is found in Ibn-'Arabi's *Tarjumán*, where the arrival of "the last third of the night" implies that the advent of
divine knowledge is at hand (95). Similarly, in his commentary on the poem "En
una noche obscura" in *La subida del Monte Carmelo*, John divides the night into
three parts: *noche del sentido* ("night of the senses"), *noche oscura del espíritu*
("dark night of the soul"), and *antelucano* ("predawn" [Vida 395]). The other
frequent way of expressing the paradox is the use of oxymoronic images com-
bining darkness and light, such as lightning flashes during the night or phrases
like "dark noon" and "midnight sun" that capture the sense in which mystical
darkness is really the only path to the true light. This widespread Sufi trope appears in John's poem in the line "más cierto que la luz del mediodía" 'clearer
than the light of midday' (López Baralt, *San Juan* 236–49; my trans.). As with
Teresa's castle, then, we have in John's *noche oscura* a symbol that, although not
unknown in the Christian tradition, nonetheless takes a form in his work that
clearly links it more closely to the Sufis.

Finally, the *pájaro solitario* ("solitary bird"), a favorite conceit of John's, re-
appears in several of his texts and was the subject of a lost treatise. The full-
est account we have is from the commentary to "Canción 14" of the *Cántico
espiritual* (103–04 [ed. Elia and Mancho]). López Baralt has demonstrated, in
painstaking detail, that all of its characteristics are present in Sufi descriptions of
a bird-king figure known as the *simurg*, who stands for the mystic's own soul. In
particular, the commentary titled *Safir-i-Simurg*, by the twelfth-century Persian
mystic Shihabudin Suhrawardi al-Maqtul, reunites all the features of John's bird
in a single text. The five features mentioned by John are that the bird seeks the
highest place, always turns his beak into the wind ("siempre tiene vuelto el pico
hacia donde viene el aire"), insists on being alone, sings a beautiful and harmonious song ("canta muy suavemente"), and has no particular color ("no es de
algún determinado color" [*Cántico* 104]). The parallels to which López Baralt
points in Suhrawardi's text sometimes seem strained, but at other times are as-
tonishingly close (*Huellas* 64–69). Suhrawardi describes the bird's preference for
high places and solitude; the *simurg*, instead of turning his head into the wind,
lifts it up to better contemplate the divine. Suhrawardi does not emphasize the
beauty of his song but focuses on its profound wisdom: "all sciences emanate
from the note of that bird." But the remarkable detail that seems to clinch the
link between the *pájaro solitario* and the *simurg* is the bird's colorlessness. Four
hundred years before John of the Cross, Suhrawardi had written of the *simurg*,
"All colors are in him, but he is colorless" (Suhrawardi al-Maqtul 29). Taken
together, the five characteristics match closely enough, given the uncanny coincidence of the strangest of all, the lack of color, that it is indeed difficult to
deny the connection altogether. Again, there is no reason to assume familiarity

with Suhrawardi's text specifically, since the *simurg* constitutes a long-standing traditional motif in Islamic writings, beginning with Avicenna (Schimmel, *Mystical Dimensions* 260–61, 306–07, 421).

This persuasive derivation of John's mysterious *pájaro solitario* from the Sufi tradition has enjoyed a special place in the discussion of Islamic influences in Spanish literature, not least because it inspired Juan Goytisolo's 1988 novel *Virtudes del pájaro solitario*. It also inspired an unusually direct challenge to López Baralt's claims from Domingo Ynduráin. Most traditionalist defenders of Catholic Spain have chosen simply to ignore attempts to link the Spanish mystics to Sufism. But in his essay "El pájaro solitario," Ynduráin puts forward an alternative hypothesis, according to which John's symbol derives from the mythical phoenix, a solitary bird indeed, since only one member of its species exists. Ynduráin quotes sixteenth- and seventeenth-century Latin texts describing the phoenix that draw together the same five characteristics described by John. He admits, though, that the psalm on which John originally based his account speaks of a sparrow, a rather ordinary bird, and a far cry from the legendary creature that rises from its own ashes every five hundred years. Another objection he does not deal with is the fact that the primary significance of the phoenix legend usually has to do with death and resurrection, themes not directly present in John's account of the *pájaro solitario*. Still, his argument raises the possibility of a purely Western derivation for one of the symbols most convincingly associated with Islamic sources.

In addition to the examples cited above, López Baralt has compiled a catalog of imagery appearing in both mystical traditions, originally published as "Simbología mística islámica en San Juan de la Cruz y en Santa Teresa de Jesús" and recently translated as *The Sufi Trobar Clus and Spanish Mysticism*. The number and specificity of these parallels create an impression that the Spanish mystics' texts, and especially those of John of the Cross, are saturated with Islamic material. She discusses the following symbols: wine and mystical drunkenness, the lamps of fire, the inner spring, the heart as a mirror of God, spiritual progress as the ascent of a mountain, asceticism as a struggle (jihad), the soul as a garden, the lily as a symbol of renunciation, the silkworm, and the mystic tree. Specific references to both Sufi and Christian texts are given, making this resource invaluable for students to pursue connections between the two traditions.

Transmission

Once students are persuaded—if they are persuaded—that Teresa's and John's texts exhibit traces of Sufism, the really difficult question arises: how did those traces get there? This question has a corollary: could Teresa and John have known they were being influenced by Islamic mysticism? The problem of transmission faces everyone who works on this topic, and it remains unresolved. It is worth pointing out that the ability of mystical symbols to move between these religions may result from the shared influence of Neoplatonic philosophy, evident even in the ninth-century origins of Sufism. In medieval Europe there was relatively open dialogue among Christian, Islamic, and Jewish traditions, but this gave way, especially in early modern Spain, to restrictions designed to impede exchange of ideas. Even so, we cannot rule out the possibility of clandestine contact, either oral or written, even during the Counter-Reformation. To begin with, then, explanations of transmission make two broad arguments: that transmission ended sometime in the Middle Ages or that influence was ongoing throughout the sixteenth century.

The simplest approach is to argue that a pervasive influence of Islamic thought in medieval Spain left traces even after ties to Muslim culture had been violently severed. This approach has the advantage of not going beyond the known facts concerning cultural relations during the period when Muslims ruled a significant portion of the Iberian Peninsula. The clearest example is undoubtedly the Majorcan lay theologian and philosopher Ramon Llull (c. 1232–1316), who wrote several treatises in Arabic and who openly acknowledges the influence of Sufi models in his mystical work *Llibre d'amic e amat* (*Book of the Lover and the Beloved*). Llull's work was available in the sixteenth century and could have influenced John. Indeed, Llull, too, multiplies the symbolic meanings of a spiritual allegory based on the Song of Songs. But his poetic language remains much more controlled and rationalized than that of John's *Cántico espiritual*. The example of Llull, as with other medieval Christian writers suggested as bridges, shows that the sixteenth-century mystics are made to depend for the Islamic element in their texts on Christian authors who are actually further from the Sufi tradition than they themselves are (López Baralt, *San Juan* 369–77, 395–401).

Another view equally acknowledges an early end to dialogue with Islamic sources but extends contact between Jewish and Christian sources well into the sixteenth century, allowing Jewish mystics to serve as a bridge between Sufism and the Carmelite school. Catherine Swietlicki argues this position in *Spanish Christian Cabala*. She primarily focuses on Teresa of Ávila, Luis de León, and John of the Cross. That the first two have been shown to be of Jewish ancestry is crucial to her argument, for that intimate, personal link strengthens the claim that contact with Jewish sources could continue after Islamic influence had ceased. In John's case, however, less is known about his ancestry. José Gómez-Menor Fuentes has tried to show that John may have had Morisco lineage. The notion that Jewish mysticism served as such a bridge implies there was a broad Islamization of both Christian and Jewish traditions in the Middle Ages that led to a submerged, unrecognized Muslim presence in early modern Catholicism.

Nonetheless, the idea that Christian authors could knowingly have appropriated Islamic texts during the period when Islam was being most firmly and thoroughly repressed on the peninsula deserves further consideration. Toward the end of his life, Asín Palacios expressed the expectation that the crypto-Muslim remnant remaining after the prohibition of Islam would in fact prove to be the missing link between the Sufis and the Carmelite mystics (*Sadilies* 25–27). Certainly, there was no lack of opportunity. Francisco Márquez Villanueva has drawn attention to the importance of the Morisco community in Ávila, and we might consider the contacts John could have made in Granada, as well as in Baeza and Úbeda, which also had large Morisco populations. But the clandestine nature of Morisco culture means we may never have a thorough enough knowledge of it to say definitively whether it could have played a role in the development of Carmelite mysticism. Manuscripts in aljamiado (Spanish written with Arabic script, incorporating numerous Arabisms) circulated clandestinely in Spain until the expulsion of the Moriscos, which began in 1609. These texts made basic tenets and practices of Islam available to crypto-Muslims. To date, however, only very minimal indications of knowledge of mysticism have been found in them. In her recent edition of the *Tafsira* (*Treatise*), a Renaissance compendium of Islamic teachings compiled by an important figure in aljamiado literature known only as the Mancebo de Arévalo ("Young Man from Arévalo"), María Teresa Narváez Córdova points to a passage employing terms referring to spiritual slumber (*innas*) and awakening (*annas*) as evidence that the mysterious author had some familiarity with Sufism (45–51). She refers specifically to texts by Ibn-ʿArabi and Suhrawardi in tracing the genealogy of these concepts. L. P. Harvey's thorough survey of aljamiado writing in *Muslims in Spain, 1500–1614* turns up only one major Sufi text, al-Ghazālī's twelfth-century *Minhāj al-ʿābidin* ("Road for Worshippers"). Harvey acknowledges that this work is not al-Ghazzālī's most advanced Sufi work but adds, "It does provide a complete outline of the [seven] stages of mystical initiation" (158). By itself, what we know about aljamiado writings would not account for the Islamic dimension of Spanish Christian mysticism. But we should not fail to take it into account as one factor among others.

We also know now, based on research done by Miguel de la Pinta Llorente and José Jiménez Lozano, that Arabic was taught in Salamanca at the time when John studied there (Pinta Llorente xlii; Jiménez Lozano 56–57; López Baralt, Prologue 46–47). Though the crown strove to withdraw Arabic manuscripts from general circulation, an undetermined number of them remained in private hands. López Baralt's latest book, "*A zaga de tu huella*," adds new archival research concerning the teaching of Arabic at Salamanca. Though López Baralt acknowledges that the cultivation of Arabic required discretion in Counter-Reformation Spain, in the light of these discoveries López Baralt now writes with greater confidence than ever that John could have studied Arabic and could have read something from a much older Sufi text, or at least talked to someone who did. "It is patently obvious that the presence of books in Arabic was more powerful in Renaissance Spain than previously thought" ("*Zaga*" 84; my trans.).

I recommend asking students which of these competing explanations for the Islamic presence seem most plausible to them. Then I would suggest that we may not ultimately want to think in terms of a single explanation but perhaps of overlapping and mutually reinforcing processes of transmission. Students can be encouraged to see whether they can articulate ways in which these different sources could have worked together in such a process.

Meanings

In trying to get students to articulate a view of the possible meanings of this hidden layer of cultural exchange, it might be most useful to begin with the question of what it would mean for our understanding of their time if we could bring ourselves to imagine Teresa and John consciously incorporating Islamic elements into their Christian mystical writings. If we think it is possible that the influence was consciously adopted, we must look at their work alongside other attempts to bridge the gap between Moriscos and Old Christians. One such attempt was the Erasmian humanist Bernardo Pérez de Chinchón's *Antialcorano* (1532), a cycle of twenty-six sermons intended for the conversion of the crypto-Muslims of Valencia. Pérez de Chinchón at times takes a derogatory tone, calling the Muslims barbarous, bestial, savage, treacherous, thieving, and describing them as "untada del vicio de sodomía" 'besmeared with the vice of sodomy' (382, my trans.). On the other hand, he devotes an entire sermon, the twenty-fifth, to explaining that converts to Christianity from Islam should hold the Virgin Mary in special veneration, since Mohammed accepted the doctrine of the virgin birth and frequently celebrates Mary in the Koran, which Pérez de Chinchón cites numerous times. Despite his approving references to Islamic scripture, Pérez de Chinchón's project of appropriation is unambiguously one-sided. He opportunistically takes advantage of whatever parallels he can to win over converts to Christianity unmingled with Islam.

Closer in time to the flourishing of the Carmelite school, another project for building a bridge between Christianity and Islam saw the light of day: the *libros plúmbeos* hoax. Uncovered on the hill above Granada subsequently known as Sacromonte in the mid-1590s, these lead tablets inscribed in Arabic were purported to be visionary writings from the first century CE, written by Arabic-speaking disciples of Christ who came to Spain to preach the gospel and were martyred there. They appear to have actually been written by Moriscos desperately seeking to create a place for themselves in an increasingly intolerant Spain. Alonso del Castillo, a court interpreter who had access to the collection of Arabic manuscripts at El Escorial, was probably the ringleader, and it is generally believed that Miguel de Luna was also involved. The version of Christianity these texts present is highly Islamized, including quasi-Koranic formulas such as "There is no God but God, and Jesus is the Spirit of God." Saturated with an atmosphere of prophecy and esoteric knowledge that at times borders on mysticism, these "lead books" project a future in which Christianity and Islam form one religion. Though the papacy recognized their dangerous syncretism from the start, many Spaniards greeted the supposed discovery with enthusiasm. It turns out that John of the Cross was in Granada at the time the first supposed

discoveries took place and was even named by the archbishop to the first com-
mision charged with investigating whether the tablets were authentic or not
(López Baralt, *"Zaga"* 14, 84). In Spain, and especially Granada, belief in their
authenticity persisted well into the seventeenth century.[3]

These contrasting attempts to incorporate Islamic elements into Catholicism,
on the one hand, or to fuse the two into one religion, on the other, provide interesting poles against which students can measure their intuitions concerning the
possible motives the Carmelite reformers could have had for drawing on Sufi
elements, if in fact they did so knowingly.

But what of the other possibility, that they unknowingly smuggled Muslim
influences into the Catholicism of Counter-Reformation Spain? Even if the Islamic inheritance is unconscious, surely it still has meaning for us in a time when
relations between Christendom and *Dar al-Islam* are increasingly strained. Teresa and John remain among the most widely read and venerated of the saints,
and their writings continue to inspire Catholics worldwide. Perhaps the Sufi
presence in their work shows that the mystical path opened their minds to acceptance of a deep affinity with writers officially viewed at the time as enemies
of the true faith. In this sense, they may serve as examples of how we ourselves
can overcome the divisive clash-of-civilizations hypothesis so widely used to explain the world situation post-9/11. Rather than Islamic terrorism, then, let us
focus some of our attention on the potential impact on our society of Islamic
mysticism—not as a panacea but as an indication that relations between cultures need not be understood in such bleak terms. We might thus conclude discussion of this topic by asking students to reflect on how studying the absorption
of Sufi ideas and images by sixteenth-century Christian authors could transform
their own relation to contemporary Islam.

NOTES

[1] The Moriscos were Spaniards of Muslim descent, nominally Christian after the prohibition of Islam in the early sixteenth century. Many took part in a clandestine Islamic
culture until their expulsion, carried out from 1609 to 1614.

[2] Citations to Teresa are to Kavanaugh and Rodríguez's *Collected Works*.

[3] Hagerty's is the only edition of the *libros plúmbeos*. Both Harvey 264–90 and Harris
provide useful background in English.

Teresa of Ávila and
the Question of Jewish Influence

Michael McGaha

In 1946 the Catholic world was stunned to learn that the great mystic and Carmelite reformer Teresa of Ávila, patron saint of Spain, was the daughter of a Jew. An article by Alonso Cortés published in Spain that year revealed that in 1485 Teresa's paternal grandfather, Juan Sánchez, had turned himself in to the Inquisition together with his children, confessing that they had committed "many and grave crimes and transgressions of heresy and apostasy" 'muchos e graues crímenes e delictos de herejía e apostasía' (Gómez-Menor Fuentes 32; see also Egido, "Familia").[1] Had the Sánchez family secretly returned to practicing Judaism? Had Juan taken this step out of fear that someone else might denounce him? Or was he motivated by the promise of more lenient treatment for those who denounced themselves during the grace period that preceded an inquisitorial visit? Whatever the case, Juan and his young son Alonso—Teresa's future father—were reconciled to the church in an auto-da-fé. Their punishment was to move in procession past all the churches in their native Toledo while wearing the yellow penitential garment, known as the sanbenito, on seven successive Fridays. The sanbenitos, prominently displaying the names of those convicted, would afterward be hung in their parish church as a perpetual reminder of their disgrace.

Not surprisingly, Juan Sánchez left town as soon as he could, moving his family about a hundred miles northwest to the much smaller town of Ávila. There he passed himself off as an Old Christian and, in 1500, purchased a forged letter-patent of nobility. By this time, Spain was officially Catholic; most of its Jews had converted either during the pogroms that ravaged the Iberian ghettos in 1391 or when given the choice of converting or being expelled from Spain in 1492. Many of these converts, however, had not been assimilated into mainstream Christian society.

Not only did the conversion of Jews fail to put an end to the anti-Semitism of the Spanish peasants, it actually exacerbated it. Formerly, the Jews had been restricted to a narrow sphere of activities by discriminatory legislation. Now that they were Christians, they could and did have successful careers in the law, the church, municipal government, and the university—all areas previously off-limits to them. Some, whether by choice or for lack of an alternative, continued to maintain a group identity, living in their own neighborhoods and doing business with, socializing with, and marrying mostly their own kind. The Old Christian masses resented the converts, considering them abnormally intelligent, arrogant, industrious, and ambitious.

After anticonvert riots broke out in Toledo in 1449, fourteen prominent New Christians were prosecuted. The prosecution alleged that these men held public offices as judges, notaries, and so forth in violation of the privilege granted to the city by King Alfonso, according to which

> no convert of Jewish origin may be allowed to hold public office or enjoy any benefice in Toledo and its area of jurisdiction, for they are not stead-fast in their Christian faith and for other reasons stated in the privilege.
> (qtd. in Beinart 351)

The verdict handed down, which ruled that converts were to be deprived of all public offices they held in Toledo, became the model for laws that would be adopted all over Spain. Known as purity-of-blood statutes (*estatutos de limpieza de sangre*), this legislation officially barred converts and their descendants from almost all careers in church and state, which would henceforth be open only to Old Christians.

Things took a dramatic turn for the worse in 1478. Fearing that recent converts were continuing to practice Judaism secretly, King Ferdinand and Queen Isabel established the Holy Office of the Inquisition, an ecclesiastical court charged with discovering and punishing alleged crypto-Jews. Although the Spanish In-quisition had the authority to punish heresy and apostasy of all kinds, during the first seven decades of its existence most of its victims were converts of Jewish descent. Those arrested by the Inquisition were considered guilty until proven innocent; they were told neither the names of their accusers nor the alleged crimes with which they were charged. Even if eventually acquitted, they might spend years in prison, during which they stood to lose all their property as well as their health and sometimes their sanity. Curiously, the only people who could be fairly certain of having no Jewish ancestry were the rural peasants, since Jews had long intermarried with the nobility and the urban professional class.

In this precarious atmosphere, Alonso Sánchez discarded the tainted patro-nymic Sánchez and adopted another of his ancestral surnames, Cepeda. Now a widower, he took Beatriz de Ahumada as his second wife in 1509. (Some scholars have speculated that Beatriz was also of Jewish ancestry, but so far have found only circumstantial evidence to support that allegation [Davies 54]). Teresa, their third child, was born in 1515. In an effort to assimilate himself into the Old Christian hidalgo class, Alonso abandoned his father's profession as a silk mer-chant, a decision that led to his eventual impoverishment. The family's Jewish origins did indeed momentarily come to light in 1519 during a lawsuit Alonso and his brothers brought against the city of Ávila in order to defend their tax-exempt status as hidalgos (Egido, "Ambiente" 83–94). Did Teresa, who was four at the time, later become aware of the history her family was trying to keep se-cret? The historian Manuel Rivero Rodríguez argues that "Saint Teresa was not aware of her status as a New Christian, and neither was the Inquisition, which never took this into account during their interrogations and investigations of her" (144). This seems highly unlikely, although there are, in fact, no documents in which Teresa or her contemporaries, whether friends or enemies, identify her as a conversa. Crucial documents (such as the requirement included in every inquisitorial interrogation to state whether one's parents and grandparents were New Christians) have been lost or destroyed. The closest we have to a definitive statement is found in a letter by Ana de San Bartolomé. Ana was Teresa's nurse and, after the foundress's death, a leader in the Discalced Carmelite Reform in France. When, in 1605, the French cardinal opposed admitting an ex-Calvinist as a Carmelite novice, Ana protested, arguing:

> I know that before Saint Teresa died, some women (and I know them) called Israelites were admitted, and afterwards some have been admitted as well. If in Spain, in the days of our holy Foundress, this was done . . . should it not be done with more reason in France?
>
> (qtd. in Weber, "Partial Feminism" 81–82)

Ana does not openly claim that Teresa was a conversa, but she makes it clear that there were many conversas among the first generation of Discalced Carmelites and that, furthermore, this policy was defended by the foundress. Much of the evidence regarding Teresa's New Christian identity is, like Ana's letter, suggestive, indirect, and subject to alternative explanations. No serious scholar doubts the sincerity of Teresa's devotion to the Catholic Church or her debt to a long tradition of Christian spirituality. But I shall show that there is considerable evidence that Teresa's converso heritage did have a significant impact on her spirituality, her social attitudes, and the imagery of her most mature mystical treatise, *The Interior Castle*.

We know very little about Teresa's parents' beliefs or religious practices, but, given her father's background, it is possible that his experience of Christianity was colored by Judaism absorbed in childhood. Such information as Teresa gives us about her father in her autobiography is tantalizing. He was scrupulously truthful, as she tells us in the first chapter of her autobiography, and avoided swearing and gossip. In other words, he minded his own business in the hope that others would do likewise. It is especially interesting that he was extremely protective of his privacy and allowed no visitors in his home other than close relatives and that he bitterly opposed Teresa's decision to enter the convent.

What are the indications that Judaism influenced Teresa's spirituality? Unlike Catholicism, Judaism had no hierarchy and no sacramental system. Each individual could have direct access to God and, at least in the case of those who were literate, could read and interpret the scriptures for themselves. Judaism was relatively tolerant of theological dissent, because it was centered on observance—"keeping the commandments"—rather than belief. Christians have often criticized Jews for adhering to the letter of the law rather than the spirit, for allowing their religion to become a lifeless, mechanical routine. In medieval Spain, however, Judaism had been invigorated and forever changed by the development of kabbalah, a mystical interpretation of the religion that stressed the duties of the heart over the duties of the limbs. Kabbalah taught that the original unity and harmony of the universe—including both the human and the divine realms, for "everything below has a counterpart above"—had been damaged by human sinfulness. The purpose of the commandments was to restore that lost unity; to achieve that, however, they must be carried out with the proper intention. When enough Jews performed the mitzvoth ("commandments") with perfect sincerity, the Messiah would come, ushering in a new golden age like that of Solomon, when the sacrifices offered in the temple would once again atone for sin and draw humanity closer to God. Many of the Spanish Jews who had been forcibly converted to Christianity comforted themselves with the thought that God would accept their intention to perform the mitzvoth in lieu of the deeds themselves. Although Teresa was rigorous in her observance of the sacraments and other exterior acts, she preferred interior silent prayer to ritual chanted prayer and argued that even vocal prayers should be recited with interior concentration and intention.

In comparison with the Judaism Spanish Jews were familiar with, Spanish Catholicism—which required conformity of its members both in their private beliefs and in their public ritual behavior—may have seemed lacking in warmth and spirituality. In her writings Teresa of Ávila, along with other New Christian authors such as the great biblical scholar Fray Luis de León—who would publish the first edition of Teresa's works after her death—and Teresa's close friend and collaborator in the Carmelite reform, the poet John of the Cross, proposed an alternative approach to Christianity that New Christians found far more appealing. Teresa, Luis, and John taught a religion based on love, one that was scripture-centered, personal, and egalitarian. These qualities were, of course, promoted by late medieval Christian movements, notably Franciscanism and the *devotio moderna*, but they may have had a special resonance for New Christians.

Much of Teresa's teaching on spirituality was inspired by her reading of books by earlier New Christian writers. For example, though very little is known about Francisco de Osuna's background, scholars have speculated that he was a converso both because of his ideology and because adopting the name of a city as a surname was almost exclusively a New Christian practice (cf. Fray Luis de León, John of Ávila). Reading Osuna's *Third Spiritual Alphabet* convinced Teresa that it was possible to communicate directly with God and to have a loving personal relationship with him even in this life, ideas that would be reinforced by her reading of John of Ávila's *Audi, Filia*, written in the form of a commentary on her beloved Psalm 45, which contains the verses: "Listen, my daughter, hear my words and consider them: forget your own people and your father's house; let the king desire your beauty, for he is your Lord" (*Oxford Study Bible*). She continued to revere John's book even after it was placed on the *Index of Prohibited Books* in 1559 (Rossi, *Teresa* 58–59).

Teresa's intimate familiarity with the Bible—especially the Old Testament, which she quotes far more often than the New—is truly noteworthy, particularly because she had no formal training in Latin and because Spanish translations of the Bible were forbidden after 1559. Did she have access to a forbidden Jewish bible, or was her knowledge pieced together from isolated verses that were accessible in approved printed books? It is impossible to say with certainty.

The egalitarian nature of Teresa's reform and her disdain for an obsession with lineage are attitudes that have been most closely linked to Teresa's converso heritage (see esp. Egido, "Ambiente" 95–119). Nothing distressed and angered Teresa more than her contemporaries' ridiculous concern with their pedigrees and with proving their pure Christian ancestry. In her writings she constantly stresses that noble, virtuous behavior is incomparably preferable to noble ancestry. Her friend Jerónimo Gracián recounts that once he told Teresa that he had just discovered, to his surprise, that she was a descendant of the Ahumadas and the Cepedas, who were "among the noblest families in town." Teresa, he says,

> got very angry with me, saying that she was content to be a daughter of the Catholic Church; and that she regretted more having committed a venial sin than if she were a descendant of the vilest, lowest born peasants and converted Jews in the whole world.   (qtd. in Castro 193)

In fact it is believed that her last words were: "I am a daughter of the Church" (Rossi, *Teresa* 287). As such, she need not concern herself with the background of her earthly parents.

The heading of chapter 27 of *The Way of Perfection* states that the chapter "[d]eals with . . . how important it is for those who want to be children of God to pay no attention whatsoever to lineage." In the chapter, Teresa states:

> [T]he one who is from nobler lineage should be the one to speak least about her father. All the Sisters must be equal . . . God deliver us, Sisters, from . . . disputes [about lineage], even though they be in jest. . . . When this concern about lineage is noticed in a Sister, apply a remedy at once and let her fear lest she be Judas among the apostles.
> (*Collected Works* 2: 137)[2]

In fact one of the most striking features of her convents was that all the nuns were equal. Unlike other Spanish convents of the period, there were—at least in Teresa's lifetime—no lay sisters, servants, or slaves in those of the Discalced Carmelites.

The convents Teresa founded were also unusual in the Spain of her time in their refusal, as Ana's letter shows, to exclude postulants of Jewish ancestry. Most of the nuns who joined her first convent, Saint Joseph's in Ávila, were New Christians, and in fact many of them were her nieces or cousins.

Although Teresa would eventually enjoy the support of some of the highest-ranking members of the Spanish nobility, and even the king himself, the Carmelite reform was initially funded and given moral support mainly by her fellow

New Christians. When the city of Toledo attempted to block a foundation because one of the convent's backers was a converso, Teresa was fortified in her resolve when a divine voice told her, "You will grow very foolish, daughter, if you look at the world's laws. . . . [A]re you to be esteemed for lineage or for virtue?" (*Collected Works* 1: 386 [*Spiritual Testimonies*, no. 5]). It now appears that as many as one-third of the seventeen convents she founded were paid for with donations from New Christians. The willingness of aristocrats like Luisa de la Cerda and the Prince and Princess of Eboli to patronize Teresa's reform is another enigma. Were they unaware of her converso background? Or did they simply not harbor anticonverso sentiments?

The British scholar Deirdre Green seems to have been the first person to argue that Teresa derived the central image of her book *The Interior Castle* from the Jewish mystical tradition. Green made this claim in several articles published in the early 1980s and more fully in her 1989 book *Gold in the Crucible: Teresa of Ávila and the Western Mystical Tradition*. In her view the source of the image of a castle with many chambers could have been the Jewish mystical texts known as Heikhalot ("Palaces"), which circulated during the third through the tenth century and elaborated on Ezekiel's vision of heaven, describing the mystic's ascent through seven different palaces to attain a vision of God or of the divine throne; the other possible source is similar passages in the Zohar, the thirteenth-century masterpiece of kabbalah. Green writes that

> in both the *Interior Castle* and the Hekhalot/Zoharic traditions we find the image of a crystal or diamond castle with seven mansions, or a group of seven crystal palaces, mansions or chambers, all inside each other, each with many doors or entrances; at the centre dwells the King, from whom shines forth an effulgent light illuminating the other mansions. The mystic's journey is one of progression from the circumference to the centre, surmounting many obstacles along the way, until in the innermost chamber she or he is united with the King, sealing the union with a kiss which is so perilous as to involve the danger of death.   (108)

Green was convinced that these parallels were "too precise and specific to arise out of a simple, non-reflective tuning in to a symbol buried in the unconscious" (86). Obviously, Teresa could not have had direct knowledge either of the Heikhalot texts or of the Zohar. Green suggests that one of Teresa's friends among the clergy might have come across the image in a Latin, Christian adaptation of the Zohar and told her about it or that Teresa might have encountered it as part of an oral folk tradition passed down by her New Christian relatives.

In a similar vein the late Spanish Arabist Miguel Asín Palacios and, after him, Luce López Baralt have argued that the image originated in Sufi mysticism. López Baralt found a ninth-century text entitled "The Castles of the Believer's Heart" by Abu'l-Husayn an-Nuri of Baghdad, which resembles Teresa's description even more closely than the passages that have been cited from the Zohar. López Baralt argues that the Muslim symbol may somehow have found its way into the popular, oral tradition of spirituality in sixteenth-century Spain ("Símbolo" 95). As Catherine Swietlicki proposes in *Spanish Christian Cabala*, Jewish mystics may have served as a bridge between Sufism and the Carmelite school.[3]

The image of the soul as a castle was common in medieval Christian literature. In the first chapter of *The Interior Castle* Teresa alludes to John 14.2—"There are many dwelling-places in my Father's house" (*Oxford Study Bible*)—as explaining how the soul can have many rooms. If we consider those two facts, Teresa's own explanation—that the image simply "came to [her] mind" as she was struggling to think of a way to write about the soul (*Collected Works* 2: 283)—is plausible, though of course she may have been subconsciously influenced by an earlier reading or conversation.

In explaining some of the ways in which Teresa of Ávila's spirituality may have been affected by her Jewish heritage and her status as a New Christian, I do not mean to imply that her devotion to Catholicism was insincere or to downplay the importance of Christian sources in her thought. Teresa's first biographers, embarrassed by her Jewish ancestry, managed to cover it up so well that it remained secret until over 350 years after her death. In today's world an understanding of what it meant to be a New Christian in sixteenth-century Spain can only enhance our appreciation of her achievement.

NOTES

[1] Unless otherwise noted, all translations from Spanish sources in this essay are my own.

[2] Citations to Teresa are from Kavanaugh and Rodriguez's *Collected Works*.

[3] See Childers' essay in this volume for further reflections on the vexed problem of the transmission of Semitic sources.

Was Teresa of Ávila a Feminist?

Bárbara Mujica

Was Teresa of Ávila a feminist? This is one of the questions my students ask most frequently. They have read that she was a valiant reformer who defended herself against the church hierarchy, the Inquisition, and hostile elements in her own order. They have heard her called a heroine and the most important Spanish woman writer of the sixteenth century. But they also have noticed her misogynistic remarks and know she founded convents where women were locked up forever, were permitted to receive few visitors, and lived under extremely austere conditions. Rather than a feminist, they argue, she sounds like just another early modern misogynist.

The issue is complex. Teresa's derogation of women occurs too frequently simply to dismiss. Much of her scorn is directed toward herself. In *The Book of Her Life* she refers to herself as a "poor little woman . . . weak and with hardly any fortitude" (*Collected Works* 1: 117). Her self-derision is undoubtedly, as Alison Weber argues, part of a strategy that allows her to appear humble while asserting spiritual authority (*Teresa of Ávila*). But why must she belittle her entire sex? "[T]he nature of women is weak," she writes in *The Book of Foundations* (*Collected Works* 3: 114). In *Interior Castle* she laments "our womanly dullness of mind" (*Collected Works* 2: 290). In *Life* she even confesses that just being a woman is enough to depress her (*Collected Works* 1: 109). Had Teresa completely assimilated the misogynistic attitudes of contemporary moralists?

To answer the question, we must keep in mind Teresa's historical context. The Middle Ages had inherited from Aristotle and other sources the notion that woman was an incomplete and defective being. In fact, some questioned whether she even had a soul. Although a few thinkers protested, notably Christine de Pizan (1365–1429), whose *City of Ladies* is an energetic defense of her sex, it was not until the sixteenth century that the worth of women became a topic of heated debate—a result, in part, of Elizabeth I's ascension to the throne of England. While the most conservative theologians saw women as daughters of Eve, whose disobedience had wrought evil on the human race, others defended women's spiritual potential. A few argued that a woman could be as lucid, composed, and valiant as a man. Although females were not supposed to aspire to intellectual excellence and few studied Latin, some moralists, such as Juan Luis Vives, Desiderius Erasmus, and Fray Luis de León, argued that women should learn to read in the vernacular so they could, through exposure to inspirational books, improve their souls and teach their children.[1]

Early modern supporters of women cannot be considered feminists in the modern sense, since they had no concern for the political, social, legal, and financial equality of the sexes. Even the most progressive thinkers assumed that women needed to be controlled by men. However, they did believe that by practicing feminine virtues such as obedience, resignation, and chastity, women could reach a degree of perfection. Since in Catholic lands celibacy was held in higher esteem than marriage, the convent was a prestigious option for women. Although, with few exceptions, women could not hope for political or intellectual glory, they could aspire to purity and even sanctity. The church offered numerous role models, starting with the Virgin Mary.

One of the most common arguments in defense of women was the androgyny of the soul. François de Billon argued in a 1555 treatise that since God is incorporeal and has both masculine and feminine attributes and since he created both man and woman in his image, the soul is androgynous. Some thinkers went so far as to argue that any person could have characteristics generally associated with the opposite sex. Thus a woman could be rational and a man sentimental. The *mujer varonil* ("manly woman") became the model of the smart, strong, courageous woman, virility being associated not with sexual identity but with moral perfection. When Teresa urges her nuns to be viril, she is promoting resoluteness and constancy among women.

Building on the notion of spiritual androgyny, Teresa reiterates throughout her works that any soul is capable of achieving a degree of perfection. Instead of insisting on sexual equality, she recognizes women's limitations, which she shrewdly twists into an advantage. Since God favors the weak, she argues, women's frailty is a blessing. Basing her argument on the notion that females are particularly susceptible to religious experience, she notes in the *Foundations* that the Lord "lets His magnificent riches show forth in us weak, little women" (*Collected Works* 3: 160) and in *Life* that "there are many more women than men to whom the Lord grants these favors" (*Collected Works* 1: 357). Teresa's censure of women is not necessarily insincere. Many talented women echoed prevailing misogynistic thought. But for Teresa, women's inferiority was a help rather than a hindrance in the quest for spiritual perfection. The biblical teaching "the last shall be first" (Matt. 20.16) was proof that God favored the lowly and humble (*New Jerusalem Bible*).

In Teresa's day convents were often overcrowded, gossipy, highly politicized, and populated by rich women who brought servants and material comforts with them. Such convents hardly offered an environment conducive to spiritual improvement. Teresa set out to provide women with truly spiritual surroundings by founding discalced, or "barefoot," convents (although the nuns actually wore sandals), where nuns would live cloistered and in poverty. As María Carrión points out, the nun's physical withdrawal into the convent reflects the inward spiritual movement of the soul seeking God. For Teresa, the cloister did not deprive women of freedom but liberated them from the distractions of everyday life, thereby enabling them to devote themselves entirely to prayer—in Teresa's view, the key to spiritual health. In *Way of Perfection* she praises conventual life, in which detachment from the world and the existence of a prayer community enable women to cultivate their souls. By adopting the unmitigated rule, Teresa affirmed that women as well as men could live in poverty in imitation of Christ.

At a time when the church was challenged not only by tepid religious practice but also by encroaching Protestantism, Teresa was anxious to play an active role in defense of the faith. Jodi Bilinkoff argues that Teresa "deeply envied male priests" because they had the freedom to preach and proselytize. She saw founding convents as a means of achieving an apostolate that she had long yearned for but, as a woman, had been denied ("Woman" 296). Carole Slade points out that Teresa aspired to model herself after Mary Magdalene, whom she saw as an apostle working tirelessly to bring Christ souls ("Social Reformer" 95).

The new convents enabled her nuns to do their part, for by praying constantly they contributed not only to their own spiritual renewal but also to the revitalization of the church. Thus Teresa saw the Discalced reform as spiritual activism. "If male clerics engaged in active apostolates, Discalced Carmelite nuns could exercise an apostolate of prayer," writes Bilinkoff ("Teresa" 174). Teresa clearly believed that women had both a duty and a right to take an active role in the defense of the faith. In the sixteenth century convents were often supported by wealthy patrons who sometimes demanded that nuns pray in perpetuity for their families. Teresa attempted to avoid accepting patronage, thereby freeing her nuns to pray for the church as a whole, not just for wealthy patrons.

For Teresa, founding convents and writing manuals such as *Way of Perfection* and *Interior Castle* were part of the same enterprise: to guide souls—especially those of her nuns—on their spiritual journeys. All of Teresa's books were written at the behest of spiritual directors, and priests sometimes manipulated the writings of their directees (Bilinkoff, "Confession"; "Confessors"). However, Weber presents evidence that Teresa maintained significant control over her writing, which she used not only to assert authority but also to provide spiritual direction to her nuns ("Three Lives"). Although Teresa casts her writing as an act of obedience, she often assumes the role of doctrinal teacher—a daring maneuver in a society that forbade women to preach. By cloaking her instruction in unassuming language—as confession, anecdote, a gloss on the paternoster, or convent history—she succeeds in articulating her views without riling the censors.

In the sixteenth century both moralists and poets defined woman in terms of her body. Vives's *The Education of a Christian Woman* (1523) and Luis de León's *The Perfect Wife* (1583), influential books that circulated widely in Spain, state that a man's priority is securing the chastity of the women under his control. Social codes of the period identified the female body as the repository of male honor and dictated that sexual transgressions by women were to be severely punished.[2] The obsession with lineage, or purity of blood, put an additional onus on women, since a man could never be certain his wife was carrying a child with "uncontaminated" blood unless he maintained absolute control over her sexuality. Poets also contributed to women's objectification. By idealizing the *dama*, whom they described in terms of generic physical attributes using an erotic vocabulary inherited from Petrarch, they robbed women of their individuality. For example, in sonnet 23 Garcilaso de la Vega portrays his lady only through metaphor: roses (lips), lilies (skin), gold (hair), and whiteness (neck).

Rather than a flesh-and-blood woman, the *dama* is a catalyst for the introspection of the male poetic *yo*.

In contrast, Teresa argues that a woman is soul as well as body; the soul is a "palace" inhabited by a "great King," God: "Well, let us imagine that within us is an extremely rich palace, built entirely of gold and precious stones; in sum, built of a lord such as this. Imagine, too . . . that you have a part to play in order for the palace to be so beautiful; for there is no edifice as beautiful as is a soul pure and full of virtues" (*Collected Works* 2: 143). She urges her nuns not to imagine that they are "hollow inside" (that is, just an outer case) but to remember their "inner richness and beauty" (2: 144). Each woman must cultivate her own soul in her own way and at her own pace. Each must find her own "way of perfection."

Teresa warns nuns repeatedly against comparing their own spiritual progress with anyone else's or resenting another sister's spiritual favors. Although Teresa preferred mental or silent prayer over ritual chanted prayers, she recognized that different methods were effective for different people. Both mental and vocal prayer had a place in her convents: "I am not speaking now about whether the prayer should be mental or vocal for everyone. In your case, I say you need both" (*Collected Works* 2: 119). She provides a commentary on the paternoster in *Way of Perfection* to help those who are not yet ready for mental prayer to derive maximum benefit from vocal prayer. At the same time, she encourages nuns who have made sufficient spiritual progress to practice mental prayer, despite the objections of some theologians who thought it too dangerous for impressionable women.

Teresa's position constitutes not only a defense of women's capabilities to pursue higher forms of prayer and contemplation but also a rejection of patriarchal social structure. Carrión defines the Teresian "palace" described in *Interior Castle* as an alcazar, a walled compound in which a woman can seek refuge, a space governed by God, into which not even her father or confessor can intrude (188). Carrión also notes that Teresa's detailed descriptions of her illnesses and physical deterioration undermine the image of woman as an "alabaster temple," replacing it with another of woman as a spiritual being. Interiority offers nuns protection not only from the temptations of the material world but also against social norms that reduce women to mere custodians of their husbands' or fathers' reputations.

Significantly, Teresa abolished the use of titles in her convents. Titles of nobility, even *doña*, signify rank derived from fathers or husbands. By abolishing titles Teresa created a society in which a woman's worth was determined not by the position of male relations but by the purity of her soul. Furthermore, of converso origin herself, she declined to investigate her postulants' lineage. Although Teresa is remembered for her religious reforms, Slade argues that such reforms have a social dimension: "Teresa also intended and indeed effected social reforms—specifically, increasing autonomy for women and integrating *conversos* . . . into Spanish society" ("Social Reformer" 91). Teresa's abolition of class and ethnic distinctions in the convent constitutes a significant act of resistance against social norms.

In Teresa's time many families were willing or able to provide a marriage dowry only for the first or second daughter. They placed younger daughters in convents, sometimes at four or five years old, since the dowry required by convents was generally lower than a marriage dowry.[3] As a result, many women with no vocation were fated for religious life. Teresa's requirement that postulants be at least seventeen reflects her desire to make certain that every Discalced Carmelite nun take vows of her own free will, thereby guaranteeing her a say in her own destiny. Furthermore, Teresa's decision to accept good postulants regardless of their ability to pay a dowry demonstrates her respect for spirituality over inherited wealth. Although Teresa originally hoped to forego convent dowries completely, financial pressures eventually forced her to accept them. Another pecuniary issue was patronage. To free her nuns from outside pressures, Teresa at first rejected patronage completely. However, practical considerations forced her to modify this stance as well.

Teresa's feminism shines through much of her writing directed toward nuns. The chattiness of her style creates a sense of intimacy and camaraderie. She envisioned her convents not as prisons but as communities imbued with love and respect for all members. Although nuns were expected to conform to the rule and punishments were stipulated for transgressors, Teresa preferred the soft touch rather than rigorous discipline. She writes in the *Constitutions* that the prioress of a Discalced Carmelite convent "should strive to be loved so that she may be obeyed" (*Collected Works* 3: 330). *Foundations* is full of such admonitions.

The concern Teresa showed for the psychological well-being of her nuns also evinces her feminism. Her comments on melancholia (depression) in women in *Foundations* suggest she possessed a deep understanding of feminine psychology, and her compassion, insight, and sense of humor undoubtedly made her an excellent spiritual director. She believed that women were perfectly capable of guiding other women. In fact, she begins *Way of Perfection* by remarking that her "age and experience" living in monasteries make her "more successful than learned men" in guiding women (*Collected Works* 2: 40).

As Alison Weber (*Teresa of Ávila*), Gillian Ahlgren (*Teresa of Ávila*), and others have noted, Teresa often appeals to her experience to assert her spiritual authority over *letrados*, or learned men, who knew theology but had little personal knowledge of God's grace. Here, her appeal goes hand in hand with a censure: "Since these learned men have other more important occupations and are strong, they don't pay attention to things that don't seem to amount to much in themselves" (*Collected Works* 2: 40). Although with considerable tact, Teresa criticizes powerful, erudite priests for their incompetence, noting that they are "too busy" to listen to women carefully. Again appealing to her experience, she then asserts her own effectiveness in this area. Teresa even wrote an instructional manual, *On Making the Visitation*, for visitators (priests who visited convents to enforce rules), teaching them how to deal effectively with prioresses and nuns. (This work is included in vol. 3 of *Collected Works.*)

Teresa taught her prioresses to guide the women in their charge. *Foundations* and *Constitutions* are full of advice to prioresses for guiding nuns, evidence that Teresa believed that women, not just priests, could minister to women's spiritual needs. In fact, Teresa thought that women could guide not only other women but also men. She herself provided spiritual direction for several men, among them her young collaborator, Jerónimo Gracián, and her brother Lorenzo.[4]

Despite the power Teresa entrusted to prioresses and other nuns, a convent cannot be entirely a society of women. Only priests can administer the sacraments, and so nuns necessarily depend on men. Having suffered at the hands of inept confessors who mortified her with allegations that her visions came from the devil, Teresa insisted that her nuns be guided by competent men. Throughout her books she reiterates the importance of compassionate, learned confessors who respect women's spiritual integrity. She believed nuns should be able to choose their confessors and even allowed them to select priests from outside the order or to change confessors if they were dissatisfied. When confessors became abusive in her convents, Teresa appealed not only to God but also to temporal authorities. She replaced the malicious Calced Carmelite confessors of Incarnation Convent in Ávila with two benevolent Discalced friars, Juan de la Cruz and Germán de San Matías.[5] When the infuriated Calced kidnapped and imprisoned these two, Teresa complained directly to King Philip II (*Collected Letters* 1: 578–81).[6]

Discalced convents offered women opportunities not only for spiritual development but also for education. From the Middle Ages convents had been centers of learning for women, but in the sixteenth century not all religious houses provided instruction. Teresa, despite her repeated assertions that she is just a poor, ignorant woman, had clearly read widely in the vernacular. She mentions the importance in her own spiritual journey of works such as the *Confessions* of Saint Augustine and the *Vita Christi* of Ludolph of Saxony, which she read in Spanish translation. Because she wanted to make such books accessible to her nuns, she required them to learn to read and, in article 40 of the *Constitutions*, charges prioresses with having them taught. In article 8 she stipulates:

> The prioress should see to it that good books are available, especially *The Life of Christ* . . . the *Flos Sanctorum, The Imitation of Christ, The Oratory of Religious,* and those books written by Fray Luis de Granada and Father Fray Pedro de Alcántara.   (*Collected Works* 3: 321)

Teresa considered literacy a protection for women against incompetent spiritual directors. The index of 1559 prohibited many devotional books popular among nuns, as well as fourteen editions of the Bible and nine of the New Testament, a move Teresa protests indirectly when she writes, "if our nature were not so weak and our devotion so lukewarm there wouldn't be any need . . . for other books" (*Collected Works* 2: 118). The implication is that since women are indeed imperfect, they do need books. Teresa's letters to her brother Lorenzo, in which she suggests schools for his sons, attest to her interest in education, and, in fact, in a letter dated 27 May 1568 to Luisa de la Cerda, she mentions plans to establish a school for girls, a project that was not carried out (*Collected Letters* 1: 48).

Although all nuns were required to learn to read, not all learned to write. White-veiled nuns, who performed menial tasks, usually learned only to read. Black-veiled choir nuns were responsible for praying the Divine Office, received a more thorough education, learning to read and write. Some used their writing skills to produce literature—hagiographies, chronicles, spiritual treatises, poetry, and plays. Many wrote *vidas,* nearly always at the command of their confessors. These were not autobiographies in the modern sense but spiritual memoirs that included prayers, descriptions of visions and locutions, and commentaries. Isabelle Poutrin says that nuns wrote so much that religious houses became "autobiography workshops" (131–34). Electa Arenal and Stacey Schlau argue that Carmelite convents developed into true intellectual communities, where women's lives were recorded and thereby validated ("Leyendo yo").

Convents offered women vocational opportunities not available elsewhere. Prioresses were responsible for the general administration of the house, including financial management, assignment of duties, and admission of postulants. A cellaress tended to the purchase of provisions. A novice mistress prepared neophytes for their profession, teaching them reading, writing, and religion. An extern (often an elderly nun not tempted by earthly delights) tended the turn, the window to the outside world. Nuns might also be chroniclers, biographers, painters, composers, singers, teachers, poets, historians, and even playwrights who composed entertainments for special occasions. In her *Constitutions* Teresa defines the duties of each of the major positions in Discalced convents.

Although Discalced Carmelite convents were egalitarian for their day, prioresses were definitely in charge, and Teresa was in charge of the prioresses. She wrote to them constantly, guiding them in their administrative duties, inquiring about their health and needs, and offering direction in the delicate area of "discernment of spirits."[7] Teresa was strict with her prioresses and could be cross with them when they failed to obey her. When María Bautista, prioress of the Valladolid Carmel, dallied in accepting a postulant that Teresa was anxious to admit, Teresa wrote her a scathing letter: "That you think you know everything is disheartening. . . . No prioress has ever taken such a stance with me, nor anyone who is not a prioress. I tell you that by acting in such a way you will lose my friendship" (*Collected Letters* 1: 223). Although Teresa could be warm and encouraging, she could also be autocratic. As founder and chief administrator, she believed her subordinates' vow of obedience bound them to abide by her decisions.

Still, Teresa was a positive role model for generations of Carmelites. Her spirituality engendered activism, impelling her to found seventeen convents in all parts of Spain. Because she was a woman, the daughter of a converso, and a mystic, Teresa was subjected to constant scrutiny. Weber has elucidated how Teresa used rhetorical strategies such as expressions of uncertainty and self-deprecation and appeals to her own experience to outmaneuver her persecutors and assert her own authority (*Teresa of Ávila*). Despite her tact when dealing with her superiors, men who dismissed women as stupid or false irritated her. In a passage from *Way of Perfection* deleted by censors, she complains, "Since the world's judges are sons of Adam and all of them male, there is no virtue in women that they do not hold suspect" (qtd. in Bilinkoff, "Woman" 298).[8] The image of Teresa that emerges from her books, particularly *Foundations*, is that of a strong, determined woman who takes on prelates, property owners, lawyers, aristocrats, workmen, and even the king himself in order to accomplish her mission.

Teresa affirmed her own authority and that of other women by creating spaces for women occupied and governed by females and devoted to their spiritual well-being. She was a brilliant politician, administrator, and fund-raiser who knew how to deal with people of all classes and ages, male and female, religious and lay. She navigated effectively through the morass of church dignitaries, inquisitors, Calced Carmelites, families opposed to their daughters' vocation, and conflicted nuns. She defended women against accusations of spiritual ineptitude. Her spiritual daughters followed her lead, bringing the reform to Portugal, France, Italy, the Low Countries, and the New World. As a saint and a doctor of the church, she continues to inspire women today.

So, to answer my students' question, I would say this: Teresa was a product of her times and undoubtedly believed women were flawed in some areas, but she turned women's supposed imperfections into a defense of their special spiritual aptitude. Furthermore, as a reformer who saw women as whole beings with spiritual needs, a foe of abusive convent confessors, a promoter of women's education, a model of leadership who provided women with the tools and experience they needed to achieve administrative excellence, Teresa was most certainly a champion of her sex—a true feminist.

NOTES

[1] For a full discussion of the topic, see Jordan.

[2] For decades scholars debated whether the seventeenth-century honor plays, in which husbands murder their wives for real or imagined sexual transgressions, reflected actual circumstances or were merely literary constructs. Recent studies by Heiple and by Black indicate that in many cases uxoricide was indeed validated by law.

[3] In 1563 the Council of Trent decreed that no girl could make formal monastic vows before the age of sixteen. However, younger girls were permitted to live in convents as students or boarders. Teresa was reluctant to accept children, although she did admit into convents her niece Teresita and her friend Jerónimo Gracián's sister Isabel while they were youngsters.

[4] See Luti, "'A Marriage Well Arranged'" and Mujica, "Paul the Enchanter."

[5] The Calced were Carmelites who observed a mitigated rule. During Teresa's lifetime, there were bitter disagreements between them and the followers of the Discalced reform.

[6] The first volume of *Collected Letters*, translated by Kavanaugh, includes letters written between 1546 and 1577. Volume 2 includes letters written between 1578 and 1582.

[7] See Weber's two studies of Teresa's attitude toward spiritual discernment: "'Dear Daughter'" and "Spiritual Administration."

[8] T. Álvarez brought this passage to light in the early 1980s. See his "Santa Teresa y las mujeres en la Iglesia" and Bilinkoff's "Woman."

After Teresa:
Mysticism in Seventeenth-Century Europe

Cordula van Wyhe

After the death of Teresa of Ávila in 1588, the order she had founded, supported by the highest echelons of European society, expanded rapidly. By the middle of the seventeenth century, Discalced Carmelite convents and monasteries had been established in France, the Low Countries, Italy, and central Europe (Wyhe, "Reformulating"; Diefendorf). The artistic, literary, and theological works produced or inspired by the second generation of Discalced Carmelites constitute a rich but little-studied source for teaching the history of seventeenth-century Catholic Europe.

Teaching the post-Teresian movement in its verbal and visual manifestations is no easy undertaking. Discalced Carmelite spirituality gained in complexity as it expanded. Moreover, suitable teaching material is scarce because research on this topic is in its infancy. Although the edited versions and collections by scholars such as Pierre Sérouet and Julián Urkiza have made the writings of post-Teresian members of the order more accessible, key texts such as those by Tomás de Jesús and Juan de Jesús María have suffered remarkable scholarly neglect.[1] Indeed, Edgar Allison Peers's *Studies of the Spanish Mystics* remains the only comprehensive discussion of the second-generation Carmelites to this day. Margit Thøfner ("'Let Your Desire Be'"; "How to Look"), Christopher C. Wilson ("Taking"), and Christine Göttler have recently undertaken pioneering studies on the visual representation of Discalced Carmelite spirituality after Teresa. However, the scarcity of superb scholarly treatments like these remains one of the obstacles for the teacher of the post-Teresian movement. Nevertheless, I regard the teaching of the second-generation Carmelites as crucial for developing a more comprehensive student awareness of how and why Teresa became a key saint of the Catholic Church and the ways in which her mysticism was conceptualized and lived by her successors. On a more general level, a class on the second-generation Carmelites can be a valuable adjunct to a seminar or lecture series on the Catholic Reformation in general. Teaching this topic can therefore be a highly rewarding experience for teachers and learners alike.

The Second-Generation Carmelites and the Spanish Netherlands

My classes on this subject focus on the Spanish-dominated ten southernmost provinces of the Low Countries that form present-day Belgium. The Hapsburg Netherlands not only coincide with my field of research as an art historian but were indeed one of the most important centers for the Teresian order in Europe during the first half of the seventeenth century. The infanta Isabella Clara Eugenia, cosovereign of the Hapsburg Netherlands with her husband, the archduke Albert, followed in the footsteps of her father, Philip II of Spain, in promoting the Discalced Carmelite order in her realm. In 1607, exactly twenty-five years after Teresa's death, her spiritual coworker, Ana de Jesús and a small group of Spanish Discalced Carmelite nuns followed the invitation from Isabella to found a convent under her patronage in Brussels. However, the archdukes believed that Ana de Jesús and her nuns required the spiritual guidance, jurisdictional authority, and practical assistance of their male brethren. Consequently, in 1610 the archdukes founded the convent of the male Discalced Carmelites in Brussels under the directorship of Tomás de Jesús. With support from the archdukes, disciples of Teresa such as Ana de San Bartolomé and Jerónimo Gracián de la Madre de Dios came to Brussels and Antwerp, where they were part of a massive, multimedia public relations offensive for the Teresian cause for canonization. The male and female convents soon became the hub for this campaign, nurturing a new generation Teresian mystics (Wyhe, "Piety").

In my seminar for undergraduates on the second-generation Carmelites, I devote special attention to Peter Paul Rubens's paintings for the altarpiece of the convent church of the Discalced Carmelite friars in Brussels. The convent church was consecrated in 1614, and it is generally assumed that the altarpiece was installed shortly afterward. The altarpiece consisted of one large painting depicting the transverberation of Teresa (fig. 1) and several predella paintings with images from Teresa's life. The painting of the transverberation was unfortunately destroyed by fire in 1940, and only a few predella paintings survive showing, among other subjects, the apparition of the holy dove (fig. 2). Nothing substantial has been published on these paintings.[2] This is all the more surprising since Rubens's images are among the earliest depictions of these scenes from the Carmelite's life on a large scale.

Given that the convent was under the direct patronage of the archdukes, it is highly likely that the commission for the altar was intended to further Teresa's cause for canonization. In fact, the installation of Rubens's paintings coincided with Teresa's beatification on 24 April 1614 by Pope Paul V. Eight years later, on 12 March 1622, Pope Gregory XV inscribed Teresa in the book of saints. Teresa's beatification did not institute a universal and obligatory cultus, but it gave Teresa international recognition and permitted her official veneration in Spain and by members of her order (Slade, *St. Teresa* 132). The rapid formation of her cult in Spain warranted the Castilian parliament to elevate her to the status of copatron of Spain in 1617, following a petition from the Discalced Carmelites (Rowe, "Spanish Minerva"). The installation of Rubens's images on the main altar of the convent church in Brussels was therefore respectful of the local restrictions imposed on Teresa's veneration by the beatification de-

Fig. 1. Peter Paul Rubens, *The Transverberation of St. Teresa of Avila* (c. 1614). Oil on canvas. Formerly London, Asscher and Welker (destroyed by fire, 1940).

cree. Nevertheless, by promoting her cult beyond the borders of Spain, Teresa's champions may have intended to put pressure on the Vatican for a swift canonization. Indeed, sermons held in support of the bid for sainthood stressed that Teresa's ubiquitous, cultic popularity was a great good to the entire church and deserving of canonization (Rowe, "Spanish Minerva" 583–86). In any case, Rubens's pioneering work certainly fueled the Low Countries' reputation as a new center for the formulation and dissemination of Teresa's visual hagiography (Thøfner, "'Let Your Desire'"; "How to Look").

In the opening discussion of the seminar, therefore, we raise some general questions regarding how far Rubens's paintings can be related to the importation of the Teresian reform into the Spanish Netherlands. Rubens's return from Italy in 1608 was opportune, in that the artist could capitalize on the new enthusiasm for the Discalced Carmelite order by helping forge a new pictorial language for the fashionable Teresian spirituality and thus buttress his position as Antwerp's foremost painter.

Fig. 2. Peter Paul Rubens, *St. Teresa of Avila's Vision of the Dove* (c. 1614). Oil on panel. Cambridge, Fitzwilliam Museum.

Visualizing Discalced Carmelite Spirituality after Teresa

Rubens painted two versions of Teresa's vision of the holy dove for the altar in Brussels (now kept in Rotterdam and Cambridge). Unfortunately, we have no means of knowing which one belonged to the original altar. Our discussion focused on the version in the Fitzwilliam Museum in Cambridge, since the students could view this painting in the original after the seminar (fig. 2). The scene represents Teresa's vision on Pentecost, when she was meditating on the feast day during her stay in the convent in Ávila in 1565. The Carmelite describes the experience as follows:

> A strong impulse seized me without my realizing why. It seemed as if my soul were about to leave the body, because it could no longer contain itself and was incapable of waiting for so great a blessing. . . . I had to seek some physical support, for so completely did my natural strength fail me that I could not even remain seated. . . . But my soul was in such a state that, as it became lost to itself . . . it remained in rapture.
>
> (*Complete Works* 1: 270–71)

The exclusive focus on the figure of Teresa, who is positioned close to the picture's surface, is immediately striking. The palette is restricted to brown, gray, and white, enhancing the impression of simplicity and austerity. Any spatial rendering is limited to a column on the right-hand side, behind the figure of Teresa, which contributes to the sense of solitude and isolation. Other visual strategies invite the beholder to share this encounter with the celestial visitor. Teresa's triangular shape guides the eye of the beholder upward to the dove. Her figure is illuminated through the celestial light entering with the dove from the upper-left-hand side. We then compared the appearance of Rubens's painting with the guidelines for religious images drawn up by sixteenth- and seventeenth-century Catholic reformers, studied in the previous class (see Freedberg). The students pointed out that the clarity, simplicity, and legibility of Rubens's portrayal of this vision clearly corresponds to post-Tridentine guidelines for religious imagery. However, on the basis of selected passages of the Teresian constitutions (*Collected Works* 3: 221–24), the students found out that the image can also be understood as encapsulating the Teresian reform ideals of poverty, enclosure, solitude, and silence. We concluded that Rubens's images promote an emotive spirituality that posits as its objective an interiorized and individualized union with the Godhead in surroundings conducive to solitude and lacking in material amenities.

That the appearance of the dove took place on Pentecost links Teresa closely to the established church in general and with Marian iconography more specifically. From an ecclesiastical point of view, Pentecost, as Carolyn Valone has pointed out, promulgates "the creation of an organized church, the institution of a priestly class, and the missionary expansion of religion based on the word of God" (801). The Virgin, who is always represented in the visual tradition as sitting in the center of the apostles, is elevated through the messianic revelation of the Pentecost from the mother of Christ to the bride of Christ and mother of the new ecclesia. Traditionally, representations of Pentecost show the dove fluttering directly above the Virgin's head, where she sits surrounded by the apostles. Was Teresa's vision perhaps inspired by this tradition in art just as Rubens's painting was inspired by her vision? No seventeenth-century viewer of Rubens's painting would have missed its direct reference to the Virgin of the Pentecost. However, while the pictorial tradition for Pentecost usually shows the Virgin seated with downcast eyes as a sign of her humility, Rubens seems to have derived Teresa's upward-looking posture and outstretched arms from Annunciation scenes and in particular from the specifically Spanish Marian iconography of Christ's apparition to Mary after his death.[3]

The apparition of the dove may already have become an iconographic theme during Teresa's lifetime (Slade, *St. Teresa* 2). On 2 June 1576 Jerónimo Gracián de la Madre de Dios commissioned Fray Juan de la Miseria to paint a portrait of Teresa from life (fig. 3). (This portrait established the physical features that would be repeated in many future depictions. Note the puffy face and the two warts.) However, the scroll framing Teresa's head is a citation from Psalm 89.1:

Fig. 3. Juan de la Miseria, *St. Teresa of Avila* (c. 1576).
Sevilla, Carmelitas Descalzos.

"I will sing of the mercies of the LORD forever" (King James Vers.). This anti-
phon was customarily sung on the second Sunday after Easter, which suggests
that this portrait represents a generic depiction of the Holy Ghost rather than
the apparition of the dove on Pentecost. Nevertheless, it is not surprising that
Teresa's supporters resorted to defensive strategies like these. The Carmelite
had constantly to justify her "unwomanly" presumption to teach Christian doctrine and to defend herself against accusations that her visions were inspired
by the devil (Thøfner, "How to Look"). The creation of a visual formula that
made her life correspond to that of the Virgin would have been, indeed, a welcome counteroffensive against these attacks. The association of Teresa with
the Virgin of the Pentecost was revived on the occasion of her beatification
in 1614, when many celebratory sermons likened her to the Mother of God.
Rubens's picture seems to have formed part of a concerted effort to affirm
Teresa's sanctity by inserting her into the venerable tradition of Marian pictorial
hagiography (Thøfner, "How to Look"). Rubens's painting is therefore not only
a stimulant to prayer or an aid to an illiterate populace to penetrate the mysteries of Teresa's life but also a validation of her visions and her status as daughter
of the church.

The transverberation of Teresa's heart, as depicted in Rubens's altarpiece, shows the saint in the company of an angel carrying a spear; at the end of the iron tip she seems to see a point of fire. Teresa narrates that the angel

> seemed to pierce my heart several times so that it penetrated to my entrails. When he drew it out, I thought he was drawing them out with it and he left me completely afire with a great love for God.
>
> (*Complete Works* 1: 193)

At the moment of Teresa's transverberation, however, her awareness of God's glory and her separation from God was so acute that it resulted in a yearning producing physical pain. The physical pain suffered by the spiritual invalid is, therefore, quite different from the agonies of ordinary, physical sufferings. The "pain of God," as Teresa calls it, is a mental pain comparable to the bittersweet torment of desire unfulfilled. Teresa explains this relation between the body and the soul: "This pain is not physical, but spiritual, even though the body has a share in it—indeed, a great share" (*Complete Works* 1: 193). In other words, the "pain of God" consists of a synchronized experience of highly contradictory emotions and feelings. The students are usually quick to point out that Rubens has conveyed this aspect of Teresa's experience in a masterful way through Christ's gesture, which is directed toward the piercing spear, with which he simultaneously wounds and comforts the spiritual invalid.

The context in which we examine Rubens's altarpiece is that of Teresa's Christ-focused mysticism. This context familiarizes students with one of the core principles of Discalced Carmelite spirituality and provides a useful perspective from which students can explore post-Teresian mysticism in general. In this way, the first part of the seminar focuses on an analysis of Teresa's *Life*. For postgraduate students I expand this discussion to include also the seventh dwelling place of the interior castle, where, according to Edward Howells, Teresa reaches the most mature formulation of the soul's mutuality with Christ in his human and divine presence (109–14). Chapter 22 of her *Life*, according to Howells, is Teresa's first attempt to establish continuity between the interior and exterior activity of the soul by placing Christ at the center of union. Teresa argues that in the highest stages of mental prayer Christ in his human and divine form takes up residence in the soul. This fusion of divine and human removes the ontological distinction between God and the soul. The reflection on the incarnate divinity is, according to Teresa, a valuable aid to attaining his presence, even at the highest levels of supernatural prayer:

> But these writers think that, as this work is entirely spiritual, anything corporal may disturb or impede it. . . . I cannot bear the idea that we must withdraw ourselves entirely from Christ and treat that Divine Body of His as though it were on a level with our miseries and with all created things. . . .
> [W]e should exert care and skill to accustom ourselves not to endeavour

with all our strength to have always before us—and the Lord grant it be always!—this most sacred Humanity.   (*Complete Works* 1: 136–40)

Teresa is possibly taking issue here with the scholastic notion that the contemplation of the humanity of Jesus was only beneficial for the early stages of meditation (Green 66). The defenders of this practice, she argues, lose much needed support when entering briefly into the most mystical stages of infused contemplation. As Deirdre Green and Thøfner ("'Let Your Desire'") have pointed out, Teresa is indeed one of the best-known writers of the Christian mystical tradition known as theism. The most significant medieval representative of this tradition is Bernard of Clairvaux, who in a similar manner to Teresa advocated the loving union of the soul with the incarnate Christ, rather than the absorption of the soul into an abstract Godhead. Theistic mysticism was directly opposed to other forms of Christian mysticism based on the writings of Pseudo-Dionysius, who defined the divinity as ineffable and unknowable (Thøfner, "'Let Your Desire'").

In this respect, Thøfner cogently has argued that the theistic or incarnational quality of Teresa's mysticism directly informed the Discalced Carmelites' "trust in the pictorial as a means for apprehending the essence of the divinity" ("'Let Your Desire'"). Teresa formulates this belief clearly when wishing to have Christ's "portrait and image always before my eyes" (*Complete Works* 1: 138). Teresa thus legitimated the use of images at all levels of religious activity, including the highest stages of mystical contemplation.

I then encouraged the students to apply their knowledge of Teresa's christocentrism to Rubens's depiction of the transverberation of her heart. Seen in relation to earlier formulations of this vision (Thøfner, "'Let Your Desire'"), Rubens's painting is highly unusual in its emphasis on the figure of Christ. While Teresa and the attending angels are subordinate to Christ, the plastic effect of his body and size makes his presence real and tangible. The centrality given to Christ, however, is entirely in keeping with Teresa's ideal of the contemplation and interiorization of the embodied deity. In this respect, Rubens's interpretation of the transverberation could be regarded as a defense of the Teresian tenet that "Christ is not an abstraction, but rather a presence simultaneously human and supra-human" (Thøfner, "'Let Your Desire'" 90). On another level, Teresa's transverberation represents an ideal mode of communication with the divinity that might have encouraged a faithful person to make Christ visible and palpable within himself or herself.[4]

Living Discalced Carmelite Spirituality after Teresa

Teresa's accounts of her visions and mystical experiences were not only visualized but also read and reexperienced by her followers. Owing to the vigorous publication campaign launched by the Brussels court in 1607, Teresa's books soon became widely available. For example, the Flemish-speaking maidservant Margarete van Noort was only able to read passages and excerpts from Teresa's writings that her employer, an aristocratic lady in Brussels, translated for her from a Spanish version. Six years later, however, Teresa's autobiography, *The Way to Perfection*, and *The Interior Castle* were all available in inexpensive Dutch translations (Thøfner, "'Let Your Desire'"). For Margarete van Noort, even the brief and limited study of the Teresian texts was instrumental for her vocation: in 1607 she became Sister Margaret of the Mother of God, the first lay sister of the royal convent of Discalced Carmelite nuns in Brussels. Between 1635 and 1637, Margaret kept an extensive diary in Spanish in which she described her path toward spiritual maturation. Soon after her death, this diary established Margaret as one of the convent's spiritual role models and earned her the reputation as a second Saint Teresa. Not surprisingly, numerous copies of her diary circulated in Discalced Carmelite convents in the Spanish Netherlands and were sent as far as Rome. Her diary is an excellent text for teaching because it offers the student unique and intimate insights into how second-generation Carmelites imitated and adapted Teresa's principles. Margaret's descriptions of the transverberations of her heart complement Rubens's visualization of this Teresian vision.

Margaret's spiritual diary became one of the most important contributions to the genre of women's religious writings in the Low Countries. It evokes a place of contest in which Margaret lived out her personal struggle to become like Teresa, while at the same time crafting her own voice. Margaret's extraordinary development responds to Teresa's belief that visionary experiences are attainable by all, irrespective of their social rank, intellectual ability, and learning. Moreover, Margaret's lowly role in the kitchen was conducive to a life truthful to the Discalced spirit, because Teresa herself famously declared that "the Lord walks among the pots and pans" (*Complete Works* 3: 22). Heeding Teresa's advice, Margaret portrays her life as uniting the active apostolate life and the contemplative life as embodied in the lives of Martha and Mary.[5]

Margaret conducts the same relentless exercises of self-examination as Teresa. Her account shows how she minutely emulates Teresa's experiential vision of God. In several passages, Margaret paraphrases the saint's account of the transverberation of her heart in order to describe a beatific vision that she believed to be identical to Teresa's:

> One day after taking communion, I suddenly saw a great radiance where I saw heaven and in it the Heavenly Father with His Son. And a flash of fire came from there, or rather like a lightning bolt, and this fiery arrow reached my heart and left me burning with a love of God and I was so undone with love, I did not know what I was doing. I became aware in my soul that God was infinite and incomprehensible, without beginning or end. One cannot say how the soul feels and understands it. It is with such delicateness and yet with the sensation of piercing, with such a great

knowledge that it is God who does this in the soul because He leaves the soul so full of light and happiness and a love of suffering for this God.[6]

Margaret clearly grapples here for the right term to describe this celestial phenomenon. After identifying it first as a "flash of fire" and a "lightning bolt," she finally resorts directly to Teresa's transverberation and calls it a "fiery arrow." By modeling her writing so closely on that of the saint, Margaret heightened the authority of her text and legitimated her own ecstatic experience. The paraphrases from Teresa's text also demonstrate the veracity and repeatability of Teresa's visions. Indeed, Margaret heightens the sense of this attainability of the Teresian transverberation by referring to it more than once. In another passage she writes:

> My love of God these days is greater than ever. Each day it grows more and more, and with such constancy that it pierces my soul and it seems as if my body is one with Him. It feels like fiery darts are thrown at me that burn my soul with a love of God and wound my whole soul with painful wounds, but very gentle, delightful and pleasant. And I would never want to be without these wounds. Although I do not hear talk of this most sweet love, later I become inflamed with love and my heart feels as if there were a brazier of burning fire in my heart from which flames of fire and sparks constantly fly out and burn and singe my whole body and soul and all my inward and outward senses.   (Margaret, *Life*)

Margaret shows here a good command of Teresa's rhetorical strategies, which testifies to her extensive study of the saint's writings. She imitates the Teresian love for oxymora to describe the "pain of God" and couples here the opposing adjectives "painful" and "pleasant." Margaret also makes imaginative use of Teresa's analogy of fire, with which Teresa explains the transformation of the soul through its consumption by divine love and its ultimate absorption into the Godhead (Slade, *St. Teresa* 94). Margaret proves herself an able master of Teresian language in another passage, in which she describes reaching the seventh chamber of the castle described in *The Interior Castle*:

> In those days I was examining the state of my soul, and it seems to me that I found it in a place that our sainted Mother Teresa speaks of when talking about the dwelling places [of her interior castle]. It seems as if I had passed through the ones that are around the outside, the ones that are in the middle, where the Husband/Christ is, and that I had begun to enjoy the fruit and rest that is not enjoyed by those outside, who are upset and disturbed. But disturbances cannot enter the middle place, since the Husband/Christ is with the soul. If they do enter, it is such a short space that it cannot be considered as having entered because the Husband/Christ does

not even glance at them. There is much to say about this, my Father. I will leave it to Your Reverence, but I am certain that this is what is happening to my soul and I speak of it with simplicity and truth, in the way God tells me to speak, and this is how I feel.

Here Margaret adopts an artless and even naive tone. This may indeed have been an intelligent adaptation of the plainness of Teresa's prose. This stylistic quality was probably meant not only to convey her sincerity and the accuracy of her account but also to ward off accusations of presumptuousness. As does Teresa, she often qualifies her conclusions with the words "in my opinion" and defers to the authority of her reader/confessor. In short, the comparative study of Margaret's text with those of the saint will both enrich the students' understanding of the Teresian heritage in general and lead them to a more detailed and nuanced understanding of Teresa's rhetorical strategies in particular.

Post-Teresian mysticism and Catholicism in general were pliable, complex, and open textured, and seminars on these subjects can revolve around different facets of the fight for the preservation of the saint's heritage.[7] Teresa's successors dealt with her legacy both as a mystic and as a foundress and legislator. The defense of Teresa's legacy extended to the governance of the order, which resulted in paradoxes and anomalies that were at odds with her vision. Ildefonso Moriones de la Visitación offers a concise overview of these developments. Ana de Jesús and Ana de San Bartolomé were intimately involved in these struggles, and an examination of their writings and images can indeed encourage an intriguing class discussion on the Teresian heritage. Happily, modern translations of these writers are now available.[8] In this respect teachers can make an invaluable contribution to stimulating generations of young scholars to pursue studies of the post-Teresian movement so that we can understand more fully the impact of Teresian spirituality and its evolution in word and image.

NOTES

[1] Sérouet has edited works by Isabel de los Ángeles; Jean de Brétigny; Leonor de San Bernardo; Beatriz de la Concepción; and Marthe de l'Incarnation, who wrote letters to Mme de Cabriès; and Marguerite du Saint-Sacrement (on Marguerite, see Diefendorf). Julián Urkiza is the editor of the complete works of Ana de San Bartolomé. Some works by Juan de Jesús María (John of Jesus Mary) are available in modern editions (*Instruction; Théologie*). See also Hoornaert.

[2] The catalog entries by Vlieghe are so far the only substantial scholarly work on these paintings. See Vlieghe, fig. 119, catalog no. 150 (pp. 159–61) and fig. 124, catalog no. 153 (pp. 163–65). Other predella paintings are discussed as catalog nos. 152 and 154.

[3] For an example of the iconography of Christ appearing to Mary, see "Apparition of Christ to the Madonna" (c. 1554), in Wethey (1: catalog 3, pl. 111). I thank Ulrich Heinen for this reference.

[4] Another valuable source for Teresian iconography is "The Idea Vitæ Teresianæ," an emblem book published in Antwerp around 1686 and widely disseminated thereafter. The 101 emblems are appended to S. López. See also Wyhe, "'The Idea.'"

[5] Teresa describes the ideal union of the active and contemplative life in *The Interior Castle* (*Complete Works* 2: 348). See also Robberechts.

[6] Translations of this text are by Susan M. Smith, from a forthcoming edition (Margaret of the Mother of God, *Life*).

[7] Space does not permit a discussion of the contributions of Tomás de Jesús, provincial of the Discalced Carmelite order for Flanders and Germany, who is generally regarded as one of the most eminent systematizers of Teresa's theology.

[8] The writings of Ana de Jesús have become more widely available, thanks to the editions by Antonio Fortes and Restituto Palmero and by Concepción Torres. Various autobiographical writings of Ana de San Bartolomé have been edited by Julián Urkiza. Darcy Donahue has translated the autobiography for the University of Chicago Press. Selections of the writings of both women are available in Arenal and Schlau, *Untold Sisters;* Mujica, *Women Writers*. For an excellent introduction to the early followers of Teresa, see *The Heirs of St. Teresa of Ávila*, edited by Christopher C. Wilson. Wilson's essay in this volume discusses artistic representations of Teresa's followers and includes numerous illustrations.

The Mystical Encounter with Extremity:
Teaching Teresa through Psychoanalytic Theory

Linda Belau

In the classes on literary theory I teach in an English department, I often use the works of mystical writers to supplement the primary theoretical texts we read. I have found that mystical writers engage students in the practical application of postmodern psychoanalytic theory. When I focus on the issue of language and mysticism, I include mystics such as Pseudo-Dionysius, Meister Eckhart, Angelus Silesius, and Jacob Boehme. In advanced courses, the autobiography of Teresa of Ávila is especially valuable as we work through the questions of language, representation, and sexual difference.

The most important issues I want my students to explore when studying the works of any mystical writer concern the idea that knowledge and understanding are two separate things. I also want them to appreciate how mystics use language to represent paradoxically that which cannot be represented. Since God exists beyond the parameters of the human (or finite) realm, the mystic's language is necessarily inadequate to express his or her divine encounters. Despite this impossibility, however, the mystic's seemingly unrepresentable relation to divinity is performed (or indicated) in the text at the level of its formal qualities rather than its content. In this sense, I want students to recognize the unconsciously performative dimension of the mystic's writing. Thus, we often discuss how we must pay attention to the form of the mystic's narrative as well as its content. That is, we direct our attention to the manner in which an account of mystical experience is written in order to discern something about the mystic's language that is not readily inscribed in the text, something that is indicated without actually being said.

Teresa's well-known autobiographical narrative, *The Book of Her Life*, is an emblematic text for such analysis. Like most mystics—who lay claim to an experience that is somehow beyond the parameters of symbolic exchange, beyond the limits of social engagement—Teresa maintains throughout her narrative that she is attempting to relay an experience that defies understanding and that the raptures she experiences are beyond comprehension: "In this fourth water the soul isn't in possession of its senses, but it rejoices without understanding what it is rejoicing in. It understands that it is enjoying a good in which are gathered together all goods, but this good is incomprehensible" (*Collected Works* 1: 157).[1] Throughout her narrative, Teresa constantly asserts that her experiences surpass her linguistic capacities or, more to the point, that she experiences the word's utter deficiency. Such experience gives her a knowledge that exceeds understanding. For example, Teresa writes:

> The glory I then experienced in myself cannot be put in writing or described, nor could anyone who hadn't experienced it imagine what it is like. I understood that everything desirable is brought together there, yet I didn't see anything. I was told, I don't know by whom, that what I could do there was understand that I couldn't understand anything and reflect upon how in comparison with that glory everything else was nothing at all. (1: 352)

As we focus on the significance of such passages, my students begin to see that there might be some reason why Teresa's prose is difficult to follow.

In fact, before the class begins a more sustained analysis of the language in the narrative, my students often complain about Teresa's writing, arguing that the text is boring, that it "doesn't say anything," or that it is difficult to follow. Initially we discuss how many of the difficulties or irregularities might be an effect of poor translation. English translations, especially of Teresa's work, have trouble dealing with the seemingly chaotic syntax and the digressions that characterize her autobiography. Because the text and her language always seem to be moving in several directions at once, students find the work difficult to follow. Frustrated students can become dismissive of the work. As we begin to theorize the possible reasons for her nonstandard syntax, however, what initially emerged as a defect in the text becomes a strength or a tool for analysis, especially if we are studying it as a performative narrative that can only approach its subject (the absolute or divinity) but can never quite meet it. In this sense, the failure of the text or any translation is exemplary.

Through such an approach, I am able to persuade my students that the text is not boring, vacuous, or pointlessly chaotic. Because her text—and its attendant "failures"—offers such a rich example of the abyssal dimensions of language, it ultimately demonstrates a certain impossibility of relation as it explores the notion of a relation to the absolute (as an experience of extremity) that can only be understood as impossible. Students usually find this notion of language and its relation to extremity stimulating. This is also the most challenging thing for students to think through since it is abstract and demands an attention to the text that goes beyond simply trying to figure out what the narrative is about.

In their approach to Teresa as a mystical writer who has something to teach them about language, my students are able to comprehend the idea that a relation with divinity (or any absolute) has to be thought of in terms of an impossibility that is nonetheless possible. My students are typically fascinated by the notion of such a paradox. Once I introduce them to the logic of this paradox, it seems a natural leap to more theoretical texts that also deal with the abyssal qualities of language.

In my classes I also teach the mystics in conjunction with Jacques Lacan's psychoanalytic theories of sexual difference. Before presenting Lacan's theories, I have found that it is important to discuss the mystic's relation to his or her social context. I often teach Teresa's *Life* from the perspective of her relation with a masculine divinity and a patriarchal church, focusing specifically on the way that Teresa's raptures bestow a knowledge that transgresses church doctrine and resists the dominant ideology. Such an approach is significant for a feminist appreciation of Teresa's work. From this perspective, it is not difficult to argue that Teresa was a radical presence in the Catholic Church. She did, after all, defy the church fathers by pursuing a direct relation with God. She was also an active reformer and is known for the monastic foundations that she made in her later years. According to J. M. Cohen, she was "a sound woman of business" and kept busy as a public figure until the last days of her life, especially as she supported the Discalced Carmelite reform (18–19).[2] One of the most traditionally aberrant women in the Catholic Church, Teresa's narrative can be read as an autobiographical record of her adventures beyond the symbolic authority of the church. Framing her narrative as confessions, Teresa is able simultaneously to support and undermine church doctrine as she writes a kind of how-to manual for transgressing its most fundamental codes requiring women's submission to male theological authority.

I use this feminist approach to move toward an analysis of Lacan's notion of the Other jouissance (what he also calls feminine jouissance).[3] My students and I consider how Teresa's mystical experiences of divine rapture expose a relation to the inadequacy of the signifier, to the fact that it is, as Lacan says, "non-all" (*Seminar* 80). In Teresa's most radical relations to divinity, there is a knowledge beyond the signifier and, therefore, beyond the mediation and the authority of the symbolic church order. In this way, Teresa was able to undergo the most aberrant of experiences—experiences so deviant, in fact, that they led to accusations of heresy—while, at the same time, she became an emblem for the very doctrine that she radically undermines.

I point out to my students that it was Teresa's reluctance to assume either of the two social roles allowed to women of her time (wife or nun) that triggered her lifelong battle with church doctrine.[4] Her refusal to slide completely under either the signifier *wife* or *nun* coincides with her aspiration to be more than something wholly relegated to her relation to a man, whether that man be a husband or God. Even though Teresa chose the convent, this decision led to twenty years of severe illness, ending with her mystical conversion at the age of thirty-nine. Both her illness and her mystical experiences were based on the constant struggle in her life with something beyond the signifier. But this something beyond the signifier—which would turn out to be the voice of God—is not so much something beyond the signifier as it is the inadequacy of the signifier itself. This notion is central to understanding Lacan's *Seminar XX*, and it is also one of the most difficult notions to bring across to my students.

Therefore, I ask my students to consider how Teresa's relation to God is remarkably different from that of traditional mystics—for example, of Boehme and Angelus—which is centered on the word of God and around God as the exceptional articulator of the master signifier. Teresa's mystical encounters, in contrast, were based on encounters with the voice of God as the incompleteness of the word. Whereas the traditional mystical experience is characterized primarily by certainty, Teresa's mystical experiences are always fraught with doubt. Although Teresa's doubt reflects awareness of her lack of theological training and uncertainty over the correct mystical vocabulary, I suggest to my class that it is also based on the inadequacy of language, on the failure of symbolic knowledge to account for her experiences of divine rapture. After reading chapters 25 and 26 of her *Life,* which focus on God's word as beyond speech, my students can begin to see how language is inadequate to describe Teresa's experiences throughout the entire narrative, especially since she constantly questions the capacity of language in her text and insists on a knowledge without understanding that grounds her relation to God. It is precisely this paradoxical knowledge that is at stake in Lacan's notion of the non-all that determines feminine jouissance.

While my students are often tempted to read this non-all simply as another figure for an unfathomable God, it is important for their understanding of Lacan that they realize that this aspect of femininity is also necessarily symbolically mediated. Once again, Teresa's narrative is absolutely elemental in bringing this point across, especially since we see the non-all for Teresa precisely in her transgression of the church's codes. In her autobiography, Teresa continuously paints herself as being between the law of the church and the unlimited and unmediated jouissance of divinity. She is, it must be remembered, a nun in the Catholic Church, a religion that views unmediated relations with God with great suspicion, especially for women and the laity.[5] The religious father, the confessor, is the one who mediates this impossible relation. And this prohibition, I point out to my students, corresponds to the paternal prohibition that forbids unmediated access to the unlimited maternal jouissance.

Thus, when she first begins to experience her divine visitations as entirely unmediated by any priest, Teresa quite naturally expects that they are temptations from the devil. Initially, the unlimited jouissance she experiences at the hands of the divine is unwelcome. She eventually comes to another mind, however, as God himself gives her the wisdom to understand that these raptures are, in fact, an impossible experience beyond the symbolic mandates of the church fathers. Not only is their mediation not necessary, it would, in fact, pose a hindrance. In this sense, Teresa finds herself beyond the symbolic doctrine of the church, even though it was her confessors who asked her to write of her experiences in the first place. Through the peculiarity of her text, however, she is able to bring the experience of feminine jouissance into the realm of church doctrine in order to maintain her aberrant relations in a traditional context.

To explore this experience of feminine jouissance more theoretically and to work back into our psychoanalytic analysis of language and the limit experience, I turn again to Lacan's *Seminar XX*. Lacan argues that Teresa's linguistic connection with God is beyond direct understanding: "God stands as the figure of the unsayable and, therefore, is intimately tied to the question of woman's jouissance" (64–77). The particular form of linguistic relation the mystic takes toward this unsayable—that is, toward the failure of the signifier—divines the mystic's relation to jouissance. And, in the same way that there are two modes of failure in the signifier, Lacan claims that there are two different pathways open to mystical experience. There is the mystical pathway situated on the side of the phallic function (76). And there is the mystical pathway situated on the side of the non-all, what Lacan calls the Other jouissance. The former mystical experience—the experience of phallic jouissance—occurs as the mystic puts himself (Lacan uses the masculine pronoun) in the place of enjoying for God. The experience of the Other jouissance consists of an experience lacking any guarantee in God—an experience, that is, bereft of parameters. While one jouissance supports the signifier, the other comes to terms with the point of the signifier's inherent lack, its own illegitimate foundation.

As we endeavor to penetrate Lacan's cryptic conclusion, I once again ask my students to read Teresa's narrative in order to consider how her autobiographical confessions represent the mystical pathway to the Other jouissance and how this jouissance is necessarily tied to the inadequacy of the signifier and the symbolic order. After reading Lacan, my students are able to appreciate the argument that Teresa's mystical experiences took bodily form precisely because words could not adequately express them. Once they are able to follow this argument, they are also able to see how her mystical experiences point to something beyond the symbolic order, something (as Lacan would say) non-all to the signifier.

By reading Lacan's theory of sexual difference alongside a rigorous analysis of Teresa's narrative, my students begin to understand the radical paradox that grounds Lacan's argument: it is only through the constraints of phallic prohibition that the freedom of the other side of the signifier, the non-all that characterizes feminine sexuality, might be encountered. It is precisely this insight that also allows my students to recognize that the non-all for Teresa manifests itself in her transgression of the church's codes, even though she never fully violates them.

Once she reconciles herself to the validity and divine origin of her raptures, Teresa finds herself split between God and the church because the various confessors and spiritual advisers around her begin to question the authenticity of her religious experience and suspect that she has been deceived by the devil. Thus, she is compelled to obey the symbolic law of the church. She does, however, find a way around this law (managing to transgress it completely) while maintaining allegiance to it. As she prays to God to deliver her from deception, she also asks him to deliver her from the constraints of her confessors. While she perpetuates this transgression of the dominant religious code, however, she will not fail to observe even the smallest ceremony of the church. In her narrative, for example, she tells how she is given conflicting messages from the symbolic and the divine realms:

> As often as the Lord commanded something of me in prayer and my confessor told me to do otherwise, The Lord returned and told me to obey my confessor; afterward His Majesty would change the confessor's mind.
> (1: 226)

This passage allows students to see that Teresa recognizes the significance of the symbolic realm. Even though her direct relation to the divine puts her at odds with the church, she nonetheless maintains absolute fidelity to her confessor's commands without denying God. In this sense, her loyalty is always on the side of the symbolic mandate. Rather than go with God and choose against her confessors, Teresa manages to side with both since God always tells her to obey her confessors. Even though she is loyal to the law of the church, then, she is not entirely subject to this law. Through this reading, my students are able to see that, while it is the symbolic order of the church fathers that ultimately commands Teresa, something else interrupts the relay of this authority. Insofar as there is this something else, Teresa is not entirely subject to the phallic symbolic order, even though the symbolic is always mediating her relations with the divine.

This is why her act of writing becomes significant in her understanding of and experience with divinity. In her writing, we are told, Teresa sits as if at holy dictation (Cohen 16). The performative dimension of writing reflects the understanding without understanding that characterizes Teresa's relations to divinity, thus allowing her to experience God negatively as something beyond the signifier, something for which the signifier is non-all. According to Lacan, "writing will show that woman's *jouissance* is based on a supplementation of this non-all" (*Seminar* 120). At the same time, Teresa's writing is firmly anchored in the economy of the symbolic order and the paternal law. Since she is writing her account at the request of some of her confessors, the very act of writing is already symbolically inscribed. What happens in the space of this writing, however, takes her beyond this inscription; it takes her to the limit of the symbolic, where she encounters this jouissance that, Lacan says, "doesn't stop not being written" (94).

In the end, what I want my students to take away from both their reading of Teresa and their engagement with psychoanalytic theory is a sense of the abyssal nature of language. This is, I believe, a basic tenet of Lacan's appropriation of linguistic theory, and it also forms the kernel of Teresa's mystical writings. As she endlessly endeavors to find the excessive and impossible meaning of her divine experience in the realm of the signifier and to have this meaning recognized in the symbolic order, Teresa is the very epitome of the ethical agent. In her writing and in her work, I want my students to see how she embraces the one ethical rule that, according to Lucie Cantin, characterized Teresa's experience: "to reveal everything, to hide nothing, without ever renouncing the attempt to force through the signifier what cannot immediately be inscribed in it" (132).

NOTES

[1] Citations to Teresa's works are from Kavanaugh and Rodríguez's *Collected Works*.

[2] For additional background reading on Teresa as a reformer, see Cantin; Slade, "Social Reformer."

[3] Lacan introduces this concept in Seminar XX, subtitled *Encore*. If time permits, I like to assign Verhaeghe's book, which provides an excellent introduction to Lacan's otherwise cryptic work on sexual difference and jouissance. Given the time constraints of most classes, I often use Evans. Fink also provides some excellent introductory information on Lacan and explains the question of jouissance from a more clinical point of view. I have also found other mystical texts and Derrida's work on negative theology illuminating. I often assign his essays "How to Avoid Speaking: Denials" or "Of an Apocalyptic Tone Newly Adopted in Philosophy."

[4] Although some women did adopt a third status, that of a beata or devout woman who lived independently of a monastic order, women of Teresa's hidalgo class generally eschewed this option. Legislation emerging from the Council of Trent after 1565 encouraged beatas to join religious orders and take binding monastic vows.

[5] Although the Catholic Church has historically recognized certain kinds of infused knowledge of the divine, during Teresa's lifetime religious experiences that appeared to bypass the sacramental system and the interpretative authority of the educated clergy were seen as philo-Protestant, if not heretical.

Teaching Spanish Women Mystics with Theories of Autobiography

Sherry Velasco

When studying texts penned by women mystics of early modern Spain, professors and students alike must inevitably confront complex issues involving gender, genre, and self-representation. As readers discover the multiplicity of voices and forms in each text as well as the diversity among different convent narratives, they soon realize that any attempt to look to critical theory as an analytic tool must be equally varied. There was no single model for monastic women's life writing: Teresa of Ávila wrote and revised her spiritual autobiography over the course of several years, whereas other nuns composed their narratives in short segments over decades and were never given the opportunity for revision. To make sense of these diverse writing and reading conditions, I have found that more than one theoretical approach to self-representation can help students engage these texts in historical context.

During the last few decades of the twentieth century, scholars began to recognize the significance of gender for autobiographical writing, and our readings have become more sensitive to the factors that shaped women's life narratives. Although I discuss the groundbreaking work of earlier theorists of autobiography (such as Dilthey; Gusdorf; and Olney), I have found that feminist theory provides a more useful analytic tool for understanding what Sidonie Smith has called the "double-voicedness" of women's autobiography (50). As Alison Weber has argued, the female mystic, facing the paradoxical imperative of proving her humility and her spiritual worth, often found herself in a double bind (*Teresa of Ávila*). The tension between the desire for narrative authority and the anxiety over claiming textual agency that characterizes women's autobiography as a genre is a particularly salient feature of women's spiritual autobiography in early modern Spain.

Any treatment of women's self-representation in mystical writing inevitably leads to discussion of language and the body. Even as we begin class discussion with traditional definitions and cultural meanings of terms such as *mysticism, asceticism, self-mortification, ecstasy*, and so forth, a lively debate soon emerges in which students are drawn toward the numerous possibilities for interpreting how early modern mystics shared a tradition of writing the body while establishing their own unique narrative strategies. That is, we consider how women's bodily practices such as self-imposed pain, hunger, and sleep deprivation served as a nonverbal means to communicate a variety of needs and desires and how bodily and textual practices are interrelated. When discussing the role of pain in mystical discourse, many students have benefited from considering critical theories of disability, trauma, and scriptotherapy (Snyder, Brueggeman, and Garland-Thomson; Caruth; and Henke). For example, I recently assigned

Encarnación Juárez's article on interpreting Teresa de Cartagena's autobiography through the lens of disability theory. Juárez's focus on Teresa de Cartagena's disability—her deafness—as an impulse for literary creation and personal insight helped students relate her autobiographical *Arboleda de los enfermos* (*Grove of the Infirm*) to personal narratives in our time written by women with disabilities. My students discovered that as the early modern life narratives became more meaningful to them personally, their analyses of these texts grew more detailed and insightful.

I have also used psycholinguistic approaches (especially those developed by the French feminists Luce Irigaray and Julia Kristeva) to encourage consideration of how language and pleasure play a central role in mystical discourse (see also P. Smith, *Body*; Swietlicki, "Writing"; Lochrie; and Slade, *St. Teresa*). While students occasionally find the psychoanalytic approach just as difficult to decipher as the original life narratives, many have been fascinated by nontraditional readings. Elizabeth Rhodes, for example, interprets some early modern nuns' life stories as texts that prefigure the pornographic dynamic, in which the desire of the subject is replaced with that of the spectator/reader. Citing Teresa of Ávila's insistence that the process was embarrassing, Rhodes suggests that the spiritual life story is a genre burdened with the writing woman's sense of obligation to please and to bare the intimacies of her relationship with God, thus producing a type of text that male ecstatics were not required to write. The *vida* thereby anticipates the pornographic dynamic ("Women"). Undoubtedly, the questions that Rhodes proposes in reference to the eroticized, fetishized body in mystical narratives invite students to reconsider the role of the interlocutor in these suggestive accounts of ascetic practices.

Given the vital and complex role of the confessor in the writing process of convent narratives, equally insightful for students' understanding of the interlocutor-writer relationship is Leigh Gilmore's description of the interdependent policing of truth when she discusses the "mutually productive performance of truth telling" in confessional discourse: "The confession must be regarded, then, as relational: neither penitent nor confessor is the 'source' of truth production. Instead, their relationship forms the locus from which confession is generated" (112). Spiritual works by women were monitored and edited by confessors, who could provide both inspiration and disapproval as well as establish the parameters for the text. The writing nun's consistent awareness of the role of her interlocutors in the process of textual authority determines what and how she narrates. In fact, as Jodi Bilinkoff reminds us, this literary collaborative partnership could provide mutual benefits, and the confessors had much to gain from recording their own role in the spiritual development of the penitent nun: "Her story became his story as well, his relationship with the saintly woman his claim to fame. Writing a hagiographical account was also a way of validating his skills as a priest" ("Confession" 180).

Theorists have also widened our conceptions of life writing by encouraging us to look for autobiographical elements in such forms as didactic treatises, letters, revelations, hagiographies, and poetry (on the autobiographical aspects of hagiography see, e.g., Greenspan). Gilmore has expanded the discussion of life writing through her term *autobiographics*, or

> [t]hose elements of self-representation which are not bound by a philosophical definition of the self derived from Augustine, those elements that instead mark a location in a text where self-invention, self-discovery, and self-representation emerge within the technologies of autobiography. Autobiographics, as a description of self-representation and as a reading practice, is concerned with interruptions and eruptions, with resistance and contradiction as strategies of self-representation. (42)

Gilmore's theory of autobiographics has encouraged my students to reexamine the diverse nature of many convent narratives, since these texts frequently include multiple genres, such as life story, spiritual doctrine, meditations on prayer, daily activities, dreams, visions, messages from God, dramatic temptations from the devil, poetry, gossip, and so forth.

A benefit of expanding our notion of autobiographical acts is that it allows students to consider generic forms that were previously excluded from traditional autobiography studies. For example, my students frequently struggle with the voluminous life narratives of nuns such as the Augustinian María de la Antigua and the Carmelite nun from Toledo, Isabel de Jesús (1611–82), whose published spiritual autobiographies consisted of approximately eight hundred large folio pages (29 centimeters) (Velasco, *Demons*). However, it is not only the length of the narratives that can intimidate the students; the apparent repetition likewise seemed to deter any close analysis of these fascinating literary documents. At times influenced by comments such as Margarita Nelken's dismissal of Isabel's writing as "monotonous due to its quantity, interchangeable due to its invariable features" (70–71), it is not surprising that students have felt more comfortable with Teresa of Ávila's *Libro de la vida* (*The Book of Her Life*). Teresa's manuscript of her *Vida*, for example, was composed of thirteen small notebooks and a few loose pages, while María de la Antigua left more than 1,300 notebooks that were compiled for the 1678 publication of her spiritual life narrative (Teresa, *Libro de la vida: Autógrafo* 544; Simón Díaz 138–40; Serrano y Sanz 42–49; Velasco, "Scatological"). Since there are no modern editions of María's text, in order to include the fascinating life narrative of this convent cook in my courses, I must either photocopy selections from the 814-page document or require students to consult the complete text on microfiche (if the library already owns the microfiche collection edited by Simón Palmer).

Despite the occasional inconveniences in organizing materials to teach early modern convent literature, I have found that by including these markedly different life narratives the students can gain a much better understanding of the variations in writing experiences for many nuns. For example, although Teresa wrote hundreds of letters as part of her spiritual and administrative activities, she did not have the same daily writing assignments required by confessors that nuns such as Isabel and María describe. Isabel de Jesús wrote extensively about the task of having to put pen to paper for one hour every day: "este tiempo de una hora, que es la que me han mandado que tome cada día" 'This period of one hour, which is what they have commanded me to write each day' (186).[1] María de la Antigua was also expected to write every day but was limited to only three pages:

> Mandóme que de oy en adelante escriva cada dia qualquiera cosa señalada que me sucediese. . . . Tienenme puesto tasa de tres hojas de una vez, y si alguna llega a quarto, me tapan la boca; esto me ha sucedido dos vezes.
>
> (44)

> He ordered me that from this day forward I should write each day anything significant that happens. . . . They have put a limit of three pages a day, and if I write four, they silence me. This has happened on two occasions.[2]

For many women, years of writing each day and handing the notebooks over to vigilant confessors resulted in the editing, compilation, and publication of the papers, almost as a complete works. In his approbation of María de la Antigua's work, Juan de Cárdenas summarizes the nature of the published version of her writings as "un compuesto de todos los papeles que por mandado de su confessor . . . escrivió la Madre María de la Antigua" 'a compilation of all the papers that the Mother María de la Antigua wrote under the command of her confessor' (Cárdenas).

Given that the dailiness of this practice of spiritual writing shares certain features with journal writing, I have found that incorporating diary theory is useful. It can guide students to ask questions of these lengthy narratives that help them go beyond assessments (such as "monotonous" or "repetitive") that fail to elucidate the writing strategies and the function of these texts in the lives of the writers and the context in which they were produced. When considering time and narrative structures in diary writing, Margo Culley reminds us that, unlike the novel and traditional autobiographies, the diary is

> always in process, always in some sense a fragment. . . . Because diaries are periodic in creation and structure, incremental repetition is an important aspect of the structure of most journals, and the dynamic of reading the periodic life-record involves attending to what is repeated. Repeated actions large and small build tension as they advance the "plot." (19)

Of course, the link between the diary and early modern convent narratives does not seem surprising when we look at the history of journal writing, since the American diary "has its roots in the spiritual autobiography that charts the progress of the pilgrim's soul toward God" (Culley 4). In fact, diary writing before the twentieth century did not aim to produce an account of the secret inner life of the writer but rather "semi-public documents intended to be read by an audience" (Culley 3). By the same token, students can benefit from how diary scholars have questioned academic assumptions about what kind of texts should be the object of serious study and how we should read and relate to these works. For this purpose, Cinthia Gannett's study *Gender and the Journal: Diaries and Academic Discourse* provides a useful model for questioning the gendered construction of the academic canon. As Suzanne L. Bunkers and Cynthia A. Huff have written, the diary

> challenges boundaries and enhances transdisciplinary thinking, by indicating how the content and form of diaries disclose how we construct knowledge, and by helping us understand how we relate to ourselves, to others, and to our culture through the mediation of language.   (1)

These remarks are equally applicable to the genre of convent life writing. Diary theory has the additional advantage of dealing with a familiar genre: many students have kept their own diary at some point in their life or were required to keep a journal as part of a composition, linguistics, or women's studies course.

For me, though, it is the complexity and variety in and among women's life narratives in early modern Spain that allow (and perhaps demand) equally diverse approaches to these texts. Whether students gain insight and become personally and critically engaged through autobiography theories focusing on pornography, psychoanalysis, collaborative confession, diary writing, or disability studies, the most rewarding part of teaching old texts comes from the possibilities that they provide for asking pertinent and challenging questions for each new generation of readers.

NOTES

[1] All translations are my own unless otherwise indicated.

[2] Approbations (*aprobaciones*) were written by ecclesiastics approving the written work for publication and appeared at the beginning of women's life narratives.

Feminist Epistemology
and Pedagogy in Teresa of Ávila

Barbara Simerka

Since the 1980s, scholars of early modern Spanish literature have used feminist thought to change the field of study in significant ways. In the earliest phase, they explored how canonical male writers represented women in their texts and documented the ways in which the era's novels, plays, and poetry supported—or occasionally questioned—male dominance. In the next phase, attention turned to women writers and to analysis of traditional criticism devoted to the few women writers already included in the canon, such as Teresa of Ávila. These studies frequently identified masculine bias in the critical canon and offered ideas derived from feminist literary and cultural criticism to present new views of women writers and their achievements. In the third and current phase, as researchers in many different fields have reconfigured their disciplines to incorporate feminism, literature professors have become more engaged in interdisciplinary studies of women and their texts. In this essay, I explore new developments in the field of philosophy to analyze Teresa of Ávila's first work, *The Book of Her Life*. In particular, I consider feminist epistemology, the study of how men and women acquire knowledge, to shed new light on the Carmelite nun's innovative teaching practices.

To teach about feminism and gender study in relation to Golden Age Spanish writers, we must first address the specter of anachronism, for on one level *feminism* is an era-specific term associated with the United States and western Europe in the late twentieth century. Four studies have been particularly effective at addressing this question. To begin, a reflection on one of the earliest feminist studies of the plight of the female author in previous eras is in order. Sandra Gilbert and Susan Gubar aptly describe the plight of the woman writer in nineteenth-century patriarchal society; her text combines an "urgent sense of her need for a female audience together with her fear of the antagonism of male readers, her culturally conditioned timidity, her dread of the patriarchal authority of art, her anxiety about the impropriety of female invention" (*Madwoman* 257). Elaine Showalter writes that this analysis of one historical moment can be used as a "general thesis" that is valid for studies of all women writers whose societies are organized around patriarchal demarcations of power and prestige (256). Showalter theorizes that as a result of a woman writer's conflicting desires to connect with the female reader by representing her own lived experience and to avoid the censure of masculine authority, "women's fiction can be read as double-voiced discourse, containing a 'dominant' and a 'muted' story" (266). In this double-voiced writing, "the orthodox plot recedes, and another plot, hitherto submerged in the anonymity of the background, stands out in bold relief like a thumbprint" (266). The scrutiny of gender and reading presented by

Teresa of Ávila is dependent on such a double-voiced discourse, for her writings must be approved by male religious figures in order to circulate among the nuns and others she wishes to educate about the mystic way.

In her introduction to the anthology *Recovering Spain's Feminist Tradition*, Lisa Vollendorf provides a nuanced view of how to redefine the term *feminism* in order to link early modern and contemporary critiques of patriarchy. She asserts that although contemporary feminisms generally define the movement in terms of working to achieve specific social and political changes that will eradicate or reduce gender inequality, it is equally legitimate to use the term *feminist* for writers of earlier generations who "critique and challenge patriarchal norms" (10).

The introductory chapter of Stephanie Merrim's comparative study, *Early Modern Women's Writing and Sor Juana Inés de la Cruz*, outlines the main areas of concern for women writing at the dawn of the Renaissance, in particular, the controversy that arose between Saint Paul's dictum that women must remain silent in the churches (1 Cor. 14.34–37), which was often interpreted as a prohibition against engaging in religious discourse, and humanist ideals of educating (noble) women, known as the quarrel about women.

In addressing the specific case of gender dynamics in the Carmelite reform movement, Alison Weber has introduced the notion of "partial feminism" to analyze both the substantial achievements and the limitations of Teresa's successors ("Partial Feminism" 82–84). I introduce these basic concepts through minilectures in a survey course where we devote just two class periods to reading selected chapters from the *Life*. For more advanced courses or seminars, students read the three essays in conjunction with the entire *Life*. In addition, for either type of course, students should consider the chapter devoted to the *Life* in Weber's groundbreaking *Teresa of Ávila and the Rhetoric of Femininity*, which explores the Carmelite's unique and gender-based use of the conventions of spiritual autobiography and rhetoric for feminist purposes.

In a course devoted to gender study, students can begin to take into consideration the many different facets of contemporary feminism. Feminist philosophers have launched a concerted attack on the moral and ethical assumptions of their discipline. Many argue that conventional approaches to philosophy do not provide a useful model for groups who have been excluded from traditional philosophy. Epistemology is the branch of philosophy that studies how knowledge is gained, evaluated, and validated. It is one of the areas of philosophy that has been most responsible for coding women's intellect and judgment as inferior, thus contributing to long-held arguments that women are not fit to play a role in serious public forums. The goal has been to develop a new epistemological system—a method for recognizing and valorizing the mental practices of women and other marginalized groups. Naomi Scheman provides a strong overview of the two main currents of feminist philosophy in her article. She identifies a "liberal" strand, which seeks to expand the membership in the current system, and a more "radical" approach, which hopes to create new modes of philosophical practice (146–47). Students can examine Teresa's reform program to find evidence of both currents. On the one hand, the Carmelite works for the liberal goal of gaining recognition for herself and her fellow mystics as legitimate participants in the Carmelite reform. However, she also seeks a more radical goal: to redefine the boundaries of acceptable thought and practice, so that mystical practice can be seen as a legitimate source of divine knowledge. In particular, students can be directed to the passages where Teresa devotes significant attention to refuting the idea that the devil is the source of mystical visions. In addition, they can analyze the way that Teresa redefines diabolical influence, asserting on several occasions that Satan is the force that goads nuns to harm their souls by abandoning mystical prayer—a complete inversion of the Counter-Reformation doctrine that the devil incites belief in visions to cause damage and lead souls astray.

One branch of feminist philosophy, standpoint epistemology, asserts that traditional philosophical knowledge is not unbiased and universal but rather that it is based on the specific lived experiences of males in hierarchical societies. In the introduction to *What Can She Know?* and in other essays, Lorraine Code uses standpoint epistemology to argue that all forms of lived experience can be a source of knowledge, including those of women who live in societies that segregate masculine and feminine activities. To explore this standpoint, students can compare Teresa's use of the word *experience* with Code's. Teresa's primary modes for justifying her authority resemble standpoint epistemology in that she repeatedly makes reference to her long years of mystical experience as the secure philosophical foundation for the reform policies she advocates.

Sandra Harding writes that standpoint epistemology provides

> a general theory of the greater objectivity that can result from research that begins in questions arising from the perspective of women's activities, . . . observing that no method, at least in science's sense of the term, is powerful enough to eliminate the kinds of social bias that are as widely held as in the scientific community itself.   (196)

Objectivity is central to the scientific method that Harding rejects here, especially when framed as a scholarly touchstone that is supposed to guarantee freedom from bias in all intellectual disciplines. Teresa does not directly question the objectivity of patriarchal philosophy and theology; however, she frequently points to the bias of confessors who have no direct mystical experience yet nonetheless believe that they are qualified to evaluate mystical visions and serve competently as spiritual advisers to those who do experience divine union. The Carmelite identifies these biased priests as one of the major obstacles to spiritual growth. After describing both beneficial and harmful experiences, Teresa defines the ideal confessor as one who has had experience in mystical prayer as well as theological training. When she characterizes the prestigious conventional theological education offered only to males as equally relevant to and legitimate as mystical experience, which is generally associated with women, Teresa offers a new philosophical paradigm that empowers women. She affirms her authority to define a good confessor and also implies that the male theologian who has learned by conventional means alone has access to only a partial truth. As an application of standpoint philosophy, students can analyze Teresa's descriptions of her positive and negative experiences with the priests who heard her confessions and identify critiques of their objectivity. Students can compare these examples of presumed objectivity with contemporary social discourses concerning marginalized groups. Students can also compare Teresa's distinction between approaches to the divine that are traditional and grounded in scholastic theology with approaches that are based on mystical union.

Alison Jaggar's reconsideration of the role of emotions in philosophical systems is also relevant to the scrutiny of objectivity. Jaggar asserts that because of the Cartesian model of a mind-body split and the positivist tradition, philosophers depict emotion as a distortion of rational processes (155). Jaggar critiques the view of emotion as a spontaneous and uncontrolled (and therefore irrational) response, pointing out that the expression of emotions is socially and culturally constructed (150). Noting that the socially prescribed emotional reactions of women (and other marginalized groups) are particularly stigmatized by dominant discourses, Jaggar offers a new paradigm for the analysis of "outlaw emotions" (160). She writes that because the life experiences of minority groups are "distinguished by their incompatibility with dominant perceptions and values," the manner in which emotions are expressed will appear deviant and thus even more suspect (160). Recognition that this variation in emotional reactions is grounded in divergent life experience, rather than in an inferior intellectual capacity, is crucial to standpoint epistemology's truth claims. Teresa's autobiography includes a defense of the role that an outlaw emotion, a particularly intense love of God, plays in mystical modes of acquiring knowledge. In fact, Teresa credits mystical practice with an intensification of her love for God and presents this emotion as an aid to her intellectual growth. Furthermore, as the Carmelite describes the steps by which she gains deeper levels of union, she emphasizes the strengthening of her love for the creator at each step of this process. For Teresa, knowledge of and love of the divine are not only compatible but even inseparable; her model of mystical knowledge breaks down the barrier between emotion and reason. Students can use these passages to explore the paradigm of outlaw emotions and gender bias, evaluating social discourses concerning both excess love and excess anger as justifications to exclude women from positions of authority in the early modern era and in our own.

Teresa's autobiography further questions conventional theology by showing that conventional religious language fails to provide the terminology necessary for comprehending the truths conveyed during mystical union. In addition, she asserts that traditional study and reading provide a slower and incomplete mode of understanding compared with the speed and clarity of the knowledge God provides during union. Thus, her life story highlights the philosophical legitimacy both of mystical prayer and of those who practice it; taking into consideration the model of double-voiced discourse, it is even possible to find indications of a carefully worded belief that mystical practice is indeed superior. Students can follow up on Teresa's critique of scholastic theology by analyzing the way that she goes on to establish her own writings, which are grounded in personal mystical experience, as a legitimate source of authority. It is important to note that she initiates this process by inscribing the key role played by Augustine's *Confessions* in her conversion, thus presenting her own reading experience as the model for her audience members, who are receptors of her autobiography, to emulate. Teresa encourages her readers to identify themselves with her as they read her work and to follow her example as she followed that of Augustine. In advocating the shift from a masculine to a feminine spiritual role model and from a canonized church father to a woman who is still alive and controversial, the reformer offers her convent readers a radical new way to think about their roles as readers and emulators of received religious dogma. Teresa notes that she inscribes her own spiritual struggles and subsequent victory as a model for discouraged readers. Students often respond to these passages with a desire to discuss the authors who have been important to their own development, and they can be encouraged to analyze their own reactions to different types of writing at different stages of development.

Feminist philosophers assert that their field must recognize the intellectual dimension of caregiving activities that women traditionally perform and that are generally characterized as instinctive rather than as a type of knowledge (Gilligan; Homiak). They advocate a balanced life of thought, physical chores, caregiving, and leisure activities as the ideal foundation for all human thought, thus eliminating the boundaries of masculine and feminine activities that separate the two genders and produce hierarchies for sources of knowledge. Students may identify this concept as they explore the reform program described in the later chapters of the *Life*. In the Discalced convents all nuns were required to work in the garden and kitchen as well as to spend time in contemplation and in recreation. This reform rejected the common practice among convents of dividing duties along hierarchical class lines and also validated the role of caretaking activities for the development of the mind and spirit. Despite the austerity of her reform, Teresa believed that periods of relaxation and social interaction each day were vital for the emotional and spiritual health of the nuns. Students are capable of applying these concepts to contemporary discussions of class, gender, and domestic labor.

Feminist pedagogy is an additional area of contemporary gender analysis that can be useful for exploring the Carmelite's transformation of her order. One of the central tenets of this movement in contemporary educational praxis is the empowerment both of the student to guide and direct his or her own learning and of the instructor, who is reconceptualized as facilitator in a collaborative process, rather than seen as a godlike figure who possesses and dispenses knowledge (Luke and Gore). The way in which Teresa redefines the roles of confessor and mystic for her reformed convents can be seen as analogous in its effort to develop a more egalitarian mode of interaction between authority figure and pupil. It is important to keep in mind that the relationship with one's confessor was crucial to a female mystic, because the church granted to the priests the power to validate visions or to condemn them as diabolic in origin.

In her second book, *The Way of Perfection*, the reformer takes a further step in the empowerment of her "students." Here, she provides guidelines so that each nun is capable of making an informed decision concerning whether her confessor serves her well as an educator or guide, and she advocates that each be given the right to change confessors. Here, Teresa places the nun rather than the priest in the seat of judgment; thus, the female learner rather than the male instructor is empowered. The Carmelite also urges that nuns be allowed to consult with spiritual men besides their confessors. Throughout the book, she often reaffirms her authority in defining a good confessor and in identifying beneficial male advisers, so that the discernment of nuns who apply her precepts in this area can be trusted. The emphasis on access to many learned men also seems to imply that each male who has learned by conventional means has access to only a partial truth. The progressive education advocated in Teresa's writings delineates a strong pedagogical base that enables her followers to synthesize the wisdom gleaned from the differing sources, from priests and spiritually gifted men as well as from union with the divine, for their own enlightenment. Students can be encouraged to use these passages to reflect on their own intellectual development and to scrutinize how they use and evaluate differing sources and forms of knowledge. For graduate students, these passages have inspired lively discussions concerning choosing and relating to academic mentors.

An additional technique that Teresa uses to empower nuns entails the development of mental prayer under unfavorable circumstances. In traditional convents, residents were required to devote several hours a day to communal prayers recited aloud; this practice was for the benefit of the souls of the convent benefactors but took away from the time that could be devoted to solitary meditation. In *The Way of Perfection*, the mystical leader creates a teaching tool to help nuns pursue the mystical path even while reciting prayers orally. Through her extended reading of the most commonly recited oral prayer, the paternoster, Teresa provides those in the beginning stages of mysticism with a series of mental exercises that are intended to help the practitioner develop her ability at recollection. The step-by-step explication of the relation between mystical practice and these well-known verses provides the reader with a base for focused thought during oral prayer, as the first step toward union, as well as structured guidance for advancing to deeper levels of communion with God. By creating tools to help nuns achieve their personal spiritual goals even in challenging contexts, Teresa facilitated the growth of her followers and also presented a model for creative learning. It is not hard to imagine that after working through the guided meditation of this first prayer, a reader could have been inspired to create her own exercises for other vocal prayers. Students can be encouraged to use this passage for their own pedagogical purposes, to understand more fully the nature of a form of devotion that differs from their own experiences and to create their own learning tools for difficult texts.

Feminist pedagogy also emphasizes the importance of student journals and personalized reflection as a key component to an emancipatory classroom; this insight can be used in two different ways (Lather). First, students can explore how Teresa describes the creation of her own autobiography in terms we might use to describe an extended form of student journal and can analyze in particular how she negotiates power dynamics between herself as writer and her confessors as validators of her insights. In addition, students can be asked to reflect on the benefits of keeping a reading or reaction journal and to analyze the power dynamics of their own authority as writers and the classroom instructor as judge.

Teresa's first two books, the *Life* and *The Way of Perfection*, reveal the masculinist biases that inform theological and philosophical systems and demonstrate that these forms of writing are, as a result of such biases, less capable of providing useful knowledge to women readers than her own text. The new poetic of reading that Teresa advocates and models validates gender-specific modes of reading and cognition, foregrounding the activity of reading as a key element of women's intellectual formation and seeking to teach women new ways to read. Sustained use of a reading journal can help students develop more awareness of their own reading habits and of the connection among gender, reading norms, and knowledge.

This essay demonstrates the homologies between Teresa's reform of the Carmelite order and contemporary feminist revisioning of the philosophy of knowledge. These innovations are central to Teresa's project, enabling her to defend mystical sources of knowledge and to inscribe herself as a model reader and teacher. Students can use her insights to evaluate their own and current cultural norms concerning reading, teaching, and knowledge.

Making Mysticism Accessible to Undergraduates

Lisa Vollendorf

Did Teresa of Ávila really want to be martyred by the Moors? Did John of the Cross have a sexual experience of God? Did Luis de León experience physical ecstasy when he heard beautiful music? Teachers of Spanish mysticism in North America likely have fielded similar questions. Perplexity about Teresa's desire for martyrdom, the sensuality of John of the Cross, and the rapturous language of Luis de León is understandable given the temporal and contextual distance separating us from the Counter-Reformation Spanish mystics. Indeed, as inhabitants of a relatively secular society in the twenty-first century, we face a problem of dual inaccessibility when reading sixteenth-century mystical texts. The barriers posed by the mystics' language and distinct spirituality can make the texts seem impenetrable to even the most engaged readers.

Like others before them, the Spanish mystics relied on language informed by Catholic tradition as well as by a desire to express the ineffable. Yet they also found themselves under scrutiny for their spiritual writings, religious practices, and reformist activities. Counter-Reformation Spain was marked by a fear of heresy and the determination to clarify doctrine and enforce orthodoxy; it was a time in which the Inquisition turned its attention toward those whose spirituality raised suspicion about possible Protestant affiliation.

The combination of aesthetic and spiritual expression produced under adverse circumstances animates the power of the Spanish texts. When Teresa writes of God's stalwart nature in "Nada te turbe" ("May Nothing Disturb You" [3: 386])—also known as "Eficacia de la paciencia"—and John writes of God's calming the soul in "Noche oscura del alma" ("Dark Night of the Soul"), the messages transcend the space and time that separate us from the authors.[1] Yet when Teresa writes, in "Vivo sin vivir en mí" ("I live without living in myself"), of dying because she cannot die (3: 375–76) and John refers to "mi pecho florido entero para él solo se guardaba" ("my flowery breast kept wholly for himself alone") in "Noche oscura" (Rivers, *Renaissance* 139), it is clear that we have moved into territory that requires a guide.

Whether included in courses on Spanish literature, early modern Europe, or religious studies, the Spanish mystics offer the opportunity for challenging and often rewarding classroom experiences. Using Teresa of Ávila as a centerpiece and focusing on gender and spirituality in Counter-Reformation Spain, this essay delineates an approach to teaching mysticism to undergraduates. The first section contextualizes mysticism within the cultural landscape of sixteenth-century Europe. This is followed by specific guidelines for choosing mystical texts for the undergraduate classroom. Section three offers pragmatic pedagogical approaches to teaching Spanish mysticism.

Mysticism in Counter-Reformation Spain

Students with little or no background in early modern European history will have difficulty appreciating why many Spanish mystics—including future saints—were viewed with suspicion during their lifetime. In my introductory lecture, I explain that in the second half of the sixteenth century in Spain, attitudes toward those who reported intense and immediate experiences of God were marked by ambivalence. On the one hand, many in the church encouraged the spirit of reform and piety that had flourished in the early decades of the century and prepared the way for flowering of Spanish mysticism. On the other hand, the rise of Protestantism had heightened distrust of religious experience unmediated by the clergy. Men and women who wanted to avoid inquisitorial scrutiny or punishment had to use great care in expressing their spirituality. In particular, it was necessary for them to affirm that they recognized the authority of the institutional church to interpret scripture and administer the sacraments essential for salvation. Internal church politics also played a role in constraining the mystics: Luis de León was imprisoned for translating the Song of Songs into the vernacular, but monastic rivalry also played an important role in his trial. Similarly, John of the Cross was imprisoned by the Calced branch of the Carmelites for his reform activities. While the Inquisition sequestered and scrutinized some of Teresa's texts and some ecclesiastics viewed her writing as potentially dangerous or unseemly, other theologians, including one grand inquisitor, deemed her work orthodox. This historical context is essential if students are to appreciate that the mystics took risks when they put pen to paper and that they often had to express themselves in indirect or coded language.

Familiarity with the status of women in Counter-Reformation Europe can also help students place mystical works in context. In response to Martin Luther's reforms and the threat of schism, Catholic leaders met at the Council of Trent (1545–63) to clarify doctrine, correct institutional abuses, and strengthen the church throughout Europe. The impact of Trent on women, as scholars have noted, was mixed. On the one hand, as the church reaffirmed the authority of the learned clergy to teach and interpret doctrine, it diminished the authority some women had enjoyed during the Middle Ages as visionaries and prophetesses. The Council of Trent also mandated strict enclosure for nuns, thereby curtailing women's access to secular society and restricting their opportunities for active charitable roles. Women who claimed a special relationship with God were considered especially suspect since they were believed to be susceptible to demonic delusions that counterfeited spiritual experiences. Yet some women managed to forge leadership roles within monasticism and developed new ways to express their spirituality. When students understand that the position of the female mystics was precarious but not hopeless, they can better appreciate the creativity with which the mystics defended their orthodoxy, deflected criticism, and camouflaged their pedagogical agendas.[2]

In this respect, Teresa occupies a unique position in Hispanic and Catholic culture. She had a profound impact on spirituality in sixteenth- and seventeenth-century Catholic Europe and Latin America (Slade, "Social Reformer"; Weber, *Teresa of Ávila*). Through her writing and with the support of her ally John of the Cross, Teresa redefined female monasticism as well as women's relation to the written word (Arenal and Schlau, *Untold Sisters*). Subsequent generations of Catholics, particularly women throughout Catholic Europe and the Americas, modeled themselves after Teresa and used her as an authorizing figure for writing and for effecting change in their communities. Thus Teresa's literary production and spiritual reform marked the beginning of the first boom in women's writing in the Hispanic world, which lasted from 1580 to 1700 (Arenal and Schlau, *Untold Sisters;* Merrim; Vollendorf, *Lives*). During this period, more women had access to education than ever before. This was due largely to the explosion in convent foundations that followed the Council of Trent and to Teresa's powerful example as a woman who made incursions into the public sphere through her writing. As an enclosed nun, she was extraordinary for the impact she had on leading a reform for both men and women in the Carmelite order. Through letters, religious texts, and the journeys she made to found convents throughout Spain, Teresa became a major figure in the Spanish religious landscape of the late sixteenth century. Thanks to the work of Luis de León, John of the Cross, Teresa of Ávila, and others who sought to free spiritual expression from the constraints of a strict Tridentine church, we have a corpus of texts that captures the complexities of the era. Inspirations to their contemporaries and to subsequent generations of male and female religious as well as to laypersons throughout the Catholic world, Fray Luis, John, and Teresa positioned themselves as leaders and teachers in a system intent on defining and enforcing orthodoxy.

Text Selection

Teaching the mystics to undergraduates can be rewarding for teachers and learners in ways that perhaps neither would anticipate. Students often respond positively to the numerous connections that can be made between the texts and the social context of the Counter-Reformation. The profound religious experiences of Fray Luis, John, and Teresa can move believers and nonbelievers alike to empathize with the difficulties faced by individuals with strong, yet sometimes controversial, religious convictions. All three mystics experienced resistance to and acceptance of their activities and writings. The complexities of their experiences as well as the varying reception they received from the Inquisition, the Calced branch of the Carmelites, and other church officials open up a world in which religion intersected with politics and the boundary lines between orthodoxy and heterodoxy were not always clearly drawn. Students can see how the mystics were partial outsiders whose loyalties were sometimes divided between their church and their own interior religious convictions.

Successful incursions into mysticism in the undergraduate classroom often hinge on one simple principle: less is more. The enterprise of narrowing the large corpus of potential texts to a desirable selection in terms of content, length, and accessibility can be difficult. Knowledge of Spanish and understanding of Catholicism in the twenty-first century give readers only a minimal advantage. Indeed, even in advanced undergraduate literature courses populated by bilingual and near-native speakers of Spanish, students from different linguistic, ethnic, educational, and religious backgrounds are equally likely to express frustration at simply not understanding the texts. While prereading exercises on the historical situation of the emerging Spanish nation and the changes in the Catholic Church (such as T. Ruiz, chs. 1, 10) can help prepare students for understanding the context of mysticism, the texts themselves often require focused, directed classroom analysis.

The process of text selection is somewhat frustrated by the varied approaches to mysticism taken by textbook editors. Selections from textbooks designed for use in Spanish literary surveys vary greatly. *Milenio*, Bárbara Mujica's third- and fourth-year textbook anthology, contains a brief introduction to mysticism, both an introduction to Teresa and chapter 11 of *Vida*, and an introduction to John of the Cross, followed by a selection of poetry. The introduction to Fray Luis de León offers helpful comments on why some scholars call him a mystic while others do not. Francisca Paredes Méndez, Mark Harprint, and José Ballesteros include one poem each from Fray Luis ("La vida retirada" 'Restful Life'), Teresa ("Muero porque no muero" 'I Die because I Do Not Die'), and John of the Cross ("La noche oscura del alma"). Mujica's *Women Writers* includes chapter 11 from Teresa's *Vida*, extensive selections from *Moradas de castillo interior* (*Interior Castle*), as well as selections from Teresa's followers. David William Foster's *Literatura española: Una antología* offers the broadest selection of mystical writing, with works by John of the Cross ("Cántico espiritual" 'Spiritual Canticle,' "Coplas a lo divino" 'Verses in the Divine Style,' "Otras canciones a lo divino" 'Other Songs in the Divine Style'), Teresa (*Vida*, chs. 1–3), and five poems by Fray Luis ("Vida retirada," "A Francisco Salinas" 'For Francisco Salinas,' "Noche serena," 'Serene Night,' "Al salir de la cárcel" 'Upon Leaving Prison,' and "Los cantares de Salomón" 'The Songs of Solomon'). Although Foster's anthology lacks explanatory notes and introductions to text selections, the book provides one of the most complete selections on mystics available in a paperback anthology. The brief bilingual selection from Teresa's *Vida* found in Amy Katz Kaminsky's *Water Lilies* offers a good introduction to the genre of the spiritual autobiography (chs. 1–2) and to Teresa's conversion in her later years (ch. 32). For those interested in teaching only poetry, Paredes Méndez, Harprint, and Ballesteros's anthology and Elias L. Rivers's *Renaissance and Baroque Poetry of Spain* are good alternatives. Rivers excludes Teresa entirely but includes poems by Fray Luis and John of the Cross, along with prose translations.

Fortunately, many Spanish mystical texts are now available on the Web (e.g., www.cervantesvirtual.com) and are available in translation. Whether through the use of electronic reserves or Web-based teaching, instructors at diverse institutions have fairly easy access to more pedagogical options. For instance, instructors might encourage students to read the Spanish original and the English translation of poetry and prose. This assignment paves the way for thorough examinations of stylistic particularities that otherwise might escape notice. Teresa's use of colloquialisms, for example, can be examined in English translation to highlight the connotations of her diminutives and self-deprecating turns of phrase. Asking students to translate a poem and then compare it with a published translation or to compare several translations of the same poem is another valuable exercise that can help students appreciate nuances of language that they might otherwise miss.

For classes in which a week or more can be spent on the mystics, teaching the poetry of Fray Luis and John of the Cross in conjunction with chapters 1–11 of Teresa's *Vida* introduces students to the spiritual and social challenges faced by the mystics. Moreover, Teresa's *Vida* provides an excellent point of entry into early modern religious life. The question of the self, so central to our modern existence in the West, occupies an important position in this autobiographical spiritual treatise. The first eleven chapters of Saint Teresa's *Vida* require at least a week to be taught effectively in an undergraduate setting. The time is well spent, however, since the chapters provide students a glimpse of an individual who fought to mold herself into a pious woman and then fought to change her church to meet the needs of women like her. The representation of a girl seeking personal fulfillment (chs. 1–3) gives way to that of an increasingly mature woman struggling to achieve spiritual fulfillment (chs. 4–10), until, in chapter 11, we find a full-fledged expression of the writer's ideas about mystical theology. Insisting that she writes only out of obedience as a "mujercita" 'silly little woman,' Teresa now daringly begins to explain—effectively to teach—the means by which one can strive for spiritual perfection. If less time is available for teaching Teresa, assigning the first three chapters of *Vida* in conjunction with chapter 11 can provide an effective overview of the shaping of the self, the pressures placed on Teresa as a woman writer, her desire to teach, and the struggle for reform that are key to understanding her life and work.

A focus on mystical poetry likewise plunges teachers and students into the key concepts of early modern spirituality. The poets' use of the language associated with the secular world—with marriage, sensuality, and sexuality—makes the personal experience of mystical union more transparent to readers today, but it also can be problematic if students view religious sentiment and sensuality as incompatible. As these examples suggest, whether instructors opt to include a few poems or chapters or to assign a more extensive selection, a positive teaching experience relies on a focused text selection and discussion of issues—such as the struggle for personal expression, spiritual enlightenment, and religious reform—that pertain to all the mystics' lives and texts.

Pragmatic Pedagogy

Even when we provide students with ample sociohistorical context, they may still find it hard to navigate the territory of Counter-Reformation spirituality and writing. It is useful, then, to think in the most basic terms when introducing students to the mystical authors. Making connections between the mystics' lives and the students' worldviews can facilitate sophisticated understanding and analysis of the pressures of spirituality in sixteenth-century Spain.

Instructors might consider providing a brief overview of the those doctrines and devotions that the post-Tridentine church emphasized, such as the importance of human effort in salvation, the seven sacraments, obedience to church authority, and the veneration of the saints. In this regard, instructors and students unfamiliar with Catholicism might consult Richard P. McBrien, Harold W. Attridge, and their colleagues, *The Harpercollins Encyclopedia of Catholicism*, which provides concise entries on key terms. For more extensive coverage, see *The Catholic Encyclopedia* (available online at www.newadvent .org/cathen/) and R. Po-chia Hsia's *The World of Catholic Renewal, 1540–1770.*

The contemporary singer Joan Osborne provides an effective point of departure for discussion about the belief in Christ's humanity and, in relation to the mystics, the quest to transcend the physical self in order to attain spiritual perfection. Osborne's "One of Us" communicates the sense of wonder surrounding Christ's life as a man. "Saint Teresa" explores mysticism and sanctity, painting a gritty picture of the saint as savior to drug addicts and prostitutes. The songs provide an excellent platform for classroom discussion, but instructors should be aware that online vendors sell numerous essays analyzing the relation between Osborne's lyrics and Spanish mysticism. To avoid receiving plagiarized student work, comparative essays on the songs and the mystics probably should not be assigned.

For classes in which Fray Luis's *La perfecta casada* (*The Perfect Wife*) has been assigned, the connections between the conduct manual for women and Teresa's *Castillo interior* or *Vida* can lead students to a vivid understanding of the cultural and theological issues at stake in Teresa's oeuvre. Fray Luis speaks from a position of authority in the church, advising women on comportment as wives and mothers. By contrast, Teresa was doubly bereft of authority: as a woman and a nun, she had to exercise great caution when presenting ideas about spirituality and theology (see Ahlgren, *Teresa of Ávila*; Bilinkoff, *Ávila of Saint Teresa*; and Weber, *Teresa of Ávila*). Her primary strategies—such as speaking from experience rather than from doctrine and adopting a rhetoric of humility rather than one of assertiveness—contrast vividly with Fray Luis's authoritative style.

To help students understand the important role of the mystics in the Catholic tradition and in the tradition of more secularly aligned scholarship, instructors can assign two short biographical narratives about authors read in class. Overviews of Teresa appear in numerous textbooks (such as Arenal and Schlau, *Untold Sisters* 8–17; Kaminsky 57–59; Paredes Méndez, Harprint, and Ballesteros 115–16; Mujica, *Women Writers* 1–12; and Rodríguez 111). To encourage students to understand the importance of the mystical saints in Catholic teachings today, instructors can compare the scholarly overviews mentioned above with religiously focused discussions of the saints (such as those found on Catholic and Carmelite Web sites or in Ahlgren, *Entering*; Luti, *Teresa*; and Williams).

Reading contrasting narratives also can generate discussion about the contexts in which the mystics lived and the legacy of their actions. For example, the analysis of Teresa as a conversa (descendant of Jews) who made the pragmatic decision to seek the protection of convent life (Arenal and Schlau, *Untold Sisters* 8–11) might be compared with the narratives constructed about her during canonization proceedings, many of which focused on her practicality in spiritual and everyday matters (Ahlgren, *Teresa of Ávila* 145–66). Similarly, Weber's analysis of Teresa's intimate collaboration with her confessors as she wrote and, with them, rewrote her *Vida* (Weber, "Three Lives") offers a very different narrative from that of a woman whose superiors "made her account for every voice and vision that came to her" (Medwick, *Teresa of Ávila* x) or who wrote her *Vida* "not for fun but because she was ordered to" (Maltz).

The suggestions above are most appropriate for undergraduate classes in which mysticism is only one of many topics covered. For courses that focus specifically on early modern Spanish literature or mysticism itself, either Gillian T. W. Ahlgren's *Teresa of Ávila and the Politics of Sanctity* or, for literature courses, Alison Weber's *Teresa of Ávila and the Rhetoric of Femeninity*, provide excellent, accessible analyses of Teresa's writings in the context of Counter-Reformation Catholicism. For both contexts, it can be a fruitful exercise to ask students to compare the role of women in the church in the sixteenth century with their role today, since official doctrine in both contexts often clashes with individual beliefs.

The success with which Teresa negotiated inquisitorial, Tridentine Spain can be highlighted through comparative readings about individuals whose heterodoxy led them to be tried and convicted by the Inquisition. Several such stories appear in Mary E. Giles's *Women in the Inquisition.* Richard L. Kagan and Abigail Dyer's *Inquisitorial Inquiries* provides English translations of several defendants' autobiographical statements and confessions. One such person, the soldier-prophet Miguel de Piedrola (c. 1540–?), was arrested in 1587 by the Toledo tribunal of the Inquisition on charges of false prophecy. Despite his arguments in favor of the legitimacy of his visions and against the Inquisition's jurisdiction over prophetic matters, Piedrola was sentenced to prison. That he was forbidden to "read the Bible or other Holy Scriptures, own paper, write letters, or speak of religious matters" captures the Tridentine emphasis on the importance of excluding laypersons from direct access to scripture and to God (Kagan and Dyer 79).

Other individuals who failed to position themselves as successfully as Teresa of Ávila include Francisca de los Apóstoles (1539– after 1578?), who established a religious community for women. In combination with her community activities, Francisca's visions and theological ideas led to her conviction in 1578. As Ahlgren notes in her English edition of the trial, Francisca's testimony about "visionary theology and the criteria she used for discernment of spirits" offers an excellent point of comparison with Saint Teresa's teachings (*Inquisition* 21). Other examples of visionaries and reformers that can be compared with Teresa of Ávila include the prophet Lucrecia de León, who is profiled in Kagan's *Lucrecia's Dreams;* the prolific seventeenth-century nun María de Ágreda (1602–65; see Colahan); Teresa's collaborator María de San José Salazar (1548–1603), whose *Book for the Hour of Recreation* is available in English translation; and Teresa's beloved nurse, Ana de San Bartolomé, whose autobiography is in English translation from the Other Voice in Early Modern Europe series.

The suggestions provided above represent only one approach to teaching the Spanish mystics. Instructors also might choose to focus on the relation between Spaniards and other mystics in different historical moments or world religions. Regardless of the course structure, teaching the Spanish mystics to undergraduates requires an accepting classroom atmosphere in which students are provided with sufficient information about the shifting religious culture of Counter-Reformation Spain and simultaneously are given the tools to decipher the intricacies of mystical expression in that context.

The more connections we as instructors make between topics related to both early modern and modern life—topics such as social control, censorship, and self-representation—the more positively students respond to the otherwise labyrinthine world of mysticism in which people "die without dying" and speak of a childhood fantasy of martyrdom. Curiosity, desire, rebellion, and compliance are as important to inhabitants of Western societies in the twenty-first century as they were to the pious Spaniards seeking to express themselves and reform their church in the sixteenth century. If instructors can help students understand the human connections between themselves and the mystics, then we have done our part to open up a world in which a handful of individuals managed to transcend cultural and religious conflict by creating aesthetically beautiful, intensely personal, and yet always politically charged records of their spiritual experiences.

NOTES

[1] Citations to Teresa's works are from *Collected Works*, edited by Kavanaugh and Rodríguez. Adrian J. Cooney is listed as the translator for the section on poetry (3: 375–410).

[2] For overviews of these issues, instructors might consult Karant-Nunn; Weber, *Teresa of Ávila* (esp. ch. 1); Wiesner, *Christianity and Sexuality*; and Lehfeldt.

Teaching Teresa of Ávila's *The Book of Her Life* in the Tradition of Western Spiritual Autobiography

Carole Slade

Students who come to Teresa of Ávila's *The Book of Her Life* by way of Augustine's *Confessions*, as they do in a course devoted to the major texts in the Western tradition of spiritual autobiography, bring assumptions and expectations to the work that sometimes cause confusion, even disappointment, but that can also yield insights not available from other avenues. Teaching the *Life* in relation to Augustine's *Confessions* provides opportunities to demonstrate Teresa's profound understanding of Christianity, her gender-inflected readings of scripture, and the role she writes for herself in the Christian narrative of salvation.

To help students put aside any preconceptions about Teresa and encourage them to take an analytical approach to the *Life*, I ask them to hand in at least one question about each chapter, the more thoughtful and difficult, the better. Many of these questions give me new ways to develop points I already intended to make, but some have been incisive enough to redirect my thinking. Despite the considerable first-rate scholarship recently devoted to Teresa's life and times, many questions about the *Life* cannot be answered definitively. Rather than try to answer students' questions directly, I discuss various ways to approach such questions, taking the opportunity to demonstrate how I use the heuristics for reading and methods of analysis that I have found productive with Teresa's texts.

I begin by making explicit the premises that inform my readings of Teresa's texts. First, I consider Teresa's texts, especially the *Life*, to be very demanding, as difficult in their own way as metaphysical poetry or modernist novels; they do not surrender very much of their meaning to the casual reader. Also, I assume that Teresa constructed her prose and chose her words with care (despite some evidence of hasty composition and scanty revision) and for specific rhetorical purposes. Before I take the surface meaning literally, I look for possibilities that her tone may be ironic or sarcastic, that an ambiguity may be intentional, and that an adjacent word or sentence might modify or negate an apparently straightforward statement. The fear, some would say "paranoia," that pervades the *Life* suggests that she wrote with the constant awareness that at least some of her readers might be hostile for any number of reasons, including suspicion of feminine spirituality, her advocacy of mental prayer, some unusual somatic manifestations of her spiritual experience, and her agitation for reform of the Carmelite order.[1] Her narratives, particularly of events in her early years, tend to be truncated and compacted. Readers can learn to untangle the meanings of most of her sentences, but some passages are so cryptic that even the most knowledgeable readers can only make educated guesses about what she intended to say, or not to say. For various reasons, among them her lack of formal training in rhetoric and her wish to disguise controversial agendas, Teresa develops some of her arguments indirectly and intermittently. I try to piece them together by tracing associational or subterranean logic between repeated words and allusions. As a literary critic myself (and in this literature course), I rely principally on close reading, but I also use whatever can be known about the particular time, place, and audience(s) to corroborate or correct those readings.[2]

In our introductory overview of theory of autobiography and of narrative in general, as well as in students' prior reading of the *Confessions*, students have learned that the term *autobiography* functions not as a prescriptive definition of a genre but as makeshift shorthand for works that read something like a first-person account of a life. I prefer the term *life writing*, and I use it interchangeably with both the long-standing and newly minted labels. Augustine intended his Latin title *Confessiones* to mean primarily a profession of faith. This witness to Christian belief entailed an account both of the occasions of sin on the trajectory away from God and of the reversal of direction made possible by the grace of God. This path with its reversal, the conversion, became a model for self-interpretation in Western life writing, religious and secular. Most Western autobiographies contain the equivalent of a conversion in one or more experiences that create a narrator with a new perspective on his or her past, or, in the vocabulary of theory of autobiography, that divide "the narrating I" from "the narrated I."[3]

Teresa did not place her own title on the writings now known as *The Book of Her Life*. Fray Luis de León created that title, which echoes the lives of the saints, for a posthumous first edition of Teresa's works in 1588.[4] In her *Life* Teresa uses several words to describe the text, all of them sometimes translated as "account" in English, but which have a range of definitions and connotations in the original Spanish. These terms include "relación" (1: 53 [prol., par. 2]; 1: 206–07 [ch. 23, par. 14]), which can be translated as "recitation," "exposition," or "deposition"; "discurso de mi vida" (1: 53 [prol., par. 2]; 1: 109 [ch. 10, par. 8]; 1: 227 [ch. 27, par. 1]), which refers generally to the systematic development of a life story and specifically to a section of the Inquisitional questionnaire; "declaración" (1: 109 [ch. 10, par. 8]), which can mean declaration, statement, or testimony; and "proceso de mi vida" (1: 226 [ch. 26, par. 6]), a phrase referring both to the process or development of a life and to a trial or judicial proceeding.[5] This array of meanings indicates that Teresa's vocabulary derives from the overlapping spheres of ecclesiastical, monastic, spiritual, judicial, and secular discourses. These various connotations also provide a useful reminder that some of the passages we normally read as narration, Teresa wrote, or at least was commanded to write, as explanation or exposition. Further, her potential audiences included some who thought her possessed by the devil and requiring exorcism (as she states openly in 1: 247–48 [ch. 29, pars. 4, 5]) and, eventually, inquisitors, who investigated numerous charges against her. A Dominican employed by the Inquisition to review the 1588 volume of her works characterized the *Life* contemptuously as "a very long story of her life, conversation, and virtues" written on "the slight pretext that she was ordered to do so by her confessors" (Fuente qtd. in Llamas Martínez, *Santa Teresa* 400; my trans.).[6] There is some truth to this accusation: Teresa was not always a reluctant writer, and she sometimes did manipulate confessors' commands for her own purposes (Weber, "Three Lives"). This eclectic work draws on many versions of life writing that were current in sixteenth-century Spain. The first-person genres Teresa evokes include Augustinian spiritual autobiography, penitential confession, spiritual testimony, account of conscience, and personal letter. The *Life* also shares characteristics with the third-person genres of hagiography, biography, and early forms of the novel.[7]

Teresa's approach to the first phase of her narrative of salvation, the confession of sin, raises numerous questions for most readers. In the first place, Teresa repeatedly complains that she has not been permitted to write about her sins: "I wish they would also have allowed me to tell very clearly and minutely about my great sins and wretched life. This would be a consolation. But they didn't want me to. In fact I was very much restricted [tied down] in those matters" (1: 53 [prol., par. 1]; see also 1: 109 [ch. 10, par. 8]).[8] A penitential confession ("confesión general"), most often made orally but occasionally requested in writing, was the first step in the sacrament of penance, the ecclesiastical ritual that in return for a confession of sin and completion of the prescribed penance conferred absolution, the kind of consolation Teresa complains she has been denied.[9] Why, then, if the priests charged with evaluating confessions of sin have not permitted her to narrate her sins, does Teresa so often condemn her own behavior as sinful? And why does she disparage herself so severely? My short, attention-grabbing answer to both these questions is that she does not.

To investigate questions about her insistent self-deprecation (one of the most frequently asked questions), I suggest that students begin by making a list of all the words Teresa uses to chastise herself. What they find, even in translation, is that she never labels herself a sinner or describes herself as sinful. The adjectives she most often uses for herself— "wretched" 'ruin,' "wicked" 'miserable,' "weak" 'flaca,' "bad" 'mala'—apply to all humanity, fallen from its original state of innocence. Similarly, her assertion that "for her sins" she deserves condemnation to hell are generic and formulaic (1: 276 [ch. 32, par. 1]; 1: 333 [ch. 38, par. 9]). I cite Elizabeth Rhodes's assessment of the limited extent of Teresa's admission of sin: "she represents herself . . . as inherently rather than specifically sinful," making a "theological statement" rather than a judgment of herself as a strategy to "offset the inquiry into her individual experience" ("What's" 95). Teresa's most negative assessments of herself often involve her feminine sex: "Just being a woman is enough to have my wings fall off—how much more being both a woman and wretched as well" (1: 109; ch. 10, par. 8). Read within the Christian narrative of sin and redemption, this despair of her gender might be an acknowledgment of her responsibility through Eve for humankind's fall into original sin. Yet Teresa never even mentions Eve in any of her works, while several times ascribing the Fall to "the sin of Adam" (not in the *Life*, but see

Interior Castle [2: 321; dwelling 4, ch. 1, par. 1]). For this reason, among others, I interpret the discouragement expressed here as a function of society instead of salvation, principally as a sarcastic reference to the negative estimation of women in the misogynistic society of sixteenth-century Spain instead of to guilt about either Eve's disobedience or her own sinfulness. That is, I locate this statement in the argument, which I find running underground through most of Teresa's writings, that men have in effect clipped women's wings, innate and God-given wings, by denying them an active role in the church.

While Teresa seems to have little problem admitting to her share of human-kind's innate sinfulness, Augustine long leaned on Manichaeism, a heretical Christian theology of dualism, to avoid acknowledging his share of the legacy of sin incurred by Adam's Fall. The actions that Augustine considers sinful from the Christian perspective he ultimately achieves—weeping over Vergil's Dido, raiding an orchard of pear trees, grieving excessively on the death of a friend, seeking material wealth and professional status, fathering a son by his longtime live-in concubine—were neither unusual nor considered immoral in his own society, but they weighed on his conscience, often for reasons he does not fully specify. These actions created emotional conflicts and intellectual problems that Augustine would eventually resolve by committing himself to a Christian ascetic vocation.

Like these actions in Augustine's life, most of those Teresa relates have a basis in biographical fact (though her convoluted narratives often make it difficult to identify), but in general these are actions that her contemporaries would have judged sinful and that would have thus tarnished her reputation rather than those for which she suffered a guilty conscience. Teresa typically deflects blame for behavior she calls "wretched" onto others or explains the hidden motives, which, had they been known at the time, would have excused her or outweighed any harm. Some of the actions Teresa renounces in the *Life* involve mistakes so trivial that they could easily be forgiven. Among the minor transgressions I include her brief addiction to reading books of chivalry, which she blames on her mother (1: 56–57; ch. 2, par. 1). Teresa takes care to uphold her mother's virtue by proclaiming her immune to the pernicious influence of these books, but she does reproach her for encouraging her more vulnerable daughter to read them.[10]

Also, Teresa confessed that during her novitiate year she did good deeds not to serve God but to please others amounts to admitting one minor sin, which attention to worldly things, in this case attention to her reputation for piety. Her admission also explains away her lengthy crying spells and frequent withdrawal from communal aspects of convent life. She reveals that the reason she so often isolated herself was not, as her sister nuns apparently assumed, her unhappiness in the convent with them but rather her intense remorse for trying to appear selflessly dutiful when the avoidance of criticism actually motivated her work (1: 70; ch. 5, par. 1). Having conceded only an excess of the spiritual virtue of scru-pulosity, she continues by alternating self-condemnation with self-exoneration:

"It all seemed to me virtue, although this will be no reason for pardon, because I knew in everything what seeking my own happiness was, and thus ignorance is no excuse." Finally she shifts the responsibility to the convent itself: "The only real excuse could be that the convent was not founded on a strict observance. I, miserable creature that I was, followed after what I saw wrong and left aside the good" (1: 70; ch. 5, par. 1). With this declaration, she has effectively retracted her confession of sin.

Other misdeeds Teresa confesses were so publicly known that she probably could not have avoided making some mention of them, even if she cannot completely exculpate herself. For example, the adolescent behavior she describes in such a garbled way in chapter 2, paragraphs 3–7 (1: 58–60), probably involved sexual activity, such as sharing newly discovered information with her cousins or experimenting to some extent.[11] Either one would have justified her father's sequestering her temporarily in a convent boarding school to prevent her from jeopardizing the family honor, which required chastity of its female members. The situation involved enough people, including the nun who counseled her at the Augustinian convent (1: 61; ch. 3, par. 1), that it could have circulated as gossip or some other report. For this lapse, whatever it was, she holds her parents responsible for letting her fall into bad company and credits her own "strong sense of honor" and her "fortitude not to do anything against the honor of God" (1: 58; ch. 2, par. 3) with preventing total destruction of her reputation.

Many other incidents involve her relationships with men, which often developed into intense emotional attachments that generated gossip, even scandal. One relationship, which she describes with such particularity that she seems to have intended contemporary readers to identify the person, involves a parish priest at Becedas who, she says, developed an extreme fondness for her: "His affection for me was not bad; but since it was too great, it came to no good" (1: 72; ch. 5, par. 4). Because her few and paltry sins required so little of his time, she explains, he began to confess "his bad moral state" to her (1: 72; ch. 5, par. 5). In these conversations she learned that a woman had given him a "charm" or "idol" to wear around his neck, perhaps as a token of affection or an act of witchcraft (1: 72–73; ch. 5, par. 5). To induce him to show her the amulet, Teresa "began to show him more love" (1: 73–74; ch. 5, par. 6). When he produced the amulet, she threw it in the river, with the result that "he stopped seeing this woman entirely." He saw Teresa more often, however, and in these encounters, they veered perilously close to mortal sin: "there were also occasions on which, if we had not remained very much in God's presence, there would have been more serious offenses" (1: 73; ch. 5, par. 6). For these lapses, which she does not describe except to say that they could have been "more serious," she does not explicitly blame this priest, but, immediately following this paragraph, she inserts a recommendation that men take advice on matters of propriety from virtuous women, presumably such as herself. Thus, while admitting enough details of their mutual infatuation to satisfy those who knew about it, she credits herself with rescuing the priest from sinful fascination with this other woman at a particularly fortuitous time, just before his death.[12] Other such incidents include chapter 7, paragraphs 5–8 (1: 85–86), in which a real or imagined toad appears to her while she converses with "this person," and chapter 8, paragraph 12 (1: 100), where she admits to developing crushes on one or more unnamed priests while listening to their sermons. For these inappropriate relationships she blames lack of discipline in the convent, absence of good role models, and bad advice from ignorant priests. When measured by the requirements of Christian asceticism, Augustine's sexual behavior was the more sinful, but the episodes Teresa narrates, particularly when she indicates that others disapproved of her behavior, had potentially more serious consequences with respect to her personal and familial honor and to her position in the Carmelite order and good standing in the church.

From this discussion of sin, we turn to the next stage of the Christian narrative of salvation, conversion. The first eight books of the *Confessions* constitute a conversion narrative. In chapter 8 Augustine describes in minute detail the last few steps toward this pivotal point, which is not the adoption of a new religion, since Augustine had already accepted Catholic Christianity, but a vow of continence in all sensual appetites, most importantly complete and permanent celibacy. Teresa's *Life* also contains a conversion narrative, but it is not nearly as fundamental to the work or as clearly demarcated. At least one critic does not find any conversion narrative in Teresa's *Life*. John Freccero contrasts "the linear conversion story of Augustine and the fragmentary, dispersed account of Teresa's life": unlike Augustine, Teresa does not "transform discontinuous moments into linear trajectory" (18). I would agree that Teresa does not compress her conversion narrative to the extent that Augustine does, but the *Life* does have a linear trajectory, albeit partly submerged, that traces a conversion experience quite different from Augustine's.[13]

Teresa begins the *Life* by comparing herself invidiously to saints, Augustine among them, who portrayed their conversions as a single, definitive reversal:

> my life has been so wretched that I have not found a saint among those who were converted to God in whom I can find comfort. . . . [A]fter the Lord called them, they did not turn back and offend Him.
>
> (1: 53; prol., par. 1)

Teresa reads Augustine's narrative as he constructed it to be read—as an abrupt, definitive intervention of divine grace modeled on Saul's confrontation with God on the road to Damascus and his transformation into the apostle Paul and following Paul, Saint Anthony, and countless others in mimetic succession.[14]

Teresa yearns to place herself in the scene of Augustine's conversion, possibly because the confessor who gave her the *Confessions* presented it as a normative account of religious experience, a role it played in devotional practice throughout the Middle Ages and beyond:

When I came to the passage where [Augustine] speaks about his conversion and read how he heard that voice in the garden, it only seemed to me, according to what I felt in my heart, that it was I the Lord called. (1: 103; ch. 9, par. 8).[15]

Augustine relates hearing a child shouting, "Pick up and read," which he initially takes as a chant in a game. When he cannot think of any game involving these words, he interprets them as instructions to pick up a book of scripture and read it. Using an ancient method of fortune telling, Augustine flips open the epistles of Saint Paul and reads the first passage on which his finger alights, Romans 13.13–14, which he takes as God's message to him: "make no provision for the flesh in its lusts" (153). Even after his conversion to Christianity, Augustine had not been able to govern his sexual and other sensual appetites, but reading this verse, which he considers to be the word of God, puts an end to his protracted, agonizing conflict of desires: "it was as if a light of relief from all anxiety flooded into my heart" (153).

In contrast to Augustine's scripture-centered conversion, which I would designate as hermeneutical (that is, relying on a theory of reading scripture), Teresa's conversion can be considered mystical, in that it centers on direct communication with God. In her interpretation of Augustine's narrative, Teresa relocates the moment of conversion away from his reading Romans back to hearing the words "pick up and read," thus identifying a shift from visual to auditory communication that expresses the manifestation of grace that she needs to relieve her of fear. Teresa strains to hear God speaking to her, but she fails— or, more accurately, the model of Augustine fails her. She continues by further distinguishing her needs from Augustine's when she describes her reading of the *Confessions* as having exacerbated rather than alleviated the fatigue and affliction that conversion typically resolves (1: 103–04; ch. 9, par. 9).

Next I call attention to her meditation on an image of a "very wounded" Christ earlier in the same chapter: "I felt so keenly aware of how poorly I thanked Him for those wounds that, it seems to me, my heart broke" (1: 101; ch. 9, par. 1). Teresa inserts herself imaginatively into the scene, not in the role of Christ, as most proponents of *devotio moderna* ("affective spirituality") advocated, but in that of Mary Magdalene. Taking the role of Mary Magdalene kneeling at the feet of Christ on the cross, a posture prefigured in her washing his feet in the house of the Pharisees, Teresa demands that he answer her prayers. She traces the beginning of her spiritual renewal to this assertion of her desire: "this was beneficial to me, because from that time I went on improving" (1: 101; ch. 9, par. 3). About two years later Teresa received the first words God spoke to her in rapture, "No longer do I want you to converse with men but with angels" (1: 211; ch. 24, par. 5),[16] which made the definitive change that characterizes Christian narratives of conversion: "From that day on I was very courageous in abandoning all for God, as one who had wanted from that moment . . . to change completely" (1: 212; ch. 24, par. 7). Teresa describes this transformation as analogous to the effect that Christ's words of forgiveness, "Go in peace," had on Mary Magdalene: "What He did in a short time for the Magdalene His Majesty does for other persons in conformity with what they themselves do in order to allow Him to work" (1: 199; ch. 22, par. 15). Teresa's conversion is not the instantaneous, definitive kind she attributes to both Augustine and Mary Magdalene, but I consider it a linear, diachronic narrative of conversion.

To represent her progression toward mystical experience, another vector in which her conversion takes place, Teresa also narrates her transformation synchronically (vertically toward God and inward to the core of her soul) in chapters 11–22, collectively known as "Ways of Watering the Garden." She diagnoses her initial obstacle to loving God as dryness of soul, by which she means the incapacity to feel. Observing the range of emotions expressed by nuns at the convent school, she discovers that she feels nothing: "so hard was my heart that I could read the entire Passion without shedding a tear" (1: 61 [ch. 3, par. 1]; see also 1: 68–69 [ch. 4, par. 9]). Her inability to feel makes her soul a wasteland of "very barren soil, full of abominable weeds" (1: 113; ch. 11, par. 6). In the initial stage of prayer, the first way of watering, the soul waters the garden entirely by its own effort, often without any result: before collecting even one drop, the soul may spend long periods "letting the pail down into the well and pulling it back up without any water" (1: 115; ch. 11, par. 10). The watering occurs with increasing ease as God repays the tears shed by the soul with increasing volumes of water from divinely replenished sources such as underground springs, mists, clouds, and, finally, drenching rains. In a mix of metaphors that articulates the paradoxes of her way, the well-watered soul has achieved the capacity to experience the passionate love for God, which Teresa represents as a spark that can be fanned into flame.

From their reading of Augustine, students have learned to look for the paradigms a writer chooses for understanding and interpreting his or her life. Augustine takes the prodigal son of Luke 15.11–32 as a figure of his life.[17] From the perspective gained in conversion, Augustine sees that his younger self pursuing sensual pleasure in Carthage and professional advancement in Milan replicated the itinerary of the prodigal son, running away from the father who loved him and squandering his inheritance. With his baptism in the Catholic Church, Augustine reenacts the homecoming of the prodigal son, receiving a forgiving welcome despite his sins, as well as the assurance that God values him particularly highly for his having strayed, just as the shepherd values the sheep that was lost more than those that stayed in the flock (Luke 15.3–7).

Teresa uses her paradigmatic stories—saints' lives from Jacobus de Voragine's *Golden Legend* and stories of New Testament women who interacted with Christ—as figures for her life and as important planks in her arguments for an apostolic role for herself and other women.[18] Teresa represents her early life as a quest to imitate the saints in the *Golden Legend*, principally their precocious piety, desire for martyrdom, and extremes of self-imposed spiritual and physical suffering. In childhood play she tries out the paths of both the martyr and the hermit (1: 55 [ch. 1, par. 4]), two versions of the "witness saint," who make their lives an imitation of the life of Christ—martyrs by suffering physical pain and hermits by suffering spiritual pain.[19] Teresa eventually rejects both of these extreme paths to sainthood, instead taking vows as a nun, a role she had rejected in childhood and adolescence (1: 55–56 [ch. 1, par. 6]; 1: 61–62 [ch. 3, par. 2]). To justify her decision to reject counsel from human beings, specifically from the priests who had failed her one way or another, she cites the saints whose model she follows instead: Paul, Francis of Assisi, Anthony of Padua, Bernard of Clairvaux, and Catherine of Siena (ch. 22, par. 7).

The most important figures Teresa uses to carve out her place in salvation history come from the New Testament, particularly the book of John, the Gospel that narrates in greatest detail the stories of women empowered by Christ. As the conversion narrative suggests and subsequent references make clear, Teresa portrays herself as Mary Magdalene, whom she sometimes conflates with Mary and Martha of Bethany, sisters of Lazarus. This conjunction of Mary and Martha, emblems of the contemplative and active lives, prefigures the dual role Teresa wishes to design for herself, a combination of the bride in mystical marriage and an apostle for Christ. She describes the way the soul can have this double focus: "the will is held fast and rejoicing [in contemplation of God]" (1: 153; ch. 17, par. 4) in the posture of Mary Magdalene or Mary of Bethany, who sat at Christ's feet while her sister Martha did the housework: "in this stage the [soul] can also be Martha in such a way that it is as though engaged in both the active and contemplative life together" (1: 153–54; ch. 17, par. 4).[20] To lead this twofold life of union with and service to God, Teresa needed to convince her contemporaries that her visions, locutions, and other spiritual experiences came to her from God. The *Life* and other writings, along with her widely remarked charisma and intelligence, helped her make that case successfully, such that she was given permission to create a reformed branch of the Carmelites, known as the Discalced Carmelites, and to found convents and monasteries based on the constitutions she wrote for them.

Reading Teresa's *Life* in the wake of Augustine's *Confessions* using the tools provided by recent theories of autobiographical narrative, then, enables a teacher to illustrate her specifically feminine Christian piety. Whether students pursue their reading of Teresa in an academic or a devotional setting, or both, these approaches to reading should enhance their understanding of her texts.

NOTES

[1] I developed these hypotheses in response to a medieval historian who observed that by comparison with other medieval women writers Teresa seemed quite paranoid.

[2] I assign very few secondary readings in this course, but for the unit on Teresa I place Bilinkoff, *The Ávila of Saint Teresa*; Slade, *St. Teresa of Ávila*; and Weber, *Teresa of Ávila* on reserve.

[3] For explanations of these terms, see Smith and Watson 59–61.

[4] Fray Luis de León created this title evoking the lives of the saints several years after Teresa's exhumed body was found to be incorrupt and talk of her sanctification had begun. For the influence of Raymond Capua's *Life of Catherine of Siena*, published in Spanish translation in 1512, see Ahlgren, "Ecstasy."

[5] Translations here are my own, culled from various English versions of the *Life* and other sixteenth-century Spanish texts. Citations to Teresa in Spanish are from the *Obras completas: Edición manual*, ed. Efrén de la Madre de Dios and Steggink.

[6] The original, from Alonso de la Fuente's "Primer Memorial," reads, "larga historia de su vida y conversación y virtudes . . . leve ocasion que dice se lo mandaron sus confesores." I have argued that Teresa had internalized the autobiographical questions on the inquisitional questionnaire and that, consciously or not, she answered many of them in the *Life* (Slade, *St. Teresa of Ávila* 9–30).

[7] Bakhtin's work on language, which he defines as responsive to other linguistic acts, or dialogical rather than referential, serves well for explaining Teresa's approach to genre. See Slade, *St. Teresa of Ávila* 12–17.

[8] Of the English translations available, I prefer the one by Kavanaugh and Rodríguez, in the *Collected Works*. While it is not as elegant as that of Peers's *Life*, it captures something of the colloquial, spontaneous nature of Teresa's prose. I would rank Cohen's version a distant third. All are available in paperback. All quotations in English and general references to her works are from Teresa's *Collected Works*, edited by Kavanaugh and Rodríguez, unless otherwise indicated.

[9] The Fourth Lateran Council (1215) formally placed full responsibility for hearing regular confession, assigning commensurate penance, and granting absolution in the ecclesiastical domain.

[10] For contemporary opinion on the books of chivalry see Slade, "'Este gran Dios'" 301–06.

[11] For the difficulty of making even an educated guess, see Teresa, *Life* (ed. Peers) 73n6.

[12] Teresa frequently emphasizes the distinction between venial sin and mortal sin, protesting to an extent that can be read to imply that others suspected she had lapsed into mortal sin. See 1: 90–91 [ch. 7, par. 17]; 1: 94–95 [ch. 8, par. 2] 1: 356 [ch. 4, par. 5].

[13] Bynum argues that because of differences based on gender medieval women wrote spiritual autobiographies that avoid the sharp turns and definitive conversions characteristic of narratives by men (*Holy Feast* 25).

[14] Augustine's conversion almost certainly did not occur as instantaneously as he indicates in *Confessions*, book 8. Rather, it probably developed in incremental changes, which he frames as a succession of philosophical positions on the origin of evil and the nature of truth. Neither was his conversion so final, for he continues to struggle with his carnal appetites, most poignantly in book 10, where he confesses to having sinful dreams about food, an appetite he deems harder to control than sex because he cannot completely banish it.

[15] It usually seems perfectly natural to students that Teresa read Augustine, just as they have, but here I try to distance their experience from hers. In fact this scene is improbable for various reasons: many women of the time were illiterate, and those who could read had their choice of books narrowed by increasingly comprehensive indexes of prohibited books. Teresa carefully specifies that she had no active role in acquiring the

Confessions: "I had not tried to procure a copy, nor had I ever seen one" (1: 103, ch. 9, par. 7). Teresa and her siblings learned to read at home from their mother and possibly a tutor, but Teresa could not even consider getting any kind of formal education. She derived most of her knowledge of scripture and theology from sermons, the daily office, and conversations with priests, though she did read many devotional books and books of chivalry on her own. On Teresa's reading see Slade, "'Este gran Dios.'"

16 Read literally and straightforwardly this sentence makes the simple declaration that Teresa has attained the privilege of interacting with heavenly rather than earthly beings. Reading with Teresa's characteristic irony and indirection in mind, I consider the sentence as obliquely stated permission from God to rely solely on Christ for spiritual guidance and companionship rather than on the priests (men) she frequently accuses of misleading her.

17 On Augustine's references to the parable of the prodigal son, see Ferrari.

18 Teresa amalgamates the saints and hermits of the *Golden Legend*, naming only Saint Catherine of Alexandria (in a dedication to a poem). She probably also drew many of her versions of New Testament women's lives from that compendium rather than from the Bible itself.

19 On the narrative motifs of the *Golden Legend*, see Boureau 68–70.

20 For a fuller discussion of the role of New Testament women in Teresa's life, see Slade, *St. Teresa of Ávila*, ch. 2.

Successful Mystics and Failed Mystics: Teaching Teresa of Ávila in the Women's Studies Classroom

Marta V. Vicente

I teach Teresa of Ávila and the Spanish mystics as part of my women's history survey class From Mystics to Feminists: Women's History in Europe, from 1500 to the Present. In this large class of about ninety-five students, we devote two weeks to exploring the relation between religion and the female body in the world of the Catholic Reformation. The title for these two weeks of lectures and class discussions is The Body in Pain: Mystics, Authority, and Sexuality, 1550–1700.

Students who take this survey course can enroll through women's studies or history. Some have a previous background in either field, but for most this is their only exposure to female religiosity and particularly to the world of Spanish mystics. Many have never heard of Teresa of Ávila and have only a vague idea of what mysticism is. Nonetheless, I have found that this audience is intrigued with the question of why some women were declared true mystics and others denounced as frauds. This issue allows me to encourage students to analyze how the interests of particular social groups intersected with widely accepted notions about female sexuality and spirituality in early modern Europe.

Students approach the topic of mystics in midsemester, after they have considered the lives of married women as described in *The Return of Martin Guerre* by Natalie Davis and the life of a nun as depicted in *The Lieutenant Nun: Memoir of a Basque Transvestite in the New World*. The latter is the autobiography of Catalina de Erauso, a seventeenth-century novice who escaped from the convent to live the life of a soldier in the New World. In the discussion of Erauso's book, students see monasticism through the eyes of the protagonist, that is, as a world that imprisons women's bodies and limits their freedom. To give students a more nuanced perspective on convent life, I provide them with images as well as short excerpts from the writings of women mystics, which suggest that for at least some women the convent was a refuge from the demands of marriage and childbearing, providing opportunities for creative and spiritual self-actualization. I explain that despite their vows of chastity and renunciation of marriage, nuns did not leave their bodies outside the convent walls. Nor did they escape the widely held Aristotelian notions of women's physical and intellectual inferiority and the attendant anxieties over female sexuality. I now introduce the paradox of how mysticism allowed some women to find a public voice through their bodies.

Notions of Female Sexuality in Historical Context

By introducing students to the world of female mystics, I want them to realize that women were able to exert authority in their communities in part by adapting notions of the sexualized female body. For some students, religion is synonymous with repression, especially sexual repression. For this reason it is important for them to see that it is precisely in the context of religion where the female body frequently transforms itself into a source of authority for women. In a cultural context in which physical pain was seen as an imitation of Christ's suffering and as a way to repay God and win his favor, women were sometimes able to use their suffering bodies to garner recognition and even political power.

After devoting time to Aristotle's notions of the female body and mind, I place the study of the female body in the context of the Spanish empire after the Catholic Reformation. I explain that the Council of Trent (1545–63) reinforced strict cloistering for nuns; that is, nuns could no longer leave the convent except in the case of extreme danger, and they could receive visitors only under very restricted circumstances. The Tridentine canonists justified these measures on the basis of their belief that women needed to be protected from the depravity of the world and from their own sensual nature. Although strict enclosure isolated women from their families and societies, it also offered them the opportunity to have a voice through informal teaching, religious writings, and, for some, their mystical experiences. Thus, the analysis of the Spanish mystics takes place at this crossroad: the unique connection between ideas about the redemptive power of women's suffering bodies and the perils that the female body represented for religious reformers. Out of this paradox students learn that sometimes women find approbation where they might otherwise find condemnation. Women could claim a certain spiritual leadership when they were able to convince authorities that the vulnerability of their weak bodies made them more spiritual rather than more sexual.

In my next lecture, I introduce the idea that although mysticism allowed some women to achieve a public voice, it was a path that was often fraught with danger. If women could receive divine messages and sensations through their bodies, many believed that female bodies were also permeable to demonic influence or evil spirits. For this unit, I assign selections from primary sources, beginning with the infamous manual for witch hunters, *Malleus Maleficarum*: "Women are naturally more impressionable, and more ready to receive the influence of a disembodied spirit; and when they use this quality well they are good, but when they use it ill they are evil" (Krämer and Sprenger 44). If, as Aristotle suggested, the way women experience the world is through their bodies, the text in *Malleus Maleficarum* implies that the way they will have access to the spiritual will be through their bodies as well. Medical texts shared this notion of the female body as vulnerable to being inhabited by outside forces. To underscore this concept, we revisit the medieval compendium of women's medicine, *The Trotula*:

> [God] created the male and the female with providen[ce], dispensing deliberation, laying out in the separate sexes the foundation for the propagation of future offspring. . . . And [God did this] so that by his stronger

quality the male might pour out his duty in the woman just as seed is sown in its designated field and so that the woman by her weaker quality, as if made subject to the function of the man, might receive the seed poured forth in the lap of Nature.   (65)

The Trotula's use of Hippocrates and Galen coincides with Aristotle's theory that physical matter dominates a woman's entire being. Moreover, because a woman was only matter and her matter controlled her will, she was more susceptible to being penetrated by other spiritual beings stronger than she.

This idea of women as mostly matter, and thus diminished in intellect, is present in one of the most influential medical treatises in Spain and Europe, Juan Huarte de San Juan's 1575 *Examen de ingenios para las ciencias* (*Examination of Men's Wits*):

> La primera mujer que hubo en el mundo . . . sabía mucho menos que Adán. Lo cual entendido por el demonio, la fue a tentar; y no osó ponerse a razones con el varón, temiendo su mucho ingenio y sabiduría. . . . Luego la razón de tener la primera mujer no tanto ingenio le nació de haberla hecho Dios fría y húmida, que es el temperamento necesario para ser fecunda, paridera, y el que contradice al saber; y si la sacara templada como Adán, fuera sapientísima, pero no pudiera parir ni venirle la regla si no fuera por vía sobrenatural.   (614–15)

> The first woman in this world . . . knew much less than Adam. When the devil learned this, he went to tempt her. And he did not dare to argue with the man, fearing his great intellectual capacity and wisdom. . . . The reason why the first woman did not have intellectual capacity was because God made her cold and wet, which is the necessary temperament to be fecund and to give birth, which is contrary to wisdom . . . ; if he had given her a tepid temperament like Adam, she would be extremely knowledgeable, but she would not be able to give birth and have her menses, except by supernatural means.   (my trans.)

According to Huarte, women should not aspire to men's tepid, dry, humoral nature and pursue an intellectual life but should remain "cold and wet" in order to be fecund and give birth.

Because of the limitations of their nature, women could not approach God through the intellectual route of scholastic theology. The pictorial image of the temptation of Saint Anthony, the good friar focused on his study while sexualized beauties tempt him, has no parallel for women. Women are temptation itself; because of their mental weakness, their flesh is the greatest impediment to achieving communion with God. How are we to explain that many mystics in early modern Europe were women? One answer is that men's intellectual pride was sometimes thought to pose an impediment to achieving this divine union, whereas women's intellectual humility made them more receptive to God's love (Mooney). During the late Middle Ages and well into the early modern age, it was not uncommon for men—including clerics—to become devotees of women whom they felt possessed some essential spiritual quality or gift lacking in themselves (J. Coakley 2).

The Road toward Authority: The Life of the Mystic

Students need to examine the role of ascetic body practices in mysticism to comprehend how what was often viewed as a dangerous, sexualized body might help women gain religious authority. The word *asceticism* as defined by the *Encyclopedia of Catholicism* means "the practice of religious discipline with an emphasis on self-control and the fostering of virtue" (McBrien, Attridge, et al.). Asceticism's emphasis on physical self-control and mortification could eliminate the negative aspects of the female body and turn it into a vehicle for a close experience with the divine.

The life of the female mystic starts with the ascetic practice, whether in the context of the convent or in the home. Strict personal self-denial for the mystic to be represents the first of the traditional three mystical stages: the purgative stage. However, the aspiring mystic will sometimes resort to extreme forms of self-imposed suffering, forms that go beyond the customary ascetic practice of curbing the appetites of the flesh. Although some Christians approved of extreme physical mortification as means of gaining proximity with God, others believed that it represented a dangerous road for those aspiring to mystical experiences. In fact, in her letters to María de San José Salazar (1548–1603), Teresa of Ávila advised her prioresses not to engage in severe ascetic practices, since they could induce false visions and ecstasies (Weber, "'Dear Daughter'").

The spiritual value of physical suffering received particular impetus from the tradition of *imitatio Christi*, a model of Christian life that underscored the imitation of Christ's own physical suffering that culminated in the passion and crucifixion. This tradition enjoyed widespread popularity during the early modern period. The extreme self-mortification of many women mystics, reinforced by an understanding of *imitatio Christi* as voluntary suffering, sometimes proved to be more appealing than Teresa's moderate asceticism. Although many canonized mystics advocated moderate asceticism, for other mystics extreme self-mortification remained an important component of their religious practice. To many of their devotees, such practices signified a crucial prerequisite for holiness.

Introducing my class to women who later will be regarded as successful mystics, I offer them examples of what exemplary ascetic practices were. For instance, the Aragonese nun and faithful correspondent of Philip IV of Spain, Sor María de Ágreda (1602–66), slept two hours daily and ate only once a day; her diet consisted of vegetables and legumes three times a week, bread and water three other days, and nothing on Fridays. She engaged in other extreme acts of self-mortification. She walked for half an hour daily on her bare knees while carrying an iron cross weighing fifty-two kilograms on her back. She also tied her hands and feet to nails on a cross on the walls of her cell while she meditated (Corteguera and Velasco). Although students are at first inclined to see these acts as evidence of pathology, I try to communicate the idea that these were culturally validated (though sometimes controversial) practices.

For the orthodox mystic, a stage of active purgation and intense meditation on Christ's life is followed by the illuminative stage, in which awareness of God's presences is increasingly infused rather than acquired through effort. The prayer of union, characterized by ecstatic assurance of God's presence, is the culmination not only of the mystic life but also of our analysis, as the class studies the interrelation of religiosity and the female body.[1]

To explore the connections between sexuality, religion, and authority, I include the case of Teresa of Ávila and the interpretation of her ecstasy by the Italian artist Gianlorenzo Bernini. We analyze Bernini's *Ecstasy of St. Theresa* (1647–52) and Jacques Lacan's interpretation of this rapture as a moment of sexual culmination (for this purpose students read Lacan's *On Feminine Sexuality*, where he describes Teresa's ecstasy as *jouissance feminine*, or female orgasm). I ask students to consider whether the final abandonment of corporeal attachment brings women, paradoxically, to the ultimate essence of marriage—sexual consummation—translated into a divine marriage. As a class we discuss whether Bernini's and Lacan's erotic interpretation of Teresa's ecstasy is valid. If the enjoyment of mystical ecstasy is sexual, as Lacan claims, is it truly liberating? Have Bernini and Lacan misinterpreted Teresa by focusing on only one aspect of her spiritual experience? At heart is whether the erotic language of the mystics refers to real sexual sentiments and desires or whether it is a metaphor for something else (or both). This, in turn, can lead to a productive discussion of whether twentieth-century notions of sexual repression and sublimation can be applied appropriately to the sixteenth century.[2]

Successful and Unsuccessful Mystics

After analyzing Bernini's sculpture, I introduce my students to the concept of the historical construction of sanctity. I ask them to contemplate the idea that the designation of sainthood is the result of the interaction between would-be saints and the men and women who observed them and judged their behavior (Delooz; Burke). History provides many examples of women who failed to prove their sanctity (Schutte; Haliczer; and Keitt). Credulity existed alongside skepticism. For example, in 1537 a Franciscan friar recommended that good Christians "should make the sign of the cross upon seeing a miracle-working female reputed to be a saint" (qtd. in Weber, "Saint Teresa, Demonologist" 172–73). And yet many female mystics did obtain approval and were exalted by their communities. The question is then, What were the factors that led some women to be declared holy while others were denounced as frauds? I approach this issue by presenting students with a cluster of successful cases followed by unsuccessful ones.

The success or failure of mystics ultimately depended on their ability to comply with the practices expected from a holy woman and to establish stable alliances with promoters and protectors. We now turn more specifically to the active life of Teresa of Ávila to see how her mystical experiences were put to the service of the reform of the Carmelite order, a reform that was supported by King Philip II and the papal nuncio. More than a half century later, another holy woman influenced royal politics directly. From 1643 until her death in 1665, María de Ágreda conducted an extensive private correspondence with the king. Expressing herself in enigmatic, humble phrases, María exerted considerable authority as the king's spiritual adviser, although the practical impact of her political influence is difficult to determine (Corteguera and Velasco). The life of Beatriz Ana Ruiz (1666–1735), a holy woman from Guardamar del Segura, provides a third example. When this impoverished washerwoman first claimed that her body was the site of a fierce struggle between God and the devil, her neighbors considered her to be simpleminded or mad. But Ruiz eventually won the admiration and support of local clerics. Her visions and prophesies, dutifully reported to her confessors and spiritual advisers, advanced various political causes advantageous for the citizens of Guardamar. By the time of her death in 1735, the town venerated her as a saint. Paradoxically, Ruiz's passivity—her conformity to expectations of docility and submission to authority—was key to her becoming a political actor (Corteguera). By comparing these three cases, students can see how women's visionary experiences could be used in support of various political-religious agendas. Teresa's visions, for the most part, were limited specifically to the future of the Discalced Carmelite reform; she tried to distance herself and her followers from local and national politics. Philip IV confided private and political problems to María de Ágreda and considered her his personal intermediary with God. Beatriz Ana Ruiz and her promoters operated on a local and regional level. These examples suggest that women mystics could exert agency and have an impact in the public sphere, but they were not solitary actors. Furthermore, their engagement with politics—whether monastic, royal, or local—could be a double-edged sword. Power and influence attracted envy and intense scrutiny. It was imperative for successful mystics to avoid any sign of sensuality, arrogance, or self-serving ambition and to conform to the feminine gender ideals of sexual purity, humility, and meekness.

Just as there are multiple factors to explain a successful mystical performance, there are many ways in which an aspiring mystic might fail to convince her public of her authenticity. María de la Visitación (1551–c.1603), known as "the nun of Lisbon," was prioress of the Convent of the Annunciation in Lisbon during the tumult associated with Spain's annexation of Portugal in 1580. María became famous throughout Europe for the stigmata she bore on her hands, feet, and forehead. Although she had many powerful devotees, including Prince Cardinal Alberto of Portugal and the famous preacher Luis de Granada, her sister nuns resented her economic control over convent funds and denounced her as a fraud. After Luis de Granada himself examined her wounds and declared them to be authentic stigmata, María continued to enjoy the support of her many devotees. But when she became associated with the Portuguese nobility who favored a Portuguese pretender to the throne, Philip II ordered the Inquisition to investigate. This time her examiners, after thoroughly washing her hands with harsh soap, discovered that the stigmata disappeared (Corteguera 174). When María's sentence was handed down, she was demoted to the position of last among her sisters and condemned to perpetual imprisonment in a convent located on the outskirts of Lisbon.[3]

Our second case of a failed mystic is from Italy. Benedetta Carlini (1590–1661), abbess of the Convent of the Mother of God, had modeled her mystic performance on that of Teresa of Ávila, just thirty years after the Spanish mystic died.[4] Yet unlike Teresa, Benedetta Carlini failed not only to prove that she was humble enough to be a good nun but also that she had sufficiently punished her sensual body—she was alleged to have a lesbian relationship with a novice in her convent. For the religious authorities who condemned Benedetta as a heretic, her body represented a tainted, sexualized, nonmaternal body.[5] The diverse fortunes of these women show that there was no simple formula for success. Sexual purity, a mortified body, humility, obedience to authority, and self-abnegation were essential for fending off charges of hypocrisy. But since mystics were often adopted as spiritual standard-bearers in political causes and partisan disputes, they could fail for reasons that had little to do with their individual performance of holiness; reputations could be won and lost according to shifting political tides. We also see that failure was not always a question of men versus women. Ecclesiastical authorities and the Inquisition had the ultimate authority to silence and punish failed mystics, but many men of all ranks—confessors, bishops, cardinals, even the king—were sometimes loyal supporters of women they deemed holy. By the same token, the aspiring mystic's worst enemies might be the sisters of her own convent. A mystic could not count on gender solidarity.

In class we conclude by discussing the irony that women's achievement of authority often came through their bodies; during their lifetime, women who made vows of virginity, who abstained from earthly pleasures, and who engaged in self-imposed suffering in imitation of Christ sometimes acquired an authority to speak, teach, and act in the public sphere or indirectly through alliances with public figures. The holy female body was also crucial in the creation of a postmortem saintly cult. After her death in 1582, pieces of Teresa's incorrupt body were dispersed among her devotees and became precious relics venerated by Philip II and later by the twentieth-century dictator Francisco Franco.

As a way of concluding these series of lectures, I ask students to write an essay comparing the life of the laywomen (such as Bertrande de Rols, the wife of Martin Guerre, or Catalina de Erauso) and the female mystics studied in class. In which ways did these women understand and see their bodies differently? What do these perceptions tell us about the changing notions of female sexuality in early modern Europe? How did men and women interact in monastic contexts in contrast to secular contexts? In what ways does this particular combination of religion and sexuality help us rethink the way people understood religion in early modern Europe? These questions leave us with the need to reconsider the elements that shaped religion and religious behavior in early modern Europe as well as the role that women—and their bodies—played.

NOTES

[1] Helpful definitions for students can be found in Downey. See esp. the entries for "Ecstasy," "Illumination, Illuminative Way," "Purgation, Purgative Way," and "Union, Unitive Way."

[2] The article by Partner, "Did Mystics Have Sex?," will be of interest to instructors who approach this topic. Partner argues that we cannot simply reduce the eroticism of mystical language to metaphor. Slade provides a provocative critique of psychoanalytic interpretations of Teresa (*St. Teresa* 133–48).

[3] The typical punishment for laywomen accused of religious hypocrisy was one hundred lashes and exile from their native town (Weber, "Demonizing"). As a nun from a noble family, María de la Visitación was spared the lashes and punished instead with extra days of fasting and limited access to communion. Even these punishments were eventually mitigated.

[4] The phenomenon of Teresa of Ávila as a model for young women aspiring to be successful mystics and saints has recently being studied (Schlau; Haliczer).

[5] Judith Brown discusses Carlini's case at length. Instructors may wish to consult the text of the Inquisition's sentence for María de la Visitación included in Imirizaldu. Another possible primary source for this unit is the inquisitorial trial of Francisca de los Apóstoles, recently edited and translated by Ahlgren.

Defiance and Obedience:
Reading the Spanish Mystics in Historical Context

María del Pilar Ryan

I teach Spanish mystical writers in a world history survey and in electives in early modern Europe, world religions, and the Roman Catholic Church from 1200 to 1700. A study of the Spanish mystics can reveal the fascinating intersection of political, social, and religious authority in early modern Spain. Among the most important issues regarding these authors for students to appreciate is how the mystics understood authority and were themselves understood in the context of the authority of the Spanish church. During an age of Catholic and Protestant reform, the fixed symbols of political, social, and religious authority were challenged on all sides, and writers such as Teresa of Ávila and Ignatius of Loyola were viewed with suspicion. These mystics wrote with a confidence in their own spirituality and in their mission to serve the church that the church itself did not share. In one of the great ironies of history, they later were canonized as leaders of Counter-Reformation Catholicism.

It is initially difficult for students to relate to early modern religion. But I have found that they become more engaged with the subject if they can see that the mystics led lives of both defiance and obedience. When students learn that the boundaries between private and public spirituality and orthodoxy and heterodoxy were ambiguous in early modern Spain, they become intrigued with the question of how some mystics were suspected of heresy and later made saints.

The historical themes of defiance and obedience are especially relevant to an audience engaged in the creation of an adult identity in the regimented environment of the United States Military Academy, West Point. While the maturation process involves rejecting elements of parental authority, students must simultaneously acknowledge the institutional authority found at West Point. In this context, young men and women experience feelings of rebellion, temptation, and doubt yet develop discipline, commitment, and a sense of purpose. Reading the Spanish mystics in historical context allows my students to understand their own experiences from a new perspective.

To ensure that the students understand the experiences of the mystics from the perspective of the sixteenth century, I often highlight the events occurring elsewhere in Europe during our discussions. I find it necessary to fix the historical timeline for these students of the postconfessional age. Students at West Point are overwhelmingly Christian, but the divide between Roman Catholics and Protestants is sometimes wide, particularly when discussing the history of Christianity. By acknowledging and emphasizing the inherent conflict between individual and institutional practices in Europe during the time of the mystics, it somehow democratizes the classroom. Roman Catholic students are not the default experts on the mystics; different elements of individual and institutional faith can be recognized and expanded on in class discussion by each student. The tension that might have developed between classmates is now projected, appropriately, onto the historical age of the mystics, and it becomes a tool for understanding the world in which the mystics negotiated.

As a historian, I frame the primary source material from Teresa of Ávila and Ignatius of Loyola with studies on the Counter-Reformation in early modern Europe. John Bossy's *Christianity in the West, 1400–1700* provides an excellent overview. Bossy was the major proponent of the thesis that the Counter-Reformation church sought to impose conformity and discipline on the diverse manifestations of medieval popular piety. His thesis has in recent years been the subject of considerable debate, and in my upper-division courses students enjoy responding to these debates. Bossy also allows students to compare the Counter-Reformation in Spain with how it operated in other European countries. Stanley G. Payne's *Spanish Catholicism*, which describes public and private faith and ritual in Spain, is also invaluable for contextualizing the Spanish mystical writers.

I usually begin the unit on Spain with a lecture on the Reconquest and the rise and fall of Erasmism in Spain. I explain that the conquest of Moorish Granada at the close of the fifteenth century solidified the union of church and state. The messianic themes of conquest were carried over into Spain's New World adventures, which later supported, both dogmatically and financially, the church against the Lutheran threat. As Ferdinand assumed greater authority in the political arena, Isabel's public piety grew in importance. For this unit, I assign selections from Peggy Liss's *Isabel the Queen: Life and Times*. This excellent biography encourages students to think about the intersection of gender, power, and religion.

The following classes are devoted to the new order that was to become one of the most successful manifestations of Catholic renewal in the sixteenth century—the Society of Jesus. Students are often surprised to learn that many in the church questioned the orthodoxy of Ignatius of Loyola and his followers. The Jesuits' emphasis on conversion from tepid Christianity to a life of inner piety raised alarm in the minds of many ecclesiastical authorities, who saw similarities among the Society of Jesus, Erasmism, and the heterodox Alumbrado movement.[1]

Two articles are particularly valuable for those leading a classroom discussion about the internal and external threats posed by mystical writers in general and by Ignatius of Loyola in particular. Both Constance Jones Mathers and Marjorie O'Rourke Boyle ("Angels") discuss the suspicions raised by the intensely personal experience of the *Spiritual Exercises*. The *Spiritual Exercises*, devised by Ignatius of Loyola, were part of a larger movement in the Spanish church fostering methodical mental prayer. One section of the *Spiritual Exercises* that in particular attracted the attention of the Inquisition concerned the "discernment of spirits"—the process of determining and following the will of God ([ed. Thornton] 202). Ignatius believed that the Rules for Discernment allowed

Christians to make decisions crucial to living and growing as spiritual beings. He used the word *contemplation* to "denote imaginative involvement in a gospel scene," capturing both the methodical mental prayer and the active missionary focus of the Jesuits (Endean 357). He maintained that it was through decision making "that we co-create with God our very selves" (Houdek 128). The individual agency these rules promoted challenged the authority of both church and state in Spain, especially when the lines of orthodoxy and heterodoxy were being more sharply drawn.

It is the action of the early Jesuits that I emphasize to my classes, since "Jesuit piety itself is decidedly aggressive; Ignatius did not call it spiritual exercise for nothing" (Rhodes, "Join" 35). One "makes" the exercises, rather than passively hearing or reading them. Students are able to identify the heroic elements in Jesuit engagement with European culture. It is at this point in every semester that my students have an epiphany and can recognize and articulate the role of the individual in creating the early modern world. To use the well-worn phrase, history comes alive for them. They see that "Ignatius' religiousness is based on the ability to endure as a functioning individual even while turning over one's will to God" (Rhodes, "Join" 35). These class discussions allow students to see a way of retaining their individual identity in an environment that demands self-lessness. These discussions about resisting homogeneity usually circle back to the nature and goals of the Inquisition and culminate in a deeper understanding of the social tensions in Spain.

How was it, then, that Ignatius emerged from his inquisitorial trials and went on to establish an influential order? Here I am able to introduce one of the many parallels between Ignatius and Teresa: both had wealthy and powerful benefactors intercede on their behalf. Indeed, both found an advocate in the same man, Francis Borgia, the Duke of Gandía, a grandee of Spain and former viceroy to Catalonia for Charles V. Borgia entered the Society of Jesus under the guidance of Ignatius and later acted as a confessor to Teresa of Ávila. A discussion of the importance of elite support for mystics helps me reinforce an important point: religious sentiment in early modern Spain was far from homogeneous. There was room for maneuver, and Ignatius and Teresa used it to their advantage.

The connections between the Jesuits and Teresa of Ávila underscore the networks of influence in early modern Spain, as well as the limitations they posed, especially to women. I have students read an account of how another Jesuit confessor to Teresa, Juan de Prádanos, instructed her "in spiritual discernment following the Jesuit paradigm: disciplined self-knowledge in God, followed by action" (Rhodes, "Join" 41). I then have them read about other Jesuits who were not open to the idea of women as spiritual teammates. The Jesuit chronicler Pedro de Ribadeneyra and other clerics in early modern Spain saw the problem of distinguishing between "true" and "false" holy women as one that could jeopardize the Jesuits' larger mission (Bilinkoff, "Many 'Lives'" 186n18). Teresa's third Jesuit confessor, Baltasar Álvarez, forbade her from discussing her mystical revelations, forcing her to choose between what she believed to be divine communication and her confessor's orders (Weber, "Teresa dì Gesù" 295–96). At this point, my students and I return to the theme of defiance and obedience, discussing what Jodi Bilinkoff terms "holy disobedience" ("Many 'Lives'" 188). Teresa could not submit humbly to both her divine communication and her confessor's orders. Obedience to one necessitates disobedience to the other. I ask my students how one resolves this dilemma. Is obedience to God more important than obedience to a Jesuit superior? To any other type of superior? My students normally say that it is, or assume that it would be for Teresa. We then discuss what the ramifications are to any organization when individuals have other, stronger loyalties. What are the consequences for a military unit? For a religious order? Where is the breaking point for the organization? At the end of the discussion, a student often remarks that the only resolution would be for God to direct the person to obey his or her temporal superior. The class is always surprised to learn that this was how Teresa's situation was resolved: she was consoled by a locution that told her to obey her confessor—for the present (Weber, "Teresa di Gesù" 296).

The vow of obedience was fundamental to the command and control of the Society of Jesus as it spread across the early modern world, yet the occasion for conflict between divine and temporal demands on obedience was great. Ribadeneyra's biography of Ignatius provided only limited examples of how the saint resolved these conflicting demands in his own life, since Ribadeneyra "may have found it extremely difficult, if not virtually impossible, to imagine Loyola in a position other than one of authority" (Bilinkoff, "Many 'Lives'" 185). Those serving under Ignatius, however, confronted the matter of disobedience guided by the lessons of spiritual discernment. One solution acknowledged an environment that demanded selflessness without negating an individual's disciplined self-knowledge in God. Holy disobedience became not an act of defiance but an act of modesty and humility (Bilinkoff, "Many 'Lives'" 193). Because it was mediated through Jesuit confessors, it allowed absolute submission to a greater good. Holy disobedience, therefore, could be "eminently praiseworthy because of its ultimate results" (Bilinkoff, "Many 'Lives'" 188). The solution reinforced both the structure and the spiritual identity of the Society of Jesus. Students find this idea fascinating, because it introduces a broker into the struggle between defiance and obedience, between the individual and the corporate entity. While the Jesuit confessor plays this role in our class readings, my students debate whether serving as a broker is the function of a leader within any organization: Is it leadership itself, an ideal quality to all who attend the United States Military Academy, that reconciles the competing needs of the individual and the corporate?

The final discussion about the Jesuits concerns the Society of Jesus's move away from mystical prayer under the Belgian Everard Mercurian, the first non-Spaniard to serve as general of the order. Mercurian was the fourth general, and his tenure, 1573–80, marked a change in the relationship between Rome and

the Jesuit provinces in Spain (Medina). "'The Strange Style of Prayer': Mercurian, Cordeses, Álvarez," by Philip Endean, is a fascinating study of the shifts
in spiritual practice and assertion of authority under Mercurian's leadership.
The formation of a Jesuit culture during this time displaced earlier openness to
mystical spirituality, and Mercurian ordered members of the Society of Jesus
to desist from being confessors to Discalced Carmelite nuns. Jesuit confessors
could no longer negotiate holy disobedience. In less than a decade, the Jesuit
understanding of obedience and defiance shifted, ending a powerful example of
male-female collaboration in sixteenth-century Spain.

I follow the units on the Jesuits and holy disobedience with one on female
monasticism. Chapter 4 from Mary Elizabeth Perry's *Gender and Disorder in
Early Modern Seville* can give students a vivid picture of why women chose (and
others were forced) to enter convents. I point out that entry into the convent
did not necessarily cut women off from interaction with the world. The walls of
the cloister were, in a sense, permeable (Lehfeldt). Teresa, while she accepted
monastic enclosure, maintained contact with family members, patrons, and
other nuns through her voluminous correspondence (Weber, "'Dear Daughter'"). Ignatius, like Teresa, was a prolific letter writer. Students can be asked to
compare and contrast selected letters. I encourage students to ask themselves
how Teresa and Ignatius tailored their letters to appeal to their particular cor-
respondents. The practical and often the political concerns reflected in the letters help students appreciate that these mystics were very much involved in the
world around them; they were involved in the business—and politics—of the
Catholic reform. Their resistance to and acceptance of authority are as much a
part of their mysticism as their corporal and spiritual struggles.

Students at the United States Military Academy, West Point, are familiar with
the structure and practice of authority. Their four-year experience as undergraduate students in an institution with a storied reputation for discipline is a
process in which they bow to authority in order to accomplish common goals
and in which they sometimes defy authority to retain their individual identity.
Part of the maturation and acculturation processes here is the recognition that
individual talents and interests can exist in a military organization. Although
they are like their contemporaries at civilian colleges and universities in many
respects, cadets are quick to recognize and appreciate the context of authority
in early modern Europe and the institutional nature of religion. The Spanish
mystics lived and wrote in a remarkable age, and knowing the historical context
for their work is fundamental to understanding it.

These strategies for teaching Teresa of Ávila and Ignatius of Loyola in the
context of the political and religious conflicts of sixteenth-century Spain have
been successful in engaging students of history at West Point. Students who
previously saw mysticism as a bizarre religious phenomenon now see mysticism
and religion itself through the lens of history. Students who viewed the literature of the mystics as quirky now find a treasure chest for understanding the
past. And those students who were curious about the mystical inner eye now

understand how it can illuminate religious, political, social, gender, and power dynamics in sixteenth-century Spain.

NOTE

[1]There are a number of excellent studies on early Jesuit spirituality and the suspicions it aroused. See, e.g., O'Malley (*First Jesuits*, "Early Jesuit Spirituality"); Hamilton; Marcocchi; and Andrés Martín ("Common Denominators").

A Transatlantic Perspective: The Influence of Teresa's Model on New World Women

Kathleen Ann Myers

The fundamental spiritual identity of midcolonial society creates a challenge for teachers and students of early Latin American culture. Living in a time and place in which the role of religion in society has been radically redefined and continues to be challenged, we need to bridge the spiritual and cultural gap that exists between the twenty-first century and colonial Spanish America. This can be a daunting task to undertake in an undergraduate classroom. Yet, if we begin by reading life stories from this period, students often become engaged with the material and curious about the colonial worldview. As student interest grows in these foreign but fascinating life stories, which often describe exotic penitential practices and visionary experiences, discussion easily moves into questions about Catholic norms for sanctity and mysticism and how this is expressed in the texts that we read. In this way, students begin to read fundamentally religious texts with an eye to comprehending the mind-set of a distant culture and society. To accomplish this goal, we need to teach students about the influential roles that Counter-Reformation spiritual practices, gender prescriptions, and religious genres played in these colonial texts and lives.

Key to initiating this learning process is to focus on the literary form of the autobiographical confessional *vida*, as popularized by Teresa of Ávila in Spain, and its biographical counterparts, the life stories of saints (hagiographies) and local holy people (biographical *vidas*). The structure and content of these life-writing genres were deeply informed by the Catholic Church's dictates for saintly behavior, especially for visionaries and women. To teach this literary-spiritual phenomenon—that is, the literary result of the spiritual practices prescribed for women—I use the life writings by or about three Spanish American colonial women: Saint Rose of Lima (1586–1617), Madre María de San José (1656–1719), and Sor Juana Inés de la Cruz (1648–95). Each text offers a distinctive view of how the Teresian model helped forge roles for women in the church and their local communities.

For centuries Teresa of Ávila's life and writings provided a powerful role model for Spanish American women who followed a religious path. Canonized and popularized in the same years that Creole urban centers were devoting mass sums of money to building religious houses and the norms established by the Counter-Reformation were being transferred to America, Teresa was upheld as the paradigm of religious orthodoxy and feminine religious behavior. Nearly every autobiographical and biographical text by or about midcolonial women (written from around 1600 to 1750) establishes a connection between the subject's life and Teresa. In late-seventeenth-century New Spain, for example, Madre María de San José writes in her confessional journals that God compared her mystical life and writings with Teresa's. In another vision, Teresa herself consoles María by promising to watch over the nun's spiritual journals. Both these visions—and María's recording of them for her confessors—illustrate the extent to which the Spanish saint had become an essential part of religious women's identity and a crucial point of reference to authorize nuns' spiritual experiences and writings. Indeed, other mystic nuns, such as María's Mexican contemporary, María Ana Águeda de San Ignacio (1695–1746), and the Colombian Madre Castillo (1671–1742), cite Teresa in their writings. Even nuns who attempted to redefine their roles as brides of Christ, such as the celebrated poet Sor Juana Inés de la Cruz and the picaresque Chilean Úrsula Suárez (1666–1749), compare themselves with Teresa. While Sor Juana claims a kinship to the Spanish saint because they are both authors, Úrsula ironically announces that she is more like Teresa every day, even though she delights in roguish behavior (165–66).

Not surprisingly, Teresa's influence also permeated the documents written by clergy about Spanish American religious women. When America's first saint, Rose of Lima, had a brush with the Inquisition, her defenders illustrated the parallels between Rose's and Teresa's visionary activity, attempting to prove the Peruvian's orthodoxy. Likewise, when examining the visions recorded in a biography about an Asian lay holy woman living in New Spain (Catarina de San Juan, c. 1607–88), a censor recalled how the church at first withheld Teresa's *Life* from circulation but later promoted it. In the New Spanish case, the censor hoped that even if Catarina's biography fell into the hands of the Holy Office of the Inquisition it would later be published and become an important spiritual text (Ramos).

The influence of Catholic teaching and practice over the writing and publishing of life stories reflects the impact of the church on every aspect of colonial Spanish American cultural life. Creole cities, especially Mexico City, Puebla, and Lima, were important sites for Catholic religious culture: dozens of churches and convents filled town centers; Catholic feast days regularly punctuated the year with religious processions, often filling city streets; and more than eighty percent of the books published in these cities were devotional texts. A large number of men and women chose to follow a religious life either by entering monastic orders or by leading rigorously devout lives as lay men and women. In seventeenth-century Lima, for instance, nearly one in four women lived in a convent or conventlike institution, such as a *recogimiento*. As the Mexican historian Edmundo O'Gorman observed, to know the epoch, one must understand that it was a time in which the latest news about the visionary activity of a local holy person was far more important than news about recent economic or political activity (qtd. in Maza 1).

The Christian precept of *imitatio Christi*, the idea that a holy life imitated the life of Jesus Christ and his saints, set this life-modeling process into motion. It served as a significant catalyst for the production of texts about the lives of the saints: by reading or listening to hagiographies, people could learn about holy behavior and then emulate it. By the seventeenth century, this relation between reading and imitation had created a strong connection between spirituality and literature. In cases of religious women writers, for example, we often see a clear spiritual-textual cycle emerge during the course of their lives. As girls they read or listened to the lives of the saints and played at being a saint. As young women they dedicated their lives to God and looked more closely to the lives of canonized nuns and mystic women for models to follow. Many of these women were required to write journals about their own lives for their confessors or spiritual directors, and they followed canonized models when writing. On a religious woman's death, her writings—if they demonstrated evidence of God's handiwork—could be used in a hagiographic biography or canonization process that would help prove her sanctity to religious officials in Rome. If successful, these texts could be published and then integrated into the textual corpus of holy lives, influencing a new generation of readers. In Spanish America, this cycle began soon after the conquest and continued throughout most of the eighteenth century. It began to decline when colonial Creole society became more secularized and the ideas of the Enlightenment became more influential. Before setting out this modeling pattern for students, I first engage them in a discussion about the models and stories that influenced their own childhood and young adult lives. This often ignites their imaginations and opens their minds to alternative life stories and their meanings.

To initiate students into this complex textual and spiritual world, I begin with America's first saint, Rose of Lima, and the dynamic process by which she was canonized. First we read selections from the popular seventeenth-century hagiography of Rose (1664), written by the English Dominican friar Leonard Hansen. Written for the explicit purpose of promoting Rose to sainthood in the Catholic Church, this document details her extreme penitential practices and good works. Hansen systematically describes Rose's birth, upbringing, vocation for the religious life, spiritual practices, death, and virtues. As students read about a woman who hung herself by her hair in order to sleep only two hours a night and who ate nothing for weeks but the holy communion wafer distributed at daily mass, we discuss ideas about models of female piety.

Growing up well before Teresa of Ávila's canonization, Rose modeled her life on the medieval Italian saint Catherine of Siena (1347–80). For centuries Catherine's example as a holy woman living outside the cloister and following a path of extreme penitential practices and visionary activity had established the ideal behavior for religious women. In her youth, Rose read the biography of Catherine and, like her model, chose the life of a third-order lay religious woman (that is, a woman who became associated with a religious order and its practices but did not enter the convent) and fasted to the point of death. Also like Catherine, Rose had visions and worked to help found a convent.

By the time Rose died in 1617, however, a new form of feminine religious behavior, as established by the Council of Trent in 1563, had taken hold. Religious women, especially mystics and visionaries, were judged safest—and most useful to the church—if they were enclosed in the convent. Lay spiritual activity had become suspect as religious sects, such as Illuminism, had begun to develop, and confessors were urged to monitor people closely. The more the church sought control over the interpretation of visionary activity and sanctity, the more closely it regulated the official designation of sainthood and the production of hagiographic texts. During this period, Pope Urban VIII reformed the canonization process, and the church promoted new models of holiness.

While Catherine of Siena would remain popular, Teresa of Ávila soon eclipsed her; by the mid–seventeenth century Teresa emerged as the definitive model for religious women in Spanish America. She was portrayed as working closely with her confessor, observing moderate penitential practices, and reigning in her visionary activity. More important, even though Teresa herself had not taken a vow of perpetual enclosure, under her convent reform she made enclosure mandatory. Two elements are noteworthy about this portrait of the saint: she represented the model of obedience to church superiors and the virtue of enclosure for religious women—two practices that would greatly help the church control religious women and visionary activity. Although Teresa herself had been deeply influenced by the life of Catherine of Siena, the church as a whole attempted to diminish the influence of the Italian saint and promote that of the Spaniard.

A telling episode in Rose's life illuminates this transition in models of holiness for women. When Rose's life and visionary activity came under scrutiny by the Inquisition in 1614—the same year Teresa was beatified—her defenders compared her mystic path not just with Catherine's but also with Teresa's. By the time Rose had become a spiritual phenomenon in Lima, many of Teresa's writings finally had been released from the Inquisition and published. Still a handful of years away from being proclaimed a saint (1622), Teresa had become a significant influence on issues about convent reform and visionary activity. Aligning Rose with Teresa thus helped establish the orthodoxy of Rose's visions. Nonetheless, Teresian spirituality was still not completely free from suspicion. Within the decade, the Inquisition had censured a treatise about Teresa's mysticism written by Rose's close lay spiritual adviser and had charged her circle of women followers with heresy for visionary activity (Iwasaki; Myers, *Neither Saints*, ch. 1).

In the same years that Teresa was canonized and increasingly represented as a Counter-Reformation saint par excellence, church officials in Peru began examining evidence for the canonization of Rose. Because of Rose's popularity at the time of her death, the church immediately began to take testimony, a required step in the canonization process. But it came to a halt within two years. More than a dozen years later, a second round of testimony for a new canonization process was taken, followed twenty years later by Hansen's official biography, written to promote Rose's cause. Notably, both the testimony and the biography revise elements of Rose's life story, bringing it closer to the new model of female sanctity. The half-century process (1617–71), characterized by dramatic stops and starts, is telling of the problem Rose's case caused in the church. The Peruvian did not fit the Counter-Reformation model of an enclosed visionary woman who observed moderate penances and remained safely under the watchful eye of her confessor. To the contrary, on several occasions Rose refused to enter the convent, and she died in her early thirties, probably as a result of her extreme fasts. Rose's canonization process showcases how the first half of the seventeenth century was a transitional period for models of feminine sanctity—and a period in which Teresa became the definitive blueprint for visionary women's lives.

To help students appreciate the lengthy bureaucratic process required for promoting an individual to sainthood, we read a selection from the document that records the church's interviews with witnesses to Rose's life. These testimonies created a collectively authored life story and were strictly controlled. The interrogators followed a conventional juridical format of questions and answers and covered specific areas of the subject's life that were considered relevant to establishing her saintly credentials, which included evidence of miracles and heroic virtue (faith, hope, and charity as well as prudence, temperance, justice, and fortitude).

In contrast to both the canonization process and Hansen's hagiography, a text by Rose herself, a two-part iconolexic (with both written text and visual imagery) collage, "The Mercies" ("Las mercedes") and "The Mystical Stairway" ("La escala mística"), illuminates her literacy and artistic abilities and her awareness of the conventions for representing a mystic's spiritual path.[1] The collage combines a series of images and text in order to represent the steps in Rose's mystical path to the divine. There are clear echoes of Teresa's work on mysticism and uses of the rhetorical devices of feminine humility and obedience so prevalent in the Spanish saint's *Life*. Like Teresa, Rose had been asked by her confessor to write about her mystical relationship with God. Rose mentions recording an account of her life, but it is now lost, and we have only her collage. While the collage never circulated to a broad public during colonial times, it was displayed at the convent she helped found and may have been examined in her canonization process. There is only one adequate, full-color reproduction of the collage, but it can be copied and displayed in class so that students can analyze the image and text (Mujica Pinilla).

The contrast between Rose's own texts, which focus on divine love (there are several simple songs and prayers attributed to her as well), and those by her biographer and witnesses, which tend to focus on her bodily mortifications, serves as a good point of departure for moving students into a discussion—and even debate—about the general roles of men and women in the church. For example, did women tend to be drawn to the corporeal aspect of Catholicism more than men? Did male witnesses (in Rose and Teresa's time and in later generations) fixate on female bodily expressions of spirituality? How did such a bias (if it existed) reflect the larger political and cultural context?

With Rose's canonization in 1671, we see that her life and the writings produced about it followed a similar path to Teresa's, with one exception. By the time Rose was canonized, for the most part the church had stopped publishing religious women's autobiographical writings.

A second set of texts, those by the Mexican mystic María de San José, who wrote nearly a century after Rose, reveals how by the mid–seventeenth century a feminine model of sanctity had crystallized in Spanish America. Although Rose had been canonized by the time María was an adolescent, María does not mention Rose anywhere in her twelve-volume collection of spiritual writings, which were mostly written at the turn of the eighteenth century and only recently published (Myers, *Word*; Myers and Powell, *Wild Country*). Nonetheless, María's extreme penitential practices as a young woman living on a rural hacienda closely reflect Rose's practices as described by Hansen. As noted earlier, Rose had been the exception to the Counter-Reformation's prescriptions for women in the church—she neither entered the convent nor observed moderate penitential practices. Thus, years later, as a nun writing about her life, María chooses to portray her life as mirroring Teresa's. Following Teresa's advice, María eagerly sought perpetual enclosure in the convent and, when she was thirty-two years old, took final religious vows in a reformed convent, where she dedicated herself to the ideals of heroic virtue. Her spiritual activity also closely followed Teresa's mystical way of purgation, illumination, and union with the divine.

Using selections from the anthology of María's twelve-volume autobiographical manuscript, I give students passages that illustrate the Mexican's use of Teresian phrases, rhetorical conventions, and imagery. Clearly following Teresa's "rhetoric of femininity," for example (Weber, *Teresa of Ávila*), María positions herself as an *escritora por obediencia*, as a humble, obedient, and ignorant religious woman writing at the behest of her confessor. To this basic structure, she adds the Spanish saint's expressions about spiritual precepts, such as "suffering or death" (*padescer o morir*), which appears dozens of times in the Mexican's journals. In addition, María often borrows the saint's mystical imagery of being filled with sweet light and experiencing a phenomenon known as enlargement (*ensanchimiento*) of the heart, among others, when describing her own mysticism. The extent of Teresa's influence is most clear when María interpolates whole passages nearly verbatim from the saint's *Life*, using the words to describe her experiences but without citing her source. The mirroring process becomes explicit when María reports that God appeared to her saying: "Your path is very similar to Saint Teresa's" 'Tu camino es mui parecido al de Santa Teresa' (1: fol. 24r). As this brief outline demonstrates, for a mystic nun who admitted "How I longed to be a saint!" '¡Como quiera ser santa' (3: fol. 40v), Teresa's example was compelling and essential. Indeed, it can be useful to have students read passages of Teresa's *Life* alongside María's text.

Notably, on María's death, one of her confessors, Sebastian Santander y Torres, wrote a lengthy hagiographic biography about the nun's life. He quotes her journals, especially the selections about mystical and penitential experiences, and ultimately compares her life with Teresa's, with the hope that the Mexican nun would be considered for canonization.

A third and final set of texts by María's contemporary, the well-known Mexican poet Sor Juana Inés de la Cruz, illustrates the extent to which a religious woman, especially a nun, had to contend with the Teresian model when writing about her life story—even when she desperately sought a different type of religious life. After decades of writing and publishing love poetry, religious verse, and dramatic secular and sacred plays, Sor Juana was called to task by the same bishop who had encouraged María de San José's mystical path, Manuel Fernández de Santa Cruz. In her famous autobiographical letter to him, the *Reply to Sor Filotea de la Cruz* (1691), Sor Juana responded to his public admonishment of a theological letter she had written and of her life as an author. Sor Juana's incursion into the clerical domain of commenting on theological issues (in this case, a scholastic debate about Christ's greatest gifts to mankind) had provoked a crisis that called into question the appropriateness of her role as an author.[2]

The best way to introduce Sor Juana's powerful, erudite response to the bishop in defense of her life is to have students first read several of the nun's secular and sacred verses—the more varied the selection, the better. I usually choose at least a few of her love sonnets and a few of her religious verses, such as the "Villancicos a Santa Catarina." By this point in the course, students have a working knowledge of the Catholic Church's expectations for nuns and their writings, so reading Sor Juana's poetry helps set the stage for students to see Sor Juana's obvious deviance from the model nun and the gap she had to close in her self-defense to the bishop.

In a tour de force, Sor Juana's *Reply* follows the bishop's recommendation to be more like Saint Teresa. She employs Teresian conventions for confessional life writings, but only in order to propose a daring new interpretation of the role of a nun. In her now famous feminist document, Sor Juana invokes Teresa's name as an example of a woman author in the church and models her highly rhetorical autobiographical story about her call to the life of letters on Teresa's *Life*. Sor Juana begins her life story at essentially the same point as Teresa did—at childhood vocation and the moment of the divine call (*vos me coegistis*)—and follows much the same process, the *imitatio Christi*. But she deliberately chooses a nonconventional way to justify her path: she shuns the culturally acceptable (though still precarious) practice of following the mystic's path. Instead, Sor Juana suggests that a woman who has been given a good intellect should use it to fashion her self-image, just as the woman who has been given visionary gifts should use them to define herself. After all, she argues, all things issue from God. By using the conventions of the *vida* for an alternative life story, Sor Juana validates the use of the genre for religious women's self-representation but changes the typical portrait of a nun. Instead of being called to the life of a mystic, Sor Juana is called to the life of letters in the church.

To complete this unit on Teresa's extensive influence in New World religious women's lives and writings, I take students through the denouement of these women's lives. While Rose was promoted to the high altars of the Catholic Church, María de San José's case never moved beyond the first stages of the canonization process, and Sor Juana was asked by church officials to renounce her life of letters. She sold her library and stopped public writing. Nonetheless, Sor Juana continued to be celebrated by some members of New Spanish and Spanish society. Soon after her death, a collection of her works was published (1700), and it even included her audacious *Reply*. The spiritual writings by the model nun María were filtered through her male biographer's words, but the poetry and prose by the supposedly deviant nun Sor Juana were published. María's life story was published in the center of Creole religious printing, Puebla, and even went into a second edition; Sor Juana's works, however, were published in Spain. During this same century, dozens more works were published about Rose of Lima. Indeed, a look at the number of publications dedicated to any individual in the Spanish viceroyalties reveals that Rose was Spanish America's most popular subject.

Even today these women continue to be significant to local, national, and pan–Latin American culture and identities. María de San José's two convents (in Puebla and Oaxaca) have been converted into religious museums, which display her portraits. Sor Juana's own convent now houses a university and her portrait is displayed on the 200-peso bill. Every August throughout many Andean towns, large processions and festivals take place in Rose's honor. Glimpsing the legacy and continued importance of these colonial women helps students appreciate the essential role that religious women played in the building of colonial Spanish American society. It also can serve as a springboard for further discussions about identity formation through the process of life writing and the legacy these lives and texts leave in a culture.

NOTES

[1] Selections from these collages are reproduced in Mujica Pinilla.

[2] For an edition of this text, see *The Answer / La respuesta.*

APPENDIX

The following list suggests primary and secondary readings for a course unit on Teresa of Ávila's influence in colonial Spanish America:

TERESA'S *LIFE*

Background and literary structure (Slade, *St. Teresa of Ávila;* Weber, *Teresa of Ávila*)
Background on the canonization process (Ahlgren, *Teresa of Ávila;* Bilinkoff, *Ávila*)

A New World context for religious women's life stories

The model nun (Lavrin, "In Search")
Life writings (Arenal and Schlau, *Untold Sisters*; McKnight; Myers, *Neither Saints*)

Church models in transition: Rose of Lima

Canonized texts (Hansen)
Canonization and testimony (Martínez Hampe [Spanish]; Mills and Taylor [English])
Rose's collages (Mujica Pinilla)

The perfect imitator: María de San José

Selections from her confessional journals (Myers, *Word from New Spain* [Spanish]; Myers and Powell, *Wild Country* [English])

The innovator: Sor Juana Inés de la Cruz

Selected secular and sacred poetry (*Obras* [Spanish]; *Answer* [English])
The Reply to Sor Filotea de la Cruz (*Answer / La respuesta*)

Conclusions

The importance of female religious to the building of colonial Creole society (Morgan; Rubial)
Rewriting lives (Myers, *Neither Saints*)

The Creation of Feminist Consciousness: Teaching Teresa of Ávila in a Women Writers Course

Alison Weber

In an undergraduate course I took in the late 1960s, I remember one professor who described Teresa of Ávila (1515–82) as a woman who was born in the wrong place at the wrong time. It was such a shame, he said, that she never had the opportunity to ride a bicycle across the Smith College campus. Although I have always been bothered by the ahistoricism and condescension implicit in this remark, I have to confess that today it does not seem entirely wrongheaded. Teresa, like the founders of Smith, believed that women (especially spiritually and intellectually gifted women) could make greater contributions to society than had been allowed to them. My aim in teaching Teresa at the heart of a course on Spanish women writers is to erase and simultaneously recall that bicycle. That is, I want students to read the Carmelite nun in the context of her historical moment and religious heritage and yet also to see the connections between that heritage and the movements that made modern feminism possible. A complementary goal is to counteract the notion of Teresa's anomalousness. I want students to realize that Teresa had literary and spiritual mothers, daughters, fathers, and sons.

Given the linguistic difficulty of some of the texts, this course works best as an advanced seminar for majors. In our first meeting, I ask students to write out their definitions of feminism and hand them in on a folded piece of paper. I tell them that I will return them, unread, at the end of the semester. Next, I ask why our department offers special courses on women writers. What is gained and what is lost when we read women in isolation from their male counterparts? Then I lay out other questions that will arise during the semester: How did women claim the authority to write or teach during periods when they were discouraged from participating in these activities? How did Christianity contribute to and constrain opportunities for women's self-actualization? What evidence is there for a separate feminine literary tradition? In what ways did women imitate, modify, or reject the models provided by male writers? For the remainder of this first class meeting, we discuss a number of Spanish proverbs about women, such as "La mujer casada, pierna quebrada y en casa" ("The married women is best kept at home with a broken leg"), "Mujer discreta, ni en ventanas ni en puertas" ("The discreet woman should not be seen at the window or in the doorway"), and "Mujer con letras, dos veces necia" ("The educated woman is doubly foolish"). I then show slides of paintings from early modern Spain that depict women dancing, looking out of windows, working, and reading. I have found that this is an effective way of presenting the difference between prescriptive discourses and social practice.

For their first assignment, students read selections from the book that inspired the subtitle for the course: Gerda Lerner's *The Creation of Feminist*

Consciousness: From the Middle Ages to Eighteen-Seventy. I ask them to think in particular about Lerner's definition of feminist consciousness:

> *Feminist consciousness* consists (1) of the awareness that women belong to a subordinate group and that, as members of such a group, they have suffered wrongs; (2) the recognition that their condition of subordination is not natural, but societally determined; (3) the development of a sense of sisterhood; (4) the autonomous definition by women of their goals and strategies for changing their condition; and (5) the development of an alternate vision of the future.   (274)

In class we compare and contrast Lerner's notion of feminist consciousness with two other views: first, that feminism is properly defined as a movement of advocacy for equal political rights for women that arose in the nineteenth century; second, that feminism is the effort to renegotiate the terms of patriarchy, an effort that has taken various forms during different historical contexts.[1] I encourage students to think of definitions not as hard-and-fast rules but as provisional scaffolding for studying complex literary and historical issues.

It is important here to discuss the concept of teleological temptation, which I introduce with this observation by Janet Todd: "We sometimes avoid listening to a past that might be annoying through its resolute refusal to anticipate us" (46). If we only look for a progressive development in a feminist consciousness, will we be tempted to ignore writers who do not fit into our schema? Does the development of a feminist consciousness always proceed in a straightforward march toward progress without making detours? This class encourages students to define terms carefully and critically and to be aware of distortions resulting from teleological expectations.

After these introductory classes, the first unit is devoted to women writers from the late Middle Ages. I begin with selections from Leonor López de Córdoba (c. 1362–1414 or later), whose *Autobiografía (Autobiography)* is a vivid account of a proud noblewoman caught up in political violence and intrigue. To help focus discussion, I give students a number of questions to consider beforehand: Why did López de Córdoba write (or rather dictate) this story of her life? In what ways does it differ from a modern autobiography? How does she describe God's workings? López protests that she personally has suffered unjustly, but does she show any awareness of Lerner's first stage of feminist consciousness, of belonging to a subordinate group of women? This work allows me to introduce the issue of class, since, as becomes clear in discussion, López felt solidarity with her extended aristocratic family rather than with women as a subordinate group. I point out that none of the writers in the course—not even the representative of the Spanish Enlightenment—will express a sense of sisterhood with women of the lower classes. Leonor's confident expression of autobiographical importance also serves as a point of comparison with other examples of life writing encountered later in the semester, which abound in protestations of humility.

We next read excerpts from *Admiración operum Dey* (*Wonder at the Works of God*), a treatise written by the conversa nun Teresa de Cartagena (mid-1400s) in response to accusations that she had plagiarized a previous treatise that, her critics claimed, exceeded the intellectual capacity of a woman.[2] This is a wonderful text for introducing students to the notion of "las tretas del débil" ("tricks of the weak"), a term coined by Josefina Ludmer to describe rhetorical strategies such as flattery and self-deprecation used by women to turn weakness to their advantage (see also Arenal and Schlau, "Stratagems"). Teresa de Cartagena offers a striking example of how women can both appeal to and subvert a patriarchal ideology of gender. On the one hand, she acknowledges gender difference (men are strong and brave; women are weak and pusillanimous), but on the other hand, she argues that gender norms are constructed through customs so long-standing that they seem natural. At the conclusion of this unit, I assign Caroline Walker Bynum's essay "The Female Body and Religious Practice in the Later Middle Ages" along with short selections from *The Book of Prayer* by María de Santo Domingo (c. 1485–1524). My aim here is to introduce students to the role of suffering (especially voluntary suffering) in the Christian ascetic-mystical tradition. The question that arises, not surprisingly, is, How can self-inflicted pain have any part in the creation of feminist consciousness? I have found students are eager to debate Bynum's provocative contention that "[c]ontrol, discipline, even torture of the flesh is, in medieval devotion, not so much the rejection of physicality as the elevation of it—a horrible yet delicious elevation—into a means of access to the divine" (182).[3] We also discuss Jo Ann McNamara's thesis that penitential asceticism in the Middle Ages represented a response to women's need to give during periods when active works of charity were limited. This is a challenging pedagogical moment. My aim is to de-pathologize female religious devotion of the past without denying the reality of the suffering that such practices entailed.

The second unit is devoted to the Carmelite school of women writers.[4] Before reading texts in this unit, it is fundamental for students to understand the impact of the Counter-Reformation on women in general and female religious in particular; there are several readings suitable for this purpose, including Gillian T. W. Ahlgren, *Teresa of Ávila* (ch. 1), Rawlings (*Church*, chs. 2–3), and Allyson M. Poska and Elizabeth A. Lehfeldt.[5] I alert students to the fact that the writers studied in this unit will have little to say about the condition of secular women, although they will express frustration over restrictions on women's spiritual autonomy and opportunities to serve the church. I suggest that we modify Lerner's schema and think about these works in terms of ecclesial feminism, that is, the consciousness of women's unjust subordination within the church and the articulation of strategies for change within the church.[6]

In my experience, students find reading Teresa in Spanish—especially her autobiography—extremely difficult. Therefore, I limit the selections from the *Libro de la vida* (*The Book of Her Life*) to the prologue and chapters 1, 2, 5, 29, and 32. Providing students with prereading questions is crucial. Sample questions include, For whom does Teresa write her *Vida* and why? Does she confess her sins, defend herself, or both? What is the source of her frustration with her confessors and how does she resolve it? How does Teresa try to reconcile her desire to be humble and obedient with her desire to be a spiritual teacher and help the church? My goal for the three or four class hours devoted to the *Vida* is to guide students through a close reading of the text so that they can understand how Teresa transformed a confession elicited by skeptical confessors into a pedagogical defense of her personal spiritual experiences and of her conviction that nuns were capable of greater service to the church. To help students appreciate how Teresa subversively embeds oppositional discourses within what might be called her discourse of submission, I hand out colored markers and ask students to highlight in different colors passages in which Teresa is performing different speech acts: confessing sins, defending herself, teaching, and criticizing. This works especially well with chapter 5, Teresa's description of her flirtatious relationship with the priest of Beceda.[7]

Readings from *Libro de las fundaciones* (*The Book of Her Foundations*) introduce the question of whether Teresa exemplifies Lerner's last three stages of feminist consciousness. Prereading questions for chapters 1 and 4–8 include, What are some of the tensions inherent in monastic life? What strategies does Teresa use to promote a sense of solidarity among her followers? Why does she insist so much on the virtue of obedience? Why is she skeptical of some nuns' ecstasies and visions? Has she become a bossy micromanager, or is she simply trying to defend her goals and strategies for change? Next, we turn to chapters 10 and 12, which narrate the stories of Casilda de Padilla, a young girl who opposes the plans of her aristocratic family to marry her off to her uncle, and Beatriz de la Encarnación, a novice who patiently endures a painful illness. Casilda's story elicits a discussion of whether Teresa's "alternate vision for the future" included aristocratic laywomen; Beatriz's narrative prompts us to reconsider the role of suffering in female spirituality. Finally, we discuss chapter 28, in which Teresa confesses her ambivalent admiration for Catalina de Cardona, a famous hermitess who indulged in extreme penitential practices. Why is Teresa attracted to Catalina's model of holiness? Does she accept or reject it?

As Electa Arenal and Stacey Schlau demonstrate in their landmark anthology *Untold Sisters*, Teresa was both a spiritual and literary mother for Discalced Carmelites and nuns from other religious orders. We turn now to Teresa's literary daughters, beginning with selections from *Libro de recreaciones* (*For the Hour of Recreation* [c. 1585]), written by one of Teresa's closest collaborators, María de San José Salazar (1548–1603).[8] I ask students to compare how Teresa and Gracia (María's fictional alter ego) respond to their confessors' command to produce a spiritual autobiography. Gracia's decision to ignore the command to write about herself and instead write (in collaboration with her sisters) a biography of "the mother foundress" illustrates how Teresa's example had given María the authority to overcome an "anxiety of authorship."[9] Students can also see that María was heir to Teresa's wit and irony. María's multivoiced dialogue invites a

discussion of the Carmelites' practice of a feminist pedagogy. There is no dominant, didactic voice; rather, the nuns narrate the history of their order and correct and tease one another, so that teaching becomes a collective enterprise.

The class now compares María de San José Salazar's dialogue with selections
from the autobiography of Ana de San Bartolomé (1549–1626), Teresa's nurse
and one of the leaders of the Discalced Carmelite reform in France. Students
immediately notice differences in style: if María de San José (who was raised in
a noble palace) is elegant and urbane, Ana (who spent her childhood herding
sheep) is ingenuous and plain spoken. I ask if there are differences in attitudes
toward women's authority. My aim is for students to appreciate that, although
both women at various times challenged their male superiors, María based her
authority on her belief that Christianity was founded on a discipleship of equals,
whereas Ana was empowered by her sense that she was a conduit for Teresa's
supernatural authority. If Ana's matriarchal feminism seems less progressive
than María's articulate defense of a feminine apostolate, the contrast between
their contemporaneous feminisms allows me to reiterate the dangers of teleological assumptions.[10]

The poetry of another Discalced Carmelite nun, Cecilia del Nacimiento
(1568–1640), allows me to raise another crucial issue in women's literary history:
How did women respond to their male forebears? I ask students to read and
compare Cecilia's "Canciones de la unión y transformación del alma en Dios"
("Songs on the Union and Transformation of the Soul in God") with "Noche
oscura" ("Dark Night") by John of the Cross. Students quickly recognize that
Cecilia's poem is a close imitation of John's. Not only are there numerous verbal
echoes, the narrative structure of the poem—the poetic persona's nocturnal
search for her lover, their secluded encounter, and the serene aftermath of their
union—is obviously modeled on *Noche oscura*. Cecilia also clearly responded
to the musicality of John's poetry, in particular his proclivity for alliteration and
interlaced assonant rhymes. But there is one important difference: the allegorical tenor of human love is explicit in the nun's poem, whereas in the friar's
poem it is confined to the rubric (which declares the verses to be "Canciones
de el alma que se goza de aver llegado al alto estado de la [perfeccion] que es
la unión con Dios, por el camino de la negación espiritual" 'Songs in which the
soul enjoys having arrived at the highest stage of perfection which is union with
God, by way of the road of spiritual negation' (John, *Poesía* [ed. Yndurain]; my
trans.). Students generally express a preference for "Noche oscura," finding it
more mysterious and less didactic, although they can also point to enigmatic,
erotic lines in Cecilia's poem. From here we can move to a discussion of why
Cecilia did not (or could not) sever the allegory from her lyrical fiction. What
were the risks and benefits—for men and for women—of using erotic language
to describe religious experience?[11]

In the final unit, we turn our attention to two secular women writers: María
de Zayas y Sotomayor (1590?–1647 or later) and María Josefa Amar y Borbón
(1749–1833).[12] We begin with a discussion of "Al que leyere" ("To the Reader")

from *Novelas amorosas* (*Stories of Love*), Zayas's passionate defense of women's intellectual equality. In the light of their previous readings, students should be able to comment on what Zayas's defense owes to the ecclesial feminists' insistence on an equality of discipleship. Students can also appreciate how Zayas, like her predecessors, deploys the seemingly incompatible arguments of difference and indifference, that is, the notion that women's talents are complementary to men's versus the position that such differences are irrelevant.

Although a number of Zayas's novellas would be suitable for the course, I have found that studying her comic play, *La traición en la amistad* (*Friendship Betrayed*), provides a welcome change of pace as the semester winds down. *La traición* tells the story of Fenisa, a coquette who betrays her female friends by trying to seduce their lovers. As Valerie Hegstrom observes, "Zayas's play is simultaneously an inversion, a subversion, and a comic copy of the *Burlador* [*de Sevilla*]" (19). Students can therefore be asked to compare and contrast Zayas's parody with the classic story of Don Juan by Tirso de Molina, a play often included in introductory survey courses. There is considerable disagreement over the nature of the feminist discourse in *La traición*; some critics stress Zayas's condemnation of the double standard and celebration of female solidarity, whereas others see Fenisa's exclusion at the end of the play as a sign of Zayas's timid or ambivalent feminism. I have found that students enjoy entering into this critical debate.[13] Finally, they can also see that women write not only within a female tradition but sometimes in ironic counterpoint to a male tradition.

The last text read in the semester is Josefa Amar y Borbón's *Discurso sobre la educación física y moral de las mujeres* (*Discourse on the Physical and Moral Education of Women* [1790]). Ending with this paragon of Enlightenment thought would seem to undermine my determination to avoid the teleological trap. Therefore, I encourage students to identify continuities as well as discontinuities: Amar insists on women's intellectual equality with men and argues for the importance of women's contribution to the public good, yet she adheres to a doctrine of separate spheres, conceding that women's education must be adapted to their primary roles as mothers and household administrators. *Discurso sobre la educación* elicits discussion of other points of comparison and contrast with earlier readings. On the one hand, Amar's esteem for physical health and her endorsement of happiness as an individual and social desideratum contrast with the values of ascetic renunciation and voluntary suffering expressed by some religious writers. On the other hand, students might find parallels with Teresa's concern to promote good health in her convents and her emphasis on the need for spiritual recreation and gentleness. Amar's idealization of the home as a feminine microsociety invites comparison with the ideal of the convent as *hortus conclusus*. Her sense of women's "domestic mission" corresponds, in some sense, to Teresa's ecclesial mission. Finally, Amar's exclusion of lower-class women from her educational agenda prompts students to consider the historical belatedness of a truly inclusive feminist solidarity. Such comparisons are designed to draw out the limitations of rigid religious-secular or benighted-progressive dichotomies.

At this point in the semester, I also like to suggest that secular feminism did not replace ecclesial feminism. We cannot trace an unambiguous trajectory from the ecclesial feminism of Teresa's era to contemporary secular feminism or even to contemporary Catholic women's movements. Throughout Christian history, some women have expressed intense frustration over the limits on their apostolic role while others have accepted it. Some have acquiesced to clerical authority with equanimity, but for others the words of Galatians 3.28 ("There is no longer Jew or Greek, there is no longer slave or free, there is no longer male and female; for all of you are one in Christ Jesus" [*New Oxford Annotated Bible*]) have resounded as a call to realize that very indifference in political and economic as well as in religious spheres. Several films beautifully illustrate the complex and paradoxical relation between Christian and feminine self-actualization: Josefina Molina's *Teresa de Jesús*; Maria Luisa Bemberg's evocative portrait of Sor Juana Inés de la Cruz, *Yo, la peor de todas* ("I the Worst of All"); and Alain Cavalier's *Thérèse*, a biography of Thérèse of Lisieux, the French Carmelite and saint who died in 1897 at the age of twenty-four. *Thérèse* in particular challenges a teleological narrative. More than three hundred years after Teresa of Ávila declared women's right to be of service to the church, and more than one hundred years after Amar declared women's right to be of service to the state, this French Carmelite embraced a soteriology of suffering.

I generally ask students to see one of these films outside class and write a short reaction paper on it. Finally, in what is usually one of the liveliest sessions of the semester, students discuss these reaction papers in the context of the larger question of whether Christian feminism is compatible with the goals of contemporary secular feminism. Depending on the class composition, students of other religious traditions can be invited to describe the relation between feminism and their faith.

At the end of the semester, I ask the class to review the strategies that the women writers studied have used to defend their access to intellectual and religious discourse. Students sometimes come up with their own amusing characterizations for different types of argument, such as "God helped me do it"; "when men fail, call in the women"; "Jesus liked women better"; "men are from Mars, women from Venus—but God needs both"; and "a happy woman is a happy citizen." This is an appropriate time to remind students that we have not seen a truly representative sample of women's experience in late medieval and early modern Spain: we have not heard the voices of Moriscas (the descendants of the Moorish inhabitants of Spain), women of the Sephardic diaspora, those who wrote in Catalan or Gallego, or (with the exception of Ana de San Bartolomé) women from the lower social orders.

Since a goal of the seminar is to give students an intensive writing experience in Spanish, I assign three papers of 700–1000 words, one of which is to be revised. Suggested topics include, (1) Was the religious realm a coercive or liberating space for women? How were women able to restructure and give new meanings to religious doctrine, symbols, and practices? (2) Compare and contrast expressions of female solidarity in works by secular and monastic women. (3) What rhetorical strategies have women writers developed to persuade their readers of their spiritual and intellectual legitimacy? (4) In what ways was Teresa a literary and spiritual model for her followers? In what ways did they modify this legacy?

Individual oral reports give students important practice in public speaking, but I have often been disappointed by the poor delivery of the speakers and the passivity of the student audience. Rather than do away with the exercise altogether, I now divide the class into groups of four and ask each student to practice delivering a condensed version of his or her revised paper. During the practice session in small groups, students rate one another on various aspects of oral presentation: clear enunciation (and correct Spanish pronunciation and grammar), eye contact, good posture, enthusiasm, and adherence to the time limit. Later we hold a *congresito*, or "miniconference," in which students deliver ten-minute papers; members of the audience are expected to ask at least one question or make one comment. Guests are welcome. The last time I taught the course, we held the conference during our regularly scheduled three-hour exam period. Sixteen students divided into four panels gave talks or *PowerPoint* presentations. Remarkably, we finished within our time limit, no one got restless, and there was still time for discussion after each panel. This format can transform a dreary series of oral reports into a lively, interactive event.

In our last class meeting, I hand back the definitions of feminism written at the beginning of the semester and invite students to make modifications on their own and on Lerner's definition. My hope is that they will appreciate that within the overarching movement from awareness of oppression to the development of an alternative vision for the future, women have drawn on a wide variety of strategies, gender norms, and notions of justice in order to renegotiate the terms of patriarchy. The contributions of Christian feminists like Teresa of Ávila are an important part of this history.

NOTES

[1] Depending on the scope and level of the class, instructors may wish to assign the essays by Nash and Gordon on the issue of the historical parameters of feminism.

[2] For López de Córdoba and Teresa de Cartagena, I teach selections from Kaminsky's bilingual anthology *Water Lilies*. Since these are the most difficult texts linguistically, allowing students to consult English translations avoids frustration at the beginning of the semester and gives me time to explain some of the features of premodern Spanish. For background reading on Teresa de Cartagena, I recommend the introduction and bibliography to Seidenspinner-Nuñez's edition and Surtz's "The New Judith: Teresa de Cartagena." See also Disse's Web site *Other Women's Voices* for information on the following writers discussed in this essay: Leonor López de Córdoba, Teresa de Cartagena,

Teresa de Jesús, María de San José, and María de Zayas. Each entry provides translated passages, information on print sources, selected secondary sources, and Internet sites, when those are available.

[3] There is an extensive and growing bibliography on the body and feminine spirituality. In preparing for this class, I have found the work by both Flynn and Reineke especially helpful.

[4] I teach Teresa's *Vida* in this unit and download selections from Álvarez's *Libro de la Vida*, which is available on the Web site maintained by the Congregation for the Clergy of the Holy See; I then add copious contextual notes and lexical glosses. For the other Carmelite writers, I have used photocopies from Arenal and Schlau's *Untold Sisters* or prepared my own annotated editions. Mujica's new anthology, *Women Writers of Early Modern Spain*, provides a welcome alternative to compiling a course packet.

[5] Poska and Lehfeldt discuss the religious experiences of laywomen as well as nuns and also address the relation between nonelites and the church.

[6] The work of Bilinkoff (*The Ávila of Saint Teresa* and "Woman with a Mission") has been fundamental in my thinking on this issue. I define ecclesial feminism in more detail in my introduction to María de San José Salazar's *For the Hour of Recreation* (23–26). See also the essay by Mujica in this volume.

[7] I am grateful to Gillian T. W. Ahlgren for this suggestion. In her essay in this volume, she discusses how she uses this technique to help students identify Teresa's theological statements when they are embedded in personal narrative.

[8] I have prepared annotated texts for my students from chapters 1, 8, and 9 based on the edition by Simeón de la Sagrada Familia. Selections are also included in Arenal and Schlau (*Untold Sisters*) and in Mujica, *Women Writers of Early Modern Spain*. Instructors may wish to consult the introduction and bibliography in my edition of *Book for the Hour of Recreation*, translated by Powell.

[9] I summarize Gilbert and Gubar's enormously influential theories on the differences between men's and women's appropriation of literary authority first articulated in *Madwoman in the Attic*. Depending on the class level, their essay "Infection in the Sentence" can also be assigned.

[10] I discuss matriarchal feminism more fully in "Partial Feminism." Instructors may wish to consult Donahue's critical study and translation of Ana's writings.

[11] Selections of Cecilia's poems and those of her sister María de San Alberto can be found in Arenal and Schlau, *Untold Sisters* ("Two Sisters"). I explore these issues in more depth in "Could Women Write Mystical Poetry?"

[12] For Zayas's play, I have taught the electronic version, *La traición*, edited by Stroud. It is also available in the bilingual edition edited by Hegstrom and translated by Larson. Mujica includes a novella by Zayas, "La inocencia castigada" ("Innocence Punished") in *Women Writers of Early Modern Spain*. This story of a woman's rape and her subsequent punishment at the hands of her husband and sister-in-law would be an excellent choice for discussing the issue of female solidarity and for comparing the role of suffering in religious and secular texts. For Amar y Borbón's *Discurso sobre la educación*, I have taught the edition by María Victoria López-Cordón. Amar y Borbón's earlier *Discurso en defensa del talento de las mugeres* (*Discourse in Defense of the Talent of Women*) is available on the Web. Lewis; Sullivan provide useful context.

[13] See Hegstrom; Vollendorf ("'No Doubt'") for an assessment of these critical positions. Students also enjoy acting out a mock trial, in which Fenisa protests her exclusion at the end of the play and argues for her reinstatement in the society of female friends.

Strictly Academic?
Teaching Religious Texts in a Secular Setting

Ralph Keen

Teaching any form of mysticism in the contemporary theater of religious studies is a demanding test in several respects. Apart from the age-old questions surrounding the definition of such terms as *mysticism* and *spirituality* and the difficulties attending any attempt to appreciate expressions of subjective experience, methodological shifts in the discipline of religious studies in recent years have required an unusual degree of critical self-scrutiny. Even the nonspecialist teaching at an introductory level is confronted willy-nilly with issues at the forefront of discourse about the nature of the discipline and the definition of the subject matter, since there are a number of distinct schools or approaches within the discipline.[1] An instructor committed more to the material than to methodology needs to be conscious of the variety of the field but conscientious about keeping students' attention on its issues.

Simply maintaining a focus on the material does not ensure against other obstacles interfering with the pedagogical process. In the formally secular setting of a state university, theological approaches to historical material, despite their potential heuristic value, have been excluded as being confessional and thus contrary to legal prohibitions against promoting religious teachings in a tax-supported institution. Since there seems to be neither consensus as to where the boundary of confessional discourse lies nor continuity over time with respect to the permissibility of the subjective, a sense of flux gradually becomes familiar but never comfortable.

There may, however, be reference points available to anchor an instructor's pedagogy amidst some of the seismic shifts in the contemporary academy. One is the intellectual autonomy inherent in academic freedom. The other is an openness to subjectivity that, when used with appropriate restraint, complements the quest for rigorous objectivity in a fashion that engages religious-studies research (and not merely methodology) in significant ways.[2]

Scholars of religion were among the first to recognize the importance of hermeneutics in interpreting texts regarded as sacred. In its contemporary form, this is the subdiscipline dedicated to weighing the circumstances under which a religious text was composed and the assumptions, whether conscious or unconscious, that are brought to bear by later interpreters. Sensitivity to these factors, especially the awareness that they cannot be grasped without the risk of reduction, has resulted in a recognition of a hermeneutical circle, in which the modern interpreter's cultural conditions shape his or her inquiry to such an extent that clarity and accuracy in deciphering a historical text are inevitably regarded as provisional at best. Hence a considerable degree of tentativeness has been written into the discipline; for any text, achieving an understanding that can be shared by a community—in this case, participants in an academic course—is in a small way a measure of success.

Courses in mysticism at the University of Iowa have become a productive laboratory for pedagogical strategies in religious studies. These courses have extended the canon to which students are introduced, given affective piety and unitive mysticism their own place in the theater of religious experience, and stimulated a degree of historical and critical evaluation beneficial in other liberal arts courses and presumably beyond.

The Setting

The Department of Religious Studies at Iowa has long been conscious of occupying a niche in the academic study of religion in America. One of the first such departments in a state university, in the 1960s the religious-studies department at Iowa, along with those at a number of peer institutions, began to embrace comparative study and critical objectivity. In the interest of moving beyond confessional approaches in teaching and research, the Iowa faculty emphasized historical work in traditions in which cultural distance might ensure dispassionate observation and analytic engagement with Western texts in which philosophical rigor is intended to eclipse the investigator's faith perspective. Not surprisingly, this resulted in dissertations from the 1960s onward reading like projects that might fit comfortably in other disciplines, history and philosophy in particular.

With a sense that methodology ought never to become dogmatic, at least regarding the possibility (or even desirability) of total objectivity in appreciating ultimate questions, new material and different approaches began to appear in the curriculum in the 1990s. Spirituality, variously defined, had gained ground in the academy as a complement or an alternative to traditional theology (Schneiders). Freedom from teaching religion normatively, instead of being restrictive, allowed for greater inclusiveness, and as a result our curriculum could extend critical scrutiny to phenomena and traditions that fall outside conventional boundaries. Heretical movements, witchcraft, and other varieties of religion that might elsewhere be dismissed as deviant or unworthy of study became legitimate material for academic inquiry. Examining contrasting viewpoints without the normative filters of anathematizations and condemnations has provided at least the opportunity for a more tolerant perspective on religious diversity.

Strong administrative support for forging connections with other units made it possible to cross-list courses with other departments, such as history and women's studies, and to create interdisciplinary certificate programs. (The undergraduate program in medieval studies, for example, regularly draws from course offerings in eight departments.) An impetus in the religious-studies department to reflect more diversity in the content of courses gave new attention to women and persons of color: Hadewijch of Brabant and Thérèse de Lisieux joined Augustine and Julian of Norwich as staples of a more inclusive under-graduate program. To prevent the inadvertent marginalization that can result from segregating course content, as well as to allow comparative discussion, women mystics have been taught alongside male theologians.

A Changing Discipline

Religious-studies courses in spirituality and mysticism began to appear at Iowa in the early to mid-1990s. Medieval mystics had been part of the curriculum in English over the years, under the able care of Valerie Lagorio and a cohort of in-vestigators associated with that department and its journal *Mystics Quarterly*.[3] The first offering of the religious-studies course, Spirituality and Mysticism, was too broad in scope to be effective, a survey built on the erroneous assumption that the same category of religion could be approached cross-culturally. There-after it became a more narrowly defined topics course, in which Song of Songs exegesis was the theme one year, medieval women mystics another, and so on. Teresa of Ávila and John of the Cross regularly appeared on the syllabus when the subject was visionary spirituality, monastic orders and their reforms, or the autobiographical dimension of religious writing.

During the same period, courses in Reformation-era religious history began to extend beyond the traditional leaders and events in the growth of magisterial Protestantism. Thus, courses in the Reformers became courses in the Reforma-tion and Counter-Reformation, with *Counter-Reformation* serving as a familiar rubric for the more inclusive category of Catholic reform. Approaching early modern Catholicism as a religious and cultural system driven by an internal momentum toward reform of piety allows the academic community to place spirituality in the foreground, with little more than a passing glance toward the Catholic polemicists and systematic theologians. Given the general preference for spirituality over old-line theology, this arrangement of the material helped draw a considerable audience to this segment of the historical tradition.

While popular appeal may be a necessary factor in planning course offerings, some of these changes were accommodations to my own interests. My training was in the academic study of theology and hermeneutics, and I was eager to test academic approaches to idiosyncratic or unconventional materials. Seek-ing continuity and extension rather than pursuing innovation for its own sake, I have tried to apply a common conceptual vocabulary and a uniform set of interpretive principles throughout my teaching portfolio, each one of which I try to keep open to critical scrutiny. The relation of experience and emotion to thought; the adequacy of texts as expressions of piety, relative to other cultural artifacts; the possibility or impossibility of adequately communicating an expe-rience of ultimate reality—these are among the topics engaged in courses on material ranging from Augustine's *Confessions* to A. J. Heschel's *Sabbath*. Texts from the Western mystical traditions are rich sources of material with which to consider these issues.

The canon of texts has shifted and expanded with my research and in response to students' critiques. The *Autobiography* of Ignatius of Loyola has been a perennial favorite, both alone and alongside the *Spiritual Exercises*. The *Dark Night of the Soul* by John of the Cross has also proved most accessible in the large introductory course. When visionary spirituality is the orienting theme, close reading of John's *Ascent of Mount Carmel* and Teresa of Ávila's *Interior Castle* allows provocative discussion of a favorite topic: the use of material space as a metaphor for paths of spiritual perfection. When properly introduced to the problem, students will readily see that buildings, mountains, pilgrimages, and the like serve both the didactic end of guiding the reader with concrete images of progress and the more elusive yet equally necessary purpose of exposing the limited ability of language and linear progression when writers attempt to depict the ineffable.

Despite the general appeal of these authors, not all the available texts have been equally successful. Longer works, no matter how important, have tested students' patience, so that, for example, the *Life* of Teresa of Ávila cannot be taught in its entirety, and neither can the *Spiritual Canticle* of John of the Cross. An instructor who is averse to compiling course packets and sensitive to undergraduates' budgets learns to assign shorter texts and make use of translations archived on various Web sites. An additional advantage of instructional technology is access to supplementary interpretive essays, background information, and valuable maps and images. Compact discs of liturgical and secular music of the early modern period add an instructive as well as entertaining dimension to the classroom experience.

Making Connections

Our students are the most valuable assets in our courses, and we try to validate the resources they bring by allowing them to capitalize on their particular abilities. Students well prepared in early modern history, for example, will be encouraged to contribute insights into the political maneuverings of the Inquisition and the dynastic policies of the Castilian-Aragonese monarchy. A background in classics will give substance to comments about antiquity when the Renaissance is the topic of discussion, but the experience from which to draw extends beyond specific historical epochs. Social history may be peripheral to the specialist in religious thought, but it is a prominent interest indeed among undergraduates, who in many cases are highly receptive to one another's contributions. An illuminating observation about Marrano religious identity and cultural assimilation, for example, may come from a student concentrating in modern American-immigration history. The instructor's task at that point is to translate the salient insight into contextually relevant terms and to invite discussion without veering off course.

Linguistic ability is an obvious resource, yet here too some guidance might be necessary. Students familiar with Spanish not only are able to contribute useful nuances of certain words and terms but also will often be familiar with the broader context of Golden Age culture, especially the secular poetry and chivalric romances that served as such a provocative foil in Teresa's religious development. A student with adequate reading knowledge of Spanish might be glad to work with some passages in the original and can often raise points that will stimulate discussion among students with and without a working knowledge of the language. Caution is required, however, if a student's Spanish is limited to modern usage, and delving into historical philology is not guaranteed to enrich students' appreciation. Similarly, an instructor who knows Latin as well as Spanish will be able to complement a student's observations and possibly draw connections to terms in the liturgical and academic language of the early modern period—but here too the risk of pedantry and irrelevance runs high.

More advanced students, especially Spanish majors, may wish to pursue textual projects, and sometimes these can be informative and beneficial. A new translation of a text, or perhaps a commentary or a comparative study of the language of two or more works, requires salutary immersion in the thought and language of an author. The supervisor of such work needs to exercise quality control beyond the ordinary bounds of the religious-studies field, but the extra work may be preferable to discouraging a bright student's interdisciplinary interests. If one is in an institution with a Renaissance or early-modern-studies working group, one might be able to draw on the expertise of specialist colleagues. At Iowa we have had some impressive undergraduate honors projects on early modern Spanish mystics by double majors; as a rule they are written in Spanish, and a faculty member in that department guides composition, while the Spanish-reading faculty member in religious studies oversees the research.

Anyone approaching early mystical texts in a religious-studies setting encounters a distinctive combination of pedagogical obstacles. For one, the authors' use of concepts and terms familiar to a majority of modern Christians invites a sense of comfort with the seemingly familiar that must be qualified by contextualizing every new figure in the canon. Hence the comfort that students have with seemingly accessible materials must be qualified in the interest of historical clarity, and the pedagogical challenge lies in finding the level of contextual detail that can sustain students' engagement with the material. As with the hermeneutical circle described earlier, intelligibility may be inversely related to the author's intention in a text, which might ultimately be irrecoverable.

All inquiry is grounded in some moral intentionality, and as researchers and instructors we are conscious of this purpose even if, to avoid being ideological, we choose not to identify it explicitly. Self-restraint in stating our agendas is essential if developing independent habits of thought is any part of our purpose. At the same time, methodological confusion will persist if *critical* and *objective* continue to be used interchangeably. Absolute objectivity being impossible, critical inquiry into religion may have to assert academic freedom against the rhetoric of church-state separation. Our own intentions in study are far more easily discernible, and the role they play in the work of investigation remains a serious question in our discipline. Feigned obliviousness to the impossibility of total objectivity will not make the problem go away, and questions about the separation of church and state cannot supersede freedom of academic inquiry. Religion is too important an element of culture to be excluded from any sector of the academy, and the critical engagement fostered by a research-intensive state university offers a potentially valuable voice in the national conversation about religion. In the field of religious studies, the secular research institution can be either the freest or the most confining venue of inquiry. The study of material both arcane and familiar, such as the early modern Spanish mystical tradition, demands and tests our tolerance and rigor.

NOTES

[1] See, for example, the essays in Connolly as well as Connolly's own introduction.

[2] As a discipline within the humanities, religious studies ideally cultivates a critical stance toward both tradition and the nonreflexive self-awareness with which most students arrive at college. See Penaskovic and Eschenback.

[3] For an appreciation of the range and impact of Lagorio's work, see the essays in Bartlett.

Teaching Teresa as a Theologian

Gillian T. W. Ahlgren

While Teresa of Ávila is one of the most accessible mystics in the Christian tradition, her theological insights are both profound and, in some senses, hidden to those not committed to ongoing spiritual growth. Approaching Teresa as a theologian places considerable demands on readers, and guiding students through her texts, with their many levels of meaning, poses unique challenges to us as teachers. Understanding her context and its theological questions is an important first step in capturing Teresa's theological message. Equally important in theological discussion of Teresa's works is clarity about one's own theological positions and the traditions and experiences that have formed and shaped them.

Let me begin, briefly, with a few notes about my pedagogical experience. I teach at a Catholic, Jesuit university committed to helping men and women discover in their own experience a point of departure for "finding God in all things." This context has certainly influenced my development as a scholar, as a theologian, and as a person of faith. Within the Jesuit tradition, education, particularly in the arts and sciences, is a point of entry into wisdom and a holistic exploration of what it means both to be human and to be in relation with the divine. That we can affirm the presence of God in the world around us and in our own lived experience suggests that learning and contemplation are natural partners. In this sense, prayer, or our loving conversation with God, allows us to see beyond the surface of things and to sense the potentiality in ourselves and others.

As she herself relates in *The Book of Her Life*, Teresa was profoundly influenced by the spiritual companionship and affirmation of the early Jesuits. Their development of meditation techniques centered around the importance of meditating on the life of Christ in ways that allowed Christians to enter, in an experiential way, into Gospel narratives and draw parallels between Christ's humanity and their own. A vital part of prayer as it was developed by Ignatius of Loyola in his *Spiritual Exercises* was to recall a Gospel story and to put oneself in the place of one of the characters, allowing the story to come to life in one's imagination. In this way, prayer and scripture worked together to convey ongoing revelation to the practicing Christian. Affirmation that Jesus's humanity could communicate something about the reality of God became the departure point for Teresa's intense dedication to the contemplative life. Indeed, a good case could be made that Teresa took Ignatian spirituality to a profoundly new level as she integrated successive insights about God into a developmental model of human personhood. By the time that she wrote *The Interior Castle* in 1577, Teresa had achieved a unique synthesis of spiritual growth and theological wisdom—one that makes this text a classic Christian mystical text. In it, she articulates the theological implications of key Christian doctrines: that humanity is created in the image of God, that it is restored into wholeness through Christ, and that we are invited, through Christ, into deeper partnership with God.

For Teresa traditional Christian doctrine was meaningful precisely because it invites us into a deeper spiritual and theological journey. Theology, or the study of God, was for Teresa an ongoing process of trying to put into words what her ever-deepening partnership with God was teaching her. In this sense, teaching Teresa as a theologian implies a particular approach to the discipline of theology, which, we could say, provides a context for the faithful, lifelong exploration of the reality of God. Christian theology grapples with the paradox that God is both ultimately unfathomable and unknowable and yet is also a God who invites us into divine mystery through the power of love. Theology, therefore, is neither an abstract science nor a catechetical project. What it teaches, first and foremost, is and ought to be an engaged, loving way of knowing and beholding the mystery of God and all that God has created. This understanding of theology is clearly operative in Teresa's works.

Teresa's affective language, her use of nuptial metaphors, and her constant reiteration of life as a journey toward union with God signal her singular dedication to the mystical life and the theological synthesis that the mystical life reveals. As current scholarship has made clear, Teresa's theological contributions to the Christian mystical tradition are extensive, but they have, at times, been difficult to decode because of the many rhetorical strategies Teresa used to work around her contemporaries' resistance to women as theological teachers (Ahlgren, *Teresa of Ávila . . . Politics* 67–84; Weber, *Teresa* 42–76). While her allusions to Scripture are extensive, for example, she is careful not to provide direct scriptural exegesis—a privilege limited to theologians and ordained men. However, a careful reading of Teresa shows how Scripture is deeply embedded in her thought and thus reveals the richness of her prayer life and the interpretive insights it provided for her.[1] Because she teaches so directly out of her personal experience, scholars have recognized Teresa more readily as a spiritual and pastoral teacher, not as a theologian. However, in a course on Teresa as a theologian, a review of current scholarship on Teresa's theological contributions would be an important point for discussion.[2]

In this essay I focus on Teresa's *The Interior Castle*, which, of all her works, contains her most mature theological reflection.[3] The book could be understood as Teresa's attempt to capture in words the shifting landscapes of the psyche (from the Greek word for soul) as it is touched by grace and commits itself to the transformative process that is the mystical journey. In it Teresa contemplates her own growth in her relationship with God and develops a nuanced characterization and analysis of the human-divine partnership, learned through Christ. The treatise is divided into seven sections, or "dwelling places," each one representing a further stage of development in the realization and integration of human potentiality. The idea that the soul consists of mansions, or "dwelling places," comes directly from John 14.2–3:

> In my Father's house there are many dwelling places; if there were not, would I have told you that I am going to prepare a place for you? And if I go and prepare a place for you, I will come back again and take you to myself, so that where I am you also may be.

In reflecting on this passage of scripture, Teresa writes, "we realize that the soul of the just person is nothing else but a paradise where the Lord says He finds His delight" (283; dwelling 1, ch. 1, sec. 1).[4] Thus the "place" that Christ prepares is as much an external space as an internal one—one that our life in Christ prepares within us, especially through prayer.

Teresa's reform of the Carmelite order had introduced contemplative prayer as a spiritual norm for her sisters. Given the suspicion of mental prayer during her day, Teresa sought to provide them both with a practical and conceptual understanding of what they might experience in prayer and with a theological understanding of how what they were experiencing was an actual living out of Christian doctrine known through scripture. The Ignatian framework for mental prayer, which encouraged intuitive correlations between scriptural narrative and human experience, was Teresa's point of departure as a spiritual guide. But women, who were considered even more susceptible to deception by the devil than men, even in prayer, were subject to some scrutiny in their capacity to interpret their own experiences. As is now widely known, Teresa herself experienced such scrutiny, and *The Interior Castle*, written on the heels of inquisitorial investigation in Seville and the review of her *Life*, contains poignant testimony to the challenges that her readers (especially women) could face from spiritual directors who sometimes cast doubt on the authenticity of their directees' spiritual experiences.[5] Indeed, much of the detail in the sixth dwelling places of *The Interior Castle*, particularly the articulation of signs of authentic visions and locutions, can be attributed to contemporary suspicion of mental prayer and paramystical phenomena associated with it. Consider, for example, the following passage:

> Let us begin with the torment one meets with from a confessor who is so discreet and has so little experience that there is nothing he is sure of. He fears everything and finds in everything something to doubt because he sees these unusual experiences. . . . Everything is immediately condemned as from the devil or melancholy. And the world is so full of this melancholy that I am not surprised. There is so much of it now in the world, and the devil causes so many evils through this means that confessors are very right in fearing it and considering it carefully. But the poor soul that walks with the same fear and goes to its confessor as to its judge,

and is condemned by him, cannot help but be deeply tormented and disturbed. Only the one who has passed through this will understand what a great torment it is.   (362–63; ch. 1, sec. 8)

For Teresa, however, conformity of a prayer experience with Scripture is a necessary affirmation of its authenticity. As she warns her readers, "[P]ay no more attention to those [words] that are not in close conformity with Scripture than you would to those heard from the devil themselves" (372; dwelling 6, ch. 3, sec. 4). Thus an attentive theological reading of Teresa reveals how she is able, through careful use of metaphor and Scripture, to recast and vivify traditional Christian teachings through her own life story.

Preparing students for such an attentive theological reading requires some pedagogical strategizing. First, because most students do not have much experience reading mystical texts, I spend some time introducing them to what is usually an entirely new genre for them. For a brief introduction to Christian mysticism, I usually ask students to read the introduction to *Foundations of Mysticism*, by Bernard McGinn, in which he defines mysticism as all that prepares and helps a person become more conscious of the presence of God. He also identifies three characteristics of mysticism: that it is a process, or way of life; that it is an element of a larger religious tradition; and that it is not so much a set of experiences as a way of coming to knowledge and apprehension of the divine. I also use the preface to Elizabeth Petroff's *Body and Soul*, where Petroff explores the link, especially for women, of mystical experience and prophetic witness, arguing that the mystical life provides women with a theological authority they otherwise would not have. I warn them that a mystical text demands more of its readers than other texts. I note that because mystics are trying to find words for the ineffable experience of God they make use of metaphors and scriptural analogies to help them convey things that defy concrete words. I suggest to them that the text is meant to be read slowly, and I introduce the concept of contemplative reading, in which reading is a form of reflection and prayer. Specifically, I review with them the monastic context of these texts, explaining the tradition of *lectio divina*, in which spiritual works were read aloud to monks and nuns in the refectory while they were eating, and the words became as much food for the soul as the meal was for the body. We read small portions of the text aloud at the outset of our reading of *The Interior Castle*, and the experience of hearing the words, not just seeing them on the page, gives the students a sense of how to approach the text more holistically.

Over the years as a reader of Teresa, I have discovered that Teresa's use of Scripture and metaphor in *The Interior Castle* is deliberate. One can identify a primary metaphor (and at times other, complementary metaphors) as well as a primary scriptural reference in each of the seven dwelling places. Teresa uses metaphor and Scripture to provide points of reference, within the context of Christian theology, for understanding what the soul is experiencing and apprehending of God through prayer. However, I have also found that students need help in recognizing a theological statement. The second step to approaching the text is to outline for students some of the major branches of Christian theology: language about God (theology proper), language about Christ (christology), language about human beings and human nature (theological anthropology), and language about the nature of the church (ecclesiology). As they read the text, I encourage them to underline, in different colors, statements that have an implication for their understanding of God, Christ, or human nature. This highlighting of the theological level of the text through each of the seven stages then paves the way for a deeper theological analysis of the overall text.

To accomplish this theological synthesis, I have found it helpful to draw a chart in which we identify the scriptural reference(s) and metaphor(s) operative in each of the seven dwelling places. We try to put into words exactly what the soul is experiencing. We also formulate, in class discussion, an integrated sense of what the soul is learning about itself (which, in addition to being a spiritual lesson, is also a theological one, forming the basis for Teresa's overall theological anthropology) and what the soul is learning about God. When we place all these things together, in a chart, the correlations between Scripture, metaphor, human experience, and theology become clearer (see fig.).[6] The chart becomes a handy way for students to remember what is happening in each stage of the soul's journey toward union with God, as well as a profound way of integrating the various levels of the text, from the function of symbols and metaphors to a psychological and spiritual analysis of experience to a deeper appropriation of the theological dimensions of the text.

In the first dwelling places, for example, we notice and read aloud Teresa's explication of the metaphor of the soul as "a castle made entirely out of a diamond or of very clear crystal, in which there are many rooms, just as in heaven there are many dwelling places" (283; ch. 1, sec. 1). We note the correlation she draws between the metaphor of the castle and the scriptural reference to dwelling places from the Gospel of John. We also observe that the soul, which is encouraged to explore its own interior, is conceptualized as a series of concentric spheres, gradually leading into a single chamber, where God resides. This concentric arrangement is reinforced by Teresa's use of another metaphor, that of a palmetto plant. She writes:

> You mustn't think of these dwelling places in such a way that each one would follow in file after the other; but turn your eyes toward the center, which is the room or royal chamber where the King stays, and think of how a palmetto has many leaves surrounding and covering the tasty part that can be eaten.   (287; dwelling 1, ch. 1, sec. 8)

As we fill in the section of the chart that pertains to what the soul is experiencing at this stage, I try to elicit the students' sense of the soul's awakening into its created nature. This nature is a new consciousness of the soul as itself inherently "precious," as Teresa writes: "But we seldom consider the precious things that can be found in this soul, or who dwells within it, or its high value. Consequently, little effort is made to preserve its beauty" (284; dwelling 1, ch. 1, sec. 2). Teresa's lament here is that it seems that we do not know how to dwell deeply within ourselves, to live in our soulfulness. Instead, we spend ourselves in movement from activity to activity. The spiritual lesson for today seems clear and pertinent:

> Absorbed in superficial movement in the world around us, we lack genuine engagement with ourselves, our internal senses and our intuitions, and therefore we do not know how to "activate" the divine life within us.
> (Ahlgren, *Entering* 23)

As we consider what the soul learns about itself as a result of this new perception of its "precious" nature, we try to articulate Teresa's deeper theological argument that "our personhood is sacred, a treasure of inestimable worth, partly because it was created by God and partly because, as God's creation, God abides in its deepest center" (23). Statements like this readily become an articulation of Teresa's theological anthropology.

Discussion of our final category, what the soul learns about God, usually begins with the observation that Teresa constantly refers to God as "his Majesty," a phrase that highlights the royal, majestic, and powerful dimensions of God's being. This sense of God's superiority to the soul is developed in the second chapter of the first dwelling place, in which Teresa describes a vision of the blackness of a soul in mortal sin. Its "precious nature" is hardly recognizable in such a state: blackened, wretched and filthy (288; sec. 2). Knowing the soul's vulnerability to sin and comparing it to the absolute purity of God induces deep humility in the soul. Teresa writes: "By gazing at His grandeur, we get in touch with our own lowliness; by looking at His purity, we shall see our own filth; by pondering His humility, we shall see how far we are from being humble" (292; sec. 9). Human beings thus recognize their dependence on God, strive to turn away from those things that lead away from God, and move toward the interior of the "castle" of the soul. This movement is the commitment to prayer, as Teresa writes: "Insofar as I can understand, the gate of entry to this castle is prayer and reflection" (286; dwelling 1, ch. 1, sec. 7). Prayer becomes the impetus for growth in self-knowledge and virtue—the point of entry into the next stages of spiritual growth. Finally, we note that as much as God and the soul appear to be radically different, Teresa refers often to God's "granting the soul favors," reiterating both God's power to do so and God's generous nature.[7]

It takes us, as a class, at least six sessions to process the text and fill in the chart. Although I always have my own notes to ensure that we cover the essential points, each year there are interesting variations in how the chart gets filled, especially in how the students translate the passages they have underlined into more integrated theological statements. In my estimation, the process of finding words to convey what Teresa is expressing about human personhood, Christ, and God is the students' initial step toward theological writing. Working on the chart together creates a communal space for exploring, with language, theological reality. The chart then serves as an important tool for students to develop longer essays about Teresa's spiritual and theological contributions.

Teaching Teresa as a theologian has certainly taught me a great deal about what it is to be a theologian. Teresa's language, which communicates a kind of intimate familiarity with God in her prayer life as well as a profound humility before all that she understands God to have revealed to her, suggests to me that Teresa did indeed touch and behold the mystery of God. The profundity of her loving encounters with God both humbled her and ignited in her a deep desire to invite others into the same experiential depths. In my own teaching of Teresa over the years, I have seen how her words resonate spiritually with students who read her works in vastly different chronological and cultural contexts from her own. Her words still have the capacity to convey to their readers God's invitation to deeper fullness of life. Witnessing the transformative effects of Teresa on her readers has taught me that to open up her theological synthesis to students is a profound blessing and a profound responsibility. To teach Teresa is, at heart, to bear witness to the reality of a God whose love is gentle, penetrating, intense, fortifying, eternal, unconditional, and absolutely transformative.

NOTES

[1] Because Inquisitor General Fernando de Valdés's *Index of Prohibited Books* banned Scripture in the vernacular, extensive vernacular commentary on Scripture was suppressed, in the writings of both men and women.

[2] Secondary readings for this section of the course might include Ahlgren, "Teresa of Ávila (1515–1582)," and sections from Luti, *Teresa*; Weber, *Teresa of Ávila*; and Williams.

[3] For a comparison of Teresa's theological views in *The Book of Her Life*, written in 1562 and redacted in 1565, and her views in *The Interior Castle*, see Ahlgren, *Entering*.

[4] All citations of *The Interior Castle* are to the translation by Kavanaugh and Rodríguez in volume 2 of *Collected Works*. The allusion is to Proverbs 8.31.

[5] For more analysis of this period of Teresa's life, see Ahlgren, *Teresa of Ávila . . . Politics* 47–64.

[6] Appendix 1 presents a chart showing how a class might fill in the chart for Dwelling Place 1 only. For suggested questions to help students complete the chart for all seven Dwelling Places, see the appendix. The usefulness of the chart as a pedagogical tool is that there is no single way to complete it, so it is different each time.

[7] For discussion of each of the seven stages in the *Interior Castle*, see Ahlgren, *Entering*. Although the chart is not contained in the book, there is ample discussion of all of the metaphors and scriptural references in each of the seven stages, as well as a description of what the soul experiences and what it learns about itself and God.

APPENDIX 1

Spiritual and Theological Analysis of Dwelling Place 1

Scriptural References	Metaphor(s) Used	What the Soul Experiences	What the Soul Learns about Itself	What the Soul Learns about God
John 14.2 Genesis 1.26	Soul as castle made of crystal Soul as diamond	*New self-perception:* awareness of an invitation to prayer and more authentic self-knowledge, awareness of itself as "flawed" and fallen	That it is "precious"—the proverbial "pearl" of great price That it is created and loved by God That it has a responsibility to care for itself and cultivate its own deepest beauty in God	That God is radically other yet in no way disdains the soul That God holds the soul in esteem and grants it favors That God invites the soul to "something more" than what it currently experiences, relationally

APPENDIX 2

Study Questions for *The Interior Castle*

First Dwelling Places

Describe the metaphors and scriptural references used in the first mansions.
Why would we want to enter the interior castle? How do we?
How does Teresa define humility?
What does the soul learn about itself and about God in this stage?

Second Dwelling Places

How would you characterize this stage and what differentiates it from the first stage?
What struggles does the soul face? What can it do to help itself?

Third Dwelling Places

What scriptural verse characterizes this stage?
How would you recognize a soul at this stage?

Fourth Dwelling Places

What scriptural verse characterizes these mansions?
What kinds of experiences does the soul have in these mansions? What do they accomplish in the soul?
Describe the metaphor of the two fountains. What does it attempt to convey?

Fifth Dwelling Places

What scriptural verse characterizes these mansions?
What is the soul's experience at this stage?

Sixth Dwelling Places

Characterize the soul and its experiences at this stage. What causes it to suffer?

Describe the experience of rapture or ecstasy as Teresa writes about it.

Seventh Dwelling Places

What characterizes the soul at this stage? What has been accomplished in it? How different is it from the way it was when it first entered the castle?

What does it learn about self and God in this section and how has that knowledge of self and God been "coalescing" through the seven stages?

Teaching Spanish Mysticism at an Undergraduate Catholic College: Issues of Relevance, Accessibility, and Self-Censorship

Dona M. Kercher

To cite Teresa of Ávila, "Soy ruin." Loosely translated, I am a lost cause. I do not presume to be the best teacher ever of Spanish mysticism, although I received positive comments from students the last time I taught the course. Indeed, to continue the mode of autobiographical confession, I have evolved from a scholar of Golden Age literature, specifically of Francisco de Quevedo's *Sueños* (*Visions*), to a film scholar. Yet precisely because I am now taking the outsider's perspective rather than that of an academic researcher in the field, some of my approaches for teaching a course on mysticism within the particular environment of an undergraduate Catholic institution may be helpful to others.

Issues of Accessibility: From Texts to Experiencing the City

Undergraduate students today struggle when faced with a scholarly edition of the Golden Age classics, such as those published by Cátedra or Castalia. Even good students read *Don Quijote* in translation—"to save time"—then are at a loss for vocabulary when they have to talk about the novel in class. There are many editions of *Don Quijote* but distinctly fewer for the Spanish mystics. I am old school in my text selection. I still believe in having students buy a modern, scholarly edition of Teresa of Ávila's *Libro de la vida* (*The Book of Her Life*). I prefer Otger Steggink's Castalia edition. It represents unparalleled scholarship, thus showing our students what graduate study in Hispanism may be all about. Importantly, there is a substantial glossary of Teresa's vocabulary, which is a good teaching tool if actively used. We eventually read the entire *Vida* over the course of the semester. This gives students a genuine sense of accomplishment.

Virtually every student who signs up for Spanish Mysticism is unsure of what mysticism is and wants me to tell him or her, right away. To address this straightforwardly, in the first class I ask students to write down anonymously an answer to the question, What is Spanish mysticism? A common response is "magic." I return to their answers at the end of the course to show them how much they have learned. In the meantime I also ask them to be alert to contemporary uses of the word *mystic* they may find.[1] To guide students to a hispanist's definition of Spanish mysticism, however, I begin with John of the Cross's "Noche oscura" ("Dark Night") in Bruce Wardropper's excellent edition *Spanish Poetry of the Golden Age*. Wardropper comments, "Mysticism is the process by which a human soul is united with divine essence on this side of the grave" (312). Now that students have their working definition, each one is asked to memorize a specific stanza of "Noche oscura" to recite for the next class.

Since my aim is to make the course Spanish Mysticism accessible, I try making it memorable with themes, visual clues, and outings. I thereby stress Teresa's emphasis on and belief in experience. In 2006 for our second class, we embarked on an early morning field trip to the Bancroft Tower, which is high on a hill overlooking the city of Worcester. Our students tend to be sheltered and seldom get out to know and appreciate the city they are in. I told them we were starting there, a memorial monument, which looks tremendously like a castle, because Teresa used the symbol of a castle in her writings, specifically in *Castillo interior* (*The Interior Castle*), as a memory device to describe the stages of contemplation to union with God. Conveniently, one side of the vast stone monument is in the darkness in the morning and the other in the light. I had the students arrange themselves according to the stanza order of "Noche oscura." We discussed when, that is, at which stanza they should be coming out into the light. They recited the first time with each person speaking in an appropriate place of lightness or darkness, and then we discussed how they could each act out their stanzas more dramatically, with more meaning—or sense of experience—with movements and gestures. Since it was a beautiful fall day and we were the only ones there to make fools of ourselves, the outing was enjoyable and a good bonding experience. Finally they each had to memorize the whole poem and recite it in my office.

Later in the semester, as a prelude to a unit on Luis de León, we reprised this exercise with Fray Luis's poem "A Francisco Salinas," which begins, "El aire se serena" 'The air becomes serene.'[2] This juxtaposed a "noche serena" ("serene night") to John of the Cross's "noche oscura" ("dark night") and thereby contrasted contemplative and mystical poetry.[3] Students indeed found the biographical story of the friendship between the two Salamancan professors—Salinas, a blind musician, and Fray Luis, marked by his five years of imprisonment—riveting. This comparative exercise, and consequent intimate familiarity with the texts, gave the students confidence to demonstrate considerable mastery of literary explication in a final essay on a poem of Fray Luis.

Magdalen: Enacting a Scene from The Da Vinci Code

Though little known nationally, Worcester, Massachusetts, has a jewel of an art museum, about two miles from our campus. Although the museum is not normally open mornings during our class period, we were permitted to enter then, funneling through the semidarkened corridors as if we were enacting the trespassing of the Louvre in *The Da Vinci Code*. My students, who had seen the movie but not read the book, pointed out that we were there legally, but I tried to bring excitement into the visit and to guide them in a tour of my favorite paintings, as the museum came alive for the day. We passed the portrait of Stephen Salisbury, who commissioned the Bancroft Tower we had visited, then went up to the European galleries to the most amazing religious portrait—El

Greco's *Repentant Magdalen* (1577). In preparation for the visit, students had read Anne Hollander's chapter on Mary Magdalen from *Feeding the Eye*, as well as the entries on this painting and its companion portrait, *Saint Peter in Tears*, which is in the Bowes Museum (Barnard Castle, County Durham, England), from the catalog to the El Greco exhibition in 2003 at the Metropolitan Museum of Art.

First, speaking in Spanish, we reviewed El Greco's iconography from perfume flask to ivy and recounted the biblical story of Mary Magdalen's washing Christ's feet. Referring to David Rosand's book with its color plate of Titian's nude, golden Magdalen (107, pl. 23), we then compared the color palette and composition of the two works. When students remarked on the prominently large proportion of the Magdalen's arm in the foreground of the picture, holding up their own forearms to their faces to compare the scale, I told them how unusual this earthy robustness was in the context of El Greco's particular style of elongated bodies. Since the *Repentant Magdalen* is considered a prime example of El Greco's "mystical religious paintings," we talked about what the visual representation of mysticism was in Teresa's Toledo.[4] You can clearly see the "don de lágrimas" 'gift of tears' in Magdalen's upward glance.[5] The immediacy of the experience is enhanced when you see this—indeed any—oil painting in person, for the light reflects off the canvas in her eyes, and the blue-greens of the picture are stunning in contrast. Furthermore, in Magdalen's transparent lace collar and her interlaced fingers—a gesture so different from the gesture in Titian that half covers, half reveals Magdalen's chest and engages in the dialogue between spiritual and profane love—one can sense both the sobriety of Teresa's times and the repose of contemplation, which is essential to the "camino de perfección" ("way of perfection"). Referring to Hollander's chapter, I told the class how the female saints, especially Magdalen, since she was considered a prostitute, allowed religious painters to represent beautiful women. The fascination with the theme of penance, seen in the pairings of Saint Peter and Mary Magdalen, situates the topic of remorse and confession for the interpretation of Teresa's autobiography. We followed up in the next class by reading the passages of *Vida* ([ed. Steggink] 307, ch. 22) in which Teresa writes about Mary Magdalen.

We were able to visit briefly the medieval galleries before leaving the museum. Traversing one gallery with a richly adorned ceiling from a fifteenth-century Spanish home, we entered a dark gallery of religious art notable for its exterior wall of stained glass windows. I directed our attention to the only Spanish window, noting that it is the most grotesque, for it depicts the literal grilling of the body of Saint Vincent on a gridiron. However, the contemporary element has a major presence in that gallery. When you spin around to the opposite wall in the same gallery, a part that is hidden from view when you enter the room,[6] you are startled by the brilliant, contemporary video installation of Bill Viola's *Union* from his series *The Passions*. This consists of two vertically mounted plasma screens, each playing eight-minute videos of a naked man and woman. Framed in three-quarter shots, they progress in tandem, but without interaction, through states of contemplation and spiritual arousal. Viola wrote that he was inspired by the imagery of Christ's Passion and by his extensive readings in the mystical literature of Europe and Asia (Walsh 25). Even more specifically, he told John Walsh that he gave his actors poems of John of the Cross to read as "historical reference points" to "the regions of the human self that I wanted them to address" (35). The video installation engages in dialogue exquisitely with the other religious art in the dark gallery. It projects a contemporary image of interiority. Is this not perhaps how we can envision mysticism today?

Without a doubt art history enhances the study of Spanish mysticism. Good digital images of El Greco, Titian, and Viola can make for a stimulating class. Although it is unlikely that others will journey to the Worcester area, the idea of venturing into the community can be duplicated creatively in other sites. For instance, each time I end the course with a December field trip to Saint Joseph's Abbey, a Trappist monastery in the Massachusetts countryside. The stillness of the chapel and the chanting of the hours are mesmerizing, a fitting recall of the life of contemplation. These trips broaden the cultural horizons of our students while reflective journal assignments reinforce the significance of their individual experiences.

Accessibility and Relevance: Teresa as Businesswoman in Medwick's Biography

Undergraduate students today are sorely challenged to understand the glorious Spanish of Miguel de Cervantes, let alone to comprehend the threat implicit in Teresa's elliptical language. How can we convince them to take a course about the more dour mystics? How is this painful process of reading their works in Spanish relevant?

By alternating reading Cathleen Medwick's secular biography in English, *Teresa of Ávila: The Progress of a Soul*, which considers the saint as a businesswoman, with *Vida* in Spanish, students gain an entryway into the text and the complexity of the literary and theological phenomenon that is Spanish mysticism. Medwick writes in an accessible, engaging style honed in her writing for popular women's magazines after studying Spanish at Columbia University. Students remember the details of Teresa's life from Medwick's distinctive, opinionated narrative. They can retell them in Spanish in class as a counterpoint and gloss on the passages of *Vida* I select for close reading according to a theme or focus for a given class. I endeavor to have students read both texts critically. For instance, in chapter 1, "Expeditions," Medwick calls Teresa an "opportunist" (9). I have students note that this is a negative assessment. I have them check on the passages of *Vida* describing her youthful escapades to find that Teresa viewed her conduct in that same negative light (*Libro* [ed. Steggink] 98–101). To me, having students retell the episodes of Teresa's life, in effect, having them translate Medwick into Spanish in class, is an effective and engaging teaching strategy. I acknowledge their limitations and at the same time expose them to the original.

Relevance in Paper Topics: The Discovery of Teresa's Letters

During a class early in the semester on the manuscript tradition of *Vida*, I had students copy Teresa's signature using a calligraphy pen and transparent vellum to sense its fluidity and speculate on her character traits from handwriting analysis. Their enthusiasm for the experiment stayed in my mind. Hence, for a paper topic I suggested that students invent an exchange of letters between Teresa and a person mentioned in Medwick's biography, alive or dead, in five pages. I mentioned they might begin with a faux scholarly introduction describing how they "found" the letters. Given that most of my class was majoring in fields other than Spanish—Latin American studies, English, social rehabilitation, psychology, sociology, and English—I thought this would give them a way to focus a paper around their academic interests. Imagine the exchange between Teresa and George Eliot as Eliot is writing *Middlemarch* or the lost letters between Teresa and her brothers when they are in the Indies. Perhaps those in business would enjoy imagining Teresa's exchange with town leaders who tried to block her foundations with frivolous accusations. She was told, for instance, to knock down stone walls because their shadows would make neighboring ponds freeze over. Others might be interested in inventing the long-lost correspondence between Teresa and John of the Cross. My mind raced. I thought this would be fun.

I was disheartened, however, since one student revealed in a ride to the museum that initially the assignment seemed too hard. The student wanted to stay with option one, to write "a conventional paper." Eventually, after we negotiated the specifics of the assignment, all the students but one chose to write a creative exchange of letters. To help them model Teresa's style, and especially to mimic the openings and closings, I distributed a few pages of her epistolary, including letters to the town officials, to her brother Lorenzo in Quito, to her patroness Luisa de la Cerda in Toledo, and to her brother Francisco de Cepeda about John of the Cross (Teresa, *Obras* [ed. Efrén and Steggink] 672–73, 681–83, 690–93).

Key to convincing the students to try the creative approach, however, was learning during an invited class by Sister Ellen Guerin, the college's former dean of undergraduate studies, that Dorothy Day looked to Teresa for guidance when she founded the Catholic Workers' Movement. Day's biography is not only inspiring, since she fully committed herself to establishing houses of hospitality for the poor in Manhattan, but also accessible to the general reader, because of the conflicts surrounding her conversion to Catholicism, which can be framed in melodrama. To become a Catholic, Day had to "give up a mate with whom I was much in love" (True 1). Subsequently, one student's exploration of what she called the "fourth dimension" of reality, in which she imagined Day and Teresa of Ávila corresponding across time on the topic of foundations, evolved into a poster presentation of their letters, which won the humanities award at the undergraduate research symposium. These extended collaborations can bring our more esoteric work in the humanities to a wider college audience and allow our undergraduates to be the stars who cross disciplinary boundaries.

Making Connections through Films

Whether students choose to engage in creative projects, which relate the readings to their field of study or not, all students partake of the final unit of the course that focuses on modern adaptations or versions of the lives of Teresa and John of the Cross. Currently Carlos Saura's *Noche oscura* is the most significant, and manageable, feature film available for this interpretative exercise. I prefer it to Josefina Molina's *Teresa de Jesús*, a multipart television series, not only because students find Molina's work slow-paced, but because *Noche oscura* allows me to reinforce earlier assignments on John of the Cross's poetry. Nonetheless, the lack of English subtitles for *Noche oscura* makes it difficult for undergraduates to view this film in its entirety. Although this rather bleak film is not my favorite Saura work, particularly effective sequences for analysis are the opening, which envisions the act of writing the poem "Noche oscura," and segments focusing on John's direct confrontations with the Calced Carmelites (those who opposed the Teresian Discalced reform).

To help students understand this film in aesthetic terms, I introduce Marvin D'Lugo's analysis in *The Films of Carlos Saura* of the film's allegorical strategies of spectatorship. D'Lugo argues that the film positions the viewer as the jailer who eventually enables John to escape his confinement, and thereby "the film as a whole invites its audience to read into the priest's struggle a meditation upon the possibility of their own liberation from physical, ideological, and spiritual confinement" (238). Further interpreting Saura within the context of post-Franco Spain, D'Lugo observes:

> Saura's contemporary reading of these events casts St. John's heresy as an implicit affirmation of the autonomy of the individual against the opposition of the collective order of the church. This provides him the occasion to posit what is finally the motivating question at the root of all his inquiries into Spanishness: the status of the individual with the cultural and political traditions of Spain. (235)

Students can research the recent political changes in Spain to see where the individual now stands vis-à-vis the institution of the church. For example, they might note that in a monumental shift, new tax law no longer makes the funding of the Catholic Church a default position on individual tax returns.

In our concluding look at images of the mystics in film, we also discuss the conflictive reappropriation of Teresa's image in Spanish culture after Franco. Here I circulate the three newspaper reviews, from *El País*, *Ya*, and *Vida nueva*, collected in Eduardo Gil de Muro's book *"Teresa de Jesús" en TVE*. I ask the students to paraphrase the critiques and then classify them on a political spectrum of right to left. Through the discussion of the specifics of these three well-chosen, short texts, I access an entire ideological discourse surrounding Teresa. As a follow-up to the newpaper reviews, I discuss the significance of Carmen Martín Gaite, who was one of the cowriters of the script to the television series, as a commentator on the submerged history of women's roles and the renewed attention to women's voices in Spain in the democratic era.[7] It helps to show a sequence from Molina's series, preferably from one of the later episodes.

In future courses I will screen and discuss Ray Loriga's *Teresa: El cuerpo de Cristo* (*Teresa: The Body of Christ* [2007]), the new feature-length film of Teresa's life, when it appears on DVD. Paz Vega, known in the United States for her role as the earth mother and maid in *Spanglish*, plays Teresa.[8] Although *Teresa: El cuerpo de Cristo* did not last long at the theaters in Spain, it nonetheless provoked a stern critique from the Catholic Church in major newspapers. In *El mundo* Juan Orellana, the director of the Departmento de Cine de la Conferencia Episcopal Española (Film Department of the Spanish Council of Bishops), deplored representing "la aproximación mística de Santa Teresa como una relación carnal" 'the mystical approximation of Saint Teresa as a carnal relationship' (qtd. in "Los obispos critican"; my trans.). For Orellana, the film's feminist viewpoint, depicting how Teresa was ahead of her time, led to a lack of understanding of Teresa's sainthood or mysticism ("Los obispos critican"). Most Spanish critics continue to prefer Molina's television miniseries, finding Concha Velasco's performance as Teresa more believable than Paz Vega's. One anonymous online reviewer for *De cine 21* argues for the originality of Rafael Gordon's *Teresa, Teresa* ("Santa distante"). As he did previously in *La reina Isabel en persona* (*Queen Isabel in Person*), Gordon imagines historical personages in a fictitious television-interview format. These new films and other media events, and especially the controversy surrounding their reception, will stimulate further dialogue on what Teresa means for Spanish national identity today.

Self-Censorship

The first semester after I arrived at Assumption College in 1990, I attended a faculty colloquium on women's studies, which made a lasting impression. At the time the women's studies minor had just been adopted after a long, hard-fought battle. Some trustees, including a woman, had opposed it. I do not need to rehearse the all too familiar arguments here. Needless to say, I was in no rush to teach Spanish mysticism. After receiving tenure, I was ready to assume more risk. I could see that unless I offered some more courses in Golden Age literature, no one else would. The *Quijote* alone was not enough. Students, particularly those facing state teacher tests, needed a curriculum of study balanced between canonical and contemporary texts. So I decided to rethink designing a course on Spanish mysticism to add balance.

As a strategy I conceived the course to include a guest speaker who would add a religious perspective, thus hopefully precluding any administrative objections to what might be perceived as a solely secular presentation. I invited the Reverend George Tavard, a member of the board of trustees whom I had met at a reception. With a glass of wine in hand, he told me he had just been in Germany meeting with Lutherans to discuss revisions to the edicts of the Council of Trent. I had never had a conversation with anyone before who mentioned the Council of Trent as something under current discussion. As we spoke, I discovered he had written books on Sor Juana Inés de la Cruz and John of the Cross.

The second time I offered the course I invited another member of the religious community, Sister Ellen Guerin. Having written her master's thesis on Teresa of Ávila, Guerin conveyed a profound understanding not only of Teresa's writings but also of how the Carmelite's life inspired others in the pursuit of justice. She unabashedly called Teresa a feminist. If possible, I highly recommend inviting representatives of the spiritual community into our classrooms with this course. They initiate a necessary dialogue within the institution.

Perhaps I proceeded with excessive caution regarding the oversight of courses with religious themes. My institution may be an isolated case. However, over the years at Hispanic film and literature conferences, I have witnessed and engaged in discussions regarding the self-censorship that lay instructors at other religious-sponsored colleges exercise when dealing with theologically sensitive topics. Job candidates are especially anxious about potential interview questions, and we need to mentor them. To further look on the positive, it is heartening that when one teaches Spanish mysticism at a Catholic college, you can discuss confession, extreme unction, or the Epistles, and the students know what you are talking about and can contribute. Recently I boldly forged ahead to pursue joint theology credit for my Spanish mysticism course. Genial conversations between our departments have led to agreement to cross-list the course, which allows the students another option to fulfill their theology requirement.

In conclusion, the emphasis on experience in teaching Spanish mysticism—from memorizing poetry for recitation to exploring the contemporary environment—is both true to the spirit of the texts and especially appropriate for a wide range of undergraduates. Despite my reservations along the way, I have found it a positive journey in teaching, whose strategies described here may inspire others. The topic indeed invites creative experimentation and collaboration.

NOTES

I would especially like to thank all the students of Spanish Mysticism at Assumption College for the generosity of their comments and their willingness to explore difficult terrain. Likewise, I owe a great debt to George Tavard and Ellen Guerin for taking the time to share their perspectives on the mystics in classroom visits. I would never have become a hispanist if I hadn't been inspired as an undergraduate by Edward Glaser at the University of Michigan and written a paper on women in Luis de León's poetry. Over the years I came to appreciate that Fray Luis's line "as I was saying yesterday," which Fray Luis uttered when he returned to teaching after his incarceration by the Inquisition—which Glaser used to say in class often with great relish—was a motto for tenacity in Glaser's own life that had been interrupted by his flight from the Nazis.

¹In fall 2006 we discovered some intriguing citations in Latin American politics. Both socialist presidential candidates Andrés Manuel López Obrador, nicknamed AMLO, in Mexico and Heloisa Helena in Brazil, who eventually lost their bids for office, received serious academic analysis as twenty-first-century mystics. AMLO called himself "místico" in his outsider "messianic" role (Krauze). Likewise a political outsider, Helena was called a mystic because of her roots in northeastern Brazil and connection to liberation theology (Rohter).

²The choice of text for Luis de León is more difficult than with "Noche oscura," given Luis's frequent revisions. I used Juan Francisco Alcina's edition (*Poesía* 80–84) and distributed Elias Rivers's prose translation of the poem (*Renaissance and Baroque Poetry* 94–96) as well. I used the occasion to discuss the evolution of poetic texts in the Golden Age and to contrast two versions of "La vida retirada." See also Wardropper 22–27.

³See the essay by Dana Buchman in this volume for a detailed analysis of teaching these poets in comparison.

⁴See the gallery image and catalog description online at the Worcester Art Museum site (www.worcesterart.org/Collection/European/1922.5.html).

⁵For this phrase, see Teresa, *Libro* (ed. Steggink) 598; my trans.

⁶A museum curator told me that its placement is in fact to allow docents to hide its presence from school tour groups if they so choose because of the shock of nudity on film. Images of a different Viola installation from *The Passions*, the five panels of *Catherine's Room*, could be introduced to a class especially if students may be uncomfortable with *Union*'s frontal nudity. Peter Sellars suggests that *Catherine's Room* is "a home and a habitation for the interior life" as described by Teresa de Ávila (qtd. in Walsh 178–79). In an interview Viola said of this installation, "I was most taken by the sense of privacy and inner strength in the image of a woman alone in a room" (qtd. in Walsh 211).

⁷Carmen Martín Gaite (1925–2000) was one of the most important Spanish novelists of the twentieth century. Her novels such as *El cuarto de atrás* (*The Backroom*), which alludes to Virginia Woolf's *A Room of One's Own*, are significant for a feminist critique of Spanish literature. Martín Gaite also wrote sociological studies of women in Spain. Her status as novelist and critic enhanced the marketing of the program *Teresa de Jesús*.

⁸To analyze *Teresa: El cuerpo de Cristo* in filmic terms, students may be asked to consider the following significant contexts for their interpretation: the global context signaled by the choice of the Japanese visual artist Eiko Ishioka as costume designer, the generic context of other Spanish films released at the same time as *Teresa* (especially of *Alatriste*, another costume drama), and the ongoing debate surrounding cultural policy in Spain, specifically the Ley de Cine (Film Law), passed in 2007, which governs the industrial model of subvention and distribution.

Where's Teresa? The Construction of Teresa of Ávila in the Visual Arts

Christopher C. Wilson

Works of art, like texts, are potent cultural indicators. Embedded within the cultures that produce them, images not only reflect the values that structure a society's identity, they simultaneously play an active role in communicating, contouring, and regulating those values. Art describes what is, what should be, and what should not be. In the study of Spanish mystics, images together with textual artifacts such as hagiographies and sermons provide windows into the aspirations and limitations imposed by early modern Catholicism.

This essay considers how visual representations of Teresa of Ávila can be used in teaching early modern constructions of female sanctity.[1] Through close scrutiny of images, students will discover that Teresian iconography is less an objective portrait of the historical individual than a careful shaping of her persona, a visual counterpart to the printed hagiographies that promoted her cult before and after her canonization in 1622. Her example demonstrates that saints are malleable, their identities adjusted in texts and images to reinforce contemporary notions of extraordinary virtue. As Frank Graziano asserts in his recent study of the cult of Saint Rose of Lima, hagiographic discourse (e.g., biographies, testimonies by those who knew the individual) and iconography produce "a packaged identity that stands in for, and ultimately displaces, the historical person on whom it was based" (33–34). Strategic selection of certain episodes stress some valued feature of the saint's (or candidate for sainthood's) identity, while other aspects that fall outside institutional perceptions of holiness are downplayed.

Baroque artists formulated images of Teresa that served the needs of her individual devotees, the Discalced Carmelite Order, and ultimately the Counter-Reformation church, with its agenda of defining appropriate parameters of female sanctity. While early modern religious men were praised for their lives of external activity—preaching, missionary work, spiritual direction, martyrdom at the hands of those perceived as infidels—female routes to sanctity typically focused on heroic retreat from the world, mystical experience, and exemplary obedience to superiors. Baroque artists depicted Teresa in conformity with these perceptions. While scholarship in recent decades has opened up an appreciation of Teresa the strategic rhetorician, energetic religious reformer, and forward-thinking feminist determined to expand women's roles in the Counter-Reformation church, in early modern art we encounter a different Teresa. Images rarely portray her as assertive administrator or teacher, deftly acquiring houses for her reform or counseling her nuns. On seeing representative samples of Teresian iconography, students who have read her texts and modern criticism may well wonder, Where's Teresa? They will find instead pointed emphasis on her as passive receptacle for the mystical experiences recounted in her *Life* and

Spiritual Testimonies: an angel pierces her heart, a white dove hovers above her head, Christ presents her with a nail of his crucifixion as a token of mystical marriage. Problematic aspects of Teresa's identity (her Jewish lineage, her role as teacher, her struggles with ecclesiastical authority, and the amount of time she spent outside the walls of the convent on her journeys) were ignored or revised to present her as a humble, obedient daughter of the church who is rewarded for her absolute orthodoxy with divine favors. The following analysis of specific examples of Teresian iconography focuses on engravings, since their wide circulation throughout Catholic Europe and Spanish America made them the most influential visual tool in constructing an early modern Teresa.

God's Compensation for Female Incompetence

The most frequently depicted image of Teresa in the decades following her death in 1582 shows her as author, holding a quill pen while a white dove, symbolizing the Holy Spirit, inspires her words. The earliest pairing of Teresa and the dove is an engraving included in the first edition of her works, printed at Salamanca in 1588 (fig. 1). Based on a 1576 portrait by Fray Juan de la Miseria (to which

Fig. 1. *Teresa as Author* with first page of Luis de León's dedicatory letter, engraving from *Los libros de la Madre Teresa de Jesús* (Salamanca, 1588).

a white dove was later added), the composition shows Teresa with hands folded in prayer, gazing up toward the Holy Spirit. Surrounding her head is a banner inscribed with words derived from Psalm 89, "I will sing of the mercies of the Lord forever" (my trans.). The image echoes Teresa's own description of her vision of a heavenly dove (*Life*, ch. 38) and at the same time visualizes the text of a dedicatory letter by the Augustinian friar Luis de León (1527–91), the first page of which faces the engraving in the 1588 volume and in subsequent printings. He wrote the letter at a moment when claims of Teresa's sanctity were on the rise. Two years earlier her corpse had undergone official inspection and had been declared incorrupt. Reports of miracles involving her bodily relics were increasing in number. Fray Luis set out to add to the list of wonders by demonstrating the miraculous nature of two great legacies that Teresa left behind on earth, her reform and her books, which attest not only to Teresa's virtues but also to the action of the Holy Spirit in her life (Chorpenning, "Fray Luis").

Fray Luis characterizes Teresa's reform of the Carmelite Order as a manifestation of the Holy Spirit's power. It is a miracle, something "outside the natural order of things" that "one woman alone should have restored perfection to a whole order, both of men and of women" (León, "Letter" 369). Fray Luis takes the view that women are inherently weak, incapable of the same endeavors for which men, by virtue of their physical and mental superiority, are well suited. Even though in the natural order of things Teresa's gender should have impeded her from reforming Carmel, God's "grace [and] the power of His Spirit" lifted her beyond the usual boundaries of femininity (370). No less miraculous than Teresa's reform, according to Fray Luis, are her books, which are also the product of the Spirit's inspiration:

> I do not doubt that in many places it was the Holy Spirit Who spoke through her and Who guided her pen and her hand. This is manifest from the light which she sheds upon dark places and the fire which her words kindle in the heart of him who reads them.   (372)

Fray Luis's words provide a theological justification for the invention and dissemination of an image that shows Teresa in the company of the Holy Spirit. The iconography evolved to depict Teresa with pen in hand, in the act of writing, as seen in a print accompanying the 1615 Saragossa edition of her works (fig. 2). An influential engraved series of Teresa's life by Adriaen Collaert and Cornelis Galle (Antwerp, 1613), printed at the request of the Spanish Discalced Carmelite nun Ana de Jesús, includes a depiction of her seated within a cell-like interior, at work on a manuscript (fig. 3). As the Holy Spirit directs a beam of illumination into the top of her head, Teresa looks up toward rays of divine light that pour down from the upper left corner, one of which is inscribed with words derived from the book of Ecclesiasticus (39.6): "The spirit of understanding fills her" (my trans.). Her act of writing here becomes a mystical experience during which God floods her with wisdom. Variations on the image of Teresa as

Fig. 2. *Teresa as Author*, engraving from *Los libros de la Beata Madre Teresa de Jesús* (Saragossa, 1615).

Fig. 3. Collaert and Galle, *Teresa as Author*, engraving (Antwerp, 1613).

divinely inspired writer multiplied rapidly. From the end of the sixteenth century through the time of her canonization in 1622, such representations nearly monopolized Teresian iconography. Why was this type of image given such preference? The answer may be found by considering attitudes toward Teresa, specifically to her achievements as writer, in the years following her death. While her books were enthusiastically received by many, their publication alarmed some in Spain's male-dominated society. At the center of the controversy was gender. Teresa engaged in theological discourse at a time when women were restricted from such activity because of their supposed intellectual inferiority and susceptibility to delusion. In 1589, one year after the publication of the first edition of Teresa's works, the Dominican Alonso de la Fuente urged the Inquisition to ban her writings, arguing that they have a diabolical origin since "they exceed the capacity of women" (qtd. in Weber, *Teresa of Ávila* 160). Similarly, Francisco de Pisa, professor of holy scripture at Toledo's university, warned that her books should be withdrawn from public consumption,

> since there are many other books from which one can safely and profitably learn of the spiritual path, without having a woman come along and

teach, for women are not given this office, but should wait in silence, as the apostle Saint Paul said.   (qtd. in Weber, *Teresa of Ávila* 161–62)

Teresa's devotees faced the problem of defending her books from those who insisted that women should not write or teach. It was against the backdrop of this controversy that the image of Teresa as divinely inspired author ascended to prominence. The iconography associated her with authors of unquestionable prestige—church fathers and doctors, such as Jerome and Gregory the Great—who were sometimes portrayed in art with pen in hand, receiving the Spirit's inspiration. In Teresa's case the visual formula, rooted in Fray Luis's argument, communicated that God compensated for her otherwise incompetent female nature, as if to say that, yes, women are intellectually feeble, but this should be of no concern to the reader, since Teresa's books are the result of the Spirit's intervention rather than of her own intellectual meddling. The Spirit's bypassing of the limitations of femininity is one of the marvels surrounding Teresa. By doggedly propagating this compositional type, promoters of Teresa's cult rebutted criticism of her books as dangerous or of diabolical origin. The surge in declarations of miracles surrounding Teresa's body and relics eventually made it inevitable that her written works would also be seen as miraculous. Supporters of her cult, who included the Spanish monarch, evidently succeeded in dissolving any controversy, since, by the time of her beatification in 1614, opposition to publication of her books had died away and printing presses across Europe were churning them out in numerous languages. The Jesuit Cipriano de Aguayo, writing in that year, sums up an attitude that might well have been shaped by contemporary images of Teresa as author:

How was it possible, except by divine inspiration, for an ignorant woman to write what she did, and in such particular style, plain and humble on the one hand, yet also grave and sententious, with such remarkable words, so pregnant with divine mysteries!
(qtd. in Weber, *Teresa of Ávila* 163–64)

Divine Love's Martyr

Another prevalent type of Teresian iconography represents her most renowned mystical experience, her vision of the piercing of her heart, known as the transverberation (C. Wilson, "Saint Teresa"; Lavin). In the *Life* Teresa describes seeing an angel in whose hands was

a large golden dart and at the end of the iron tip there appeared to be a little fire. It seemed to me this angel plunged the dart several times into my heart [leaving me] all on fire with great love of God.   (1: 252)[2]

Seraphinii vultu decorum, ignito ad summitatem aureo spiculo, cor et viscera sibi traijcientem, flammisque cœlicis accendentem, mirabiliter experitur; vnde seraphico amore, toto deinceps vitæ decursu languida, ad sponsum anhelat.

Fig. 4. Collaert and Galle, *Transverberation of Teresa of Ávila*, engraving (Antwerp, 1613).

One widely disseminated depiction of this episode was a 1613 engraving by Collaert and Galle (part of the above-mentioned print series of Teresa's life, produced in Antwerp [fig. 4]). It served as a compositional point of departure for many subsequent representations, including Gian Lorenzo Bernini's famous mid-seventeenth-century statue in the Cornaro Chapel of Rome's Santa Maria della Vittoria. An angel supports Teresa from behind as another aims the fiery point of an arrow at her heart. In a state of physical collapse, Teresa leans backward and gazes toward heaven. The architectural setting suggests a convent interior, with an altar visible through a doorway in the background. Margit Thøfner has called attention to the repeated use of this pictorial device in the Collaert and Galle series ("How to Look"). The altar's presence connects Teresa to the liturgy and sacraments, communicating that her pursuit of holiness takes place within the institutional church. Her mystical experiences, then, are monitored and church-approved.

In his survey of Counter-Reformation saints, Peter Burke asserts that "a key factor in the imputation of sanctity to an individual is the 'fit' between his or her career and the best-known stereotypes of sanctity" (50–52). Individuals were matched with certain roles or routes to sanctity (such as the missionary, mystic, or founder of a religious order) and were likened to exemplars of those roles that had already been recognized as saints. It was the job of biographers and artists, including engravers of devotional prints, to contour the life of the would-be saint to fit the pattern of the canonized model. Portrayals of Teresa's visions and levitations (constituting half of the twenty-five prints in the Collaert and Galle series) firmly anchored her in the role of mystic; as seen earlier, even her act of writing was presented as a mystical experience rather than as an intellectual effort. Images of the transverberation favorably compared her to earlier female saints who had undergone similar piercings: Catherine of Siena, transfixed with the stigmata, and Gertrude of Helfta, who saw herself wounded after begging Christ to "transfix my heart with the arrow of your love" (102). Highlighting Teresa's resemblance to these models validated claims of her sanctity. Her first hagiographer, Francisco de Ribera, "was at pains to compare Teresa's visions and revelations" to those of Gertrude, among other saints, in order to situate her within an accepted paradigm of piety, thereby making "her appear less like a dangerous innovator" (Haliczer 43).

The iconography also evoked associations with two other saintly precedents, the martyrs Sebastian and Ursula, both of whom were depicted in art transfixed with arrows. In the baroque imagination Teresa's transverberation became inextricably linked with the notion of martyrdom through love, an idea that lay at the heart of Teresian spirituality. In *The Way of Perfection*, addressed to the nuns of her reform, Teresa contends that the austerities practiced in each of her houses—poverty, silence, enclosure, penance—can lead to an interior death that is nothing less than "a long martyrdom" (2: 82). She often compares ecstasy to death, suggesting that mystical experience gives the aspirant a glimpse of union with God, the anticipated culmination of inner martyrdom. The experience of union with God during prayer is "delightful" death (2: 337 [*Interior Castle*]). Describing the effects of being wounded with love for God, as during the moment of her transverberation, she writes,

> You can't exaggerate or describe the way in which God wounds the soul and the extreme pain this wound produces, for it causes the soul to forget itself. Yet this pain is so delightful that there is no other pleasure in life that gives greater happiness. The soul would always want, as I said, to be *dying of this sickness.*   (1: 251 [*Life*]; emphasis added)

A hymn by Pope Urban VIII, dating to the second quarter of the seventeenth century, calls Teresa a "victim of love" and suggests that the transverberation was the actual wound by which she was eventually martyred: "But a sweeter death awaits you / A milder penance calls / With the dart of divine love / Thrust into your wounds you will fall" (qtd. in Lavin 1: 116–17). Promoters of Teresa's cult must have favored transverberation iconography not only because it presented her as another Gertrude or Catherine but also because it effectively characterized her as one of the Counter-Reformation church's martyrs. Her experience, moreover, was paradigmatic: in images she modeled a brand of martyrdom—death through love—that could be pursued by audiences such as female contemplatives for whom literal martyrdom, the prize awarded to some male missionaries, was unattainable.

The Visual Rhetoric of Female Subordination

One nagging problem with the promotion of Teresa's cult was the criticism of her as an inappropriately independent and strong-willed woman, traveling from convent to convent, moving from confessor to confessor. During her lifetime the papal nuncio, Felipe Sega, condemned her as "a restless, gadabout, disobedient, and contumacious woman" (qtd. in Teresa, Complete Works 3: 150n2). To counter such opposition, witnesses in the beatification and canonization proceedings pointed to key instances of Teresa's obedience to superiors, citing for example her immediate willingness to burn her written commentary on the Song of Songs at a confessor's request (Ahlgren, Teresa of Ávila 153). An engraving by Arnold van Westerhout (Rome, 1716) showing Teresa (assisted by other nuns) tossing manuscript pages into a fire calls attention to this episode. Such efforts—visual and textual—fostered the characterization of a humble, absolutely obedient Teresa who immediately trampled on her own inclinations at the request of male superiors.

Images of Teresa with John of the Cross further illustrate this taming of what some had perceived as her dangerously authoritative persona (C. Wilson, "Masculinity Restored"). In a print from the Collaert and Galle series, Teresa bids farewell to John as he leaves the Valladolid convent where he learned about the rule from the founding mother (The Book of Her Foundations, ch. 13 [fig. 5]). In the background she vigorously points to the first monastery established for the new Discalced friars. This composition frankly acknowledges Teresa as the founder of an order composed of both women and men. As the early modern period continued, however, artists downplayed Teresa's leadership and gave John a more prominent position in subsequent images, elevating him as a co-reformer or a spiritual adviser to Teresa. Van Westerhout's 1716 print series, a Discalced Carmelite commission, is the most comprehensive cycle of images of Teresa's life in any artistic medium, yet it eliminates the Valladolid episode; Teresa's interaction with John at the time of the formation of the male branch of the order is visualized instead by a scene of her visit to the friars' first monastery at Duruelo (Foundations, ch. 14 [fig. 6]). John stands elevated above her at the entrance, welcoming her to the new foundation. Awed by his performance of holiness, Teresa tilts her head to the side in a gesture that conveys deference and admiration. There is little hint here of the dynamic, instructive Teresa who was depicted a century earlier in the Collaert and Galle engraving. As comparison of these two prints reveals, Teresa and John were gradually rescripted in accordance with acceptable notions of gender relations.

Fig. 5. Collaert and Galle, *Teresa of Ávila with the First Two Friars of the Carmelite Reform* (John of the Cross and Anthony of Jesus), engraving (Antwerp, 1613).

The constructed Teresa was not static. Occasional representations of her as a more active, interventionist figure—as virile woman (Rowe, "Disrupting") or rescuer of souls from the flames of purgatory (Göttler), for example—further attest to the extraordinary malleability of her image. It should be pointed out to students, finally, that early modern audiences must have perceived the various Teresian images discussed here in different ways. For certain viewers, portrayals of Teresa no doubt encouraged imitation. Some nuns—Sor Juana Inés de la Cruz (1648–95) in Mexico, for example—who pointed to Teresa as a female literary exemplar must have interpreted the depiction of her with pen in hand as a visualization of a historical precedent, giving them license to write (Juana Inés de la Cruz, *Answer* 9; Arenal and Schlau, Introduction 10; Myers, *Neither Saints* 14–15). For other more cautious viewers, such as some male clerics suspicious of errant Teresa imitators, images of her and the marvels she experienced underscored the saint's exceptionality. In a treatise on discerning true and false mysticism written during the 1630s, the Mexican Discalced Carmelite friar Juan de Jesús María warns that there are, in his times, "very few Bridgets, Catherines of Siena, or Teresas" (*Guía Interior* 251). Teresian iconographers

Fig. 6. Van Westerhout, *John of the Cross Greeting Teresa of Ávila at the Monastery at Duruelo*, engraving (Rome, 1716).

could not completely control audience reaction. They could only work to suppress that which was problematic and to accentuate that which was useful about the Spanish nun, to satisfy the needs of individual or institutional promoters of her cult; viewers, in turn, read the images with varying responses of admiration and imitation.

NOTES

[1] For illustrations of Teresian iconography that can be used in preparing class lectures, see Gutiérrez Rueda; Lavin; and C. Wilson, "Masculinity" and "Saint Teresa."

[2] Citations to Teresa's works are to the *Collected Works*, translated by Kavanaugh and Rodríguez.

Reading "Noche oscura" Twice

Howard Mancing

When I teach "Noche oscura" ("Dark Night") by John of the Cross to undergraduates, I have often used a method that affords the students an opportunity to read and contextualize the poem in multiple ways. Most often I teach the poem in our undergraduate Introduction to Literature class required of majors and minors. This is the first literature class for most of the students, and it consists of about five weeks devoted to prose fiction, poetry, and drama. There is not much time to do anything in depth, but I place emphasis on metrics and look at some poems (from different time periods and different countries) in more depth. Even when the poem is included in the anthology that we might be using for class, I prepare a separate handout with the text of "Noche oscura" under the name of Juan de Yepes (the saint's birth name, and therefore only slightly misleading). Then we read and discuss the poem in which a young woman sneaks out of her quiet house one dark night and travels along a secret path to a place where she meets her lover. The two of them make love, and then they lie back in contentment and exhaustion. During the discussion, attention is called to the surreptitious nature of the affair, the alliteration with the letter *s* to stress the silence and secrecy, the sexual tension and anxiety in the narrator's voice, and the pleasure of anticipation. The highlight takes place in lines 24–25: "amado con amada, / amada en el amado transformada" 'the loved and lover, / the loved one wholly ensouling the lover' ("Noche oscura" [ed. Blecua]; "Dark Night" [trans. Nims]). These lines perfectly capture the intensity of the rhythm of copulation and orgasm ("amado," "amada," "amada," "amado," "transformada"), and the calm intimacy of postcoital relaxation and contemplation.

After some comparison of the erotic theme with other love poetry we have already read (such as that of Garcilaso de la Vega), I summarize the life of the author: his humble origins, his religious vocation in the Carmelite order, his relationship with Teresa of Ávila, his work as a monastic reformer, his mysticism, and his posthumous beatification and canonization. Then I wait for the one question that always, without exception, comes from someone in the class— something along the lines of, If he was such a great religious man, why did he write so graphically about sex? This may be followed by some giggling and cynical speculation about relations between John and Teresa and why it is that priests preach abstinence and chastity but do not practice it themselves. A few students are sometimes made slightly uncomfortable by this turn in the discussion, but most of them enjoy the slightly naughty titillation of the topic.

But, I suggest, maybe there is more to the poem than is at first apparent. Next, I return to the subject of mysticism and make a brief, broad-brush attempt at a description of what the motivating force behind mysticism is—direct, unmediated contact with the divine. Without attempting any detailed description (time is of the essence; I only have one fifty-minute class period), I make a few comments about mystical traditions in Judaism, Islam, and Buddhism, suggesting that it is a widespread, virtually universal human tendency. I comment briefly on Teresa and her graphic descriptions of her own mystical trances, including mention of the angel with the sharp (phallic) arrow thrust into her body and the painful ecstasy the experience produces. Particular attention is drawn to the mind-body dualism inherent in this type of experience: the soul leaves the body, ascends to heaven, and is united directly with God. At this point, the students begin to see the relation, and this brings the subject back to John's poem.

With this, we return to the poem and read it again. This time, everything is symbolic, and a different understanding emerges:

> It is the soul that leaves the dormant body, not the woman who leaves the quiet house.
> The secret path is a (metaphoric) vertical ascent into a realm of the spirit, not a (literal) horizontal journey across land.
> The union is a divine, spiritual one, not a biological, sexual one.
> The beloved is Christ himself, not a human lover.
> The ecstatic feeling is spiritual, not physical.
> The final repose is spiritual grace, not physical satiation.

Some passages that might have been unclear now take on a more meaningful role: the inner light that guides the young woman is her faith and spiritual conviction; the lilies at the end of the poem symbolize innocence and marriage (of the soul with Christ).

In effect, what happens in "Noche oscura" is that one story is told in terms of another one. The literal story is, in effect, the pretext for the metaphoric story.

I explain to students that this is called allegory, the systematic correspondence of one element to another in an extended narrative context so that the story told on the surface is often only a pretext for the (more profound or serious) story told at a deeper level or by implication.

I then discuss John's other poetry, especially his other two poems on the same theme. I summarize his *Cántico espiritual* ("Spiritual Canticle") as a much longer, more detailed allegory of the lover's search for the beloved. Normally, I play at least part of the music compact disc on which Amancio Prada performs the poem, set to his own music. Sometimes a student will remember the biblical Song of Solomon—if not, I bring it up—and I use a passage from that book to show the deep roots of the erotic motif in the Judeo-Christian tradition. John's contemporary Benito Arias Montano (1527–98) is the author of a paraphrase of the Song of Solomon, proof that the ideas of a loving relationship between Christ and the soul was a currently popular one (see the excerpt in the Blecua anthology). Then I turn to John's short poem "Llama de amor viva" ("Living Flame of Love"), usually passing out a copy for on-the-spot reading and discussion. If "Cántico" is a greatly elaborated version of "Noche oscura," "Llama" is nothing but an expansion of its fifth stanza. "Llama" is a series of ecstatic exclamations expressing pain and pleasure. The poem is, in effect, nothing but a description of an orgasm (i.e., the mystical union with the divine).

This leads to a discussion of how and why we tell stories in this complicated, indirect manner. With a little prompting, the students can usually come up with their own examples of such double-layered storytelling: biblical parables, Aesop's fables, novels like George Orwell's *Animal Farm*, films like *The Matrix*. We give some consideration to how effective this type of storytelling is, and I introduce Mark Turner's thesis from his important book *The Literary Mind*—that the basic mode of human cognition is narrative:

> *Story* is a basic principle of mind. Most of our experience, our knowledge, and our thinking is organized as stories. The mental scope of story is magnified by *projection*—one story helps us make sense of another. The projection of one story onto another is *parable*, a basic cognitive principle that shows up everywhere. . . . We interpret every level of our experience by means of parable. . . . Parable is the root of the human mind—of thinking, knowing, acting, creating, and plausibly even of speaking.   (v)

If Turner is right, parable (or, here, allegory) is part of standard, everyday human cognition. The reason authors write one thing in order to communicate another is simply that that is how our mind works. Besides, story is more appealing than sermon. A good story entertains us and lets us draw our own conclusions, while a sermon tends to be explicit. We are active in determining the meaning of a story, and there are more possible ways of interpreting the story.

Again, it is time to go back to the poem. How original was John, I ask, in talking about the soul being a separate nonmaterial entity different from the material body? Almost everyone can draw from personal religious teachings to talk about eternal soul and mortal flesh. The discussion of body and soul often reminds a student of Descartes's distinction between the material body and the immaterial mind (and if no one mentions this, I do), and then we can discuss how mind-body dualism is a fundamental characteristic of Western thought, both religious and secular. To illustrate that John was by no means unique in his metaphors of soul/person and body/house in a religious context, I usually next distribute (if it is not in the text we are using in the class) and discuss Lope de Vega's sonnet about the failure to respond to God's call, "¿Qué tengo yo, que mi amistad procuras?" using Henry Wadsworth Longfellow's English translation. Here, the speaker is in her house, and Christ comes to call on her, exactly opposite of what happens at the beginning of "Noche oscura." An angel, God's messenger, speaks to the inhabitant (the soul) to look out the windows of the house (the eyes of the body) and admit her lover (Christ). She fails to do so, however, and promises to respond tomorrow, only to repeat the same promise the next day. All the important imagery in Lope's "¿Qué tengo yo?" is the same as it is in John's "Noche oscura": house/body, inhabitant/soul, lover/Christ, and so forth. But here the result is diametrically opposed to what happens in the poem by John: the soul never leaves the body; there is no union. Lope is both too cerebral and too human to merge with the divine, while John uses feeling and conviction alone to achieve the greatest of all possible religious experiences. The ultimate mystical experience is not an intellectual one; it is, rather, an emotional and physical one.

If the subject has not already come up during discussion, I attempt to draw out from the students some consideration of the legitimacy of discussing the spiritual relationship with God in terms of sex. Sometimes, a few students are not comfortable with the idea that directly and intensely experiencing God's love can be like having an orgasm. Those students who are willing to talk about their own religious experiences, at least to some degree, will often claim that they have had the feeling of being in direct contact with their God. But I have yet to have a student in one of my classes who claims that he or she has ever had the sort of out-of-body, intense encounter we have been discussing. When pressed to explain how they would describe—in human words and in human terms—what must be the most sublime, profound, and moving spiritual experience that it would be possible for a person to have, they rarely come up with a convincing, compelling description. Then I ask if John's metaphor is not perhaps the most appropriate: having the most direct, intense, personal contact with God is like having an orgasm—that is, like having the most direct, intense, personal contact with another person.

Finally, to convince the students that John's imagery is less original and less controversial than what they might at first have thought, I summarize for the students some recent discoveries in brain research. The neuroscientists Andrew Newberg and Eugene D'Aquili, for example, conducted brain scans on subjects who had induced mystical experiences, and what they found, as they explain in a book cowritten with the science writer Vince Rause, was "solid evidence" that these experiences were accompanied by

> a series of observable neurological events, which, while unusual, are not outside the range of normal brain function. In other words, mystical experience is biologically, observably, and scientifically real.
>
> (Newberg, D'Aquili, and Rause 7)

This led them to ask, "Could evolutionary factors such as sexuality and mating have influenced the biological development of religious ecstasy?" (9). Their answer is affirmative:

> We believe, in fact, that the neurological machinery of transcendence may have arisen from the neural circuitry that evolved for mating and sexual experience. The language of mysticism hints at this connection: Mystics of all times and cultures have used the same expressive terms to describe their ineffable experiences: *bliss, rapture, ecstasy*, and *exaltation*. They speak of losing themselves in a sublime sense of union, of melting into elation, and of the total satisfaction of desires.
>
> We believe it is no coincidence that this is also the language of sexual pleasure. Nor is it surprising, because the very neurological structures and pathways involved in transcendent experience—including the arousal, quiescent, and limbic systems—evolved primarily to link sexual climax to the powerful sensations of orgasm.
>
> The mechanism of orgasm is activated by repetitive, rhythmic stimulation. Significantly, orgasm requires the simultaneous stimulation of both the arousal and quiescent systems. As we have seen, the simultaneous activation of those two systems are intimately involved in the process that sets in motion the mind's machinery of transcendence; mystical union and sexual bliss, therefore, use similar neural pathways.   (125)

The first paragraph seems specifically to summarize what happens in John's poem, but in fact his name is never mentioned in the book. The authors' point is that mystical experiences seem to be a universal part of human biology and cognition. Their comparison of mystical ecstasy with sexual ecstasy, and in particular with an orgasm, makes the imagery in "Noche oscura" more understandable and may justify the mysticism-sex relation. The suggestion, based on neuroscience, is that John used that set of images because it was the most accurate way he could describe what he was experiencing.

Note that D'Aquili and Newberg do not say or even imply (nor does anyone else, as far as I know) that mystical union is nothing but a sexual orgasm. What they say is that many of the same areas of the brain, and many of the same neurotransmitters (brain chemicals) are involved in much the same way. The *feeling* of the mystical union is very much *like* the *feeling* of sexual orgasm. If this is so, as it appears to be, how else to describe the former if not in virtually the same terms as the latter (see also D'Aquili and Newberg, *Mystical Mind*)?

At this point, students are encouraged to consider the possibility that religious experiences of all kinds, and especially mystical experiences, may indeed have a biological and evolutionary explanation. The breathless swoons of Teresa and John may not be direct divine intervention (and certainly are not, as Freud has suggested, some sort of infantile neurotic urge). They may simply be perfectly explainable, if extraordinary, biological processes. Since the rise of cognitive science in the 1960s and the subsequent discoveries of neuroscience, together with what we are learning from neuroimaging (PET scans, functional MRI, and so forth) and recent sophisticated advances in the understanding of human evolution, we in the humanities need to be ready to look to entirely new fields for ways of understanding literary texts. It is our duty to encourage students to read further into these fields as they continue their education in the twenty-first century and not rely on methods and concepts from the nineteenth and twentieth centuries.

If your students are still in doubt about the relation between spirituality and sex, send them to read chapter 74 of Dan Brown's *The Da Vinci Code*. If nothing else convinces them, surely a wildly popular piece of schlock fiction will.

Teresa of Ávila and Ignatius of Loyola: A Gender-Based Approach to Spiritual Autobiography

Darcy Donahue

Although it may seem at first consideration that gender does not figure largely in the mystical goal of union with the divine, in fact the opposite is true. Social norms of masculinity and femininity inevitably affect the individual's vision and experience of mysticism. In the mysticism of Teresa of Ávila and Ignatius of Loyola, contemporaries who did not know each other but who wielded enormous influence on the spirituality and religious politics of their time, a gender-based analysis seems particularly appropriate.[1] In what follows, I provide some suggestions for a comparison of their writing using gender as a primary category of analysis. More specifically, I focus on the ways in which these two powerful icons of mystical spirituality represent their experiences in their autobiographies. While both of these writers offer more than sufficient material for separate analysis, much can be gained from a comparison. The juxtaposition of their voices raises a range of issues that will enable students to understand each writer's mystical identity as influenced by complex social ideologies. The following suggestions are intended for an advanced undergraduate special-topics class on Spanish mysticism but could be adapted to the graduate level or to an advanced-level high school class. The material could compose a two- to three-week section within the larger course.

Before students examine the works themselves, it would be advantageous to engage the class in exploring the larger issue of gender and how it affects writing. Such a discussion might begin with the idea of masculinity and femininity as socially constructed categories of identity and could serve as an introduction to the notion of the gendered voice in writing. The extent of these preliminary considerations would depend on the level of the class but could draw on recent theories of gendered reading and writing. Though written some time ago, the portion of Elaine Showalter's article "Feminist Criticism in the Wilderness" dealing with women's writing and women's culture is still useful in this regard (259–66). Similarly, Mary Mason's study of autobiographical writing by women would contribute to a better understanding of gendered writing.

It would also be important to indicate to students that identity categories are not static but vary widely across time and cultures. This introductory discussion of social identity could lead naturally into background material on the gender ideologies of the early modern period. At this point selected excerpts from texts like Juan Luis Vives's *The Education of a Christian Woman* (the first two or three chapters of book 1 provide a good idea of beliefs concerning the nature of women), Juan Huarte de San Juan's *Examen de ingenios para las ciencias* ("The Examination of Men's Wits"; chapters 19 and 20 explain early modern ideas concerning the biological basis of gender differences), and Luis de Leon's *La perfecta casada* ("The Perfect Wife," introduction and chapter 1) would provide a useful introduction to some of the principal handbooks of gender construction in sixteenth- and seventeenth-century Spain.

Many students, particularly women, may comment that the idea of femininity in these books seems highly misogynistic and will be chagrined to hear that for their time these works were considered liberal in their advocacy of education and increased responsibilities for women. It may be necessary to remind students that what they perceive as blatant misogyny was simply the continuation of Aristotelian notions of gender that still prevailed, if not always in practice, at least in theory. Not all women were constrained by the rigid confines of femininity set forth in this prescriptive literature, but the final effect of such literature was to reinforce existing gender roles. Certainly women's roles at the time were limited in ways that are not easily conceivable for college-age women, who are used to the idea that they can have both career and family. For the women of Teresa's day and social class, the choice was family or career, and the career was religious. The convent, surprising as it may seem to today's students, was often a supportive community in which women could express their artistic, intellectual, and spiritual inclinations, as Electa Arenal and Stacey Schlau have demonstrated in their excellent studies of convent culture ("'Leyendo yo'"; *Untold Sisters*).

While a life in religion may seem somewhat alien to modern readers, it was the all-consuming passion of both Ignatius and Teresa, whose evolution as mystics and religious reformers was similar in some ways and widely divergent in others. The similarities, such as the desire to reform and to imitate the lives of the saints as closely as possible, are certainly the product of the fervently religious culture in which they lived as well as personal inclination. The ways in which they went about carrying out their goals, particularly in their interaction with authorities, both secular and religious, undoubtedly reflect their socialization as woman and man. Similarly, their writing, particularly their writing of self, reveals a discourse that is conditioned by contemporary expectations concerning language, self-representation, and a gendered identity. Although both saints wrote many kinds of texts, the autobiographies are probably the most engaging for the undergraduate student and provide ample material for analysis. The reasons for writing and the actual construction of the works themselves are as good a way as any to begin discussing how the two life narratives reflect the influence of early modern attitudes about men, women, and religious authority. The origins and evolution of the texts raise many questions about the nature of life writing and the literary fashioning of a mystical identity, male or female. There are significant differences between the two works with regard to these issues.

Ignatius's story formed a link in the chain of memoirs that would compose a history of the Society of Jesus and provide exemplary lives of the founding fathers for the edification of future members. Ignatius did not actually write his life at all but rather dictated it to a handpicked associate, the Portuguese Jesuit Luis Gonçalves da Câmara, who took notes and then dictated it to an amanuensis, who in turn wrote the final version.[2] Of the eleven chapters, the first eight were written from Câmara's notes by a Spanish scribe in Rome, and the last three were originally written in Italian by a different scribe. This process of dictation, note taking, dictation, and transcription began in 1553 and continued for a period of over two years. Although Câmara states that he faithfully transcribed the Jesuit general's exact words, his own intervention and that of the anonymous scribes create a double layer between the source and the reader that inevitably distances the latter from the source himself. The resulting narrative is the third-person account of Ignatius's conversion to a life of mystical spirituality and the years following it, a work that originally had no title but has come to be known as *Autobiografía* (*Autobiography*), *Relato del peregrino* (*The Pilgim's Story*), *Memoria* (*Memoir*), and *Confesión* (*Confession*).

It is worth noting that Ignatius was the last of the Jesuit founders to tell his story and that he had read the memoirs of his associates before he dictated his own. One of these memoirs, written by Juan Polanco, was itself based on information that Ignatius had given him during their years together, so in essence Ignatius may have been reworking his own previous oral versions. The Jesuit memoirs and the hagiographies that were prime reading at the time are powerful subtexts of Ignatius's account. Having pointed out these aspects of the work's creation, it would be useful to ask students for their reaction. Is this really an autobiography? Why or why not? Did Ignatius even tell his own story? How important is it that his sources and reading public are male?

The origins of *El libro de la vida* (*Life*) reveal some of the differences between Teresa's text and that of Ignatius. As occurred with so many other religious women authors, the writing itself was not entirely voluntary but rather an act of obedience mandated by Teresa's confessors when she was close to fifty years old, after she had been experiencing mystical visions for many years. As Alison Weber has convincingly established in her now classic analysis of Teresa's rhetoric of femininity, though her confessors were not necessarily hostile to her experiences, her awareness of their eventual scrutiny conditioned her narration (*Teresa of Ávila*). This brings to the fore the question of readers and their expectations and the narrator's awareness of both, which is clearly different for Teresa and Ignatius. For students to better understand the nature of the reader-narrator relationship in Teresa, in which the first readers will not be admiring exdisciples and associates of the same sex as in Ignatius but rather suspicious authorities who have the power to determine the acceptability of one's most intense spiritual experiences, I strongly recommend that they read and discuss the first two chapters of Weber's book, which remains the best source for understanding the power differential involved and the rhetorical strategies that result from it. If time allows, even before reading these chapters, students could undertake a short writing exercise in which they imagine themselves in such a situation, attempting to explain a certain action to a skeptical listener of the other sex, perhaps a parent. How would their awareness of their own sex and the sex of their potential censor affect what they tell? What might they say differently if the censor were of the same sex? Why?

Issues of writer, reader, and literary and religious authority will remain central as students begin to read the works themselves. The narratives differ enormously in tone, structure, and content, and the best way for students to see this is to read them in juxtaposition. Although it is always preferable to read works in their entirety, doing so would not be necessary in order to compare the two lives. Teresa's text is much longer and recounts her life from childhood through the foundation of the first Discalced Carmelite convent in a total of forty chapters. Ignatius's story begins when he is twenty-six, after he had been wounded in the French siege of Pamplona in 1521 and continues through his mystical conversion to the confirmation of the Jesuit order in eleven chapters of varying length. The class could read chapter 1 of *Autobiography* and chapter 1 of *Life* for the first reading assignment as a way of juxtaposing the two texts from the outset.

Beginnings are important because they create a first impression of how each writer views her or his career and the autobiography itself. In reading the first chapters of these works, students should be encouraged to look for the obvious differences, which also reflect subtle divergences in experience and vision. What is the effect of the impersonal third-person narrator in *Autobiography*, and how does it affect our understanding of Ignatius's story to know that he referred to himself as "the pilgrim?" Are we aware that he is dictating and not writing? According to Cámara, Ignatius had originally intended to tell "about his whole life and his youthful escapades clearly and distinctly" (Ignatius, *Autobiography* 16). Although it is not clear whether Ignatius himself chose to eliminate these details or, as Joseph F. O'Callaghan suggests, Cámara omitted them because he did not deem them relevant to the narrative (16n2), the absence of any reference to his childhood is significant. How does this absence affect our understanding of his life?

Ignatius's experience of physical injury—his leg was maimed in battle—was clearly the catalyst for his conversion, and his description of the excruciating pain and his endurance of it in chapter 1 bespeak a preoccupation with the masculine values of physical strength and valor that were evident in his career as a soldier and continue in his religious career. What do these values tell us about Ignatius's self-concept? As his story progresses, it becomes evident that Cámara and presumably Ignatius are reducing the details to a minimum, focusing on physical movement and the exterior social world at least as much as the complex spiritual metamorphosis that the young soldier experienced while convalescing from his fractured leg.

Students should be encouraged to imagine what is being excluded from this collaborative narration and for what possible reasons and should keep in mind that all narrators are conscious of possible reader reactions and that Ignatius (and his transcribers), like Teresa, was aware that he was narrating for posterity as well as contemporary readers. In her excellent study of the autobiography, Marjorie O'Rourke Boyle maintains that Loyola employs an epideictic rhetoric in which the primary purpose is to praise God rather than convey personal information. The intent of this rhetoric is "the persuasion of judgment. Its import was moral not empirical. . . . The Jesuits had petitioned an explanation from Loyola of how the Lord had governed him. Like Augustine he responded as a prudent confessor of values" (*Loyola's Acts* 3).

Teresa's work begins with a prologue acknowledging her obedience to her confessors and recognizing the work as divinely ordained. The focus of her first chapter is her parents and her pious upbringing as the source of her early religious inclination. She recounts her childhood desire to imitate the martyr saints and also the effect of her mother's death. The details of family life in this and the following chapters communicate a relational capacity and the impact of home and family that is mostly absent from Ignatius's narrative. Furthermore, these initial chapters provide important insights into the social and emotional environment that contributed to Teresa's spirituality. The writer herself clearly considers her childhood and adolescence as inseparable from her subsequent development. Instead of the rupture with a previous self suggested by Ignatius's elimination of his preconversion life, Teresa seems to be indicating that her religious vocation is the natural consequence of her early years.

The first chapter ends with a characteristic topos; the author addresses God directly, recognizing her own unworthiness. As Weber has observed, this humility topos was part of Teresa's larger defensive rhetoric of femininity, and the consequence of her status as woman, mystic, and conversa.[3] Repeated references to her gender form part of this rhetoric (Weber, *Teresa of Ávila*, esp. ch. 2). It would be worth asking students to consider Ignatius's book from the perspective of overt recognition of gender. Does the narrator make any reference to the importance of the pilgrim's sex as part of his self-concept? Does he ever use topics of humility? If so, in what contexts?

The conversion from a worldly to a spiritual existence that is at the center of the mystical experience is narrated in the first chapter of *Autobiography* with the same spareness of language and seeming lack of emotion that characterize the work as a whole. The narrator describes a vision of the Virgin Mary that marked the critical turning point:

> Estando una noche despierto, vido claramente una imagen de nuestra Señora con el santo Niño Jesús, con cuya vista por espacio notable recibió consolación muy excesiva y quedó con tanto asco de toda la vida pasada, y especialmente de cosas de carne, que le parecían habérsele quitado del ánima todas las especies que antes tenía en ella pintadas. Así, desde aquella hora hasta el agosto de 53, que esto se escribe, nunca mas tuvo ni un mínimo consenso en cosas de carne. . . .   (*Autobiografía* 64)

> While he was awake one night, he saw clearly an image of Our Lady and the holy child Jesus. From this sight he received for a considerable time very great consolation and he was left with such loathing for his whole past life and especially things of the flesh, that it seemed that all the fantasies

he had pictured in his mind were driven from it. Thus, from that hour until August of 1553, when this was written, he never made the slightest consent to things of the flesh. . . .   (*Autobiography* 24–25)

He continues to mention that this interior or spiritual change is recognized by members of his family in his interaction with them. Again, given the significance of this event for the rest of his life, the condensation and scarcity of detail are surprising yet utterly in keeping with the rest of the narrative.

It should be interesting for the class to compare the above description with Teresa's more gradual conversion experience. Before doing so, however, it would be appropriate to read Saint Augustine's moment of final conversion as he describes it in *Confessions* (bk. 8, ch. 12), because it was widely considered the paradigm for such experiences and because Teresa mentions *Confessions* as a decisive influence in her own conversion. Yet unlike the experience described by Augustine, as Carol Slade observes, there is no real "turning point" in Teresa's story but rather a series of situations that progressively intensify and seem to culminate in chapter 9 in her emotional reaction to a statue of the passion of Christ (*St. Teresa* 35). If Ignatius's account is terse, Teresa communicates the emotional intensity of this incident:

> Acaecióme que entrando un día en el oratorio, vi una imagen que havían traído allí a guardar, que se havía buscado para cierta fiesta que se hacía en casa. Era de Cristo muy llagado, y tan devota, que en mirándola, toda me turbó de verle tal, porque representava bien lo que pasó por nosotros. Fue tanto lo que sentí de lo mal que havía agradecido aquellas llagas, que el Corazón me parece se me partía, y arrojéme cabe Él con grandísimo derramamiento de lágrimas, suplicándole me fortaleciese ya de una vez para no ofenderle.
>
> (*Obras completas* [ed. Éfren de la Madre de Dios and Steggink] 53)

> It happened to me that one day entering the oratory I saw a statue they had borrowed for a certain feast to be celebrated in the house. It represented the much wounded Christ and was very devotional so that beholding it I was utterly distressed in seeing Him that way, for it well represented what He suffered for us. I felt so keenly aware of how poorly I thanked Him for those wounds that, it seems to me, my heart broke. Beseeching Him to strengthen me once and for all that I might not offend Him I threw myself down before Him with the greatest outpouring of tears.
>
> (*Collected Works* 1: 100–01)

Despite the relative suddenness of this occurrence, it does not resolve Teresa's conversion: it is one more step in an ongoing process rather than the single life-changing incident of the Augustinian model. In fact, Ignatius's vision of the Virgin is much closer to Augustine's conversion experience. According to Caroline Bynum, "When women recount their own lives, the themes are less climax, conversion, reintegration, and triumph . . . than continuity" ("Women's Stories" 108). At this point students could consider why the patterns of conversion might differ. How do norms of gender and lived experiences condition women to perceive their lives as process rather than a series of discrete events characterized by triumph or defeat?

Specific visions in the works might also be compared. Students find diabolical encounters interesting for many reasons—the obvious fascination that evil and its manifestations continue to hold, the fact that even such saintly figures do not escape temptations and doubts, and the saints' constant awareness of the "enemy" as a tangible presence in their lives. Teresa's oft-cited dream journey to hell in chapter 32 is a graphic account of the physical horrors of the damned. It was undoubtedly influenced by contemporary visual representations and is one of many instances in which the saint admits to finding words inadequate to describe experience. At the undergraduate level, before reading this passage students could be asked to write their own brief imagination of hell to compare it with that of Teresa. It would also be helpful to use one of Hieronymus Bosch's horrific paintings (or another visual image) to illustrate how closely Teresa's description reflects contemporary popular images of the infernal. Throughout her *Life*, Teresa depicts herself as beset by doubts concerning the source of her visions and the decision to leave her original convent community and occasionally attributes these misgivings to the devil.

Ignatius experiences a more seductive vision of the diabolical. It occurs in chapter 3, which recounts his stay at Manresa, during which "the pilgrim" apparently experienced suicidal thoughts or temptations. The vision, "que tenía forma de serpiente, y tenía muchas cosas que resplandecían como ojos, aunque no eran" 'seemed to him to have the form of a serpent with many things that shone like eyes, though they were not eyes' (*Autobiografía* 75; *Autobiography* 33), initially delights him, but it becomes evident that its source is evil. The vision recurs and is often accompanied by Ignatius's grave doubts concerning his vocation and the difficulty of his chosen life. He recognizes that this is a form of the devil appearing to him and chases it away with a staff. Unlike Teresa's many references to the possible intervention of the devil throughout her career, this is Ignatius's only allusion to such a presence. The impression created is that it was a temporary and ultimately surmountable hindrance to his spiritual progress. It was, however, a vision that remained with him for several years, according to W. W. Meissner (342). Furthermore, Ignatius's *Spiritual Exercises* (first week, exercise five) contains a meditation on hell that is similar to Teresa's vision ([ed. Mullan] 26). Ignatius has clearly chosen to minimize the influence of the demonic in *Autobiography*. Using their supplementary readings, students could compare possible reasons for this decision with Teresa's frequent references to the devil and discuss how this difference might be gender related.

Both works conclude with the founding of new religious orders that represents the culmination of the saints' career as religious visionaries and activists. In both cases the founders experienced personal hardships and even persecution as a result of their reformist activities. Teresa describes the experience of founding the convent of Saint Joseph's in Ávila, the first Discalced Carmelite convent, in chapters 32–36 of *Life*. She is careful to present the varied tribulations of the foundation as indications of its divine ordination rather than to focus on the highly political and personal nature of the attacks she suffered from various sources. Students may be surprised to learn that as seemingly praiseworthy a project as religious reform involved such worldly concerns. For historical background on the religious and political climate of Ávila before and including the Saint Joseph's foundation, I recommend Jodi Bilinkoff's *The Ávila of St. Teresa* and chapters 1 and 2 of *Teresa of Ávila and the Politics of Sanctity* by Gillian Ahlgren. Bilinkoff provides a detailed analysis of the sociocultural conditions that made Ávila ripe for the type of reform that Teresa enacted, while the Ahlgren chapters focus more on the gender politics of religious orthodoxy and Teresa's reform.

Ignatius's narrative also ends with some degree of success, the confirmation of the Society of Jesus. As in the case of Teresa, however, this seeming triumph occurs only after he has undergone considerable personal anguish; he underwent an inquisitorial investigation and trial for suspicions of Illuminist heresies, and at one point he was prohibited from preaching. In a letter to one of his principal female benefactors, Isabel Roser, Ignatius describes these tribulations in more detail than in *Autobiography* (*Letters* 97–101). For instructors who wish to read more about the historical context of Ignatius and the founding of the Jesuit order, I recommend works by Cándido de Dalmases and by John W. O'Malley, who offers an excellent study of the company's founding in *The First Jesuits*.

An interesting point of comparison in the difficulties encountered by each writer-narrator is their interaction with the opposite sex. Given the patriarchal structure of secular and religious culture in early modern Spain, it is an interaction that is heavily weighted in favor of the male in terms of authority and voice. Teresa voices her dissatisfaction with confessors on numerous occasions and even expresses openly the idea that women are more favored by God for piety than men. Similarly, at the end of chapter 10 of her autobiography, she counterposes the experience of interior prayer to pure erudition, the domain of men. Cumulatively these passages constitute Teresa's dissent from the absolute authority exercised by the male religious establishment. Students could discuss the implications of such passages. What effect might such statements have on male readers? Female readers? How does she soften her critique of religious power relations? In chapter 5, Teresa provides evidence of her own spiritual superiority over her confessor in the town of Becedas. Through the power of her religious conviction and her commitment to his salvation as well as her savvy understanding of popular culture, she saves him from what seems to be a spell cast on him by his lover. Students will enjoy this episode for its clever inversion of the roles of confessor and penitent and its rather salacious content.

Ignatius benefited enormously from wealthy women followers and patrons, yet he was also viewed with suspicion as a result of his role as spiritual counselor and teacher to women.[4] He was well aware of the dangers that such contact might entail and this was undoubtedly one of the key factors in his decision not to admit women to the Jesuit order. While in Rome and subject to the scrutiny of the Inquisition, he even advised his closest followers that they must not be spiritual counselors to any but women of the highest social rank. His own experience with a number of women had brought him under suspicion of sexual misconduct and, despite his obvious financial and emotional dependence on several female supporters, he clearly adheres to existing stereotypes of the female as a source of temptation and weakness.[5] Whereas Teresa must deal with men as superiors and powerbrokers, Ignatius can choose the women with whom he will associate. Since the references to women in *Autobiography* are brief and uninformative, students might enjoy reading some letters between Ignatius and women of varied backgrounds and intentions. Hugo Rahner's edition of Ignatius's letters to women provides a useful introductory analysis of the different types of correspondence (*Letters*). Teresa's correspondence with male counselors and confessors would also be of interest in considering the gender politics of religious activism. The transcriptions are available in Spanish in Efrén de la Madre de Dios and Otger Steggink's edition *Obras completas* and can be consulted in the English translation by Kieran Kavanaugh in *Collected Letters*.

It should be apparent from the readings that both Teresa and Ignatius were subject to official scrutiny and control. As a way of concluding their comparative analysis, students could read the *censura* of *Life* by the Dominican friar Domingo Báñez.[6] Teresa, writing from obedience, clearly did some self-censorship, but her text was still subject to the approval of the male arbiters of orthodoxy. How do Báñez's comments reflect establishment attitudes about women visionaries and their writing? Ignatius's self-surveillance is also evident, though in a somewhat different fashion from that of Teresa. At the very end of *Autobiography,* Câmara enters in the first person to recount his unsuccessful attempt to obtain Ignatius's personal writings concerning the Jesuit *Constitutions.* We can conclude from his refusal to provide Câmara with the requested documents that the Jesuit general was very concerned about the possible consequences of making his personal writings available, perhaps rightly so, given the suppression of his autobiography ten years after its publication. What evidence does his *Autobiography* provide of self-censorship? At this point students could act as censors-critics. What more would they like to know about each writer's mystical experiences? What questions would they like to ask them? If time allows, they might even imagine a conversation between these two great mystics and reformers. They would have had much to say to each other.

NOTES

[1] Although Teresa never met Ignatius, she was deeply influenced by her many Jesuit confessors. For an overview and bibliography on the topic, see the entry for Jesuits in *Diccionario de Santa Teresa* (Álvarez).

[2] For an analysis of the interaction between Câmara and Ignatius during the recitation, see Boyle's introduction to *Loyola's Acts* (8–21).

[3] For a study of Teresa's Jewish ancestry, see Márquez Villanueva, "Santa Teresa y el linaje."

[4] For an interesting comparison of Teresa and Ignatius as spiritual directors of women, see Raitt.

[5] There are a number of intriguing studies of the relation between the early Jesuits and women. See, for example, Bilinkoff, "Many 'Lives'"; Hufton; and O'Malley, *First Jesuits* (147–49).

[6] Báñez did not, in fact, censure Teresa on doctrinal or theological grounds, although he warned against the circulation of her writing.

Teaching Imagery and Allegory in Teresa of Ávila's *The Interior Castle*

Joan Cammarata

Preeminent among mystical writers, Teresa of Ávila is perhaps the simplest, most natural, and yet most accurate narrator of personal experiences in the various degrees of spiritual life. Teresa is foundress of the reformed Discalced Carmelite order, and her doctrine of mystical teachings has come to be known as the Carmelite school of spirituality. She emphasizes mysticism as a way of life, not as a singular ecstatic experience. In obedience to her confessors, Teresa writes of her progress in the spiritual life so that she may transform her personal experience into a collective spiritual teaching. For this reason she is recognized as a "psychagogue," a leader of souls (Hatzfeld 19). Teresa's *Moradas del castillo interior* (*The Interior Castle* [1577]) develops the ideas of her major works, *El libro de la vida* (*The Book of Her Life* [1562]) and *Camino de perfección* (*The Way of Perfection* [1565]). Written when her *Life* was sequestered by the Inquisition and unavailable to her followers, *The Interior Castle* is the most mature expression of her intimate spiritual experience. Teresa provides her sisters a masterful allegorical account of the soul's journey in prayer through seven dwellings of a castle to reach the innermost chamber, which represents the mystical marriage of the soul-bride with the Christ-bridegroom, the ecstatic union with God.[1]

The topic of mysticism can be intimidating to students in the twenty-first century, who require a framework that contextualizes mysticism in relation to the Spanish Inquisition, the Council of Trent, and the Counter-Reformation. John H. Elliott's *Imperial Spain* provides an excellent overview of the historical situation. Students should know that Teresa's reform was in part motivated by the threat of Protestantism. Teresa urges her contemplative nuns to be an army of women who oppose the Reformation in northern Europe. Their mission is to fight evil from within and temptation from without through their life of prayer, as Philip II enjoined Spaniards to do in 1561. Teresa realized that a mission of prayer was the only apostolic mission available to women in the mid–sixteenth century. The Council of Trent (1545–63) imposed strict enclosure on all religious women, thus excluding them from public preaching and an active apostolate in the world. Teresa expresses distress over these restrictions in *The Interior Castle* (dwelling 6, ch. 6), but in *The Way of Perfection* (chs. 1–3) she had already conceived of an alternative apostolate of prayer for her sisters. They were to be the elite soldiers who fight to save souls through prayer from inside the cloister as the Catholic armies and clergy fight in the outside world to defend the church from schism. Teresa exhorts her cloistered nuns to be strong like men not weak like women and to use their contemplative lives of prayer to convert souls by their example. Students can be assigned Jodi Bilinkoff's essay

"Woman with a Mission: Teresa of Ávila and the Apostolic Model," which lays out this fundamental background succinctly.

Students are often surprised to learn that Teresa is not a visionary who is remote from the work of the world but a mystic who moves from the private sphere of contemplative prayer out to the public sphere of intense social involvement in her reform (Donnelly 126). In 1970 Pope Paul VI named Teresa the first woman Doctor of the Church and praised her in his homily as "a most congenial and fecund author, master of the spiritual life, incomparable contemplative and indefatigably active." Students will enjoy reading Carole Slade's excellent essay on Teresa as a social reformer.

Most of our students are already sensitive to issues of gender politics that address patriarchal attitudes toward women, and they soon realize that Teresa recognizes the marginalized status of women, whether lay or religious, in her society. The spiritual life of enclosure does offer religious women a different kind of freedom, the emancipation from family and societal obligations. Paradoxically, the church provides the conditions for Teresa to achieve that which a secular woman of her time could never have accomplished. Students are aware of women's exclusion from leadership positions in the church today, and they can learn more about the church's subordination of women in Mary Daly's classic study, *The Church and the Second Sex.*

When students are asked about their impressions of convent life in Teresa's time, their notions are mostly informed by contemporary reality. They are amazed that often women who were not able to marry entered the convent without any vocation for the spiritual life. The first convent that Teresa lived in, La Encarnación in Ávila, was similar to a hotel for women, with worldly amenities and class distinctions. The laxity of the Carmelite order permitted the more aristocratic nuns to live in the relative comfort of their own quarters with their servants or slaves and to receive visitors of both sexes. Teresa's reform restored the primitive Carmelite rule and imposed a vow of radical poverty. She always disapproved of those who boasted of their illustrious lineage (perhaps in recognition of her converso origins) and recommended detachment from family identity and rank: "Let the sister who is of the highest birth speak of her father least; we must all be equals" (*Complete Works* 2: 112 [*Way of Perfection*]).

Students can also appreciate how Teresa's writing is circumscribed by gender. In the persona of an obedient nun, Teresa functions within ideological cultural conventions when she calls on the stereotypes of feminine passivity and psychological fragility. Yet at other times she asserts herself with bold self-confidence. In her writings, Teresa reiterates her good faith by constant professions of loyalty to the doctrines of the church. She attributes any errors to her ignorance and proclaims her willingness to be corrected. This circumspection, often expressed through humility topoi, is not only an acknowledgment of her supposedly inferior status as a woman but also possibly a recollection of another aspect of cultural otherness, her Jewish ancestry. While Teresa makes no explicit reference to her Jewish heritage in any of her writings, it is worthwhile to explain that

Teresa's lineage and her role as reformer put her in a doubly precarious position in an environment where it was necessary to avoid investigation by an Inquisition suspicious of so-called New Christians.

Teresa avoids censure in her writings by negotiating a space for female speech through rhetorical strategies that garner acceptance by the male ecclesiastical hierarchy. An essential and indispensable text for students to become familiar with Teresa's gender-inflected rhetoric is Alison Weber's *Teresa of Ávila and the Rhetoric of Femininity*; chapter 4 of this study is devoted to the *The Interior Castle*. Teresa's professed incompetence as she narrates her personal experiences in the various degrees of spiritual life is what Weber terms a "rhetoric of obfuscation," which Teresa uses to conceal her choice of erotic and sensual imagery in the spiritual marriage (99). Students become adept at identifying Teresa's references to the inadequacies of women and her rhetorical strategies that express uncertainty, such as "it seems to me" and related phrases, which she repeatedly uses to avert patriarchal criticism.

Teresa's language is accessible to students. They relate to the images, as Teresa hoped her original readers would, and they respond to the personal intimacy, simplicity, and sincerity of her expression. Students can be familiarized with the commonplace gender stereotypes of Teresa's time that associated women with the sewing needle and men with the pen. According to much prescriptive literature of her day, only men could produce authoritative written discourses, while women were consigned to silence or identified with unreliable oral discourse. In their reading of the prologue to *The Interior Castle*, students see that Teresa herself appeals to the association between women and orality when she says that she will "speak" with her sisters while she writes. Her sisters will better understand prayer, she claims, if another woman who shares their language explains it to them in a way appropriate for her nuns.

We should inquire why Teresa writes as if she were having a discussion with her community. She adopts the conversational mode of a mentor and spiritual director, thus drawing readers to her. Considering her own prayer a conversation with God, Teresa engages her sisters in an imaginary dialogue with colloquial spontaneity to catch their attention. This method would have been especially effective if the text were read aloud, as was often the custom in monastic communities. In her role as a spiritual teacher, Teresa relies on repetition to allow readers to assimilate her ideas and to reassure herself they have done so. Students who wish to explore Teresa's style and imagery can consult Víctor García de la Concha's landmark study, *El arte literario de Santa Teresa* and Elizabeth Howe's *Mystical Imagery: Santa Teresa de Jesús and San Juan de la Cruz*.

Teresa's mystical journey is formalized in the architectonic symbol of a diamond castle with numerous concentric rooms that represent the different stages in the development of contemplative prayer. Students can be asked to describe their own ideas of how a castle is constructed. This prepares them to understand how Teresa's choice of the imagery of the seven dwellings of the castle has a pedagogical role and an organizational function. Teresa simplifies for her sisters a way of remembering the successive stages in the evolution of the interior life. As Michael Gerli points out, architectural metaphors constituted an important mnemonic technique in Teresa's day; Teresa uses the seven rooms of the castle to help the nuns visualize and remember the different levels of prayer. Students will also profit from Joseph Chorpenning's lucid essay "The Literary and Theological Method of the *Interior Castle*."

In the circular edifice of the castle where Teresa's soul will have its transformation from sinful mortal to bride of Christ, the students are introduced to Teresa's secondary images for the soul, such as the tree of life, the pearl, the palmetto bush, and the silkworm, whose metamorphosis into the butterfly introduces the bridal imagery. In Teresa's love mysticism, two become one but retain their identity as two: the flames of two candles join into one but recover their singularity. If the scope of the course permits, teachers can use the image of the flames to present the concept of theistic mysticism, in which there is differentiated unity, in contrast to monistic mysticism, in which there is a total fusion with God. Like Teresa's sisters, students can be guided through the didactic exposition of the seven dwelling places to discover the three phases of mystical theology: purgative, illuminative, and unitive. Students will benefit from exploring specific studies on Teresa's mysticism: Edgar Allison Peers's *Studies of the Spanish Mystics* and Deirdre Green's *Gold in the Crucible*.

I prefer to spend less class time on the first dwellings of the castle and devote most time on dwellings 5 through 7, where the interpretation of imagery is vital to an understanding of the mystical way. It is appropriate to assist the students with the key points of each dwelling to ensure comprehension before they proceed to integrate the textual analysis with their personal views.

In dwellings 1 and 2, Teresa illustrates the purgative state in which humankind is cleansed of sin by sacraments and the voluntary denial of passions through the practice of prayer. The third and fourth dwellings show the passive purification of the soul and enlightenment of the mind in the illuminative stage. The prayer of recollection prepares the soul to listen to God in the prayer of quiet, wherein the faculties of the soul and consciousness are suspended and the betrothal of the soul and God begins.

The unitive stage is reached in the fifth through seventh dwellings. The fifth dwelling compares the prayer of union with spiritual betrothal. For Teresa, there is an interior and intuitive knowing, but there is an inability to express either the nature of God or the exact quality of the experience of knowing. Teresa speaks of the spiritual transformation of the prayer of union by using the metaphor of the silkworm that dies in its cocoon to produce the butterfly. Through this metaphor Teresa teaches her sisters to relinquish self-love and self-will and practice detachment. Students find the silkworm's passage from larval to pupal stage a convincing explanation for the mystical experience. Like a moth drawn to the flame, the soul-butterfly will later, in the seventh dwelling, go toward the symbolic light of Christ to achieve purification by the fire of love in mystical marriage.

The sixth dwelling is the dwelling of spiritual betrothal, in which mystical phenomena—such as locutions, visions, raptures, ecstasy, and trance—are experienced through interior senses with greater frequency. Teresa admonishes against false visions engendered by the devil throughout the work. Students might inquire why Teresa is so anxious about spiritual delusions. They find the answer in the historical moment: incidences of fraudulent visions are detrimental to the reform and arouse the suspicion of the Inquisition.

In the seventh dwelling Teresa experiences the spiritual marriage, the final stage of mystical union where she is inseparably united with Christ in the deepest center of the soul. For the Christian mystics, whose contemplation of the Incarnate Christ is an essential element of spiritual perfection, the union as bridegroom-Christ and bride-soul is best expressed in human terms, in the language of passion and carnal love in a spiritual marriage consummated with the kiss that unites the soul to the bridegroom.

Occasionally students express uneasiness and disapproval over this use of erotic language to denote the sacred union with God. Those who have strict conservative religious training even consider such language irreverent. After a discussion that explores the tradition of idealized human love as expressed in the courtly love tradition of the sentimental romance and in books of chivalry, which Teresa read, the apprehensive students become more engaged. It is helpful to explain that the tension between celibacy and the use of erotic language is one of the distinguishing marks of Christian mysticism. The conventions of human love and the language of sexuality can then make sense as a mystical language of suggestion to concretize the human relation with God.

Students benefit from some knowledge of the long tradition of Christian nuptial mysticism. I point out that Origen, the second-century theologian and biblical commentator, legitimated erotic imagery in Christian mysticism by transforming the language of love to serve the mystical path to God, identifying the kiss with the gift of the Holy Spirit that Christ the bridegroom bestows on his bride, the soul. The language of profane love is further justified for students when they learn that Teresa takes her inspiration from Bernard of Clairvaux, the twelfth-century Cistercian whose unfinished eighty-six sermons on the Song of Songs draw from the medieval tradition of allegorical interpretation. Scriptural commentators designate the kiss of transforming union as the pinnacle of communion with God. Teresa deletes the *ad litteram* sense of the corporeal images to provide only the spiritual meaning for her sisters. This is another opportunity to rely on Weber's explanation of a "rhetoric of obfuscation" to show how Teresa masks the risky erotic imagery of the spiritual marriage with conflicting comparisons. Some suggested background readings on the traditions of nuptial mysticism and of the allegorical exegesis of commentary include Bernard McGinn's *The Foundations of Mysticism* and his "The Language of Love in Christian and Jewish Mysticism"; Irving Singer, *The Nature of Love*; and Nicolas Perella, *The Kiss Sacred and Profane*.

Teresa's pedagogical goal is to teach her religious community how to live an integrated spiritual life by the example of her own inner spiritual journey. The students in our literature courses are mainly Catholic; however, not all of them have been instructed in Christian doctrine. Students are generally forthcoming and comfortable sharing their religious beliefs. The study of *The Interior Castle* becomes student-centered through group discussions that address how this self-knowledge is relevant to students' personal lives. The topics I have used include the following: Are there parallels with Teresa's emotions in the students' own lives? Can students' personal experiences in spirituality, or lack of them, be related or connected to the readings? Since Teresa's journey acknowledges the struggle between Christ and the devil (temporal pleasures), do the students see this journey as the more familiar battle between good and evil that individuals fight against their natural instincts? Why have Teresa's spiritual values and teachings had a lasting impact on subsequent generations? Some students who are also studying psychology are interested in exploring the human conditions that have been ascribed to the psychological states of the mystics (for example, introspection, hysteria, depression, melancholy, delirium, and euphoria).

The scope of the course and the abilities of the students will determine the amount and depth of the material that will work. If the entire text of *The Interior Castle* cannot be covered, the reading can be successfully limited.[2] My students read this text in Spanish in undergraduate Spanish literature courses that include native and nonnative, upper- and lower-level students, so achievement can vary based on each student's degree of experience in language comprehension and critical analysis. I recommend that students read for context and avoid the English translations of the text because this is a Spanish literature course. However, they are encouraged to bring up any linguistic concerns during class and, of course, they know that translations are available.

The subject matter of mysticism can be overwhelming for students. I have found that they work best with unfamiliar concepts when provided with questions such as these that guide their reading and give them direction for class discussion:

> What is the relevance of Teresa's mystical writings in the context of her reform of the Carmelite order? (Students will more readily grasp the historical moment of Teresa's reform by consulting Bilinkoff's *The Ávila of Saint Teresa*.)
>
> How does Teresa fulfill her role as spiritual director and mystical psychagogue?
>
> In her guidance and directives for attaining spiritual perfection, how does Teresa counsel her readers to achieve detachment and to attain humility and the love of God?

What is the social status of women in sixteenth-century Spain? What are the dynamics of being a woman writer in Teresa's society and what rhetorical strategies give women a voice?

How can the knowledge of God be communicated through finite words and figurative language when it is only revealed in the spiritual sense of intuition?

What images and symbolism from the natural world does Teresa use to describe her spiritual journey and ultimate union?

How does the metamorphosis of the silkworm illustrate the prayer of union?

How does Teresa's spiritual quest to achieve union with God find expression through the image of the castle and the traditional symbolism of spiritual marriage?

Is human carnal love a proper or appropriate explanation for religious experience that is only spiritual?

How would you present the ineffable as a reflection of reality?

Personal reflection helps students internalize the material and share their perceptions. Students write a few sentences on each dwelling about something they learned, liked or disliked, a personal experience, a comparison with another work, or a feeling that is similar to the content of the work. These reflections, read at the beginning of class, constitute a course journal that is collected at the end of the semester. The benefit is that it requires the student to write every day and to record and share a personal interpretation of the material. These thoughtful contributions often initiate productive conversations among students.

By following this approach to the study of Teresa's *The Interior Castle*, students come to appreciate and comprehend Teresa's pedagogical methodology, the distinctiveness of women's writing, and the problematic nature of mysticism.[3]

NOTES

[1] "Moradas" is sometimes translated as "mansions." I follow the usage of Kavanaugh and Rodríguez, who prefer "dwellings."

[2] Recommended sections include the prologue and dwellings 1 (ch. 1); 4 (chs. 1–3); 5 (chs. 1–3); 6 (chs. 4–6, 8–9); 7 (chs. 1–2, 4); epilogue.

[3] This essay was written before I was aware of Ahlgren's *Entering Teresa of Ávila's Interior Castle: A Reader's Companion*. Her study will certainly be of interest to teachers of this text.

Teaching Teresa's *Libro de las fundaciones* (*The Book of Foundations*)

Helen H. Reed

Teresa of Ávila's's last work, *Libro de las fundaciones* (*The Book of Foundations*) is often said to be her least read and is presumably her least taught.[1] What an undeserved neglect! As Alison Weber demonstrates, it is Teresa's most ironic and humorous text (*Teresa of Ávila* 123–57). Here Teresa narrates the founding of fifteen Discalced Carmelite convents and shares with the reader her plans, problems, ingenious solutions, and adventures in doing so. It is a memoir often not written in the recollection of tranquility but rather in the middle of the fray, something like a soldier's tale partly penned while still at war. She wrote it in three phases between 1573 and 1582, the year she died, with an intense sense of purpose and idealism, her lofty aims often adjusted and tempered by pragmatism. By whatever crafty and necessary means, Teresa usually accomplished what she wished, although not always. Her heroism and cleverness as a woman of action, the liveliness and intimacy of the narration, and her portrayal of the lives of Renaissance women make this text both entertaining and timely. It is amenable to the "agency" model of analysis proposed by some feminist historians as opposed to the older "oppressed victims of patriarchy" paradigm.[2] Moreover, recent scholarship provides new data on some of the historical figures represented.[3]

Teresa's story really begins in chapters 32–36 of her *Libro de la vida* (*The Book of Her Life*), where Teresa describes the founding, from 1562 to 1565, of the first Discalced Carmelite convent, San José of Ávila, against great opposition and with poor odds for success. An energetic woman in her late forties, she subsequently set out to found more reformed convents on the instructions of the new head of the Carmelite order. With the help of John of the Cross, Jerónimo Gracián, and others, she also extended the reform to Carmelite friars, founding or influencing the foundation of fifteen monasteries. Her role is that of reformer and apostle, inspired by the New World conquest of souls, as she describes in the first chapter of *Fundaciones*. She also writes in response to the threat of Protestantism in Europe and in hopes of strengthening the faith in Spain (Slade, *St. Teresa* 109–11). *Fundaciones* represents the socialization of Teresa's mystical experience, her effort to provide enclosed spaces that might enable others to achieve salvation, especially women. To do so, she built on her reputation as a mystic, her network of supporters within and outside the church, and her own indefatigable spirit. The text is infused with the energy of someone who has changed her life and set out on both a mission and quixotic adventure.

Fundaciones is the only book Teresa claims to be divinely inspired, "written in compliance with a direct order from heaven" (Chorpenning, *Divine Romance* 120), but she also records that she writes in obedience to her Jesuit confessor, Jerónimo Ripalda, in undertaking to write chapters 1–20 in 1573 and 1574.

There, she describes her earliest foundations subsequent to San José of Ávila, at Medina del Campo, Malagón, and Valladolid in 1568; Toledo and Pastrana in 1569; Salamanca in 1570; and Alba de Tormes in 1571. The second part, chapters 21–27, was written in 1576. It describes Segovia in 1574, the Andalusian convents, Beas and the problematic Sevilla foundation in 1575, and Caravaca in 1576. Later in 1576, Teresa was ordered into reclusion in the convent of San José of Ávila and forbidden to found more convents. In 1580, the political climate changed for the better. Now frail and ill, she wrote part 3, chapters 28–31, even as she founded the last four convents, Villanueva de la Jara in 1580, Palencia in 1581, Soria in 1581, and Burgos in 1582 (Chorpenning, *Divine Romance* 118).[4]

Teresa describes the hardships she incurs with optimism and self-deprecating humor. She travels widely, cleans filthy houses that are to become convents, and manipulates parents, patrons, and homeowners. Her favorite strategy is to rent a house in secret and take possession of it in the middle of the night before anyone knows what happened. She recounts many controversial anecdotes and vignettes, often related to an issue, using the experiences of individual nuns as examples. Teresa's narrative is often sensory or visual. One can well imagine her sweltering under the Sevillian sun (ch. 24), struggling to cross the Guadalquivir against the tide (ch. 24), negotiating the precipices and rocky roads in the mountains of Segovia (ch. 30), being stranded with her cart stuck in the mud as she approaches Burgos (ch. 31), or sleeping on a pile of straw in a house hastily abandoned by sloppy students in Salamanca (ch. 19).[5]

Fundaciones is a hybrid text that recounts the story of Teresa's foundings, often in opposition to the wishes of towns' citizens, as well as the stories of the professing nuns and patrons of the foundations. The autobiographical narrative is interspersed with advice for prioresses, biographies of nuns or patrons, and a few digressions on prayer and other subjects. The narrative structure is episodic, and the principal addressees are the present and future nuns of the Carmelite order, as well as the ecclesiastical hierarchy. It is a didactic and purposeful memoir, meant to teach how future convents might function successfully. Teresa expresses doubts, meditates extensively, and introduces several thorny issues: obedience, melancholy, the devil, and false ecstatic visions, for example. She ostensibly obeys both God and her confessors but often expresses a lack of confidence in the human intellect, which she sees as prone to being clouded by emotion, illness, or caprice. This "skepticism," a natural inclination to accept limits to human knowledge and rely on experience and faith in God, enables her to undermine the authority of the educated ecclesiastics that might disagree with her plans.[6]

An underlying assumption of the narrative is that the convents will strive to be utopian societies on earth that prepare the nuns to deserve heaven in the afterlife. The nuns' obedience to the prioress and Teresa's obedience to superiors are the ideal means to achieve this state. Still, Teresa's attitude to obedience is ambivalent. She herself is disobedient in leaving the convent of La Encarnación in Ávila, where she had lived for over twenty-five years, and setting out to establish the reformed convent of San José and later the Andalusian convents. She supports disobedient daughters who often defy their parents' wishes in leaving home to enter her convents, just the way Teresa did as a teenager (Weber, *Teresa of Ávila* 149–52).

Why did she now decide to act as she did? The worldly and noisy convent of La Encarnación had grown to house 150 nuns under the mitigated rule. The social stratification, meaning luxury for some and virtual starvation for others; petty squabbles and gossip; and visitors and visits to home increasingly dissatisfied her. Teresa had lived in luxury, as the daughter of a wealthy converso wool merchant, and had partaken of all the customs she now was beginning to abhor. Shocked by a terrifying vision of hell, influenced by her readings of Francisco de Osuna and the religious movement of *recogimiento* (the prayer of recollection, quiet meditation, and reflection), admiring of Pedro de Alcántara and the Franciscan reform, encouraged by conversations with her relative María de Ocampo and the beata (holy woman) María de Yepes, and aware of the new guidelines set by the Council of Trent in 1563, Teresa came to realize what she wanted: poverty, strict enclosure, silence, and meditation (Bilinkoff, "Teresa of Jesus" 166–71).[7] She would return to the primitive rule of the Carmelites, as practiced by a group of twelfth-century European hermits living on Mount Carmel in Palestine (Slade, "Relationship" 229). Her nuns were to practice meditation and silent prayer. The convents would be small, ideally with thirteen novices and a prioress. The nuns would wear habits of coarse wool and sandals. They would abandon family names and adopt religious ones, such as Ana de Jesús, María de San José, Ana de la Madre de Dios, María de la Encarnación, to name a few future notables of the order (Bilinkoff, *Ávila* 112–37).

Teresa's program of reform was radical in that it challenged the prevailing social and financial system. Her convents were to be founded in poverty and to avoid endowments by aristocratic patrons. The nuns should live by charity, accepting donations with no strings attached. The aristocracy traditionally patronized religious foundations to enhance their reputations and to ensure their place in heaven through perpetual prayers recited on their behalf. Bereaved or emotionally needy people often sought solace from the company of friars and nuns and sometimes even professed themselves. Patrons expected to select relatives and friends as nuns and even prioresses for their convents. In short, their economic contributions led to political and spiritual control.

Teresa, on the other hand, wished to free the convents from this patronage system, which she had experienced for so many years at La Encarnación. In regard to selection of novices, her criteria were egalitarian. She would consider potential novices without regard to their "blood purity," nobility, or dowry. (Many convents required postulants to prove blood purity—that they had no Moorish or Jewish ancestors.) Rather, her entrance requirements were vocational, a penchant for holiness and prayer, some education, and a suitable disposition devoid of melancholy.

Very early on and in order to succeed, however, Teresa was obliged to compromise her ideals. Her foundations needed a sound economic basis in order to thrive and even to survive. In towns she often received the backing of wealthy converso merchants, sympathetic to the Catholic reform and to the practice of *recogimiento*. But in country villages and small towns she had to rely on endowments from aristocratic women and their husbands. Otherwise, there were simply not enough people willing to provide alms. Her first such compromise was the founding of Malagón in 1568 with her patron Luisa de la Cerda from Toledo. In 1567, Luisa, recently widowed, had requested Teresa's presence in Toledo to comfort her, and Teresa remained in her household for six months. The noblewoman financed the Malagón convent completely and provided the dowry for one of the novices, who soon became prioress. She sometimes found it difficult to leave convent decision making in Teresa's hands (Weber, "Saint Teresa's Problematic Patrons" 361–64). In 1569, Teresa was to have similar difficulties with Luisa de la Cerda's cousin, Ana de Mendoza, Princess of Eboli. Malagón was far away from its patron's domicile, but the convent founded by Ana de Mendoza at Pastrana was but a stone's throw from the palace where she lived, a formula for trouble, as we shall see. Teresa sometimes even sought nuns with good dowries in urban centers, as letters concerning a potential convent in Madrid reveal.[8]

Teresa had good fortune in being able to build on her first success in Ávila. Still, without her charm, delicacy, diplomatic skills, and powers of persuasion, she might never have founded more convents. In February 1566, Giovanni Batista Rossi, known in Spain as Rubeo, the newly elected general of the Carmelite order, visited Spain. Rubeo and Teresa were like-minded reformers, as was King Philip II, who had invited Rubeo to Spain.[9] Teresa wisely introduced Rubeo to Álvaro de Mendoza, bishop of Ávila (later of Palencia) and one of her staunchest supporters. She also invited them to visit San José of Ávila. Impressed, Rubeo issued her a patent that allowed her to found convents in Old and New Castile (ch. 2). The provincial heads of the Carmelites, often conservative and against reform, would now be unable to stop her (Haliczer 97).

Teresa's second good strategic move was to found monasteries for friars. The first foundation at Duruelo, soon moved to Mancera, where the friars had unexpectedly found water, and the monastery at Pastrana were founded in 1568 and 1569. Ruy Gómez and his wife, Ana de Mendoza, the Prince and Princess of Eboli, patronized the foundation of both a convent and a monastery at Pastrana. Ruy Gómez also supported a Discalced Carmelite college at the University of Alcalá de Henares, which in turn sent well-educated novices to Pastrana. The monastery at Pastrana grew to house thirty-two friars in two years and became too large and too ascetic in its practices. A friar from Pastrana founded a friary at Altomira, Cuenca, also backed economically by Ruy Gómez.[10] From 1571, Ana de Mendoza supported the development of a Discalced Carmelite priory,

Nuesta Señora del Socorro. It was founded by the ascetic hermit Catalina de Cardona in La Roda, Cuenca, and populated by some of the friars from Pastrana. Thus the Prince and Princess of Eboli were consistently major, wealthy patrons of the Discalced Carmelites and other orders as well, even though Teresa later moved the nuns' convent from Pastrana to Segovia.

Had Ruy Gómez not died leaving his thirty-three-year-old widow with six young children and devastated by grief, his tact and Teresa's respect for his power as secretary of state might have continued to maintain an uneasy peace between the two women. But on his death, their interests clashed dramatically. Ana wanted typical aristocratic privileges in return for her patronage, to have perpetual vocal prayers for the soul of Ruy Gómez and solace from the nuns. She wished not only to live in the convent as a Carmelite under the name of Ana de la Madre de Dios but also to receive visitors and conduct business as owner of the town. Teresa finally moved the convent to Segovia rather than cope with the behavior of her now not so powerful yet still demanding patroness, the antithesis of her ideal obedient nun.[11]

Just as each foundation presented different economic and logistical problems, so each novice entered with a different social rank, personality, and family situation. Teresa's minibiographies are among the most thoughtful studies in the text and present us with a variety of girls who become suitable novices, some seeming unlikely candidates, others amazing for the bizarre details of their sanctity. This "city of women" (Slade, *St. Teresa of Ávila* 123), inhabited by the women religious that Teresa parades before us, demonstrates many ways to live a religious life in the sixteenth century and introduces issues of governance, belief, and gender. The chapters on Casilda de Padilla, Catalina de Beas, Catalina Godínez, Teresa de Laíz, and Ana de Mendoza are particularly good for class discussion. The last four chapters also make an interesting unit to teach. Teresa's "specular" meditation on Catalina de Cardona's asceticism is especially poignant.[12]

The ideals of contemplation, enclosure, and silent prayer caused some problems in the administration and guidance of the novices in their spiritual journey. *Recogimiento* theoretically led to divine revelation. But the experience of *arrobamiento* ("ecstasy") was difficult to evaluate in others, particularly in impressionable young girls. False ecstasies inspired by the devil instead of God or ecstasies brought on by melancholy or excessive asceticism, of which Teresa did not approve, were often suspected and sometimes investigated by the Inquisition. Some girls did not have the disposition to endure the strict rule of poverty, chastity, and obedience. Teresa discusses melancholy at some length, manifested as inability to endure convent life, proneness to false ecstasies, excessive fasting and other forms of extreme asceticism, disobedience, and gloomy feelings. In her girls, Teresa wished to avoid extreme behaviors and the raptures through which she herself had experienced God. They were disruptive to convent governance and dangerous in the political climate of the time. Obedience to their voices from God might challenge the authority of the prioress.

Teresa's version of the novices' lives is shaped by her narrative's purpose and by contemporary political concerns. Her letters or other sources often reveal different takes on the same characters—for example, Beatriz Chávez, who with another nun from the Seville convent later denounced Teresa and Jerónimo Gracián to the Inquisition for sexual misconduct. Teresa does not mention these problems or change her earlier version of events in *Fundaciones* (Weber, *Teresa of Ávila* 152–54). The happy endings, compliant nuns, and generous benefactors that abound are sometimes belied by subsequent developments mentioned in her letters. Teresa silences or underplays some of the worst conflicts within the convents to present positive models worthy of emulation.[13]

I recently taught selections from *Fundaciones* in a survey course of medieval through Golden Age Spanish literature. I included two other texts by women writers, Leonor López de Córdoba's autobiographical memoir and María de Zayas's exemplary novel, *La fuerza del amor* ("The Force of Love"). A leitmotif of the course was heroes and heroines, antiheroes and antiheroines. The women's texts lent themselves to this sort of character analysis and to discussions of gender issues and rhetoric, juxtaposed to *Cantar del Mío Cid* (*The Song of the Cid*) and *Lazarillo de Tormes*. In a *PowerPoint* presentation with slides I explained the historical information and issues outlined in this essay, as well as mysticism and the Counter-Reformation. I cited examples of Teresa's "rhetoric of femininity" and asked the students to look for others. Next, I assigned selections to read and discuss for the following class, asking everyone to write about which characters they most identified with and why. My instinct was that the difference in the novices' and my students' vocational interests might make this exercise stretch their historical imaginations. It would teach them about the religiosity of the age and women's life options in an intimate way. Most chose to write about Teresa herself, noting her courage and the good she did in the world. One student wrote that he also liked to work with his hands and had a strong faith in God, though not as profound as hers. Another student felt connected to Teresa partly because her own second name was Teresa. Her interest in Spanish religious history was also inspired by her eighty-year-old grandparents' recent pilgrimage to Santiago de Compostela. They had walked to the holy city for nearly a month, all the way from the French border. Another student chose the nun Ana de la Madre de Dios (the name in religion chosen by Ana de Mendoza, Princess of Eboli), stating that, although she was not as wealthy, she understood Ana's reasons for founding a convent and admired her civic-minded goodness.[14] The overriding response of the students was to consider Teresa a heroine worthy of emulation.

She might well evoke a similar response in a class of retirees. For Teresa, life began at forty with her mystical ecstasies and continued with her foundations, consuming the last twenty years of her life. At the same time, she produced five books and numerous other writings. Both author and activist, she overcame gender restrictions to embark on an apostolic mission, albeit in a much more limited geographic space than her male counterparts, the missionaries and conquistadors in the New World. With Ignatius of Loyola and John of the Cross, she spearheaded the Catholic Reformation in Spain. Her self-portrait and narration in *Fundaciones* is both amazing and inspirational.

NOTES

[1] Teresa sent her original manuscript to Fray Luis de León, who did not include it in the publication of her other works in 1588. Jerónimo Gracián, her spiritual adviser, who was made provincial head of the Discalced Carmelites in 1581, organized a system of pagination, later cancelled by Domingo Ibáñez. The first edition was prepared by Gracián and Ana de Jesús and published in Brussels in 1610. They did not include part of chapter 10 and all of 11, eliminating the story of the runaway Casilda (Kavanaugh and Rodríguez).

[2] For a discussion of these models, see Schutte and Kuehn viii, xii.

[3] See, e.g., Weber, "Saint Teresa's Problematic Patrons" and Introduction; the essays in Nader; Slade, "Relationship"; and Reed, "Catalina." Teresa's letters and accounts such as Gracián's *Peregrinación* complement and enrich Teresa's narrative, making us aware of her particular focus.

[4] For a more detailed chronology and discussion of the individual foundations, see García de la Concha's edition of the *Fundaciones* or the introduction to Kavanaugh and Rodríguez's edition.

[5] See the maps of Teresa's foundations with dates and routes of her many travels in Aguado's edition (1: 91–92, 2: 101–02) and in the introduction by Kavanaugh and Rodríguez.

[6] Mujica, "Skepticism" 63–71. Teresa ranks experience and intuition over book learning and erudition, often doubts whether God or the devil is the source of visions, and suspects others' visions of being corrupted. Mujica associates Teresa's views with skepticism, an attitude also reflected in the "rhetoric of femininity" (Weber, *Teresa of Ávila*) with which Teresa often expresses doubts and belittles herself with wit, modesty, and charm—the result being that she often gets her way.

[7] For a more detailed discussion of *recogimiento*, see the essay by Rhodes in this volume.

[8] See letters written in 1579 to or about Isabel de Osorio, a potential novice from Madrid, in Peers, *Letters* 2: 688–90, 700, and 738.

[9] Teresa's four existing letters to Philip II were perhaps written to impress other influential persons and neither read nor answered by the king. See Slade, "Relationship."

[10] See Gracián 174; Boyden 142; Reed, "Catalina" 439–41.

[11] See *Fundaciones*, ch. 12; Weber, "Saint Teresa's Problematic Patrons" 370–79; Reed, "Mother Love" 157–60.

[12] Slade offers a sensitive analysis of Teresa's particularly enigmatic description of this ascetic female hermit (*St. Teresa of Ávila* 124–27). The word "specular" comes from her discussion.

[13] See Weber, "Saint Teresa's Problematic Patrons" (367) on the patron of Alba de Tornes, Teresa de Laíz, and her disagreements with Teresa about selection of novices and a prioress, which are silenced in *Fundaciones*. Teresa's heart and left hand still reside in the church's reliquary in Alba de Tormes.

[14] With special thanks to Paul Álvarez, Libby Kent, Jessica Rojo, and Kirsten Salazar.

Comparing Humanist and Mystical Understanding in Luis de Leon's "Noche serena" and John of the Cross's "La noche oscura"

Dana Bultman

Instructors who wish to provide their students with literary material that can exemplify how a mystical experience might surpass an intellectual understanding of God could chose to do a comparative exploration of two lyric poems. A comparison of Luis de Leon's "Noche serena" ("Still Night") and Saint John of the Cross's "La noche oscura" ("The Dark Night") provides a precise and appealing pathway for students into the complexities of sixteenth-century Spanish humanism and mysticism. Elias Rivers includes both poems in *Renaissance and Baroque Poetry of Spain with English Prose Translations*. On a first reading, these short texts present students with representations of strong desires, both intellectual and sensual, for knowledge of the divine. They also promise plentiful allusive and intertextual meanings to those who, like Renaissance philologists and interpreters, examine the poems more closely.

While John is generally recognized as a mystic, Fray Luis is not. Fray Luis never claimed to have achieved a mystical comprehension of God, although he did share John's dedication to disseminating spiritual teachings to the laity. Comparing these two authors' works closely can thus be an intriguing process: what does each poem suggest about individual human beings' limitations and capacities for understanding the divine? The speaking voices in both poems express deep longing as the works begin. In both texts the fears and worries of human life are seen as obstacles to spiritual progress. Fray Luis and John also similarly contrast night versus light and soul versus body. Additionally, the two poems end similarly with imagery of nature and the female breast as a place of peace and repose. But when one compares the works more closely, the references to night that link the titles of the two poems may lead students to note each work's different representation of the night. The word *night* is positive in John's poem because of its promise for a possible individual union with God. In contrast, *night* is negative in Fray Luis's poem because of its association with sleep and humanity's forgetfulness of ultimate truths. Thus these poets' uses of *night* exemplify the potential of individual words to unfold with rich, multiple, even contradictory meanings.

Both poems were produced in the 1570s but are difficult to date. Tradition accepts that the composition of "La noche oscura" coincided with the year John escaped from his imprisonment, 1578. Scholars vary in their opinions over Fray Luis's poem, speculating that he wrote "Noche serena" sometime between 1570 and 1580 (*Obras* 2: 758n [1991]). To provide a context for studying the meanings of Fray Luis's and John's poetry it should be explained that throughout the Middle Ages biblical scholarship had been based both on the authority of the Vulgate (the Latin Bible) and on the tradition of interpreting scripture in the fourfold manner: literal; allegorical; moral; and anagogical, or mystical. In this interpretive method one first focused on the literal meaning of the words in a passage of scripture, then a more important allegorical sense was assigned to the text. Next, one reasoned out moral teachings based on the passage, and last the fortunate reader might eventually be infused with an anagogical understanding of the passage if God so chose.

Written in the context of the traditional fourfold textual interpretation of scripture, both Fray Luis's and John's poems affirm that spiritual understanding is progressive and that experience of the divine can be achieved not through the intellect's powers of reason but only through direct intervention by the forces of God's grace. On this point the main difference between the two poems becomes apparent. The poetic subject that speaks in Fray Luis's "Noche serena" remains at a moral level of understanding the divine, a level that can still be reached by the intellect. In contrast, the speaking subject in John's "La noche oscura" expresses an experience of God that surpasses logic and testifies to having received a higher spiritual knowledge that cannot be fully conceptualized or communicated.

Close readings of Fray Luis's and John's poems show that despite the similarities between these two works, the authors emphasize different threads of their shared cultural traditions. Although each poem is technically a *lira* (the metrical form favored by the courtly poet Garcilaso de la Vega that mixes and alternates seven-syllable and eleven-syllable verses), Fray Luis calls his work an ode, in imitation of the classical Latin poet Horace, while John calls his a song in keeping with popular, oral tradition. This difference provides evidence that, as poets, they base their intertextual allusions on separate source material. Fray Luis draws from the classical tradition, Greek philosophy and myth in particular, and John draws mainly from scripture and Spanish popular poetry.

Readers, once they delve into the poem's verses, can observe that the title of Fray Luis's poem, "Noche serena," presents a paradox. On first considering the title one might think that serenity will be positively experienced in the context of the night. Instead there is an absence of serenity experienced by the speaker of the poem, who burns with longing to awaken from his inability to transcend the material world. The poem presents a deep division between heaven and earth that alludes to a platonic separation between transcendent idea and inferior matter. The poetic I cannot overcome his state of separation from what he desires; he yearns to transcend the grief of the world and unite his soul with divine truth, yet he cannot.

The poetic subject in Fray Luis's poem speaks in the present tense of a feeling he has whenever he looks up at the stars at night and notices their beauty. He sees that at the same time the earth is surrounded and buried by night and forgetfulness. He feels a mixture of love and pain, which causes him to weep and implore heaven itself to answer his questions. In keeping with the platonic view of the human body as a snare, or cage, of the spirit, he asks why his soul is trapped in the prison of his body. What imperfection is he guilty of that causes his soul to seek out false shadows instead of the highest good? But heaven does not respond, and the speaker is left to reason out his own answers.

Like a sermon turning from personal experience to a general moral message for all, the speaking voice in the poem asserts that human beings live in a kind of sleep, not realizing that their lost time is being quietly marked by the planet's rotations. The voice warns all mortals to awaken, to see that shadow and deception cannot sustain their souls. The solution is to look to the heavens in contemplation in order to put the smallness of worldly life's empty worries and fears in perspective. The earth is just a poor vantage point from which to observe the grand, eternal, rhythmic concert of the shining spheres, which are proportionate to the grandeur of their planned and systematic movements.

Fray Luis's speaker notes the beauty of the moon; of Mercury, the light of wisdom; of Venus, the star of love; of blood-red Mars; of peaceful Jupiter; and of Saturn, the deity of the paradisiacal golden age in classical mythology, before asking, Who can esteem the exile of a soul's life on earth compared to this perfection? Once again, there is no one to answer this rhetorical question in the poem. Reason and the authority of the classical tradition step in to help him deduce logically that divinity must be present among the stars. The solitary speaker concludes that there in the heavens peace and contentment reign, sacred love and the pure light of beauty shine in a timeless springtime where night never comes. The starry sky provides an image of the true fields, he declares, the true meadows of pleasant sweetness, the delightful breasts and valleys of blessings. However, this transcendent place of delight is shown to be inaccessible, increasing the speaker's longing instead of assuaging it. Night and forgetfulness hinder human comprehension of the soul's true nature, like the body that traps the soul inside.

Fray Luis, a humanist familiar with Greek mythology and the texts of Plato, expresses a desire for direct experience of the divine in this poem but does not claim to have achieved this sort of mystical knowledge. Although the poetic voice wants contact with the transcendent realm, he does not get it; his questions go unanswered and he can only theorize intellectually. On the one hand, it could be argued that "Noche serena" may simply have been a humanist exercise in writing lyric poetry and imitating classical authors rather than a reflection of Fray Luis's personal beliefs or experience. On the other hand, he was undoubtedly familiar with the practice of *recogimiento*, or methodical mental prayer, and greatly admired Teresa of Ávila. If we bear this in mind, it is not unreasonable to assume that the poem resonated on some level with his own spiritual experiences.

In contrast to the sentiments expressed in "Noche serena," John's "La noche oscura" is characterized by joy. Instead of an unbridgeable separation between matter and spirit, there is hope for sensual union with the divine. In fact, through the exemplary experience it portrays, the poem promises the reader that God, as divine beloved, can be found within oneself.

When one studies "La noche oscura," it is helpful to first clarify the literal meaning of the poem and then work with the allusive nature of text to develop more complex interpretations. The poetic subject is a female speaker who says that one dark night, inflamed with the anxiety of love, she left her house once it was still and quiet. She is full of joy at her good fortune because she left without being detected (and potentially stopped, one might assume). She explains that despite the darkness she felt secure, leaving her house in disguise and with her face covered, by way of a secret stair. She praises the fortune the night brought her, explaining that no one saw her, nor did she look at anything, having as her only guide the light that burned in her heart. As in "Noche serena," the darkness provides a contrast against which the brightness of light can be better appreciated. But instead of the speaker's being separated from the desired light, as in Fray Luis's poem, in "La noche oscura" the speaker finds light within her heart that guides her better than midday sun would to the private place where she was sure that someone was awaiting her.

Instead of equating night with the negativity of sleep, delusion, and ignorance, the poetic voice rejoices in the night; it is even more favorable than the dawn because it brought together the female beloved, "amada," and the male beloved, "amado," and transformed her into him when they were united (139, lines 24–25 [ed. Rivers]). On the literal level this could be read as sexual union. The speaker says her beloved then fell asleep on her "pecho florido" 'flowery breast' (139, lines 26–29 [ed. Rivers]) that she had saved only for him, and, as the cedars fanned a breeze on the lovers, she delighted and caressed him. As the breeze spread out the strands of his hair, it also touched her neck and left her in a state of sensual suspension. She remained there, forgetting herself, touching her face to his, and at that moment everything stopped and she left her self behind, with all her thoughts and fears, among the lilies.

The literal level of interpretation of John's poem reveals what seems to be secret lovers meeting each other at night when they cannot be caught. There is no overtly moralizing element in the poem that censures their desire, only the appreciation of lovely sensuality. But when a reader attempts to relate this literal meaning to the explanatory heading that accompanies the poem, he or she will be challenged to come up with another layer of interpretation beyond the literal. John's heading reads, "De el alma que se goza de haber llegado al alto estado de la perfección que es la unión con Dios por el camino de la negación espiritual" 'Songs of the soul rejoicing at having reached the highest state of perfection, which is union with God, by means of spiritual self-denial' (138 [ed. Rivers]). It is the only place in the text that explains what the poem represents allegorically: the soul's enjoyment of the high state of perfection that is the union with God by means of the path of spiritual negation.

Just as one can read scripture on multiple levels, so too John fashioned his poem to be read on several levels. Reading allegorically, students may conclude that the female beloved is a representation of the soul and that the male beloved is God. But in approaching this level of interpretation, one must also ask what meaning to assign to such elements as the house and secret stair. Why does the soul go disguised? Why does the soul not look at anything and why is it not seen by anything? What are the allegorical values of the cedars, the lilies, and the breeze that suspends the senses? In the last stanza, what is the positive mystical value of forgetfulness and the leaving of the self referred to by "dejéme" 'I abandoned myself' (139, line 38 [ed. Rivers])? These questions lead the reader to a deeper knowledge of the poem's relation to mystical traditions of meditative prayer.

The allusions John makes in his poem are not limited to allegorical, one-to-one correspondences that become transparent once the reader cracks the code with the help of John's explanatory heading. Instead, the reference to spiritual marriage between the soul and God in his heading refers both to ways of reading the Bible and to mystical teachings circulating in the cultural environment of Spain. These allusive meanings would not be readily apparent to the reader without further knowledge of theology and spiritual treatises. Since the study of theology was prohibited to women in sixteenth-century Spain, "La noche oscura" can potentially be seen as an indirect way of encouraging the dissemination of such knowledge to readers who did not have official access to it.

The poetic voice's reference to not looking and not being seen can be interpreted as an aspect of John's mystical method mentioned in the heading, "por el camino de la negación espiritual" 'by means of spiritual self-denial.' Self-loss was a spiritual practice associated with the *via negativa*, or negative theology, which held that God could not be truly conceptualized or described. A method to achieve self-loss, based on the withdrawal from the exterior senses and on turning one's attention within had been detailed in 1527 in the influential book by the Franciscan friar Francisco de Osuna, the *Tercer abecedario espiritual* (*Third Spiritual Alphabet*), a text well known by John's friend Teresa of Ávila. In this text Osuna explains how to achieve an experience of the divine and he recommends that one shut down the exterior senses and make an effort to be deaf, mute, and blind in order to journey inward to the self and beyond ([ed. López Santidrián] 184). For Osuna the night represents the state of solitude and quiet that allows the soul to journey toward the beloved, or God. He uses the term "noche oscura" in his writings to imply the need for an interior light of faith, not just the light visible to the eyes, to find one's way.

In John's "La noche oscura" the soul desires God, but, before being able to move toward this goal, the soul has to quiet down its "house." Paola Elia and María Mancho explain in "Notas complementarias" that John may have meant the reader to understand "house" allegorically as the lower impulses of the body, the passions and the appetites (627). The soul has access to a ladder leading to a higher state of being, the "secret stair," which allows the soul to proceed toward the goal unhindered. According to the critic Domingo Ynduráin, the fact that the reader understands the soul to descend the stair, instead of to ascend, demonstrates the paradoxical techniques of John's method in achieving mystical union (qtd. in Elia and Mancho, "Notas" 631). In Osuna's writings the stair also appears and represents a neoplatonic understanding of the progressive steps that emanate from divine spirit and become manifested on the lowest levels of earthly reality as pure matter. Descending the stair in John's poem may indicate that instead of rejecting the material world in one's attempt to ascend toward the divine, to find God one should fully accept one's humanity and descend, as did Christ.

The enigmatic meanings that can be assigned to the cedars, the lilies, and the breeze suggest that John may have followed Osuna's method of meditative prayer while developing his own allusive vocabulary based on his understanding of the Song of Songs. John's use of the cedars is an intertextual reference that recalls moments from the Song, such as 1.4, 1.16, 5.14, and 8.9. In the biblical text the cedars are protective enclosures, like tents and houses, or like the door built to protect a young sister before she is ready for marriage. The cedar is also used to refer to the body of the male beloved. The lilies, on the other hand, refer to the body of the female beloved in 2.16, 4.5, 5.13, 6.1, 6.2, and 7.2. They signify beauty and a place for feeding. The female beloved's breasts are twin goats grazing among the lilies. This repeated use of lilies to suggest the comfort and nourishment offered by the female breast is emphasized by a single comparison of lilies in the Song to the lips of the male lover dripping with myrrh. Whereas in Fray Luis's "Noche serena" the "deleitosos senos" 'breasts of delight' (101, line 79; my trans.) referred to at the poem's end are inaccessible, in John's "La noche oscura" the place of pleasurable union is one's own soul's "pecho florido" 'flowery breast,' where God rests in comfort.

At the end of the poem the breeze enters as an active agent; it is the breeze that strikes the soul and suspends the senses. This action is read by Dámaso Alonso as the dynamic intervention of the Holy Spirit, the Christian God's way of bestowing the grace of mystical knowledge (qtd. in Elia and Mancho, "Notas" 653). In this context forgetfulness is positive because it is precisely the forgetting of the self, and with it one's intellect, that is necessary for the reception of divine grace and the union with God to take place. In losing the self one also loses one's cares and worries. The practice of *dejamiento*, or "abandonment," was linked to Osuna's work and associated with the Alumbrado movement condemned by the Inquisition in the 1520s. John's use of "dejéme" 'I abandoned myself' (139, line 38 [ed. Rivers]) recalls this tradition of letting the divine enter through a negation of the self (Hamilton 30).

The contrast between John's and Fray Luis's treatments of cosmic mysteries offers a basis for defining their different mystical and humanist approaches to spiritual understanding in these two poems. It is also interesting to note that the two authors are explicitly connected in many ways, some coincidental, such as their deaths the same year in 1591, some intensely studied, such as their similar heritage as descendants of conversos, Jews converted to Christianity. They inhabited the same intellectual environment; Fray Luis was a professor at the University of Salamanca while John was a student from 1564 to 1568 (Elia and Mancho, prol. xxxi). They both had important commitments to the mystic and reformer Teresa of Ávila. John left the University of Salamanca in 1568, without finishing his degree in theology, to accompany Teresa to found a convent in Valladolid. Later John would be imprisoned for nine months beginning in 1577 for defending and participating in her Discalced Carmelite reform. For his part, Fray Luis edited and wrote an introduction for the first edition of Teresa's works published six years after her death in 1582. Fray Luis suffered imprisonment also, from 1572 to 1576, for upholding the value of using Hebrew texts to correct errors in the Vulgate (Thompson, *Strife*).

The comparative study of "Noche serena" and "La noche oscura" prepares students to go further into such topics and, for example, to consider Fray Luis's and John's engagement with scripture. To contextualize further study of their writings, instructors should point out that Spanish scholars of the sixteenth century had increased access to knowledge of Greek because in 1453, when Constantinople was taken by the Turks, many erudite Greek scholars fled westward to Italy where they began teaching Greek language and Byzantine culture. Added to the Iberian Peninsula's traditionally strong Hebrew scholarship, this created the potential in Spain for new humanist forms of scriptural study to flourish. On the basis of this knowledge of language and culture, scholars like Fray Luis challenged the accuracy of the Latin Bible, provoking controversy by claiming that it could be corrected and improved through comparison with Greek and Hebrew versions. Why did study of the accuracy of scriptural texts pose a threat? If the text of the Latin Bible needed revision, then these corrections would result in changes to the long-accepted literal meaning. Such changes in the literal meaning would then cast doubt on the authority of traditional interpretations on the other three levels: the allegorical, moral, and anagogical. Greek and Hebrew philology thus presented a challenge to the integrity of the inherited theological tradition in Latin. The Catholic Church officially responded by reasserting the authenticity of Jerome's Vulgate at the Council of Trent (1545–63).

While John is recognized as a mystic and Fray Luis is not, both were versed in mystical theology and shared an innovative understanding of the importance of the Song of Songs. As poets and interpreters of scripture, Fray Luis and John's connection to this biblical text traverses the academic year of 1565–66 in Salamanca when the Song was explicated as a part of the Hebrew curriculum (Elia and Mancho, prol. xxxi). Equally important, both writers believed in the active power of the Holy Spirit in scripture and endorsed the humanist ideal of extending their knowledge of scripture to others, including women. In 1561 Fray Luis began translating the Song into Spanish using the Hebrew text as well as the Vulgate, writing his line-by-line commentary on it, the *Exposición del Cantar de los Cantares*, for his cousin Isabel Osorio, a nun who could not read Latin. At the request of Ana de Jesús, a follower of Teresa of Ávila, in 1584 John wrote a detailed commentary on his poetic work *Cántico espiritual*, inspired by the Song, for the nuns of her Discalced Carmelite convent.

Through their more complex works and commentaries, both Fray Luis and John disseminated their controversial spiritual understandings to readers of

Spanish and to nuns in particular. In the sixteenth century the Catholic Church considered the literal meaning of the Song of Songs as a sensual marriage poem in the form of a dialogue between spouses to be not only secondary but almost irrelevant. The best interpretation, it was held, was an allegorical one. The bridegroom and bride were primarily viewed as representing Christ and his church. Fray Luis and John had in common a preference for an alternative allegorical interpretation: one that saw the bridegroom and bride as God and the human soul. In his exposition of the Song, Fray Luis made the humanist gesture, radical when applied to scripture, of setting aside allegory altogether in order to first focus on the correct literal meaning of the Hebrew. He treated the text as he did classical literature, translating it and commenting on its aesthetic and historical qualities. John of the Cross, in his *Cántico espiritual* preferred poetic imitation to translation. For both men, however, a close engagement with the literal meaning of scripture was crucial for opening a path to its anagogical meaning.

Instructors who wish to read more may want to consult Ángel Alcalá's essay, "Fray Luis de León, maestro de S. Juan de la Cruz," which provides detailed insight into Fray Luis and John's relationship and approaches to scripture. Colin Thompson's *The Strife of Tongues* offers an excellent introduction to Fray Luis's life, his inquisitional trial, his humanist scholarship, and his poetic and theological writings. Paola Elia and María Jesús Mancho's edition of John's poetry, *Cántico espiritual y poesía completa*, includes an updated biography and detailed critical commentary on John's verses gleaned from numerous sources. Kieran Kavanaugh and Otilio Rodríguez have translated John's works into English in *The Collected Works of St. John of the Cross*. Those who wish to read more about the tradition of the exegesis of the Song may want to consult Richard A. Norris's The Song of Songs: *Interpreted by Early Christian and Medieval Commentators*. For more information on Francisco de Osuna, Laura Calvert's reading of all of his spiritual alphabets is very useful. The most recent edition of Osuna's *Tercer abecedario* was edited by Saturnino López Santidrián, and Mary E. Giles has provided us with an English translation of this work by Osuna. Melquíades Andrés Martín's book on the *recogidos* explains in detail Osuna's and others' spiritual teachings. For an introduction to the Spanish Illuminists, or Alumbrados, Alastair Hamilton's book is a good point of departure.

Teaching Luis de León's
Mystical Poetry as Pilgrimage

David H. Darst

The two words that seem to define best the mystic atmosphere of late-sixteenth-century Spain are *camino* ("way") and *subida* ("ascent"). They both belong to long spiritual and literary traditions that go back to the Greek and Latin fathers of the Christian Church and existed throughout the Middle Ages and the Renaissance as commonplace phrases: "peregrinatio vitae," 'pilgrimage of life' and "ascensus mysticus dei," 'mystic ascent to God.' The notions behind these words and phrases initiate my lectures on the mystical poetry of Fray Luis de León (1527–91) to the undergraduate and graduate students in my Renaissance and Baroque Poetry of Spain class and constitute my strategy to acquaint them with sixteenth-century mystical poetry in the intellectual traditions of the time.

Some would argue that it is inaccurate to describe Luis de León as a mystic, since his poems do not describe the experience of union with the godhead. Obviously, we can never know how far Fray Luis went on the mystical path of prayer. But as Dana Bultman's essay in this volume shows, he was conversant with mystical theology and *recogimiento* (the method of interior prayer practiced by the mystics). Like the mystics, he conceived of life as a continuing inner journey toward God. Although his poems do not use the language of nuptial mysticism, they do convey an intellectual and aesthetic experience of the divine that can be called rapturous in its intensity.

In my opening lectures, I point out the ubiquity of the terms of pilgrimage: Teresa of Ávila called her second work *Camino de perfección* ("The Way to Perfection"), and one of John of the Cross's commentaries on his mystical poetry is titled "Subida al Monte Carmelo" ("Ascent to Mount Carmel"). Fray Luis dedicated one chapter of *Los nombres de Cristo* (*The Names of Christ*) to *camino*, which he relates directly to the idea of *subida*:

> Es verdad que todos los que caminan por Cristo van altos y van sin estropiezos. Van altos, lo uno porque suben; suben, digo, porque su caminar es propiamente subir; porque la virtud cristiana siempre es mejoramiento y adelantamiento del alma. (*Obras* 1: 459)

> It is true that all who follow the way of Christ go up and go without stumbles. They go up, for one because they ascend; they ascend, I say, because their way is properly to ascend; because Christian virtue always is a betterment and an advancement of the soul.[1]

I next establish Fray Luis's acute awareness of the importance of the pilgrimage as a physical act of religious piety, expressed in Fray Luis's ode 21 to Santiago, whose eponymous burial place in northwestern Spain, Santiago de Compostela, remains today a popular pilgrimage destination. Fray Luis describes the saint's life with Jesus, his martyrdom, the transfer of his bones to Spain, his appearances as Santiago Matamoros (Saint James the Moor Slayer) to save the Gothic remnant from domination by the Moors, and his body's fame as an object of veneration, closing the poem with praise for the people who come to visit the site:

> El áspero camino
> vence con devoción, y al fin te adora
> el franco, el peregrino
> que Libia descolora,
> el que en Poniente, el que en Levante mora.   (*Obras* 1: 166–70)

> The harsh roadway
> is conquered with devotion, and you are finally adored
> by the Frenchman, by the pilgrim
> browned by the Libyan sun,
> by he who in the West and he who in the East resides.

Teaching this notion of the pilgrimage needs little ancillary material. I introduce the metaphoric correlation of *Peregrinatio vitae* to one's life experiences from cradle to grave with a handout of the statement by Saint Augustine of Hippo in *On Christian Doctrine* that the things of this world are to be used to assure our safe arrival at our spiritual destination rather than enjoyed for themselves along the way:

> For to enjoy a thing is to rest with satisfaction in it for its own sake. To use, on the other hand, is to employ whatever means are at one's disposal to obtain what one desires, if it is a proper object of desire; for an unlawful use ought rather to be called an abuse. Suppose, then, we were wanderers in a strange country, and could not live happily away from our fatherland, and that we felt wretched in our wandering, and wishing to put an end to our misery, determined to return home. We find, however, that we must make use of some mode of conveyance, either by land or water, in order to reach that fatherland where our enjoyment is to commence. But the beauty of the country through which we pass, and the very pleasure of the motion, charm our hearts, and turning these things which we ought to use into objects of enjoyment, we become unwilling to hasten the end of our journey; and becoming engrossed in a factitious delight, our thoughts are diverted from that home whose delights would make us truly happy. Such is a picture of our condition in this life of mortality. We have wandered far from God; and if we wish to return to our Father's home, this world must be used, not enjoyed, so that the invisible things of God may be clearly seen, being understood by the things that are made—that is, that by means of what is material and temporary we may lay hold upon that which is spiritual and eternal.   (625)

When I present this material to a class, I stress the view of life as a journey in which the traveler is expected to use the material world to reach the heavenly abode but not to tarry along the way, distracted by those things actually meant to lead the traveler to the desired end. I especially emphasize the last phrase about being able to perceive invisible things by means of the visible creation (which I summarize with the Latin topos *per visibilia ad invisibilia*).

After this general introduction to the pilgrimage's traditional purpose, I attempt to acclimate the students to its mystic ramifications with a handout of two pages from the *Summa theologica* of Thomas Aquinas (20: 610–11). Citing Augustine as his source, Thomas presents a straightforward and simple idea that my students have little difficulty relating to Spanish mystical poetry. Thomas asks himself, what is the goal of the contemplative life and how can one achieve it? Clearly, the goal must be the contemplation of God alone, as stated by Augustine: "that 'the contemplation of God is promised us as being the goal of all our actions and the everlasting perfection of our joys'" (qtd. in Aquinas 20: 611). Yet since God's presence is not here on earth, but rather in heaven, the spiritual pilgrim must start at the beginning, as it were, with contemplation of those things furthest from God, and move steadily forward from the creation to the creator or, in Thomist terminology, *ab effectu*, from the effects, since "God's effects show us the way to the contemplation of God Himself" (Aquinas 20: 611). Thomas again quotes Augustine as his authority: "Hence Augustine says that 'in the study of creatures we must not exercise an empty and futile curiosity, but should make them the stepping-stones to things imperishable and everlasting'" (20: 611). Thomas then gives two examples of intellectual journeys to reach God that move from the outer edge of God's creation to God himself. He notes "that four things pertain, in a certain order, to the contemplative life: first, the moral virtues; second, other acts apart from contemplation; third, contemplation of the divine effects; fourth, the complement of all, which is the contemplation of the divine truth" (20: 611). He then offers a more elaborate six-stage intellectual journey:

> For the first step consists in the perception of sensible things themselves; the second step consists in going forward from sensible to intelligible things; the third step is to judge of sensible things according to intelligible things; the fourth is the absolute consideration of the intelligible things to which one has attained by means of sensibles; the fifth is the contemplation of those intelligible things that are unattainable by means of sensibles, but which the reason is able to grasp; the sixth step is the consideration of such intelligible things as the reason can neither discover nor grasp, which pertain to the sublime contemplation of divine truth, in which contemplation is ultimately perfected.   (20: 611)

The class discusses how these spiritual stepping-stones to God function. The first pathway simply requires a process of abstraction based on practicing initially the virtues of justice, fortitude, temperance, and prudence; then other acts such as faith, hope, and charity; then active contemplation of God's creation, which reflects the divine being; and finally contemplation of God as Creator. The six-stage path is even more direct: one begins with the world perceived by the five senses of taste, touch, smell, sight, and hearing then advances progressively through more abstracted intellectual stages beyond the rational faculties to a sublime contemplation of God.

We next examine the specific case of Fray Luis, in whose writings the usage of the metaphoric roadway is startlingly consistent. We concur that the *camino* is always a *subida*, and the *subida* is always a physical ascent from the most humble to the most sublime aspects of God's handiwork. Furthermore, Fray Luis maintains a clear notion of space and time (however extended upward both may be), so the reader of his poetry never experiences an "out-of-body" state dissociated from everyday existence. Fray Luis describes his pilgrimage to God, in other words, as if it were a physical journey with real stepping-stones (which are the celestial orbs), so the readers of his poetry—and those attempting to teach it—can easily make the voyage with him without having to undergo a rigorous course in mystical hermeneutics.

The mystical poems of spiritual pilgrimage I have used most successfuly are, in this order, ode 10 to Felipe Ruíz, ode 3 to Francisco Salinas, and ode 8 to Diego Oloarte. It is easy to convey the meaning of ode 10 to students because it describes the entire *camino-subida* motif in the first stanza:

> ¿Cuándo será que pueda
> libre de esta prisión volar al cielo,
> Felipe, y en la rueda
> que huye más del suelo
> contemplar la verdad pura, sin velo?   (1–5)

> When will it be that I can,
> free from this prison, fly to Heaven,
> Philip, and in the sphere
> that flees most from the Earth
> contemplate pure truth without a veil?

The only metaphor here is "prisión," which stands for the body. In the long-standing platonic-Christian notion the body is a prison house that entraps an eternal soul that descended to the body at birth and—as the poet notes here and in all his poetry—that longs to return to its natural abode in heaven. There is one use of periphrasis: "la rueda / que huye más del suelo," which refers to the realm of heaven in the prevalent Ptolemaic celestial system, to which Fray Luis refers in all his mystic poems because it is the pathway of ascent for the soul and is beyond the Pauline veil of the material world. Again, there are no arcane, cabalistic notions here the students have to understand other than the placement of Earth at the center of the Ptolemaic universe, followed by the seven planets (the moon, Mercury, Venus, the sun, Mars, Jupiter, Saturn), the fixed stars (because they are always in the same position relative to one another while the planets appear to wander throughout the sky), and the permanent realm of heaven (the outermost sphere).

The Ptolemaic system as constructed by Fray Luis can be presented with anything from a blackboard sketch to a student presentation. I emphasize that Fray Luis sees this celestial hierarchy as merely a *camino* and never attempts to describe its mathematical convolutions or speculate about the number of other wheels or wheels within wheels that make its function match apparent motions. He never mentions, for example, the crystalline sphere or the empyrean or the primum mobile or any other astronomical constructions of the Christian Ptolemaic system. Furthermore, he describes the ascent and its goal in the most traditional terms possible, mirroring the Thomist terminology of his day to such an extent that his goal ("contemplar la verdad pura") is the same "contemplation of divine truth" that Aquinas described as the final step and complement of all in the ascent cited earlier from the *Summa theologica*.

The point to make, then, is that the poet's mystical impulses are traditional and unencumbered by esoteric matters beyond the scope of an educated lay reader. The poems are meant to be understood easily and to inspire a desire in the reader to accompany the poet (as Fray Luis will insist in many of them) on his mystical journey to God's presence. This can be illustrated to students with one more ancillary text from a commentary by Fray Luis on the Song of Songs, apparently one of his first literary efforts (c. 1562). In a relatively short paragraph, the young friar explains both why the metaphor of the ascent through the celestial orbs is appropriate for the journey of the soul to God and how standard and traditional the metaphor is:

> En el sentido espiritual, en decir el Esposo que siga, si quiere hallarle, la huella del ganado, avisa a las almas justas que le desean de dos cosas muy importantes: la una, que para hallar a Dios, aun en las cosas brutas y sin razón, tenemos bastante ayuda y guía, porque, como se dice en el salmo [Psalms 17.1–2], *los cielos dicen la gloria de Dios, y el cielo estrellado cuenta sus maravillas, un día tras otro día revoca esta palabra, y una noche tras otra nos da este aviso*. La grandeza, dice, y lindeza del cielo, con ser cosas sin alma y sin sentido; las estrellas con sus movimientos en tanta diversidad, tan concertados y de tanta orden, los días y noches con las mudanzas y sazones de los tiempos que siempre vienen a tiempo, nos dicen a voces quién sea Dios, porque no quede disculpa alguna a nuesto descuido. Lo segundo que nos avisa es que el camino para hallar a Dios y la virtud no es el que cada uno por los rincones quiere imaginar y trazar para sí, sino el usado ya y el trillado por el bienaventurado ejemplo de infinito número de personas santísimas y doctísimas que nos ha precedido.
>
> (1: 89)

In the spiritual sense, when the husband says that she should follow, if she wishes to find him, the footprints of the herd, he advises the just souls who love him of two very important things: one, that to find God, even among inanimate and mindless things, we have sufficient help and guide because, as it says in Psalm 17.1–2 [Psalm 19 in the King James Version]: "The heavens declare the glory of God; / And the firmament showeth his handiwork. / Day unto day uttereth speech, / And night unto night showeth knowledge." The greatness, it says, and the beauty of the heavens, being things without soul and feeling; the stars with such diverse motions, so well organized and with such order; the days and the nights with the changes and seasons of the year that always come on time proclaim to us who God is, so there cannot be any blame for our neglect. The second thing that it advises us is that the way to find God and virtue is not one that people in every corner may want to imagine and plan for themselves but rather the one well used and frequently traveled by the blessed example of the infinite number of holy and learned persons who have preceded us.

The corpus of the stanzas in ode 10 thus describes this celestial creation as something that Fray Luis hopes to see (he uses the verb "veré" 'I will see' eight times) when he arrives at the heights of the universe: the structure of Earth with its four elements of earth, water, air, and fire stacked one above the other; the planets with their strange motions; the fixed stars; and the motionless highest realms, "de espíritus dichosos habitadas" 'inhabited by the fortunate spiritual beings' (70).

Ode 3 describes the same journey and ascent, but in this poem Fray Luis actually makes the pilgrimage himself and, having arrived, invites his readers to join him. Students should be told that the poem (a verse epistle, as are all the mystical poems) is dedicated to Francisco Salinas, the famous Salamancan professor of music theory, who was blind. The ode thus uses music as the catalyst for the initiation of the mystical pilgrimage through the heavenly spheres and as the component that merges the soul with the divine being. The traveler, however, is not the corporeal Fray Luis but rather his soul, "el alma," which is the subject of fourteen active verbs: "está sumida" 'is submerged,' "torna" 'returns,' "se conoce" 'recognizes itself,' "se mejora" 'improves itself,' "desconoce" 'does not recognize,' "traspasa" 'goes beyond,' "oye" 'hears,' "ve" 'sees,' "está compuesta" 'is composed of,' "envía" 'sends,' "navega" 'navigates,' "se anega" 'drowns itself,' "oye" 'hears,' and "siente" 'feels.' These verbs describe the awakening of the soul by the harmonies of Salinas's music and the soul's recognition of its true origin and destination and turning from earthly things and subsequent pilgrimage through the skies to the highest sphere, where the soul contemplates God and responds with spiritual chords that vibrate in harmony with the divine music. Then follows the total oblivion of mystical ecstasy in which the soul loses itself to all sensible things. The poem ends with Fray Luis urging his friends to undertake the same spiritual journey and Salinas to play forever, since it is his music that awakens the soul to the divine, closing the senses to all else. The way is thus the same ascent through the heavens to God as in all of Fray Luis's thought, but here the poet's soul undertakes the journey and the initial conveyance is Salinas's earthly music, which transports Fray Luis's soul to God's celestial harmonies, with which the soul—being of the same immaterial substance—vibrates in unison. Students have had no difficulty discussing this poem with the contexts of the handouts from Augustine and Aquinas.

Next we examine ode 8, a verse epistle directed to Fray Luis's friend Diego Oloarte. It begins where ode 3 left off, with the poet speaking as if he were at the end of his pilgrimage in heaven with the angelic chorus. He looks below at the earth wrapped in the metaphoric sleep and oblivion that comes with ignorance of one's divine goal, weeps in pity for the wayward souls, and speaks to heaven, "morada de grandeza" 'dwelling place of greatness' (11). Why, he asks, does the soul, whose destination is to be with God, persist in inhabiting its earthly prison, ignorant of heaven above? He then calls on human beings to awaken, to lift their eyes to the eternal sphere and to marvel at its ethereal structure: the silvery moon, wise Mercury, amorous Venus, impetuous Mars, benign Jupiter, and ancient Saturn, followed by the choir of fixed stars. Here (Fray Luis will use the adverb "aquí" five times in the next ten lines) is where the soul belongs, in the truly eternal meadows and fields of paradise.

The three poems are thus taught as a repetitive progression of Fray Luis's pilgrimage through the heavens to the divine mansion. In his epistle to Felipe, he imagines what it will be like. In his epistle to Francisco, he undertakes the ascent and reaches union with the divine being. In his epistle to Oloarte, he addresses all human beings from his lofty abode to urge them to undertake the same pilgrimage. This is an effective way to teach quickly these popular poems, and in my classes, which cover all Golden Age poetry, I do not attempt to enrich the material with biographical matters or with discussion of contemporary ecclesiastical controversies. My principal goal is to work to ensure the students' understanding of the content and purpose of these specific mystical poems, and an effective methodology uses traditional statements on pilgrimages of the soul so students see these poems within the context of such statements.

In summary, teaching Fray Luis de León's mystical poetry in this way has the advantage of focusing on the essential components of mystical thought, components, as Fray Luis himself observes, that are part of the well-trodden pathways of Christianity. Furthermore, they are the same components one finds in the basic notions of Teresa of Ávila's and John of the Cross's mysticism, which allows the Salamancan teacher to be read and appreciated within the cultural context of Spain's two most famous saints.

NOTE

[1] Citations to the *Obras* are to the 1957 edition; all translations are mine.

Mysticism and Early Modern Musical-Cosmological Paradigms

Mario A. Ortiz

One of the greatest challenges in teaching the mystics is to help students approach the texts without the interference of their own religious beliefs. What students hold as religious truth affects their critical evaluation of the subject matter. I overcome this challenge by focusing on the aesthetics of mysticism. Yet a new challenge emerges: are our twenty-first-century students willing to accept an aesthetic paradigm? Aren't questions about beauty just as relative as those regarding mysticism? My essay focuses on a model for approaching an aesthetic paradigm that was central to the overall aesthetic discourse of the early modern period: the musical-cosmological paradigm of harmony. Harmony is then studied as a metaphor for beauty and perfection and as something human beings need to become one with. Furthermore, my examination of the rhetorical devices used to describe listening to the music of the spheres provides an appropriate introduction to the aesthetics of describing the mystical experience. I have found that students feel less threatened when examining a nonreligious metaphor from the ancient pagan world as a preamble to discussing Christian mysticism.

In this essay I present the outline for a fifty-minute lesson on an early modern musical-cosmological paradigm that has some striking parallels with the mystical experience. This lesson has been designed for an undergraduate survey course on early modern Hispanic literature, in which mysticism is studied for two weeks, or four lessons. The central early modern text that I analyze is Luis de León's "Oda a Salinas" ("Ode to Salinas"). I examine the "Oda a Salinas" as a text that bridges the musical-cosmological paradigm and mystical writings from the period. Fray Luis's poem is a tribute to Francisco de Salinas's music, the power of which elicits a mystical rapture on the lyrical voice of the ode.

I divide this lesson into three sections. Before class students receive three handouts, one for each section, with a title, a small selection of quotations from primary sources (for the first two handouts), the ode's complete text (for the third handout), and a few terms to investigate. The titles of the sections are "Pythagorean, Platonic, and Neoplatonic Traditions: The Mystical Power of Music," "Francisco de Salinas and Sixteenth-Century Musical Humanism: The Quest for Lost Ancient Music Lore," and "Luis de León and the 'Oda a Salinas': (subtitle to be completed by the students)." The titles are meant to suggest to the students a mystical quest. Using these materials as pieces of evidence, students are asked to reconstruct the story being told. When we meet to analyze the materials, students then present their findings, and I assist them by filling in the missing pieces of information. What follows is a reconstruction of such a narrative. I will be referring to the same texts and terms that the students have in their handouts.

Pythagorean, Platonic, and Neoplatonic Traditions: The Mystical Power of Music

Throughout its history music has been filled with images of its supernatural powers, more so than any other art form. Examples include the musical accomplishments of mythological heroes such as Orpheus, the biblical accounts of David's ability to cure Saul when he was tormented by an evil spirit (1 Sam. 16.14–17), and the miracle of the fall of the walls of Jericho after the Israelites marched around the city for seven days with seven trumpets (Josh. 6.2–5). Furthermore, ancient Greco-Latin writers inform us that music was used ritually to reach a spiritual state of perfection. According to the Pythagoreans, for example, harmony was a science of numbers that was an earthly reflection of a divine order. As such, music had the power to unite the dissonance of the self with the harmonious divine essence. Iamblichus, an influential neoplatonic writer,[1] tells us in his *Life of Pythagoras*:

> The whole Pythagoric school produced by certain appropriate songs, what they called [adaptation, elegance of manners, and contact], usefully conducting the dispositions of the soul. . . . They purified their reasoning power . . . and . . . liberated themselves. . . . By musical sounds alone, unaccompanied with words, they healed the passions of the soul and certain diseases.   (61)

Music thus has the power to purify the intellect and heal the soul from its passions. We may then say that according to Iamblichus, music has a purgative function. It works as a preparatory stage for the higher aesthetic experience of hearing what is unheard by most, as Simplicius, another neoplatonic author, reminds us: "If any one . . . should have his . . . senses . . . purified . . . through a perfection arising from sacred operations, such a one . . . will hear things inaudible by others" (qtd. in Iamblichus 33).

The Pythagoreans also believed that through the use of the proper type of music, the gods would manifest themselves in the music itself. As Iamblichus writes:

> There is, also, an alliance in these sounds and melodies to the proper orders and powers of the several Gods, to motions of the universe itself, and to the harmonious sounds which proceed from the motions. Conformably, therefore, to such like adaptations of melodies to the Gods, the Gods themselves become present.   (qtd. in Mathiesen 44)

Commenting on this passage, Thomas J. Mathiesen calls to our attention the notions of mimesis and emanation:

> Mimesis takes place through emanation by the attraction of like to like and causes the Gods to be actually present in the music itself. For Iam-

blichus, this is not a psychic condition but rather an actual reunion of the
soul with the Gods.   (44)

There is an illuminative function that takes place through the actual presence
of the gods.

Although music is able to purify the passions and make the gods present, the
goal of music was to allow the individual to partake fully of the divine essence.
Plotinus, yet another neoplatonic author, discusses this possibility:

> Harmonies unheard create the harmonies we hear and wake the soul to
> the consciousness of beauty, showing it the one essence. . . . For the mea-
> sures of our music . . . are determined by the [Divine] Principle.   (43)

Being able to hear the "[h]armonies unheard" or being shown "the one essence" involves a unitive experience that only a select few were said to have
accomplished. One such individual was none other than Pythagoras. Iamblichus
points out how Pythagoras "fixed his intellect in the sublime symphonies of the
world, he alone hearing and understanding, as it appears, the universal harmony
and consonance of the spheres, and the stars that are moved through them"
(qtd. in Mathiesen 43).

The "universal harmony and consonance of the spheres" became an aesthetic
principle, more commonly called the music of the spheres, which would have a
long-lasting influence in Western culture. This Pythagorean theory postulated
that the planets were positioned in certain harmonious proportions and therefore produced consonant sounds. This heavenly model of perfection was the
subject of much attention since Greek classical antiquity. One of the earliest and
most influential accounts comes from Plato's *Republic*, in the passage known
as the "Myth of Er."[2] However, it is Cicero's "Dream of Scipio" from his *De re-
publica* that gives us the best synthesis of this Pythagorean doctrine. According
to Cicero, "The whole universe is comprised of nine circles, or rather spheres.
The outermost of these is the celestial sphere, embracing all the rest, itself the
supreme god, confining and containing all the other spheres." The spheres produce a pleasing sound that Cicero explains as "a concord of tones separated by
unequal but nevertheless carefully proportioned intervals, caused by the rapid
motion of the spheres themselves. . . . [The spheres] produce seven different
tones, this number being, one might almost say, the key to the universe." He
then explains that this music is inaudible: "The ears of mortals are filled with
this sound, but they are unable to hear it." However, the possibility exists for
mortals to hear this music: "Gifted men, imitating this harmony on stringed
instruments and in singing, have gained for themselves a return to this region"
(qtd. in Godwin 10–11).

From the previous examples, it becomes clear that for Greco-Latin authors
there was a distinct separation between the divine music of the spheres and
human vocal and instrumental music. For the Pythagoreans, we mortals have

received the gifts of the gods to create music. Furthermore, Pythagoreans were precise in distinguishing between a low kind of music, which pleased only the senses, and a higher kind of music, which aimed at imitating the celestial model. Pythagoras has been traditionally credited with the legendary discovery of the mathematical proportions of music. The Pythagorean scale, which was a cosmic-aesthetic ideal based on strict mathematical principles, was nonetheless considered imperfect, since any object of divine origin, when it comes into contact with our material world, suffers a fall from its heavenly archetype. Aristides Quintilianus, also a neoplatonic author, explains this imperfection:

> Surely music itself also has a beginning from the whole universe . . . and by its mixture with bodily matter falls away from its precision and excellence in numbers, since at least in the regions above us, it is strict and incorruptible. So also we are powerless to make the divisions of the intervals equal, and we have defective consonances of scales because our bodily density is a hindrance.   (qtd. in Mathiesen 55)

Despite this imperfection, the proper use of these divinely inspired scales allowed a few gifted mortals to ascend into the heavenly spheres and partake of the primordial sound.

Francisco de Salinas and Sixteenth-Century Musical Humanism: The Quest for Lost Ancient Music Lore

The musical-cosmological paradigm was a constant of the Greco-Latin tradition. It would nevertheless be forgotten until the advent of musical humanism in the sixteenth century, which was strongly dominated by Pythagorean, platonic, and neoplatonic thought. Just as with other humanistic pursuits, music theorists sought to rediscover the lost musical wisdom of Greek classical antiquity. The fascination with that lost knowledge attained mythical dimensions and became a quest for a musical holy grail. Although much of the writing of musical humanists reiterated the same general aesthetic concepts already discussed here, its true focus became the search for the mathematical reconstruction of those Greek musical scales that were credited with having mystical powers. Close study of Greek sources led sixteenth-century theorists to speculate about the divisions of tones and compositions of scales.

Throughout the Middle Ages, some of the original neoplatonic works had been modified and Christianized by writers such as Augustine, perhaps the most influential Christian writer, who borrowed extensively from the neoplatonic authors. In the sixteenth century, however, most musical humanists overtly rejected those Christian overtones and attempted to return to the original roots of Greek theory. A central concern for theorists of the Renaissance was the reconstruction of Greek musical scales. The Greeks had classified their scales according to three *genera* of tetrachords (groups or scales of four notes), which were called the diatonic, the chromatic, and the enharmonic. Of these three, musical humanists became increasingly concerned, if not obsessed, with the enharmonic *genus*, since it seemed to be the source of the mystical qualities of music. There were as many interpretations of the mathematical divisions of the enharmonic *genus* as there were theorists writing about it. There was at the same time a growing interest in proving the proposed findings in actual musical practice. New instruments were created to accommodate the tonal possibilities of the newly rediscovered scales. The quest consisted of not only rediscovering the perfect scale but also creating the perfect instrument.

Francisco de Salinas (1513–90), the greatest Spanish musical humanist, was a very accomplished organist. After having studied Latin, Greek, philosophy, and arts, he spent twenty years in Rome (1538–58), during which time he studied Greek music theory from ancient sources. His most notable contribution to the development of humanism was his masterwork, the treatise *De musica libri septem* (1577 ["The Seven Books on Music"]). While a professor at the University of Salamanca, he became a close friend of Luis de León, on whose behalf he testified when the poet was incarcerated by the Inquisition.

In many regards Salinas followed the mainstream musical humanism of the period. Nevertheless, he departed from his contemporaries in a few significant ways. For example, he modified the traditional division of music by Boethius, which was dominant throughout the Middle Ages. Boethius had divided music into three categories: *musica mundana*—music of the cosmos; *musica humana*—music of the soul; and *instrumentis constituta*—music in the practical sense of being performed by instruments (Godwin 46–47). Although Salinas claimed that he did not mean to reject a division that had been adopted by "such great authors," he proposed a new tripartite division that best suited his theoretical exposition:

> [First,] that music which is perceived only by the senses . . . such as the singing of birds, which one can hear with pleasure but without any participation of the intellect, because it lacks harmonic reason. [Second,] the one that is perceived only by the intellect [Boethius's *musica mundana* and *humana*] . . . in which the ear is not delighted . . . because it is not learned from combination of sounds, but only through the logic of numbers. [And finally,] the one that is perceived by the senses and the intellect at the same time. . . . This is the one the ancient writers called *instrumentis constituta*. . . . Man alone perceives this harmony, because man alone, among the living beings, has reason. . . . And this music, which is practiced by men, can be said to be harmonic.   (*Musica libri septum* 34–35)[3]

It is significant that Salinas's tripartite division highlights his preference for instrumental or human-made music, because it is perceived equally by the senses and the intellect. In fact, he went even further in following Aristotle's rejection of the notion of the music of the spheres. He makes it clear that the music of the spheres exists not as actual musical sound but as an aesthetic idea.

Given his preference for instrumental music, Salinas devoted eleven chapters of his treatise to postulate his theories on the chromatic and enharmonic Greek *genera*. To him the enharmonic *genus* was the most important:

> It is the most exact, the most dense, and most perfect, because it contains in itself the other two genera [diatonic and chromatic] . . . to the point of the other two abandoning their own being and name, to become one with the most perfect, namely the enharmonic.   (229)[4]

Salinas strongly refutes some humanists who had concluded that the enharmonic *genus* could not be put into practice, or who had even denied its existence: "[the enharmonic *genus*] is the most difficult to sing and cannot be performed except by the most experienced and skilled in the art" (252).

After highly complex mathematical divisions of the tones, he proposed new solutions to the reconstruction of the chromatic and enharmonic *genera*. These perfect models could only be performed on a perfect type of instrument. Therefore, he clearly distinguished between "imperfect instruments," which were tuned according to artificial means, and "the perfect instrument" (199). Following the example of some of his contemporaries, he had an organ built, which according to him was most suitable for the enharmonic *genus*: "Many keyboard instruments are likewise set up according to this [enharmonic] genus (I remember having heard them played in Florence). But I have one here in Salamanca that I had built in Rome, which is the most perfect of them all" (238).

The musical performances of Salinas were legendary. We can infer that those who left a written record of them were referring to his performances on his "perfect" organ. Ambrosio Morales, for example, compared Salinas with Pythagoras:

> He has such a profound understanding of music, that I have seen him playing and singing, making in a small space the most varied movements of sadness, happiness, impetus and repose, with such power, that it no longer awes me what they write about what Pythagoras was able to do with music, nor what Saint Augustine says can be done with it.
> (qtd. in Alcalá, "'Aquesta inmensa cítara'" 253; my trans.)

Only Luis de León was able to surpass such praise when he paid tribute to his friend's musical accomplishments in the "Oda a Salinas."

Luis de León and "Oda a Salinas"

In analyzing "Oda a Salinas," we may divide it into four parts of one, two, three, and four stanzas each, namely, stanzas 1, 2–3, 4–6, and 7–10. This division is not arbitrary but rather a reflection of the ode's internal thematic organization, one that echoes the main components of the cosmological paradigm here examined and, by analogy, its debt to mysticism. Furthermore, the division into 1, 2, 3, and 4 has a direct correspondence to the Pythagorean *tetraktys*, which represented the quintessential numerical paradigm and symbol of the perfection of number.

The first stanza focuses on Salinas, emblem of the perfect musician. His "perfect music" is clearly not an abstract idea, such as the music of the spheres, but a concrete phenomenon that "resounds." Luis de León starts by acknowledging Salinas's aesthetic postulate about the superiority of music that is perceived by the senses and the intellect as it is being played by a "skillful hand."

> El aire se serena
> y viste de hermosura y luz no usada,
> Salinas, cuando suena
> la música extremada,
> por vuestra sabia mano gobernada.

The air becomes serene and puts on an unusual beauty and light, Salinas, when that exceptional music resounds which is controlled by your skillful hand.

Stanzas 2 and 3 shift the focus from Salinas to the actual effects that his "divine sound" has on the listener's soul. Luis de León echoes the neoplatonic doctrine of the power of certain appropriate music to purify the "reasoning power" and heal "the passions of the soul" that Iamblichus, among others, wrote about. Salinas's music allows the listener's soul to recover its lost memory, to know itself, and to disavow gold, the symbol of deceptive beauty. In short, the soul undergoes a purgative process that makes it better.

> A cuyo son divino
> mi alma, que en olvido está sumida,
> torna a cobrar el tino
> y memoria perdida,
> de su origen primera esclarecida.

> Y como se conoce,
> en suerte y pensamientos se mejora;
> el oro desconoce
> que el vulgo ciego adora,
> la belleza caduca, engañadora.

At that divine sound my soul, buried in forgetfulness, recovers its bearings and the lost memory of its primeval, noble source.

And as it gets to know itself, it betters its condition and thoughts; it forgets gold, which the blind mob worships, and impermanent, deceptive beauty.

Once the soul has been purified, it may now transcend the material world, the bodily hindrance to the aesthetic enjoyment of the divine musical archetype. In this illuminative stage, the soul travels to the highest sphere to come in contact with the paradigmatic musical scale and witnesses the meeting of the two numerically composed manifestations of music: Salinas's earthly enharmonic model and the grand master's divine primal sound. Interestingly, although Salinas rejected in his theories the existence of an actual, physical sound produced by the movement of the spheres, Luis de León reconciles this issue by placing in the heavenly sphere a concrete musician, the grand master, with a concrete musical instrument, a kithara. In other words, in the middle of the poem (stanza 5) Luis de León anthropomorphizes the concept of the music of the spheres, not only to conform to Salinas's aesthetics but also, and perhaps more significantly, to create the divine counterpart of the perfect music of the first stanza of the poem. The poem confirms what Iamblichus had written about mimesis and emanation: "to such like adaptations of melodies to the Gods, the Gods themselves become present" (qtd. in Mathiesen 44).

Traspasa el aire todo
hasta llegar a la más alta esfera,
y oye allí otro modo
de no perecedera
música, que es de todas la primera.

Ve cómo el gran maestro,
a aquesta inmensa cítara aplicado,
con movimiento diestro
produce el son sagrado,
con que este eterno templo es sustentado.

Y como está compuesta
de números concordes, luego envía
consonante respuesta;
y entrambas a porfía
mezclan una dulcísima armonía.

It passes through the whole atmosphere until it reaches the highest starry sphere, and there it hears another mode of imperishable music, which is the prime source of all musics.

It sees how the great Musician, leaning over this immense harp, with dextrous movement produces the sacred sound which sustains this eternal temple.

And since it is itself composed of harmonizing elements, it then sends forth a reply in tune; and as they compete, they both compound a very sweet harmony.

Finally, the soul enters the unitive stage as it drowns in the "sea of sweetness" of the union of the two kinds of music. The language is explicitly mystical. In keeping with Salinas's aesthetics, even at this climactic point the senses enjoy a superior status. Although the lyrical I explicitly condemns the "low and vile sense," he nonetheless calls on his friend to let the sound continue indefinitely, since it makes his senses awaken to the divine good, or in Plotinus's words: "Harmonies unheard create the harmonies we hear and wake the soul to the consciousness of beauty, showing it the one essence" (43).

> Aquí la alma navega
> por un mar de dulzura, y finalmente
> en él ansí se anega
> que ningún accidente
> extraño y peregrino oye o siente.
>
> ¡Oh, desmayo dichoso!
> ¡Oh, muerte que das vida! ¡Oh, dulce olvido!
> ¡Durase en tu reposo,
> sin ser restituído
> jamás a aqueste bajo y vil sentido!
>
> A aqueste bien os llamo,
> gloria del apolíneo sacro coro,
> amigos a quien amo
> sobre todo tesoro;
> que todo lo demás es triste lloro.
>
> ¡Oh! suene de contino,
> Salinas, vuestro son en mis oídos,
> por quien al bien divino
> despiertan los sentidos,
> quedando a lo demás amortecidos.

Here the soul swims in a sea of sweetness, and finally so drowns in this sea that it does not hear or perceive any accidental note which is alien or foreign.

Oh, happy swoon! Oh life-giving death! Oh, sweet forgetfulness! If only I could continue in your repose, without ever being restored to this low, inferior mode of feeling!

To this delight I summon you, glory of Apollo's sacred choir, friends whom I love more than any treasure; for everything else is sad tears.

Oh, let your music sound forever, Salinas, in my ears, for it awakens to divine delight one's senses and makes them deaf to all else.

If Salinas truly succeeded in rediscovering a lost musical paradigm, Luis de León's merit is in synthesizing in exquisite poetic language his friend's accomplishment. In other words, the ode elevates in mystical rhetoric the transcendent nature of Salinas's performance.

The exercise outlined in this essay has given me successful results in the classroom. The texts and terms (once they have been investigated) are self-explanatory. Therefore, students are capable of reconstructing the paradigm from ancient as well as early modern writings and Luis de León's ode. Furthermore, at the end of the lesson, students have had significant exposure to some fundamental aesthetic concepts that they will encounter in mystical writings. In subsequent lessons, I have seen students establishing insightful connections between the musical paradigm and the mystical experience: the existence of a divine object (music of the spheres or God) with which certain gifted humans aspire to be united; the use of specific practices (music or mental prayer) to achieve such union; the role of the senses and the intellect in the musical and mystical experiences; the relation between the purgative, illuminative, and unitive properties of music and the corresponding mystical stages; and most important, the poetic language employed to describe the aesthetic and the mystical experiences.

The only thing that I intentionally left out in my description of this classroom exercise is the subtitle for the third section. Following our discussion, students work in small groups to reach a consensus of what that subtitle should be. Their responses, such as "The Regaining of the Mystical Nature of Music" and "The Mystical Musician," invariably reveal that they successfully grasped the main objective of the lesson. During the last few minutes of the class period, I ask them about modern ideas about the power of music: new age music (which interestingly borrows much, although in distorted ways, from neoplatonic sources), Christian fundamentalist views of certain types of music as being evil (i.e., rock), the power of music to affect our emotions, the now growing field of music therapy, and so on. Although we still have some notions about the power of music, we conclude, what we have lost is an aesthetic paradigm to hold them together.

NOTES

[1] At this point it is important to clarify that the neoplatonic authors here quoted belong to the philosophical school beginning in the third century AD and not to the later neoplatonist school of the Renaissance.

[2] Plato describes the music of the spheres: "Through the middle of the light from heaven, the extremities of its ligatures extended . . . by which all the revolutions were turned round, whose spindle and point were both of adamant, but its whirl mixed of this

and of other things. . . . The whirls were eight in all, as circles one within another. . . . And the circle of the seventh is the brightest. . . . And whilst the whole is turning round, the seven inner circles are gently turned round in a contrary motion to the whole. . . . And on each of its circles there was seated a Siren on the upper side, carried round, and uttering a single sound on one pitch. But the whole of them, being eight, composed a single harmony" (qtd. in Godwin 4–8).

[3] Interestingly, in an earlier, unpublished version of his treatise, Salinas had included a fourth type of music: "the one that we believe is performed by the angels when they serve our Almighty God, and they play their citharas, which we cannot hear nor understand in this life, unless it were a miracle; but we believe in it only through faith, and we wait to hear in the afterlife" (*Musices liber tertius* 213). Salinas probably follows here the practice of his contemporaries in removing Christian symbols from his theoretical discussion.

[4] English translations of Salinas's treatise are mine.

NOTES ON CONTRIBUTORS

Gillian T. W. Ahlgren is professor of theology, Xavier University. She is the author and editor of four books: *Teresa of Ávila and the Politics of Sanctity, Human Person and the Church, The Inquisition of Francisca: A Sixteenth-Century Visionary on Trial*, and *Entering Teresa of Ávila's* Interior Castle: *A Reader's Companion. The Inquisition of Francisca* received the 2006 Best Translation of the Year Award from the Society for the Study of Early Modern Women.

Linda Belau is associate professor of English, University of Texas, Pan American. She has edited two collections of essays and written extensively on trauma and psychoanalysis. Her articles have appeared in the *Cardoza Law Review, A: Journal of Culture and the Unconscious, Vitalpoetics, Postmodern Culture*, and Gramma: *Journal of Theory and Translation*.

Dana Bultman is associate professor of Spanish, University of Georgia. She is the author of *Heretical Mixtures: Feminine and Poetic Opposition to Matter-Spirit Dualism in Spain, 1531–1631* and has written articles on Góngora and early modern Spanish poets.

Joan Cammarata is professor of Spanish, Manhattan College. She has written widely on Teresa of Ávila, Cervantes, and Spanish Renaissance poetry. She is the author of *Mythological Themes in the Works of Garcilaso de la Vega* and has edited *Women in the Discourse of Early Modern Spain.* Her book on the epistolary production of Teresa of Ávila, "Letters from Teresa: The Cultural Politics of Feminine Epistolography in Early Modern Spain," is forthcoming.

William Childers is associate professor of Spanish, Brooklyn College, City University of New York. He is the author of *Transnational Cervantes*, awarded in 2007 the MLA's Katherine Singer Kovacs Prize, as well as articles on Cervantes and other topics relating to the Spanish baroque. His current book project is tentatively titled "Spain's Last Moors: A Cultural History of the Morisco Question."

David H. Darst is professor of Spanish at Florida State University, Tallahassee. He is the author of *The Comic Art of Tirso de Molina, Juan Boscán*, and *Converting Fiction: Counter-Reformational Closure in the Secular Literature of Golden Age Spain.* He has written articles on the poetry, drama, and intellectual traditions of the Spanish Golden Age.

Darcy Donahue is associate professor of Spanish and women's studies at Miami University. Her scholarly interests include early modern Spanish narrative, biography, and cultural studies. She has published articles on Cervantes, Teresa of Ávila and spiritual autobiography and is the author of a translation and critical study of the autobiography of Ana de San Bartolomé.

Ralph Keen is associate professor of religious studies, University of Iowa. His publications include *Divine and Human Authority in Reformation Thought: German Theologians on Political Order, 1520–1555* and *The Christian Tradition: An Historical Introduction.* The editor and translator of Johannes Cochlaeus's *Responsio ad Johannem Bugenhagium Pomeranum*, he has written extensively on Thomas More and Philipp Melanchthon. Part of his current research addresses the role of tradition in early modern Catholic thought.

Dona M. Kercher is professor of Spanish and chair of modern and classical languages and cultures, Assumption College. She has published articles on the cultural politics of the Cervantine films of Manuel Gutiérrez Aragón in *Refiguring Spain* and in *Cine-Lit* and *Arizona Journal of Hispanic Cultural Studies*. Her essays on the films of Alex de la Iglesia and media history have appeared in *Post-Script* and *Alternative Europe*. She is currently working on a book on the appreciation of Hitchcock in Spain and Latin America.

Howard Mancing is professor of Spanish, Purdue University. He is the author of *The Chivalric World of Don Quijote: Style, Structure, and Narrative Technique*, *The Cervantes Encyclopedia*, and *Cervantes' Don Quixote: A Reference Guide*. He is coeditor of *Text, Theory, and Performance: Golden Age Comedia Studies*. He has published articles on Cervantes, the picaresque novel, and literary theory and cognition.

Michael McGaha is professor of Spanish, Pomona College, emeritus. The former editor of the journal *Cervantes* and the author of numerous articles and translations of Spanish Golden Age literature, his most recent book is *Autobiographies of Orhan Pamuk: The Writer in His Novels*.

Bárbara Mujica is professor of Spanish, Georgetown University. She has published eight anthologies of Spanish and Spanish American literature and written extensively on mysticism, the pastoral novel, and seventeenth-century theater. Her most recent books are *Women Writers of Early Modern Spain: Sophia's Daughters*; *Teresa de Jesús: Feminismo y espiritualidad*; *Sister Teresa*, a novel; and *Teresa de Ávila: Lettered Woman*.

Kathleen Ann Myers is professor of Hispanic studies, Indiana University, Bloomington. She is the author of two books on María de San José and of *Neither Saints nor Sinners: Writing the Lives of Women in Spanish America*. Her most recent book is *Fernandez de Oviedo's Chronicle of America: A New History for a New World*.

Mario A. Ortiz is assistant professor of Spanish, The Catholic University of America. He has published a collection of essays, *Representationes modernas de Sor Juana*, and articles on Unamuno, Ana Caro, and Sor Juana; is currently working on a monograph, "Music in the Life and Works of Sor Juana Inés de la Cruz"; and is editing a collection of essays, "Representaciones modernas de Sor Juana."

Amanda Powell is senior instructor of Spanish at the University of Oregon. She is author, with Kathleen A. Myers, of *A Wild Country Out in the Garden: The Spiritual Journals of a Colonial Mexican Nun*, which is a study of the writer Mariá de San José Palacio Berruecos, and editor and translator, with Electa Arenal, of *The Answer / La Respuesta*, by Sor Juana Inés de la Cruz. Her translations of sixteenth- and seventeenth-century Spanish and Spanish American women writers include works of poetry and prose in *Book for the Hour of Recreation* by Mariá de San José Salazar (ed. Weber) and *Untold Sisters: Hispanic Nuns in Their Own Works* (ed. Arenal and Schlau). Her essays address early modern women's spiritual and secular writings, including baroque neoplatonism and the pan-European fashion for women's love poetry to women.

Helen H. Reed is professor emerita of Spanish, State University of New York, Oneonta. She is the author of *The Reader in the Picaresque Novel* and articles on early modern Spanish literature and history. She has nearly finished a short biography, "The King's Captive: The Life and Letters of Ana de Mendoza, Princess of Eboli." Her other research interests include Cervantes, literary theory, and women's studies.

Elizabeth Rhodes is associate professor in the Department of Romance Languages and Literatures, Boston College. She teaches writing, film, women's studies, and early modern Spanish culture. She recently translated and edited, with Margaret Greer, selected stories by Mariá de Zayas and edited, with Juan Montero, the poetry of Jorge de Montemayor. Her latest articles appear in *Caliope, Bulletin of the Comediantes*, and *Hispanic Review*.

María del Pilar Ryan is associate professor and chief, International Division, Department of History, United States Military Academy, West Point. Her research interests include Jesuit history, politics in early modern Spain, and the history of sainthood.

Emily E. Scida is associate professor of Spanish linguistics, University of Virginia, where she is also the director of the Spanish and Italian language programs. Her research interests include comparative and historical Romance linguistics, foreign language teaching, and second language acquisition. She has contributed chapters in *The Romance Languages: A Historical Introduction* and in *El español a través de la lingüística: Preguntas y respuestas*. She is the author of *The Inflected Infinitive in Romance Languages*.

Barbara Simerka is associate professor of Spanish, Queens College, City University of New York. She is the author of *Discourses of Empire: Counter-epic Literatures in Early Modern Spain* and the editor of *El arte nuevo de estudiar comedias*. Her articles have appeared in *Bulletin of Hispanic Studies, Hispanic Review*, and *Comparative Literature Studies*. She is currently working on a book on cognitive theory and gender.

Carole Slade is adjunct associate professor of English and comparative literature at Columbia University. She is the editor of the MLA's *Approaches to Teaching Dante's Divine Comedy* and the author of *St. Teresa of Ávila: Author of a Heroic Life*. Her articles include studies of Teresa of Ávila, medieval mysticism, gender, and autobiography as genre. She is writing a book on spiritual autobiography.

Sherry Velasco is professor of Spanish literature and culture, University of Southern California, Los Angeles. She is the author of *Male Delivery: Reproduction, Effeminacy, and Pregnant Men in Early Modern Spain, The Lieutenant Nun: Transgenderism, Lesbian Desire, and Catalina de Erauso*, and *Demons, Nausea, and Resistance in the Autobiography of Isabel de Jesús (1611–1682)*. Her research interests include the literature of self-representation, sexuality and literature, and iconography and literature.

Marta V. Vicente is associate professor, Women, Gender, and Sexuality Studies Program and history department, University of Kansas. She is the editor, with Luis Corteguera, of *Women, Texts and Authority in the Early Modern Spanish World* and the author of *Clothing the Spanish Empire: Families and the Calico Trade in the Early Modern Atlantic World*.

Lisa Vollendorf is professor of Spanish at California State University, Long Beach. She is the author of *The Lives of Women: A New History of Inquisitional Spain* and *Reclaiming the Body: María de Zayas's Early Modern Feminism* and the editor of *Recovering Spain's Feminist Tradition* and *Literatura y feminismo en España*. Currently she is editing, with James A. Parr, *Approaches to Teaching Cervantes's* Don Quixote and preparing a book on Cervantes and his women readers.

Alison Weber is professor of Spanish at the University of Virginia. She is the author of *Teresa of Ávila and the Rhetoric of Femininity* and the editor of *For the Hour of Recreation,* by María de San José Salazar. Her work concentrates on gender and religious experience in early modern Spain.

Christopher C. Wilson, a specialist in the art of Spain, the Spanish Netherlands, and colonial Latin America, teaches at the Holton-Arms School in Bethesda, Maryland. His work concentrates on the iconography and artistic patronage of the Discalced Carmelite order.

Cordula van Wyhe is lecturer in art history at the University of York. She has published articles on religious iconography, seventeenth-century court culture, and Netherlandish art. Her edition of the spiritual autobiography of the venerable Margaret of the Mother of God is forthcoming.

SURVEY PARTICIPANTS

Grace Aaron, *University of North Carolina, Chapel Hill*
Elizabeth Adams, *Temple University*
Johnnie Ruth Adams, *Southwest Tennessee Community College*
Gillian T. W. Ahlgren, *Xavier University*
Julio Baena, *University of Colorado, Boulder*
Linda Belau, *University of Texas, Pan American*
Jodi Bilinkoff, *University of North Carolina, Greensboro*
Dana Bultman, *University of Georgia*
Joan Cammarata, *Manhattan College*
William Childers, *Brooklyn College, City University of New York*
Sarah Coakley, *Harvard Divinity School*
David H. Darst, *Florida State University, Tallahassee*
George Greenia, *College of William and Mary*
Helen Hills, *University of Manchester*
Cleveland Johnson, *Spelman College*
Ralph Keen, *University of Iowa*
Patricia Manning, *University of Kansas*
Howard Mancing, *Purdue University*
Bárbara Mujica, *Georgetown University*
Kathleen Ann Myers, *Indiana University, Bloomington*
Mario Ortiz, *The Catholic University of America*
Amanda Powell, *University of Oregon*
Dale Pratt, *Brigham Young University*
Helen Reed, *State University of New York, Oneonta*
Roy Rosenstein, *American University of Paris*
María del Pilar Ryan, *United States Military Academy, West Point*
Ann Sittig, *Metropolitan Community College*
Sherry Velasco, *University of California, Los Angeles*
Marta V. Vicente, *University of Kansas*
Lisa Vollendorf, *California State University, Long Beach*
Carole Slade, *Columbia University*
Cordula van Wyhe, *University of York (United Kingdom)*

WORKS CITED

Ahlgren, Gillian T. W. "Ecstasy, Prophecy, and Reform: Catherine of Siena as a Model for Holy Women of Sixteenth-Century Spain." Boenig 53–65.

———. *Entering Teresa of Ávila's* Interior Castle: *A Reader's Companion*. New York: Paulist, 2005.

———, ed. and trans. *The Inquisition of Francisca: A Sixteenth-Century Visionary on Trial*. The Other Voice in Early Modern Europe. Chicago: U of Chicago P, 2005.

———. "Teresa of Ávila (1515–1582)." Lindberg 311–24.

———. *Teresa of Ávila and the Politics of Sanctity*. Ithaca: Cornell UP, 1996.

Alcalá, Ángel. "'Aquesta inmensa cítara': An Aesthetics of Musical Ecstasy in Fray Luis de León's (1527–1591) *Ode to Salinas*." *Libraries, History, Diplomacy, and the Performing Arts: Essays in Honor of Carleton Sprague Smith*. Ed. Israel J. Katz. Festschrift Ser. 9. Stuyvesant: Pendragon, 1991. 247–92.

———. "Fray Luis de León, maestro de S. Juan de la Cruz: De la *Exposición del Cantar de los cantares* al *Cántico espiritual* y los tratados místicos." *Boletín de la Biblioteca de Menéndez y Pelayo* 74 (1998): 33–64.

Allen, Prudence. "Soul, Body and Transcendence in Teresa of Ávila." *Toronto Journal of Theology* 3 (1987): 252–66.

Alonso, Dámaso. *La poesía de San Juan de la Cruz (desde esta ladera)*. 1958. 4th ed. Madrid: Aguilar, 1966.

———. *Poesía española: Ensayo de métodos y límites estilísticos*. Rev. ed. Madrid: Gredos, 1976.

Alonso, Martín. *Evolución sintáctica del español*. Madrid: Aguilar, 1962.

Álvarez, Tomás, ed. *Diccionario de Santa Teresa: Doctrina e historia*. Burgos: Monte Carmelo, 2002.

———. "Santa Teresa y las mujeres en la iglesia: Glosa al texto teresiano de Camino 3." *Monte Carmelo* 89 (1981): 121–32.

Amar y Borbón, María Josefa. *Discurso en defensa del talento de las mugeres*. 1786. 29 Aug. 2005 <http://www.fh-augsburg.de/~harsch/hispanica/Cronologia/siglo18/Amar/ama_intr.html>.

———. *Discurso sobre la educación física y moral de las mujeres*. 1790. Ed. María Victoria López-Cordón. Madrid: Cátedra; Valencia: U de Valencia, 1994.

Amelang, James S. "Autobiografías femeninas." Ortega, Lavrin, and Pérez Cantó 155–68.

Ana de Jesús. *Anne de Jésus: Carmélite déchaussée*. Ed. Antonio Fortes and Restituto Palmero. Toulouse: Editions du Carmel, 2001.

———. *Cartas (1590–1621): Religiosidad y vida cotidiana en la clausura femenina del Siglo de Oro*. Ed. Concepción Torres. Salamanca: U de Salamanca, 1995.

Ana de San Bartolomé. *Ana de San Bartolomé: Discípula y heredera de S. Teresa: Obras Completas*. Ed. Julian Urkiza. Burgos: Monte Carmelo, 1998.

———. *Autobiography and Other Writings*. Ed. and trans. Darcy Donahue. The Other Voice in Early Modern Europe. U of Chicago P, 2008.

Andrés Martín, Melquíades. "Common Denominators of Alumbrados, Erasmians, 'Luterans,' and Mystics: The Risk of a More 'Intimate Spirituality.'" *The Spanish Inquisition and the Inquisitorial Mind*. Ed. Ángel Alcalá. New York: Columbia UP, 1987.

———. *Historia de la mística de la edad de oro en España*. Madrid: Católica, 1994.

———. *Los místicos de la edad de oro en España y América: Antología*. Madrid: Católica, 1996.

———. *Los recogidos: Nueva visión de la mística española (1500–1700)*. Madrid: Fundación U Española, 1975.

Antony, Louise, and Charlotte Witt, eds. *A Mind of One's Own: Feminist Essays on Reason and Objectivity*. Boulder: Westview, 1993.

Arenal, Electa, and Stacey Schlau. Introduction. Arenal and Schlau, *Untold Sisters* 1–17.

———. "'Leyendo yo y escribiendo ella': The Convent as Intellectual Community." *Journal of Hispanic Philology* 13 (1989): 214–29.

———. "Stratagems of the Strong, Stratagems of the Weak: Autobiographical Prose of the Seventeenth-Century Hispanic Convent." *Tulsa Studies in Women's Literature* 9 (1990): 25–42.

———. "Two Sisters among the Sisters: The Flowering of Intellectual Convent Culture." Arenal and Schlau, *Untold Sisters* 131–89.

———, eds. *Untold Sisters: Hispanic Nuns in Their Own Works*. Trans. Amanda Powell. 1989. Rev. ed. Chicago: U of Chicago P, forthcoming.

Arias Montano, Benito. "Paráfrasis sobre el Cantar de los Cantares de Salomón." Blecua, *Edad* 1: 207–08.

Asín Palacios, Miguel. "Un precursor hispanomusulmán de San Juan de la Cruz." *Obras escogidas*. Vol. 1. Madrid: CSIC, 1945. 243–326. Rpt. of *Al-Andalus* 1 (1933): 7–79.

———. *Sadilíes y alumbrados*. Introd. Luce López Baralt. Madrid: Hiperión, 1990.

———. *Saint John of the Cross and Islam*. Trans. Howard W. Yoder and Elmer H. Douglas. New York: Vantage, 1981.

Augustine. *Confessions*. Trans. Henry Chadwick. Oxford: Oxford UP, 1991.

———. *On Christian Doctrine*. Trans. J. F. Shaw. Great Books of the Western World 18. Chicago: Encyclopedia Britannica, 1952.

Bakhtin, Mikhail. *The Dialogic Imagination: Four Essays*. Ed. Michael Holquist. Trans. Caryl Emerson and Holquist. Austin: U of Texas P, 1981.

Báñez, Domingo. "Report Made by the Master Fray Domingo Báñez on the Spirit of Saint Teresa and on the Autograph Narrative of Her Life." Teresa of Ávila, *Complete Works* 3: 333–36.

Barnstone, Willis. "Mystico-Erotic Love in 'O Living Flame of Love.'" *Revista hispánica moderna* 37 (1972–73): 253–61.

Barrientos, Alberto, et al., eds. *Introducción a la lectura de Santa Teresa*. 2nd rev. ed. Madrid: Espiritualidad, 2002.

Bartlett, Anne Clark, ed. *Vox Mystica: Essays on Medieval Mysticism in Honor of Professor Valerie M. Lagorio*. Cambridge: Brewer, 1995.

Bastons Vivanco, Carlos. "Ética y estética en la estilística del *Libro de la vida* de Santa Teresa." *Actas del I Congreso Internacional sobre Santa Teresa y la Mística Hispánica.* Ed. Manuel Criado de Val. Madrid: EDI, 1984. 229–41.

Bataillon, Marcel. *Erasmo y España: Estudios sobre la historia espiritual del siglo XVI.* Trans. Antonio Alatorre. México, DF: Fondo de Cultura Económica, 1966.

Beatriz de la Concepcíon. *Lettres choisies de Béatrix de la Conception.* Ed. Pierre Serouet. Paris: Desclée de Brouwer, 1967.

Beinart, Haim. "The Great Conversion and the *Converso* Problem." *The Sephardi Legacy.* Ed. Beinart. Vol. 1. Jerusalem: Magnes, 1992. 346–82. 2 vols.

Benjamin, Walter. "The Task of the Translator / Die Aufgabe des Ubersetzers." *Delos: A Journal on and of Translation* 2 (1968): 76–99.

Bilinkoff, Jodi. *The Ávila of Saint Teresa: Religious Reform in a Sixteenth-Century City.* Ithaca: Cornell UP, 1989.

———. "Confession, Gender, Life-Writing: Some Cases (Mainly) from Spain." *Penitence in the Age of Reformations.* Ed. Katharine Jackson Lualdi and Anne T. Thayer. Aldershot: Ashgate, 2000. 169–83.

———. "Confessors, Penitents, and the Construction of Identities in Early Modern Ávila." *Culture and Identity in Early Modern Europe (1500–1800).* Ed. Barbara B. Diefendorf and Carla Hesse. Ann Arbor: U of Michigan P, 1993. 83–100.

———. "The Many 'Lives' of Pedro de Ribadeneyra." *Renaissance Quarterly* 52 (1999): 180–96.

———. "A Peasant Visionary and Her Audience." *Studia Mystica* 18 (1997): 36–59.

———. *Related Lives: Confessors, Female Penitents, and Catholic Culture, 1450–1650.* Ithaca: Cornell UP, 2005.

———. "Teresa of Jesus and Carmelite Reform." *Religious Orders of the Catholic Reformation: Essays in Honor of John C. Olin on His Seventy-Fifth Birthday.* Ed. Richard De Molen. New York: Fordham UP, 1994. 166–86.

———. "Woman with a Mission: Teresa of Ávila and the Apostolic Model." *Modelli di santità e modelli di comportamento.* Ed. Giulia Barone, Marina Caffiero, and Francesco Scorza Barcellona. Turin: Rosenberg, 1994. 295–305.

Black, Georgina Dopico. *Perfect Wives, Other Women: Adultery and Inquisition in Early Modern Spain.* Durham: Duke UP, 2001.

Blecua, José Manuel. *Poesía de la edad de oro.* 2 vols. Madrid: Castalia, 1982.

Boenig, Robert, ed. *The Mystical Gesture: Essays on Medieval and Early Modern Spiritual Culture in Honor of Mary E. Giles.* Aldershot: Ashgate, 2000.

Bossy, John. *Christianity in the West, 1400–1700.* Oxford: Oxford UP, 1985.

Boureau, Alain. "Les structures narratives de *La Legenda aurea*: De la variation au grand chant sacré." *Legenda aurea, sept siècles de diffusion. Actes du colloque international sur la* Legenda aurea, *texte latin et branches vernaculaires à l' Université de Québec à Montréal, 11–12 mai 1983.* Ed. Brenda Dunn-Lardeau. Montreal: Bellarmin, 1986. 57–76.

Boyden, James M. *The Courtier and the King: Ruy Gómez da Silva, Philip II, and the Court of Spain.* Berkeley: U of California P, 1995.

Boyle, Marjorie O'Rourke. "Angels Black and White: Loyola's Spiritual Discernment in Historical Perspective." *Theological Studies* 44 (1983): 241–57.

———. *Loyola's Acts*. Berkeley: U of California P, 1997.

Brétigny, Jean de. *Quintanadueñas. Lettres*. Ed. Pierre Sérouet. Louvain: Bureaux de la R. H. E., 1971.

Brown, Dan. *The Da Vinci Code*. New York: Doubleday, 2003.

Brown, Jonathan. *Painting in Spain: 1500–1700*. New Haven: Yale UP, 1991.

Brown, Judith. *Immodest Acts: The Life of a Lesbian Nun in Renaissance Italy*. Oxford: Oxford UP, 1986.

Bunkers, Suzanne L., and Cynthia A. Huff. Introduction. *Inscribing the Daily: Critical Essays on Women's Diaries*. Ed. Bunkers and Huff. Amherst: U of Massachusetts P, 1996. 1–20.

Burke, Peter. "How to Be a Counter-Reformation Saint." *Religion and Society in Early Modern Europe, 1500–1800*. Ed. Kaspar von Greyerz. London: Allen, 1984. 45–55.

Bynum, Caroline Walker. "The Female Body and Religious Practice in the Later Middle Ages." *Fragmentation and Redemption: Essays on Gender and the Human Body in Medieval Religion*. New York: Zone, 1991. 181–238.

———. *Holy Feast and Holy Fast: The Religious Significance of Food to Medieval Women*. Berkeley: U of California P, 1987.

———. "Women's Stories, Women's Symbols: A Critique of Victor Turner's Theory of Liminality." *Anthropology and the Study of Religion*. Ed. Frank Reynolds and Robert Moore. Chicago: Center for the Scientific Study of Religion, 1984. 105–25.

Calvert, Laura. *Francisco de Osuna and the Spirit of the Letter*. Chapel Hill: U of North Carolina P, 1973.

Cantin, Lucie. "Femininity: From Passion to an Ethics of the Impossible." *Topoi* 12 (1993): 127–36.

Cárdenas, Juan de. "Aprobación." *Desengaño de religiosos, y de almas que tratan de virtud....* By María de la Antigua. Sevilla: Cabeças, 1678. N. pag.

Carpenter, J. A., and Come Carpenter. "La experiencia y la escatología mística de Santa Teresa y sus paralelos en el islam medieval de los Sufis." *Santa Teresa y la literatura mística hispánica: Actas del I Congreso Internacional sobre Santa Teresa y la Mística Hispánica*. Ed. Manuel Criado de Val. Madrid: EDI–6, 1984. 159–87.

Carpi, Elena, Antonina Saba, and Manuela Sassi. "Los diminutivos orgánicos en la obra de Teresa de Ávila." *Epos* 12 (1996): 159–76.

Carrión, María. *Arquitectura y cuerpo en la figura autorial de Teresa de Jesús*. Barcelona: Anthropos, 1994.

Caruth, Cathy, ed. *Trauma: Explorations in Memory*. Baltimore: John Hopkins UP, 1995.

Castro, Américo. *De la edad conflictiva*. Madrid: Taurus, 1961.

Certeau, Michel de. *The Mystic Fable: The Sixteenth and Seventeenth Centuries*. Trans. Michael B. Smith. Chicago: U of Chicago P, 1992.

Chorpenning, Joseph. *The Divine Romance: Teresa of Ávila's Narrative Theology.* Chicago: Loyola UP, 1992.

———. "Fray Luis de León's Writings on St. Teresa of Jesus." *Teresianum* 43 (1992): 133–74.

———. "The Literary and Theological Method of the *Interior Castle.*" *Journal of Hispanic Philology* 3 (1979): 121–33.

Christian, William A., Jr. *Local Religion in Sixteenth-Century Spain.* Princeton: Princeton UP, 1981.

Coakley, John W. *Women, Men, and Spiritual Power: Female Saints and Their Male Collaborators.* Columbia: Columbia UP, 2006.

Coakley, Sarah. *Powers and Submissions: Spirituality, Philosophy and Gender.* Oxford: Blackwell, 2002.

Code, Lorraine. "Experience, Knowledge, and Responsibility." Garry and Pearsall 157–72.

———. *What Can She Know? Feminist Theory and the Construction of Knowledge.* Ithaca: Cornell UP, 1991.

Cohen, J. M. Introduction. *The Life of St. Teresa of Ávila by Herself.* Trans. Cohen. New York: Penguin, 1957. 11–20.

Colahan, Clark. "María de Jesús de Agreda: The Sweetheart of the Holy Office." Giles, *Women* 155–70.

Coleman, David. "Moral Formation and Social Control in the Catholic Reformation: The Case of San Juan de Ávila." *Sixteenth Century Journal* 26 (1995): 17–30.

Coloquio de amor. Perf. Sonnia L. Rivas-Caballero and Octavio Lafourcade Señoret. RTVE-Música, 2003.

Concha, Víctor García de la. *El arte literario de Santa Teresa.* Barcelona: Ariel, 1978.

Concha, Víctor García de la, and María Álvarez Pellitero, eds. *Libro de romances y coplas del Carmelo de Valladolid (c. 1590–1609).* 2 vols. Salamanca: Consejo General de Castilla y León, 1982.

Connolly, Peter, ed. *Approaches to the Study of Religion.* London: Cassell, 1999.

———. Introduction. Connolly, *Approaches* 1–9.

Corteguera, Luis R. "The Making of a Visionary Woman: The Life of Beatriz Ana Ruiz, 1666–1735." Vicente and Corteguera 165–82.

Corteguera, Luis R., and Sherry M. Velasco. "Authority in the Margins: Reexamining the Autograph Letters between Sor María de Ágreda and Philip IV of Spain." *Women's Voices and the Politics of the Spanish Empire: From the Convent Cell to the Imperial Court.* Ed. Jennifer L. Eich, Jeanne L. Gillespie, and Lucia Harringdon. New Orleans: UP of the South, 2008. 223–48.

Coward, Harold, and Toby Foshay, eds. *Derrida and Negative Theology.* Albany: State U of New York P, 1992.

Criado de Val, Manuel. "'Ser' y 'estar' en Santa Teresa y en San Juan de la Cruz." *Actas del I Congreso Internacional sobre Santa Teresa y la Mística Hispánica.* Ed. Criado de Val. Madrid: EDI, 1984. 119–211.

Crow, John A. *Spain: The Root and the Flower: An Interpretation of Spain and the Spanish People.* 3rd ed. Berkeley: U of California P, 1985.

Culley, Margo. Introduction. *A Day at a Time. The Diary Literature of American Women from 1764 to the Present*. Ed. Culley. New York: Feminist, 1985. 3–26.

Dalmases, Cándido de. *Ignatius of Loyola, Founder of the Jesuits*. Saint Louis: Inst. of Jesuit Sources, 1985.

Daly, Mary. *The Church and the Second Sex*. New York: Harper, 1968.

D'Aquili, Eugene, and Andrew Newberg. *The Mystical Mind: Probing the Biology of Religious Experience*. Minneapolis: Fortress, 1999.

Davies, Gareth. "Saint Teresa and the Jewish Question." *Teresa de Jesús and Her World*. Ed. Margaret Rees. Leeds: Trinity and All Saints Coll., 1981. 51–73.

The Da Vinci Code. Dir. Ron Howard. USA, 2006.

Davis, Natalie Zemon. *The Return of Martin Guerre*. Cambridge: Harvard UP, 1983.

Delooz, Pierre. *Sociologie et canonisations*. Liège: Faculté de Droit, 1969.

Derrida, Jacques. "How to Avoid Speaking: Denials." Coward and Foshay 73–142.

———. "Of an Apocalyptic Tone Newly Adopted in Philosophy." Coward and Foshay 25–72.

Dicken, E. W. Trueman. *The Crucible of Love: A Study of the Mysticism of St. Teresa of Jesus and St. John of the Cross*. New York: Sheeds, 1963.

Diefendorf, Barbara B. *From Penitence to Charity: Pious Women and the Catholic Reformation in Paris*. New York: Oxford UP, 2004.

Dilthey, Wilhelm. *Selected Writings*. Ed. and trans. H. P. Rickman. New York: Cambridge UP, 1976.

Dinan, Susan E., and Debra Meyers, eds. *Women and Religion in Old and New Worlds*. New York: Routledge, 2001.

Disse, Dorothy. *Other Women's Voices: Translations of Women's Writing before 1700*. 10 Sept. 2007. 22 Dec. 2007 <http:www.home.infionline.net/~ddisse>.

D'Lugo, Marvin. *The Films of Carlos Saura: The Practice of Seeing*. Princeton: Princeton UP, 1991.

Donahue, Darcy. "Writing Lives: Nuns and Confessors as (Auto)biographers in Early Modern Spain." *Journal of Hispanic Philology* 13 (1989): 230–39.

Donnelly, Dorothy. "The Sexual Mystic: Embodied Spirituality." Giles, *Feminist Mystic* 120–41.

Downey, Michael, ed. *New Dictionary of Catholic Spirituality*. Collegeville: Liturgical, 1993.

Dupré, Louis, and Don E. Saliers, eds. In collaboration with John Meyendorff. *Christian Spirituality: Post-Reformation and Modern*. New York: Crossroad, 1991.

Efrén de la Madre de Dios and Otger Steggink. *Tiempo y vida de Santa Teresa*. 3rd ed. Madrid: Católica, 1996.

Egido, Teófanes. "Ambiente histórico." *Introducción a la lectura de Santa Teresa*. Ed. Alberto Barrientos, et al. 2nd rev. ed. Madrid: Espiritualidad, 2002. 63–155.

———. "La familia judía de Santa Teresa (Ensayo de erudición histórica)." *Studia Zamorensia* 3 (1982): 449–79.

Elia, Paola, and María Jesús Mancho. "Notas complementarias." John of the Cross, *Cántico* 408–785.

———. Prologue. John of the Cross, *Cántico* xxi–clii.

Elliott, John H. *Imperial Spain, 1469–1716.* London: Penguin, 1990.

Endean, Philip. "'The Strange Style of Prayer': Mercurian, Cordeses, and Álvarez." McCoog 351–97.

Erauso, Catalina de. *The Lieutenant Nun: Memoir of a Basque Transvestite in the New World.* Trans. Michele Stepto and Gabriel Stepto. Boston: Beacon, 1996.

Evans, Dylan. *An Introductory Dictionary of Psychoanalysis.* New York: Routledge, 1997.

Ferrari, Leo Charles. "The Theme of the Prodigal Son in Augustine's *Confessions.*" *Recherches Augustiniennes* 12 (1977): 105–18.

Fink, Bruce. A *Clinical Introduction to Lacanian Psychoanalysis.* Cambridge: Harvard UP, 1997.

Flynn, Maureen. "The Spiritual Uses of Pain in Spanish Mysticism." *Journal of the American Academy of Religion* 64 (1996): 257–77.

Foster, David William, ed. *Literatura española: Una antología.* 2 vols. New York: Garland, 1995.

Fray Luis de León: Un intellectual comprometido. Television Española. RTVE, 1991. Videodisc. Films for the Humanities and Sciences, 2001.

Freccero, John. "Autobiography and Narrative." *Reconstructing Individualism: Autonomy, Individuality, and the Self in Western Thought.* Ed. Thomas C. Heller, Morton Sosna, and David Wellbery. Stanford: Stanford UP, 1986. 16–29.

Freedberg, David. *Iconoclasm and Painting in the Revolt of the Netherlands, 1566–1609.* New York: Taylor, 1988.

Frohlich, Mary. *The Intersubjectivity of the Mystic: A Study of Teresa of Ávila's* Interior Castle. New York: Oxford UP, 2000.

Gannett, Cinthia. *Gender and the Journal: Diaries and Academic Discourse.* Albany: State U of New York P, 1992.

Garry, Ann, and Marilyn Pearsall, eds. *Women, Knowledge, and Reality: Explorations in Feminist Philosophy.* New York: Routledge, 1992.

Gaylord, Mary Malcolm, and Francisco Márquez Villanueva, eds. *San Juan de la Cruz and Fray Luis de León: A Commemorative International Symposium.* Newark: Juan de la Cuesta, 1996.

Gerli, Michael. "'El castillo interior' y el arte de la memoria." *Santa Teresa y la literatura mística hispánica.* Ed. Manuel Criado de Val. Madrid: EDI–6, 1984. 331–37.

Gertrude of Helfta. *The Herald of Divine Love.* Trans. and ed. Margaret Winkworth. New York: Paulist, 1993.

Gilbert, Sandra M., and Susan Gubar. "Infection in the Sentence: The Woman Writer and the Anxiety of Authorship." 1979. *Feminisms: An Anthology of Literary Theory and Criticism.* Ed. Robyn R. Worhol and Diane Price Herndl. Rev. ed. New Brunswick: Rutgers UP, 1997. 21–32.

———. *The Madwoman in the Attic: The Woman Writer and the Nineteenth-Century Literary Imagination.* New Haven: Yale UP, 1979.

Gil de Muro, Eduardo. Teresa de Jesús *en TVE.* Burgos: Monte Carmelo, 1985.

Giles, Mary E. *The* Book of Prayer *of Sor María of Santo Domingo: A Study and Translation.* Albany: State U of New York P, 1990.

———, ed. *The Feminist Mystic.* New York: Crossroad, 1982.

———. Introduction. Osuna, *Third Spiritual Alphabet* 1–34.

———, ed. *Women in the Inquisition: Spain and the New World.* Baltimore: Johns Hopkins UP, 1999.

Gilligan, Carol. *In a Different Voice: Psychological Theory and Women's Development.* Cambridge: Harvard UP, 1982.

Gilmore, Leigh. *Autobiographics: A Feminist Theory of Women's Self-Representation.* Ithaca: Cornell UP, 1994.

Godwin, Joscelyn. *Music, Mysticism and Magic: A Sourcebook.* London: Routledge, 1986.

Gómez-Menor Fuentes, José. *El linaje familiar de Santa Teresa y de San Juan de la Cruz: Sus parientes toledanos.* Toledo: Gráficas Cervantes, 1970.

Gordon, Linda. "What's New in Women's History." *Feminist Studies / Critical Studies.* Ed. Teresa de Laurentis. Bloomington: Indiana UP, 1986. 20–30.

Göttler, Christine. "Securing Space in a Foreign Place: Peter Paul Rubens' *Saint Teresa* for the Portuguese Merchant-Bankers in Antwerp." *Journal of the Walters Art Gallery* 57 (1999): 133–51.

Gracián, Jerónimo. *Peregrinación de Anastasio.* Barcelona: Flores, 1966.

Graziano, Frank. *Wounds of Love: The Mystical Marriage of Saint Rose of Lima.* New York: Oxford UP, 2004.

Greco, El. *Repentant Magdalen.* Worcester Art Museum, Massachusetts.

El Greco. Exhibition catalog. London: Natl. Gallery, 2003.

Green, Deirdre. *Gold in the Crucible: Teresa of Ávila and the Western Mystical Tradition.* Longmead: Element, 1989.

Greenspan, Kate. "Autohagiography and Medieval Women's Spiritual Autobiography." *Gender and Text in the Later Middle Ages.* Ed. Jane Chance. Gainesville: UP of Florida, 1996. 216–36.

Grendler, Paul, gen. ed. *Encyclopedia of the Renaissance.* 6 vols. New York: Scribner's, 1999.

Guillén, Jorge. "The Ineffable Language of Mysticism." *Language and Poetry: Some Poets of Spain.* Cambridge: Harvard UP, 1961. 79–156.

Gusdorf, Georges. "Conditions and Limits of Autobiography." *Autobiography: Essays Theoretical and Critical.* Ed. and trans. James Olney. Princeton: Princeton UP, 1980. 28–48.

Gutiérrez Rueda, Laura. "Iconografía de Santa Teresa." *Revista de espiritualidad* 90 (1964): 5–237.

Hagerty, Miguel José, ed. *Los libros plúmbeos del Sacromonte.* Granada: Comares, 1998.

Haliczer, Stephen. *Between Exaltation and Infamy. Female Mystics in the Golden Age of Spain.* Oxford: Oxford UP, 2002.

Hamilton, Alastair. *Heresy and Mysticism in Sixteenth-Century Spain: The Alumbrados.* Toronto: U of Toronto P, 1992.

Hansen, Leonard. *Vida admirable de Sta. Rosa de Lima: Patrona del Nuevo Mundo.* 1664. Trans. Jacinto Parra. Manila, 1671.

Harding, Sandra G. "Feminist Justificatory Strategies." Garry and Pearsall 189–202.

Harris, A. Katie. *From Muslim to Christian Granada: Inventing a City's Past in Early Modern Spain*. Baltimore: Johns Hopkins UP, 2007.

Harvey, L. P. *Muslims in Spain, 1500–1614*. Chicago: U of Chicago P, 2005.

Hatzfeld, Helmut. *Santa Teresa de Ávila*. New York: Twayne, 1969.

Hegstrom, Valerie. Introduction. Zayas y Sotomayor, *La traición en la amistad* [1999] 13–29.

Heiple, Daniel. "The Theological Context of Wife-Murder in Seventeenth-Century Spain." *Sex and Love in Golden Age Spain*. Ed. Alain Saint-Saëns. New Orleans: UP of the South, 1996. 105–21.

Henke, Suzette. *Shattered Subjects: Trauma and Testimony in Women's Life-Writing*. New York: St. Martin's, 1998.

Herpoel, Sonja. *A la zaga de Santa Teresa: Autobiografías por mandato*. Amsterdam: Rodopi, 1999.

Hillerbrand, Hans J., gen. ed. *Oxford Encyclopedia of the Reformation*. 4 vols. New York: Oxford UP, 1996.

Hollander, Anne. "Mary Magdalen." *Feeding the Eye: Essays*. Berkeley: U of California P, 1999. 240–52.

Hollywood, Amy. *Sensible Ecstasy: Mysticism, Sexual Difference, and the Demands of History*. Chicago: U of Chicago P, 2002.

Hollywood, Amy, and Patricia Beckman, eds. *Cambridge Companion to Christian Mysticism*. Cambridge: Cambridge UP, forthcoming.

Homiak, Marcia. "Feminism and Aristotle's Rational Idea." Antony and Witt 1–17.

Hoornaert, Piet. "The Contemplative Aspiration: A Study of the Prayer Theology of Tomás de Jesús." *Ephemerides Theologicae Lovanienses* 56.4 (1980): 339–76.

Houdek, Frank J. *Guided by the Spirit: A Jesuit Perspective on Spiritual Direction*. Chicago: Loyola UP, 1996.

Howe, Elizabeth. *Mystical Imagery: Santa Teresa de Jesús and San Juan de la Cruz*. New York: Lang, 1988.

Howells, Edward. *John of the Cross and Teresa of Ávila: Mystical Knowing and Selfhood*. New York: Crossroads, 2002.

Hsia, R. Po-chia. *The World of Catholic Renewal, 1540–1770*. Cambridge: Cambridge UP, 1998.

Huarte de San Juan, Juan. *Examen de ingenios para las ciencias*. Ed. Guillermo Serés. Madrid: Cátedra, 1989.

Huerga, Alvaro. *Fray Luis de Granada, una vida al servicio de la iglesia*. Madrid: Católica, 1988.

Hufton, Olwen. "Altruism and Reciprocity: The Early Jesuits and Their Female Patrons." *Renaissance Studies* 15 (2001): 228–53.

Iamblichus. *Iamblichus' Life of Pythagoras*. Trans. Thomas Taylor. London: Watkins, 1926.

¡Iberia!: Spanish and Portuguese Music of the Golden Age. Perf. Waverly Consort. Wave, 2002.

Ibn-'Arabi, Muhyi'ddīn. *The* Tarjumán al-ashwáq: *A Collection of Mystical Odes*. Bilingual English-Arabic. ed. 1911. Ed. Reynold A. Nicholson. London: Theosophical, 1978.

Ignatius of Loyola. *Autobiografía. La autobiografía de San Ignacio: Apuntes para una lectura.* Ed. Manuel Mazas. Rome: Centrum Ignatianum Spiritualitatis, 1984. 57–115.

———. *The Autobiography of St. Ignatius of Loyola, with Related Documents.* Trans. Joseph F. O'Callaghan. Ed. John C. Olin. New York: Fordham UP, 1992.

———. *Letters to Women.* Ed. Hugo Rahner. New York: Herder, 1960.

———. *Obras completas.* Ed. Ignacio Iparraguirre and Cándido de Dalmases. Rev. ed. Madrid: Católica, 1982.

———. *El peregrino: Autobiografía de San Ignacio de Loyola.* Ed. Josep María Rambla Blanch. Bilbao: Mensajero, 1983.

Ignatius of Loyola. The Spiritual Exercises *and Selected Works.* Ed. George E. Ganss. With the collaboration of Parmanada R. Divarkar, Edward J. Malatesta, and Martin E. Palmer. New York: Paulist, 1991.

———. *The Spiritual Exercises of St. Ignatius.* Trans. John F. Thornton. New York: Vintage, 2000.

———. *The Spiritual Exercises of St. Ignatius of Loyola.* Trans. Elder Mullan. New York: Kennedy, 1914.

Imirizaldu, Jesús, ed. "Sentencia de María de la Visitación." *Monjas y beatas embaucadoras.* Ed. Imirizaldu. Madrid: Nacional, 1977. 179–97.

Irigaray, Luce. "La mystérique." *Speculum of the Other Woman.* Trans. Gillian C. Gill. Ithaca: Cornell UP, 1985. 191–202.

Isabel de Jesús. *Tesoro del Carmelo, Escondido en el campo de la iglesia, hallado, y descubierto en la muerte, y vida que de si dexó escrita. . . .* Madrid: Paredes, 1685.

Isabel de los Ángeles. *Cartas de la M. Isabel de los Ángeles (1556–1644).* Ed. Pierre Sérouet. Burgos: Monte Carmelo, 1963.

Iwasaki, Fernando. "Mujeres al borde de la perfección: Rosa de Santa María y las Alumbradas de Lima." *Hispanic American Historical Review* (1993): 581–613.

Jaggar, Alison M. "Love and Knowledge: Emotion in Feminist Epistemology." *Gender / Body / Knowledge: Feminist Reconstructions of Being and Knowing.* Ed. Jaggar and Susan Bordo. New Brunswick: Rutgers UP, 1989. 149–63.

Jantzen, Grace M. *Power, Gender and Christian Mysticism.* Cambridge: Cambridge UP, 1995.

Jehle, Fred. *Antología de poesía española.* 6 Jan. 2004. 5 Mar. 2008 <http://users.ipfw.edu/jehle/poesia.htm>.

"Jewish History Sourcebook: The Expulsion from Spain, 1492 CE." *Internet Jewish History Sourcebook.* Ed. Paul Halsall. July 1998. 26 Nov. 2007 <http://www.fordham.edu/halsall/jewish/1492=jews=spain1.htm>.

Jiménez Lozano, José. "Estudio preliminar." *Poesía completa.* By John of the Cross. Ed. Jiménez Lozano. Madrid: Taurus, 1983. 9–81.

John of Ávila. *Audi, Filia.* Trans. and introd. Joan Frances Gormley. New York: Paulist, 2006.

———. *Epistolario.* Ed. Luis Sala Balust. Rev. ed. Francisco Martín Hernández. Vol. 5 of *Obras completas.* Madrid: Católica, 1970.

John of the Cross. *Cántico espiritual y poesía completa.* Ed. Paola Elia and María Jesús Mancho. Barcelona: Crítica, 2002.

———. *The Collected Works of St. John of the Cross*. Trans. Kieran Kavanaugh and Otilio Rodríguez. Washington: Inst. for Carmelite Studies, 1991.

———. *The Collected Works of St. John of the Cross: A Digital Library (Version 1.0)*. Ed. Discalced Carmelite Fathers of Washington, D.C. CD-ROM. Washington: Inst. of Carmelite Studies, 2003.

———. *The Complete Works of St. John of the Cross*. Trans. E. Allison Peers. 3 vols. London: Burns, 1934–35.

———. "The Dark Night." *The Poems of St. John of the Cross*. Trans. John Frederick Nims. New York: Grove, 1959. 19–21.

———. "*The Living Flame of Love*," Versions A and B. Trans. Jane Ackerman. Birmingham: Medieval and Renaissance Texts and Studies, 1995.

———. "Noche oscura." Blecua, *Poesía de la edad* 1: 302–03.

———. "Noche oscura." *Poesía*. Ed. Domingo Ynduráin. Madrid: Cátedra, 1983. 259–61.

———. "Noche oscura." Rivers, *Renaissance and Baroque Poetry* 138–39.

———. *Obra completa de San Juan de la Cruz*. Ed. Luce López Baralt and Eulogio Pacho. 2 vols. Madrid: Alianza, 1991.

———. *The Poems of Saint John of the Cross*. Trans. and introd. Willis Barnstone. Bilingual ed. Bloomington: Indiana UP, 1968.

———. *The Poems of St. John of the Cross*. Trans. Roy Campbell. 4th ed. New York: Pantheon, 1956.

———. *Poesía*. Ed. Domingo Ynduráin. Madrid: Cátedra, 2000.

———. *Vida y obras*. Madrid: Biblioteca de Autores Christianos, 1964.

Jordan, Constance. *Renaissance Feminism: Literary Texts and Political Models*. Ithaca: Cornell UP, 1990.

Juana Inés de la Cruz. *The Answer / La respuesta. Including a Selection of Poems*. Ed. and trans. Electa Arenal and Amanda Powell. 1994. Rev. ed. New York: Feminist, forthcoming.

———. *Obras completas*. Ed. Georgina Sabat de Rivers and Elias Rivers. Madrid: Espasa Calpe, 2004.

Juan de Jesús María. *Guía Interior, verdadera y falsa mística: Criterios de discernimiento*. Ed. Daniel de Pablo Maroto. Madrid: Fundación U Española, 1987.

———. *Instruction des novices*. Ed. Giovanni Strina. Brussels: Soumillion, 2000.

———. *La théologie mystique*. Trans. Cyprien de la Nativité de la Vierge. Brussels: Soumillion, 1994.

Juárez, Encarnación. "The Autobiography of the Aching Body in Teresa de Cartagena's *Arboleda de los enfermos*." Snyder, Brueggemann, and Garland-Thomson 131–43.

Kagan, Richard L. *Lucrecia's Dreams: Politics and Prophecy in Sixteenth-Century Spain*. Berkeley: U of California P, 1990.

———. *Spanish Cities of the Golden Age: The Views of Anton van den Wyngaerde*. Los Angeles: U of California P, 1989.

Kagan, Richard L., and Abigail Dyer, eds. and trans. *Inquisitional Inquiries: The Secret Lives of Jews and Other Heretics*. Baltimore: Johns Hopkins UP, 2004.

Kamen, Henry. *Spain, 1469–1714: A Society of Conflict*. 2nd ed. London: Longman, 1991.

——. *The Spanish Inquisition: A Historical Revision*. New Haven: Yale UP, 1997.

Kaminsky, Amy Katz, ed. *Water Lilies / Flores del agua: An Anthology of Spanish Women Writers from the Fifteenth through the Nineteenth Century*. Minneapolis: U of Minnesota P, 1996.

Karant-Nunn, Susan. "The Reformation of Women." *Becoming Visible: Women in European History*. Ed. Renate Bridenthal, Susan Mosher Stuard, and Merry E. Wiesner. 3rd ed. Boston: Houghton, 1997. 175–201.

Kavanaugh, Kieran. "The Spanish Sixteenth Century: Carmel and Surrounding Movements." Dupré and Saliers 69–92.

Kavanaugh, Kieran, and Otilio Rodríguez. Introduction. *The Book of Her Foundations: The Collected Works of St. Teresa of Ávila*. Trans. Kavanaugh and Rodríguez. Washington: Inst. of Carmelite Studies, 1985. 3: 3–93.

Keitt, Andrew. *Inventing the Sacred: Imposture, Inquisition, and the Boundaries of the Supernatural in Golden Age Spain*. Leiden: Brill, 2005.

King, Ursula. *Women and Spirituality: Voices of Protest and Promise*. London: Macmillan, 1989.

Krämer, Heinrich, and Jacob Sprenger. *Malleus Maleficarum*. 1486. Trans. Montague Summers. New York: Dover, 1971.

Krauze, Enrique. "López Obrador, el mesías tropical." *Letras libres* 57 (2006): 5.

Kristeva, Julia. *Revolution in Poetic Language*. Trans. Margaret Waller. New York: Columbia UP, 1984.

Lacan, Jacques. *The Four Fundamental Concepts of Psycho-analysis*. New York: Norton, 1998.

——. *On Feminine Sexuality: The Limits of Love and Knowledge. Encore, 1972–1973*. Ed. Jacques-Alain Miller. Trans. Bruce Fink. The Seminar of Jacques Lacan 20. New York: Norton, 1998.

——. *The Seminar of Jacques Lacan, Book XX: Encore*. Trans. Bruce Fink. New York: Norton, 1998.

Lapesa, Rafael. *Historia de la lengua española*. Madrid: Gredos, 1983.

Lather, Patti. *Getting Smart: Feminist Research and Pedagogy with/in the Postmodern*. New York: Routledge, 1991.

Lavin, Irving. *Bernini and the Unity of the Visual Arts*. 2 vols. New York: Oxford UP, 1980.

Lavrin, Asunción. "Las Esposas de Cristo en Hispanoamérica." Ortega, Lavrin, and Pérez Cantó 667–94.

——. "In Search of the Colonial Woman in Mexico: The Seventeenth and Eighteenth Centuries." *Latin American Women: Historical Perspectives*. Ed. Lavrin. Westport: Greenwood, 1978. 23–59.

Lehfeldt, Elizabeth. *Religious Women in Golden Age Spain: The Permeable Cloister*. Aldershot: Ashgate, 2005.

León, Luis de. *A Bilingual Edition of Fray Luis de León's* La perfecta casada: *The Role of Married Women in Sixteenth-Century Spain*. Ed. John A. Jones and Javier San José Lera. Lewiston: Mellen, 1999.

————. "Letter from the Master Fray Luis de León to the Mother Prioress Ana de Jesús and the Discalced Carmelite Nuns of the Convent at Madrid." 1588. Teresa of Ávila, *Complete Works* 3: 368–78.

————. *The Names of Christ*. Trans. Manuel Durán and William Kluback. New York: Paulist, 1984.

————. "Noche serena." Rivers, *Renaissance and Baroque Poetry* 99–101.

————. *Obras completas castellanas*. Ed. Félix García. 4th ed. 2 vols. Madrid: Católica, 1957.

————. *Obras completas castellanas*. Ed. Félix García. 5th ed. 2 vols. Madrid: Católica, 1991.

————. "Oda III: A Francisco Salinas, Catedrático de Música de la Universidad de Salamanca / "Ode III: To Francisco Salinas, Professor of Music at the University of Salamanca." Rivers, *Renaissance and Baroque Poetry* 94–96.

————. *Poesía*. Ed. Juan Francisco Alcina. Madrid: Cátedra, 2000.

————. *Poesía completa de Fray Luis de León*. Ed. José Manuel Blecua. Madrid: Gredos, 1990.

————. *La poesía de fray Luis de León*. Ed. Oreste Macrí. Salamanca: Anaya, 1989.

————. *Poesías completas: Obras propias en castellano y latín y traducciones e imitaciones latinas, griegas, bíblico-hebreas y romances*. Ed. Cristóbal Cuevas. Madrid: Castalia, 1998.

————. *The Unknown Light: The Poems of Fray Luis de León*. Trans. Willis Barnstone. Albany: State U of New York P, 1979.

Leonor de San Bernardo. *Lettres*. Ed. Pierre Sérouet. Paris: Desclée de Brouwer, 1981.

Lerner, Gerda. *The Creation of Feminist Consciousness: From the Middle Ages to Eighteen-Seventy*. New York: Oxford UP, 1993.

Lewis, Elizabeth Franklin. "Feijoo, Josefa Amar y Borbón, and the Feminist Debate in Eighteenth-Century Spain." *Dieciocho* 12 (1989): 188–203.

Lindberg, Carter, ed. *Reformation Theologians: An Introduction to Theology in the Early Modern Period*. London: Blackwell, 2002.

Liss, Peggy. *Isabel the Queen: Life and Times*. Oxford: Oxford UP, 1992.

Llamas Martínez, Enrique. *Santa Teresa de Jesús y la Inquisición española*. Madrid: CSIC, 1972.

————. "Teresa de Jesús y Juan de la Cruz ante la Inquisición: Denuncias, procesos, sentencias." *Cuadernos de pensamiento* 7 (1993): 179–206.

Llull, Ramon. *Llibre d'amic e amat / The Book of the Lover and the Beloved*. Trans. Mark D. Johnston. Warminster: Aris, 1995.

Lochrie, Karma. "The Language of Transgression: Body, Flesh, and Word in Mystical Discourse." *Speaking Two Languages: Traditional Disciplines and Contemporary Theory in Medieval Studies*. Ed. Allen J. Frantzen, Jr. Albany: State U of New York P, 1991. 115–40.

López, Santiago Sebastián. "Iconografía de la vida mística Teresiana." *Boletín del Museo e Instituto Camón Aznar* 10 (1982): 15–38.

López Baralt, Luce. *Huellas del Islam en la literatura española. De Juan Ruiz a Juan Goytisolo*. Madrid: Hiperión, 1985.

————. *Islam in Spanish Literature: From the Middle Ages to the Present.* Trans. Andrew Hurley. Leiden: Brill, 1992.

————. Prologue. *Obra completa de San Juan de la Cruz.* Madrid: Alianza, 1991. 7–52.

————. *San Juan de la Cruz y el Islam.* 2nd ed. Madrid: Hiperión, 1990.

————. "El símbolo de los siete castillos concéntricos del alma en santa Teresa y en el Islam." López Baralt, *Huellas del Islam* 73–97.

————. "Simbología mística islámica en San Juan de la Cruz y en Santa Teresa de Jesús." *Nueva revista de filología hispánica* 30 (1981): 21–91.

————. *The Sufi Trobar Clus and Spanish Mysticism: A Shared Symbolism.* Trans. Andrew Hurley. Lahore, Pakistan: Iqbal Academy, 2000.

————. *"A zaga de tu huella": La enseñanza de las lenguas semíticas en Salamanca en tiempos de san Juan de la Cruz.* Madrid: Trotta, 2006.

López de Córdoba, Leonor. *Autobiografía/Autobiography.* Kaminsky 19–32.

Ludmer, Josefina. "Las tretas del débil." *La sartén por el mango: Encuentro de escritoras latinoamericanas.* Ed. Patricia Elena González and Eliana Ortega. Rio Piedras: Huracán, 1984. 47–54.

————. "The Tricks of the Weak." *Feminist Perspectives on Sor Juana Inés de la Cruz.* Ed. Stephanie Merrim. Detroit: Wayne State UP, 1991. 86–93.

Luis de Granada. *Of Prayer and Meditation.* Trans. R. Hopkins. Menston: Scholars, 1971.

Luke, Carmen, and Jennifer Gore. Introduction. *Feminism and Critical Pedagogy.* Ed. Luke and Gore. New York: Routledge, 1992. 1–12.

Luti, J. Mary. "'A Marriage Well Arranged': Teresa of Ávila and Fray Jerónimo Gracián de la Madre de Dios." *Studia Mystica* 10 (1989): 32–46.

————. *"Teresa of Ávila's Way.* Collegeville: Liturgical, 1991.

Lynch, John. *Spain 1516–1598: From Nation State to World Empire.* 3rd ed. Oxford: Blackwell, 1991.

"Los obispos critican la visión de Ray Loriga sobre la relación entre Cristo y Santa Teresa." *El pais.com.* 2 Aug. 2007. 31 Jul. 2008 <http://www.elpais.com>.

MacPherson, Ian. "'Rompe la tela de este dulce encuentro': San Juan's 'Llama de amor viva' and the Courtly Context." *Studies in Honor of Bruce W. Wardropper.* Ed. Dian Fox, Harry Sieber, and Robert ter Horst. Newark: Juan de la Cuesta, 1989. 193–203.

Maltz, Terry. "St. Teresa of Avila: Doctor of the Church." *Catholic Online.* 1996. 15 June 2007 <http://www.catholic.org/saints>. Path: Browse saints, T; St. Teresa of Avila.

La Máquina del estado. Television Española. RTVE, 1998. Videocassette. Films for the Humanities and Sciences, 2003.

Marcocchi, Massimo. "Spirituality in the Sixteenth and Seventeenth Centuries." *Catholicism in Early Modern History: A Guide to Research.* Ed. John W. O'Malley. Saint Louis: Center for Reformation Research, 1988. 163–92.

Marcos, Juan A. *Mística y subversiva: Teresa de Jesús (Las estrategias retóricas del discurso místico).* Madrid: Espiritualidad, 2001.

Margaret of the Mother of God. *The Life of the Venerable Margaret of the Mother of God, Lay Sister at the Royal Convent of Discalced Carmelites Nuns in Brussels.* Introd. Cordula van Wyhe. Trans. Susan M. Smith. The Other Voice in Early Modern Europe. Chicago: U of Chicago P, forthcoming.

María de la Antigua. *Desengaño de religiosos, y de almas que tratan de virtud.* . . . Sevilla: Cabeças, 1678.

María de San José. Oaxaca Manuscript. John Carter Brown Library, Providence. Spanish Codex 39–41.

María de San José Salazar. *Book for the Hour of Recreation.* Ed. Alison Weber. Trans. Amanda Powell. The Other Voice in Early Modern Europe. Chicago: U of Chicago P, 2002.

———. *Libro de recreaciones: Escritos espirituales.* Ed. Simeón de la Sagrada Familia. Rome: Postulación General O.C.D., 1979.

Márquez Villanueva, Francisco. "Ávila, ciudad morisca y cuna de espiritualidad cristiana." *Mélanges María Soledad Carrasco Urgoiti.* Ed. Abdeljelil Temimi. Zaghouan, Tunisia: FTERSI, 1999. 209–19.

———. "Santa Teresa y el linaje." *Espiritualidad y literatura en el siglo XVI.* Madrid: Alfaguara, 1968. 141–205.

Marthe de l'Incarnation. *Lettres spirituelles: Suivies de treize lettres de la mère Marthe de l'Incarnation à Mme de Cabriès. / Marguerite du Saint-Sacrement.* Ed. Pierre Sérouet. Paris: Cerf, 1993.

Martínez Hampe, Teodor. *Santidad e identidad criolla: Estudio del proceso de canonización de Santa Rosa.* Cuzco, Peru: Centro de Estudios Regionales Andinos Bartolomé de las Casas, 1998.

Mason, Mary. "The Other Voice: Autobiographies of Women Writers." *Autobiography: Essays Theoretical and Critical.* Ed. James Olney. Princeton: Princeton UP, 1980. 207–36.

Mathers, Constance Jones. "Early Spanish Qualms about Loyola and the Society of Jesus." *Historian* 53 (1991): 679–90.

Mathiesen, Thomas J. "Music, Aesthetics, and Cosmology in Early Neo-Platonism." *Paradigms in Medieval Thought: Applications in Medieval Disciplines: A Symposium.* Ed. Nancy van Deusen and Alvin E. Ford. Mediaeval Studies 3. Lewiston: Mellen, 1990. 37–64.

Mayberry, Nancy. "Beatriz de Silva: An Important Fifteenth-Century Visionary." *Vox Benedictina* 4 (1987): 169–83.

Maza, Francisco de la. *Catarina de San Juan.* 1970. Mexico, DF: Cien de México, 1990.

McBrien, Richard P., Harold W. Attridge, et al., eds. *HarperCollins Encyclopedia of Catholicism.* San Francisco: Harper, 1995.

McCoog, Thomas M., ed. *The Mercurian Project: Forming Jesuit Culture, 1573–1580.* Rome: Inst. Historicum Soc. Iesu and the Inst. of Jesuit Sources, 2004.

McGinn, Bernard. *The Foundations of Mysticism.* New York: Crossroad, 1995. Vol. 1 of *The Presence of God: A History of Western Christian Mysticism.* 5 vols.

———. Introduction. McGinn, *Foundations* xi–xx.

———. "The Language of Love in Christian and Jewish Mysticism." *Mysticism and Language.* Ed. Steven T. Katz. Oxford: Oxford UP, 1992. 202–35.

———. "Love, Knowledge, and *Unio mystica* in the Western Christian Tradition." *Mystical Union and Monotheistic Faith: An Ecumenical Dialogue.* Ed. Moshe Idel and McGinn. New York: Macmillan, 1989. 59–86.

McGrath, Alister E. *Christian Spirituality: An Introduction*. Malden: Blackwell, 1999.

McKennit, Loreena. *The Mask and the Mirror.* Compact disc. Warner Bros., 1994.

McKnight, Kathryn Joy. *The Mystic of Tunja: The Writings of Madre Castillo, 1671–1742*. Amherst: U of Massachusetts P, 1997.

McNamara, Jo Ann. "The Need to Give: Suffering and Female Sanctity in the Middle Ages." *Images of Sainthood in the Middle Ages*. Ed. Renate Blumenfeld-Kosinski and Timea Szell. Ithaca: Cornell UP, 1991. 199–221.

Medina, Francisco de Borja. "Everard Mercurian and Spain: Some Burning Issues." McCoog 945–66.

Medwick, Cathleen. *Teresa de Jesús, una mujer extraordinaria*. Trans. Marcelo Covián. Maeva: Madrid, 2002.

———. *Teresa of Ávila: The Progress of a Soul*. New York: Doubleday, 2001.

Meissner, W. W. *Ignatius of Loyola: The Psychology of a Saint*. New Haven: Yale UP, 1993.

Menéndez Pidal, Ramón. "El estilo de Santa Teresa." *La lengua de Cristóbal Colón*. 2nd ed. Buenos Aires: Espasa-Calpe, 1944. 129–53.

Merrim, Stephanie. *Early Modern Women's Writing and Sor Juana Inés de la Cruz*. Nashville: Vanderbilt UP, 1999.

Mills, Kenneth, and William B. Taylor. *Colonial Spanish America: A Documentary History*. Wilmington: Scholarly Resources, 1998.

Monjas coronadas: Vida conventual femenina. Madrid: Real Academia de Bellas Artes de San Fernando, 2005.

Mooney, Catherine M. "Voice, Gender, and the Portrayal of Sanctity." *Gendered Voices: Medieval Saints and Their Interpreters*. Ed. Mooney. Philadelphia: U of Pennsylvania P, 1999. 1–15.

Morgan, Ronald J. *Spanish American Saints and the Rhetoric of Identity, 1600–1810*. Tucson: U of Arizona P, 2002.

Moriones de la Visitación, Ildefonso. *Teresian Carmel: Pages of History*. Trans. S. C. O'Mahony. OCD General House. 2 June 2003. 9 May 2008 <http://www.ocd.pcn.net/histo_16.htm>.

Mujica, Bárbara, ed. *Antología de la literatura española: Renacimiento y Siglo de Oro*. 1991. 2nd ed. Eugene: Wipf, forthcoming.

———, ed. *Milenio: Mil años de literatura española*. Hoboken: Wiley, 2001.

———. "Paul the Enchanter: Jerónimo Gracián and Teresa's Vow of Obedience." C. Wilson, *Heirs* 21–44.

———. "Skepticism and Mysticism in Early Modern Spain: The Combative Stance of Teresa of Ávila." *Women in the Discourse of Early Modern Spain*. Ed. Joan E. Cammarata. Gainesville: UP of Florida, 2003. 54–76.

———, ed. *Women Writers of Early Modern Spain: Sophia's Daughters*. New Haven: Yale UP, 2004.

Mujica Pinilla, Ramón. "El ancla de Santa Rosa de Lima: Mística y política en torno a la Patrona de América." *Santa Rosa y su tiempo*. Ed. José Flores Araoz et al. Lima: Banco de Credito, 1995. 54–215.

Myers, Kathleen Ann. "Crossing Boundaries: Defining the Field of Female Religious Writing in Colonial Latin America." *Colonial Latin American Review* 9 (2000): 151–65.

———. *Neither Saints nor Sinners: Writing the Lives of Spanish American Women.* Oxford: Oxford UP, 2003.

———. *Word from New Spain: The Spiritual Autobiography of Madre María de San José (1656–1719).* Liverpool: Liverpool UP, 1993.

Myers, Kathleen Ann, and Amanda Powell. "Gender, Tradition, and Autobiographical Spiritual Writings." Myers and Powell, *Wild Country,* 289–336.

———. *A Wild Country Out in the Garden: The Spiritual Journals of a Colonial Mexican Nun.* Bloomington: Indiana UP, 1999. 298–340.

Nader, Helen, ed. *Power and Gender in Early Modern Spain: Eight Women of the Mendoza Family, 1450–1650.* Urbana: U of Illinois P, 2004.

Nalle, Sara T. *God in La Mancha: Religious Reform and the People of Cuenca, 1500–1650.* Baltimore: Johns Hopkins UP, 1992.

Narváez Córdova, María Teresa. "Estudio preliminar." *Tratado [Tafsira].* By Mancebo de Arévalo. Ed. Narváez Córdova. Madrid: Trotta, 2003. 13–96.

Nash, Mary. "Experiencia y aprendizaje: La formación histórica de los feminismos en España." *Historia social* 20 (1994): 151–72.

Nelken, Margarita. *Las escritoras españolas.* Barcelona: Labor, 1930.

New American Bible. Trans. Catholic Biblical Assn. of Amer. Patterson: Saint Anthony Guild, 1970.

Newberg, Andrew, Eugene D'Aquili, and Vince Rause. *Why God Won't Go Away: Brain Science and the Biology of Belief.* New York: Ballantine, 2001.

The New Catholic Encyclopedia. 2nd ed. 15 vols. to date. Detroit: Thomson, 2003–.

The New Jerusalem Bible. New York: Doubleday, 1990.

The New Oxford Annotated Bible with the Apocrypha. Michael Coogan, gen. ed. New Revised Standard Version. 3rd ed. New York: Oxford UP, 2001.

Nicholson, Reynold A. 1914. *The Mystics of Islam.* London: Arkana, 1989.

La noche oscura. Dir. Carlos Saura. Iberoamérica Films and Genérale d'Images, 1989.

Norris, Richard A., trans. and ed. *The Song of Songs: Interpreted by Early Christian and Medieval Commentators.* Grand Rapids: Eerdmans, 2003.

Nurī, Abū'l-Husayn an-. *Moradas de los corazones* [Maqamat al-qulub]. Trans. Luce López Baralt. Madrid: Trotta, 1999.

"Los obispos critican que el filme *Santa Teresa* retrate el misticismo como una relación carnal." *El mundo* 8 Feb. 2007. 23 Jul. 2008 <http://www.elmundo.es/elmundo/2007/02/08/cultura/1170930381.html>.

Olney, James. *Metaphors of Self. The Meaning of Autobiography.* Princeton: Princeton UP, 1972.

O'Malley, John W. "Early Jesuit Spirituality: Spain and Italy." Dupré and Saliers 3–27.

———. *The First Jesuits.* Cambridge: Harvard UP, 1993.

———. "Ignatius of Loyola (1491–1556)." Lindberg 298–310.

O'Malley, John W., and Gauvin Alexander Bailey, eds. *The Jesuits and the Arts: 1540–1773*. Philadelphia: Saint Joseph's UP, 2005.

O'Neill, Charles, and Joaquín María Domínguez, eds. *Diccionario Histórico de la Compañía de Jesús: Biográfico-temático*. Rome: Inst. Historicum S.I., 2001.

Ortega, Margarita, Asunción Lavrin, and Pilar Pérez Cantó, eds. *El mundo moderno*. Madrid: Cátedra, 2005. Vol. 2 of *Historia de las mujeres en España y América Latina*. Gen. ed. Isabel Morant. 4 vols.

Osborne, Joan. *Relish*. PolyGram, 1995.

Osuna, Francisco de. *Tercer abecedario espiritual*. Ed. Melquíades Andrés Martín. Madrid: Católica, 1972.

———. *Tercer abecedario espiritual de Francisco de Osuna*. Ed. Saturnino López Santidrián. Madrid: Católica, 1998.

———. *The Third Spiritual Alphabet*. Ed. and trans. Mary E. Giles. New York: Paulist, 1981.

The Oxford Study Bible. Ed. M. Jack Suggs, Katharine Doob Sakenfeld, and James R. Mueller. New York: Oxford UP, 1992.

Pacho, Eulogio, ed. *Diccionario de San Juan de la Cruz*. Burgos: Monte Carmelo, 2000.

Paredes Méndez, Francisca, Mark Harpring, and José Ballesteros, eds. *Voces de España: Antología literaria*. Boston: Heinle, 2005.

Partner, Nancy F. "Did Mystics Have Sex?" *Desire and Discipline: Sex and Sexuality in the Pre-modern West*. Ed. Jacqueline Murray and Konrad Eisenbichler. Toronto: U of Toronto P, 1996. 297–311.

Pattison, Walter T., and Donald W. Bleznick, eds. *Representative Spanish Authors*. 3rd ed. 2 vols. New York: Oxford UP, 1971.

Paul VI. "Homily." *Catholic.net*. 19 Sept. 2008 <http://www.us.catholic.net/rcc/Periodicals/Dossier/MARAPR99/homily.html>.

Payne, Stanley G. *Spanish Catholicism*. Madison: U of Wisconsin P, 1984.

Payne, Steven. *John of the Cross and the Cognitive Value of Mysticism: An Analysis of Sanjuanist Teaching and Its Philosophical Implications for Contemporary Discussions of Mystical Experience*. Dordrecht: Kluwer, 1990.

Peers, Edgar Allison. *Handbook to the Life and Times of St. Teresa and St. John of the Cross*. London: Burns, 1954.

———. "Saint Teresa in Her Letters." *"Saint Teresa of Jesus" and Other Essays and Addresses*. London: Faber, 1951. 35–80.

———. *Studies of the Spanish Mystics*. Vol. 1: London: Sheldon, 1927; vol. 2: London: Sheldon, 1930; vol. 3: London: SPCK, 1960.

Penaskovic, Richard, and John F. von Eschenback. "Infusing Critical Thinking into the Study of Religion." *Spotlight on Teaching* 1 (1992): 1–3.

Perella, Nicolas. *The Kiss Sacred and Profane*. Berkeley: U of California P, 1969.

Pérez de Chinchón, Bernardo. *Antialcorano: Diálogos christianos*. Ed. Francisco Pons Fuster. Alicante: U de Alicante, 2000.

Perry, Mary Elizabeth. *Gender and Disorder in Early Modern Seville*. Princeton: Princeton UP, 1990.

Petroff, Elizabeth Alvilda. *Body and Soul: Essays on Medieval Women and Mysticism.* New York: Oxford UP, 1994.

Pfeiffer, Heinz. "The Iconography of the Society of Jesus." O'Malley and Bailey 199–228.

Pinta Llorente, Miguel de la. *Proceso criminal contra el hebraísta salmantino Martín Martínez de Cantalapiedra.* Madrid: CSIC, 1946.

Plotinus. *The Essence of Plotinus: Extracts from the Six* Enneads *and Porphyry's* Life of Plotinus. Ed. Grace H. Turnball. New York: Oxford UP, 1948.

Poska, Allyson M., and Elizabeth A. Lehfeldt. "Redefining Expectations: Women and the Church in Early Modern Spain." *Women and Religion in Old and New Worlds.* Ed. Susan E. Dinan and Debra Meyers. New York: Routledge, 2001. 21–42.

Pountain, Christopher J. *A History of the Spanish Language through Texts.* London: Routledge, 2001.

Poutrin, Isabelle. *Le voile et la plume: Autobiographie et sainteté féminine dans l'Espagne moderne.* Madrid: Velázquez, 1995.

Prada, Amancio. *Cántico espiritual.* Compact disc. RTVE, 1991.

Raitt, Jill. "Two Spiritual Directors of Women in the Sixteenth Century: St. Ignatius of Loyola and St. Teresa of Ávila." *Renaissance and Reformation Studies in Laudem Caroli for Charles G. Nauert.* Ed. James V. Mehl. Kirksville: Thomas Jefferson UP, 1998. 213–31.

Ramos, Alonso. *De los prodigios de la Omnipotencia y milagros de la Gracia en la vida de la venerable Sierva de Dios Catharina de S Joan.* 3 vols. Puebla and México, 1689–92.

Ranft, Patricia. *Women and Spiritual Equality in Christian Tradition.* London: Macmillan, 1998.

Rawlings, Helen. *Church, Religion and Society in Early Modern Spain.* Basingstoke, Eng.: Palgrave, 2002.

———. *The Spanish Inquisition.* London: Blackwell, 2005.

Raymond of Capua. *La vida de la bien aventurada santa Caterina de Sena.* Trans. Antonio de la Peña. Alcalá de Henares: Brocar, 1511.

Real Academia Española. *Diccionario de la lengua española.* 22nd ed. <http://www.rae.es.>

Reed, Helen H. "Catalina de Cardona, 'la Mujer Pecadora' and Her Auto/Biographies." *Essays in Honor of Robert Fiore.* Ed. Chad M. Gasta and Julia Domínguez. Newark: Juan de la Cuesta, 2009. 429–46.

———. "Mother Love in the Renaissance: The Princess of Eboli's Letters to Her Favorite Son." *Power and Gender in Early Modern Spain: Eight Women of the Mendoza Family, 1450–1600.* Ed. Helen Nader. Urbana: U of Illinois P, 2004. 152–76.

La reina Isabel en persona. Dir. Rafael Gordon. Hardy, 2000.

Reineke, Martha J. "'This Is My Body': Reflections on Abjection, Anorexia, and Medieval Women Mystics." *Journal of the American Academy of Religion* 58 (1990): 245–65.

Rhodes, Elizabeth. "Join the Jesuits, See the World: Women and the Society of Jesus." *The Jesuits II: Cultures, Sciences and the Arts, 1540–1773.* Ed. John W. O'Malley et al. Toronto: U of Toronto P, 2006. 33–47.

————. "Spain's Misfired Canon: The Case of Fray Luis de Granada's *Libro de la oración.*" *Journal of Hispanic Philology* 15 (1990): 3–28.

————. *The Unrecognized Precursors of Montemayor's Diana.* Columbia: U of Missouri P, 1992.

————. "What's in a Name: On Teresa of Ávila's *Book.*" Boenig 79–106.

————. "Women on Their Knees: The Pornographic Nature of Sixteenth-Century Religious Discourse." Wesleyan Renaissance Seminar. Wesleyan U. 4 May 1994.

Riffaterre, Michael. "The Poem's Significance." *Semiotics of Poetry.* Bloomington: Indiana UP, 1978. 1–22.

Rivero Rodríguez, Manuel. *La España de don Quijote: Un viaje al Siglo de Oro.* Madrid: Alianza, 2005.

Rivers, Elias L. *Fray Luis de León: The Original Poems.* Critical Guides to Spanish Texts. London: Grant, 1983.

————, ed. *Poesía lírica del Siglo de Oro.* Madrid: Cátedra, 1979.

————, ed. *Renaissance and Baroque Poetry of Spain with English Prose Translations.* 1966. Prospect Heights: Waveland, 1988.

Robberechts, Catherine. "La fin d'une tradition mystique quelques exemples de manuscripts du 17ᵉ siècle dans les communautés religieuses." *Le jardin clos de l' ame; l' imaginaire des religieuses dans les Pays-Bas du Sud, depuis le 13e siecle.* Ed. Paul Vandenbroek. N.p.: Brussels, 1994. 271–81.

Rodríguez, Rodney T., ed. *Momentos cumbres de las literaturas hispánicas: Introducción al análisis literario.* Upper Saddle River: Prentice, 2004.

Rohter, Larry. "In Brazil, a Firebrand Unsettles Brazil's Presidential Race." *New York Times* 4 Sept. 2006. 18 Sept. 2008 <http://www.nytimes.com>.

Rosand, David. *Titian.* New York: Abrams, 1978.

Ros García, Salvador, et al., eds. *Introducción a la lectura de San Juan de la Cruz.* Salamanca: Junta de Castilla y León, 1991.

Rossi, Rosa. *Juan de la Cruz: Silencio y creatividad.* Trans. Juan Ramón Capella. Madrid: Trotta, 1996.

————. *Teresa de Ávila: Biografía de una escritora.* Trans. Marieta Gargatagli and Albert Domingo. Barcelona: Icaria, 1983.

Rowe, Erin Kathleen. "Disrupting the Republic: Santiago, Teresa de Jesús, and the Battle for the Soul of Spain, 1617–1630." Diss. Johns Hopkins U, 2005.

————. "The Spanish Minerva: Imagining Teresa of Ávila as Patron Saint in Seventeenth-Century Spain." *Catholic Historical Review* 92 (2006): 574–96.

Rubial, Antonio. *La santidad controvertida.* México, DF: Fondo de Cultura Económica, 1999.

Ruiz, Federico, et al. *God Speaks in the Night: The Life, Times, and Teaching of St. John of the Cross.* Trans. Kieran Kavanaugh et al. Washington: Inst. of Carmelite Studies, 1991.

Ruiz, Teófilo F. *Spanish Society, 1400–1600.* New York: Longman, 2001.

Ruiz de Loizaga, Francisco Javier. "La grafía fonológica de Santa Teresa." *Boletín de la Real Academia Española* 77 (1997): 261–78.

Salinas, Francisco de. *De musica libri septem: Siete libros sobre la música.* Trans. Ismael Fernández de la Cuesta. Madrid: Alpuerto, 1983.

———. *Musices liber tertius: Estudio preliminar, facsímil, edición y traducción.* Ed. and trans. Antonio Moreno Hernández. Pref. J. Javier Goldáraz Gaínza. Madrid: Biblioteca Nacional, 1993.

Sánchez, Manuel Diego, comp. *San Juan de la Cruz: Bibliografía sistemática.* Madrid: Espiritualidad, 2000.

Sánchez Lora, José Luis. *Mujeres, conventos y formas de la religiosidad barroca.* Madrid: Fundación Universitaria Española, 1988.

———. "Mujeres en religión." Ortega, Lavrin, and Pérez Cantó 131–52.

Sánchez Moguel, Antonio. *El lenguaje de Santa Teresa de Jesús.* Madrid: Clásica, 1915.

"La santa distante." *De cine 21.* 14 Jan. 2008 <http://www.decine21.com/FrmPeliculas .asp?id=7994>.

Scheman, Naomi. "Though This Be Method, yet There Be Madness in It: Paranoia and Liberal Epistemology." Antony and Witt 145–70.

Schimmel, Annemarie. *Mystical Dimensions of Islam.* Chapel Hill: U of North Carolina P, 1975.

———. *The Triumphal Sun: A Study of the Works of Jalaloddin Rumi.* London: East-West, 1980.

Schlau, Stacey. "Following Saint Teresa: Early Modern Women and Religious Authority." *MLN* 117 (2002): 286–310.

Schneiders, Sandra M. "The Study of Christian Spirituality: Contours and Dynamics of a Discipline." *Minding the Spirit: The Study of Christian Spirituality.* Ed. Elizabeth A. Dreyer and Mark S. Burrows. Baltimore: Johns Hopkins UP, 2005. 5–24.

Schutte, Anne Jacobson. *Aspiring Saints: Pretense of Holiness, Inquisition, and Gender in the Republic of Venice, 1618–1750.* Baltimore: Johns Hopkins UP, 2001.

Schutte, Anne Jacobson, and Thomas Kuehn. Introduction. *Time, Space, and Women's Lives in Early Modern Europe.* Ed. Schutte and Kuehn. Trans. Silvana Seidel Menchi. Kirkville: Truman State UP, 2001. vii–xvii.

Seidenspinner-Nuñez, Dayle, ed. *The Writings of Teresa de Cartagena.* Cambridge: Brewer, 1998.

Serrano y Sanz, Manuel. *Apuntes para una biblioteca de escritoras españolas.* Madrid: Atlas, 1975.

Showalter, Elaine. "Feminist Criticism in the Wilderness." *The New Feminist Criticisms.* Ed. Showalter. New York: Pantheon, 1985. 243–70.

Silverio de Santa Teresa, ed. *Procesos de beatificación y canonización de Santa Teresa de Jesús.* 3 vols. Burgos: Monte Carmelo, 1934–35.

Simón Díaz, José. *Bibliografía de la literatura hispánica.* Madrid: CSIC, 1950.

Simón Palmer, María del Carmen, ed. *Spanish Women Writers (1500–1900).* Microfiche. Madrid: Chadwyck-Healey, 1992.

Singer, Irving. *The Nature of Love.* Chicago: U of Chicago P, 1984.

Slade, Carole. "'Este gran Dios de la cavallerías' [This Great God of Deeds]: St. Teresa's Performances of the Novels of Chivalry." *The Vernacular Spirit: Essays on Medieval Religious Literature.* Ed. Renate Blumenfeld-Koskinski, Duncan Robertson, and Nancy Bradley Warner. New York: Palgrave, 2002. 297–316.

———. "The Relationship between Teresa of Ávila and Philip II: A Reading of the Extant Textual Evidence." *Archive for Reformation History* 94 (2003): 223–42.

———. "Saint Teresa's *Meditaciones sobre los Cantares*: The Hermeneutics of Humility and Enjoyment." *Religion and Literature* 18 (1986): 27–44.

———. "St. Teresa of Ávila as a Social Reformer." *Mysticism and Social Transformation*. Ed. Janet K. Ruffing. Syracuse: Syracuse UP, 2001. 91–103.

———. *St. Teresa of Ávila: Author of a Heroic Life*. Berkeley: U of California P, 1995.

Smith, Paul Julian. *The Body Hispanic: Gender and Sexuality in Spanish and Spanish American Literature*. Oxford: Clarendon, 1989.

———. "Visions of Teresa: Lacan, Irigaray, Kristeva." *Representing the Other: "Race," Text, and Gender in Spanish and Spanish American Narrative*. Oxford: Clarendon, 1992. 97–127.

Smith, Sidonie. *A Poetics of Women's Autobiography: Marginality and the Fictions of Self-Representation*. Bloomington: Indiana UP, 1987.

Smith, Sidonie, and Julia Watson. *Reading Autobiography: A Guide for Interpreting Life Narratives*. Minneapolis: U of Minnesota P, 2001.

Snyder, Sharon L., Brenda Jo Brueggemann, and Rosemarie Garland-Thomson, eds. *Disability Studies: Enabling the Humanities*. New York: MLA, 2002.

La sonora soledad de Juan de Yepes. Screenplay by José Jiménez Lozano. Videocassette. Madrid: Videolibro, 1994.

Spitzer, Leo. "Three Poems on Ecstasy (John Donne, St. John of the Cross, Richard Wagner)." *A Method of Interpreting Literature*. 1949. New York: Russell, 1967. 1–63.

Starr, Mirabai. Introduction. Teresa of Ávila, *Interior Castle* 1–27.

Suárez, Úrsula. *Relación autobiográfica*. Ed. Mario Fericcio Podesta. Introd. Armando de Ramón. Santiago, Chile: Editorial Universitaria de la U de Concepción, 1984.

Suhrawardi al-Maqtul, Shihabudin. *Three Treatises on Mysticism*. Trans. Otto Spies and S. K. Khatak. Stuttgart: Kohlhammer, 1935.

Sullivan, Constance. "The Quiet Feminism of Josefa Amar y Borbón's Book." *Indiana Journal of Hispanic Literatures* (1993): 49–73.

Surtz, Ronald E. *The Guitar of God: Gender, Power, and Authority in the Visionary World of Mother Juana de la Cruz (1481–1534)*. Philadelphia: U of Pennsylvania P, 1990.

———. "The New Judith: Teresa de Cartagena." Surtz, *Writing Women* 21–40.

———. *Writing Women in Late Medieval and Early Modern Spain*. Philadelphia: U of Pennsylvania P, 1995.

Swietlicki, Catherine. *Spanish Christian Cabala: The Works of Luis de León, Santa Teresa de Jesús, and San Juan de la Cruz*. Columbia: U of Missouri P, 1986.

———. "Writing 'Femystic' Space: In the Margins of Saint Teresa's *Castillo interior*." *Journal of Hispanic Philology* 13 (1989): 273–93.

Talbot, John Michael. *The Lover and the Beloved*. Compact Disc. Sparrow, 1989.

Teresa de Cartagena. *Admiración operum Dey*. Kaminsky 37–53.

Teresa de Jesús. Dir. Josefina Molina. Screenplay by Víctor García de la Concha, Carmen Martín Gaite, and Josefina Molina. Videodisc. RTVE, 1984; Devisa, 2006.

Teresa de Jesús y el siglo XVI. Comp. José Ignacio Piera Delgado. Ávila: Catedral de Ávila, 1994.

Teresa: El cuerpo de Cristo. Dir. Ray Loriga. Azeta, 2007.

Teresa of Ávila. *The Book of Her Life*. Trans. Kieran Kavanaugh and Otilio Rodríguez. Introd. Jodi Bilinkoff. Indianapolis: Hackett, 2008.

———. *Cartas de Santa Teresa*. Ed. Tomás Álvarez. 4th ed. Burgos: Monte Carmelo, 1997.

———. *The Collected Letters*. Trans. Kieran Kavanaugh. 2 vols. Washington: Inst. of Carmelite Studies, 2001–07.

———. *The Collected Works*. Trans. Kieran Kavanaugh and Otilio Rodríguez. 3 vols. Washington: Inst. of Carmelite Studies, 1976–87. Vol. 1, 1976; rev. 1987.

———. *The Complete Works of Saint Teresa of Jesus*. Trans. E. Allison Peers. 3 vols. London: Sheed, 1946. Rpt. as *The Complete Works of St. Teresa of Ávila*. London: Continuum, 2002.

———. *Epistolario de Santa Teresa de Jesús*. Ed. Luis Rodríguez Martínez and Teófanes Egido. 2nd ed. Madrid: Espiritualidad, 1982.

———. *The Interior Castle*. Trans. Mirabai Starr. New York: Riverhead, 2003.

———. *The Letters of Saint Teresa of Jesus*. Trans. E. Allison Peers. 2 vols. London: Sheed, 1962.

———. *Libro de las fundaciones*. Ed. José María Aguado. 2 vols. Madrid: Espasa Calpe, 1950.

———. *Libro de las fundaciones*. Ed. Víctor García de la Concha. Madrid: Espasa Calpe, 1982.

———. *Libro de la vida*. Ed. Dámaso Chicharro. Madrid: Cátedra, 1997.

———. *Libro de la vida*. Ed. Otger Steggink. Madrid: Castalia, 1986.

———. *Libro de la vida*. Ed. Tomás Álvarez. <http://www.clerus.org/clerus/dati/2000-12/29-7/LIBROI.html>.

———. *The Life of Teresa of Jesus*. Trans. E. Allison Peers. 1944. New York: Image, 1991.

———. *The Life of Teresa of Ávila by Herself*. Trans. J. M. Cohen. New York: Penguin, 1988.

———. *Las moradas*. Ed. Tomás Navarro Tomás. Madrid: Espasa Calpe, 1962.

———. *Obras completas*. Ed. Alberto Barrientos et al. Madrid: Espiritualidad, 1984.

———. *Obras completas de Santa Teresa de Jesús*. Ed. Tomás Álvarez. 12th ed. Burgos: Monte Carmelo, 2002.

———. *Obras completas: Edición manual*. 1954. Ed. Efrén de la Madre de Dios and Otger Steggink. Madrid: Católica, 1997.

———. *La vida / Las moradas*. Ed. Antonio Comas. Barcelona: Planeta, 1989.

———. *The Way of Perfection*. Trans. E. Allison Peers. New York: Image, 1964.

Teresa, Teresa. Dir. Rafael Gordon. Rafael Gordon, 2003.

Thérèse. Screenplay by Alain Cavalier. Dir. Daniel Deschamps. Videocassette. Circle, 1986.

Thøfner, Margit. "How to Look Like a (Female) Saint: The Early Iconography of St. Teresa of Ávila." Wyhe, *Female Monasticism* 59–78.

———. "'Let Your Desire Be to See God': Teresian Mysticism and Otto van Veen's *Amoris Divini Emblemata*." *Emblematica* 12 (2002): 83–103.

Thomas Aquinas. *Summa Theologica*. Trans. Fathers of the English Dominican Province. Chicago: Encyclopedia Britannica, 1952. Vols. 19–20 of Great Books of the Western World.

Thompson, Colin P. *St. John of the Cross: Songs in the Night*. Washington: The Catholic U of America P, 2003.

———. *The Strife of Tongues: Fray Luis de León and the Golden Age of Spain*. Cambridge: Cambridge UP, 1988.

Todd, Janet. *Feminist Literary History: A Defense*. Oxford: Polity, 1988.

Tomlinson, Janis A. *From Greco to Goya: Painting in Spain, 1561–1828*. New York: Abrams, 1997.

Trigilio, John, and Kenneth Brighenti. *Catholicism for Dummies*. Hoboken: Wiley, 2003.

The Trotula: *An English Translation of the Medieval Compendium of Women's Medicine*. Ed. and trans. Monica H. Green. Philadelphia: U of Pennsylvania P, 2002.

True, Michael. *Justice Seekers, Peacemakers: Thirty-Two Portraits in Courage*. Mystic: XXIII, 1985.

Tuana, Nancy. *The Less Noble Sex: Scientific, Religious, and Philosophical Conceptions of Woman's Nature*. Bloomington: Indiana UP, 1994.

Turner, Mark. *The Literary Mind*. New York: Oxford UP, 1996.

Valone, Carolyn. "The Pentecost: Image and Experience in Late Sixteenth-Century Rome." *Sixteenth Century Journal* 24 (1993): 801–28.

Vega, Lope de. "¿Qué tengo yo, que mi amistad procuras?" Blecua, *Poesía de la edad* 2: 103.

———. "Tomorrow." Trans. Henry Wadsworth Longfellow. *An Introduction to Spanish Literature*. Ed. George Tyler Northup. 3rd rev. ed. Nicholson B. Adams. Chicago: U of Chicago P, 1960. 271.

Velasco, Sherry. *Demons, Nausea, and Resistance in the Autobiography of Isabel de Jesús (1611–1682)*. Albuquerque: U of New Mexico P, 1996.

———. "Scatological Narratives in the Kitchen of Sor María de la Antigua (1566–1617)." *Letras Femeninas* 21 (1995): 125–37.

Verdejo López, María Dolores, ed. *Proceso Apostólico de Jaén . . . San Juan de la Cruz: Informaciones de 1616*. Jaén: Archivo Histórico Diocesano de Jaén, 1984.

Verhaeghe, Paul. *Does the Woman Exist? From Freud's Hysteria to Lacan's Feminine*. New York: Other, 1999.

Vicente, Marta, and Luis Corteguera, eds. *Women, Texts and Authority in the Early Modern Spanish World*. Aldershot: Ashgate, 2003.

Viller, Marcel, gen. ed. *Dictionnaire de spiritualité ascétique et mystique, doctrine et histoire*. 17 vols. Paris: Beauchesne, 1937–95.

Viola, Bill. *Union*. 2000. Worcester Art Museum, Massachusetts.

Virgillo, Carmelo, Teresa Valdivieso, and Edward H. Friedman, eds. *Aproximaciones al estudio de la literatura hispánica*. 5th ed. Boston: McGraw, 2004.

Vives, Juan Luis. *The Education of a Christian Woman*. Ed. and trans. Charles Fantazzi. Chicago: U of Chicago P, 2000.

Vlieghe, Hans. *Saints, Corpus Rubenianum Ludwig Burchard*. Vol. 2. London: Phaidon, 1972.

Vollendorf, Lisa. Introduction. Vollendorf, *Recovering* 1–27.

———. *The Lives of Women: A New History of Inquisitional Spain*. Nashville: Vanderbilt UP, 2005.

———. "'No Doubt It Will Amaze You': María de Zayas's Early Modern Feminism." Vollendorf, *Recovering* 103–22.

———, ed. *Recovering Spain's Feminist Tradition*. New York: MLA, 2001.

Walsh, John, ed. *Bill Viola: The Passions*. Los Angeles: Getty, 2003.

Wardropper, Bruce, ed. *Spanish Poetry of the Golden Age*. New York: Meredith, 1971.

Weber, Alison. "Between Ecstasy and Exorcism: Religious Negotiation in Sixteenth-Century Spain." *Journal of Medieval and Renaissance Studies* 23 (1993): 221–34.

———. "Could Women Write Mystical Poetry? The Literary Daughters of Juan de la Cruz." *Tras el espejo la musa escribe: Studies on Women's Poetry of the Golden Age*. Ed. Julián Olivares. London: Tamesis, forthcoming.

———. "'Dear Daughter': Reform and Persuasion in St. Teresa's Letters to Her Prioresses." *Form and Persuasion in Women's Informal Letters: 1500–1700*. Ed. Ann Crabb and Jane Couchman. Aldershot: Ashgate, 2006. 241–61.

———. "Demonizing Ecstasy: Alonso de la Fuente and the *alumbrados* of Extremadura." Boenig 147–65.

———. Introduction. María de San José Salazar, *Book* 1–26.

———. "The Partial Feminism of Ana de San Bartolomé." Vollendorf, *Recovering* 69–87.

———. "Saint Teresa, Demonologist." *Culture and Control in Counter-Reformation Spain*. Ed. Anne J. Cruz and Mary Elizabeth Perry. Minneapolis: U of Minnesota P, 1991. 171–95.

———. "Saint Teresa's Problematic Patrons." *Journal of Medieval and Early Modern Studies* 29 (1999): 357–79.

———. "Spiritual Administration: Gender and Discernment in the Carmelite Reform." *Sixteenth Century Journal* 31 (2000): 127–50.

———. "Teresa di Gesù e la direzione spirituale." *L'età moderna*. Ed. Gabriella Zarri. Brescia: Morcelliana, 2008. 289–309. Vol. 3 of *Storia della direzione spirituale*.

———. *Teresa of Ávila and the Rhetoric of Femininity*. Princeton: Princeton UP, 1990.

———. "Teresa's 'Delicious' Diminutives: Pragmatics and Style in *Camino de Perfección*." *Journal of Hispanic Philology* 10 (1986): 211–27.

———. "The Three Lives of the *Vida*: The Uses of Convent Autobiography." Vicente and Corteguera 107–25.

Wethey, Harold E. *The Paintings of Titian*. 3 vols. London: Phaidon, 1969.

Wiesner, Merry E. *Christianity and Sexuality in the Early Modern World: Regulating Desire, Reforming Practice*. New York: Routledge, 2000.

———. *Women and Gender in Early Modern Europe*. Cambridge: Cambridge UP, 1993.

Williams, Rowan. *Teresa of Ávila*. Harrisburg: Morehouse, 1991.

Wilson, Christopher C., ed. *The Heirs of St. Teresa: Defenders and Disseminators of the*

Founding Mother's Legacy. Washington: Inst. of Carmelite Studies, 2006.

———. "Masculinity Restored: The Visual Shaping of St. John of the Cross." *Archive for Reformation History* 98 (2007): 134–66.

———. "Saint Teresa of Ávila's Martyrdom: Images of Her Transverberation in Mexican Colonial Painting." *Anales del Instituto de Investigaciones Estéticas* 74–75 (1999): 211–33.

———. "Taking Teresian Authority to the Front Lines: Ana de San Bartolomé and Ana de Jesús in Art of the Spanish Netherlands." C. Wilson, *Heirs* 72–106.

Wilson, Margaret. *San Juan de la Cruz: Poems.* Critical Guides to Spanish Texts. London: Tamesis, 1975.

Worcester Art Museum. <http://www.worcesterart.org/Collection/European/1922.5.html>.

Wyhe, Cordula van, ed. *Female Monasticism in Early Modern Europe. An Interdisciplinary View.* Aldershot: Ashgate, 2008.

———. "'The Idea Vitæ Teresianæ' (1686): The Teresian Mystic Life and Its Visual Representation in the Southern Netherlands." Wyhe, *Female Monasticism* 173–207.

———. "Piety and Politics in the Royal Convent of Discalced Carmelite Nuns in Brussels 1607–1646." *Revue d'histoire ecclésiastique de Belgique* 100 (2005): 457–87.

———. "Reformulating the Cult of Scherpenheuvel: Marie de'Médicis and the Regina Pacis Statue in Cologne." *The Seventeenth Century* 22.1 (2007): 41–74.

Ynduráin, Domingo. "El pájaro solitario." *Actas del Congreso Internacional Sanjuanista, I: Filología.* Ed. María Jesús Mancho Duque and José Antonio Pascual. Valladolid: Junta de Castilla y León, Consejería de Cultura y Turismo, 1993. 143–61.

Yo, la peor de todas. Dir. María Luisa Bemberg. GEA Cinematográfica, 1990.

Zayas y Sotomayor, María de. "Al que leyere." *Tres novelas amorosas y tres desenganos amorosos.* Ed. Alicia Redondo Goicochea. Madrid: Castalia, 1989. 47–50.

———. *La traición en la amistad.* Ed. Matthew D. Stroud. 29 Aug. 2005 <http://www.trinity.edu/mstroud/comedia/traic1a.html>.

———. *La traición en la amistad / Friendship Betrayed.* Ed. Valerie Hegstrom. Trans. Catherine Larson. Lewisburg: Bucknell UP, 1999.

INDEX

Modern Language Association of America

Approaches to Teaching World Literature

Joseph Gibaldi, series editor

Achebe's Things Fall Apart. Ed. Bernth Lindfors. 1991.
Arthurian Tradition. Ed. Maureen Fries and Jeanie Watson. 1992.
Atwood's The Handmaid's Tale *and Other Works*. Ed. Sharon R. Wilson,
    Thomas B. Friedman, and Shannon Hengen. 1996.
Austen's Emma. Ed. Marcia McClintock Folsom. 2004.
Austen's Pride and Prejudice. Ed. Marcia McClintock Folsom. 1993.
Balzac's Old Goriot. Ed. Michal Peled Ginsburg. 2000.
Baudelaire's Flowers of Evil. Ed. Laurence M. Porter. 2000.
Beckett's Waiting for Godot. Ed. June Schlueter and Enoch Brater. 1991.
Beowulf. Ed. Jess B. Bessinger, Jr., and Robert F. Yeager. 1984.
Blake's Songs of Innocence and of Experience. Ed. Robert F. Gleckner and
    Mark L. Greenberg. 1989.
Boccaccio's Decameron. Ed. James H. McGregor. 2000.
British Women Poets of the Romantic Period. Ed. Stephen C. Behrendt and
    Harriet Kramer Linkin. 1997.
Charlotte Brontë's Jane Eyre. Ed. Diane Long Hoeveler and Beth Lau. 1993.
Emily Brontë's Wuthering Heights. Ed. Sue Lonoff and Terri A. Hasseler. 2006.
Byron's Poetry. Ed. Frederick W. Shilstone. 1991.
Camus's The Plague. Ed. Steven G. Kellman. 1985.
Writings of Bartolomé de Las Casas. Ed. Santa Arias and Eyda M. Merediz. 2008.
Cather's My Ántonia. Ed. Susan J. Rosowski. 1989.
Cervantes' Don Quixote. Ed. Richard Bjornson. 1984.
Chaucer's Canterbury Tales. Ed. Joseph Gibaldi. 1980.
Chaucer's Troilus and Criseyde *and the Shorter Poems*. Ed. Tison Pugh and
    Angela Jane Weisl. 2006.
Chopin's The Awakening. Ed. Bernard Koloski. 1988.
Coleridge's Poetry and Prose. Ed. Richard E. Matlak. 1991.
Collodi's Pinocchio *and Its Adaptations*. Ed. Michael Sherberg. 2006.
Conrad's "Heart of Darkness" and "The Secret Sharer." Ed. Hunt Hawkins and
    Brian W. Shaffer. 2002.
Dante's Divine Comedy. Ed. Carole Slade. 1982.
Defoe's Robinson Crusoe. Ed. Maximillian E. Novak and Carl Fisher. 2005.
DeLillo's White Noise. Ed. Tim Engles and John N. Duvall. 2006.
Dickens's Bleak House. Ed. John O. Jordan and Gordon Bigelow. 2009.
Dickens's David Copperfield. Ed. Richard J. Dunn. 1984.
Dickinson's Poetry. Ed. Robin Riley Fast and Christine Mack Gordon. 1989.
Narrative of the Life of Frederick Douglass. Ed. James C. Hall. 1999.
Duras's Ourika. Ed. Mary Ellen Birkett and Christopher Rivers. 2009.

Early Modern Spanish Drama. Ed. Laura R. Bass and Margaret R. Greer. 2006

Eliot's Middlemarch. Ed. Kathleen Blake. 1990.

Eliot's Poetry and Plays. Ed. Jewel Spears Brooker. 1988.

Shorter Elizabethan Poetry. Ed. Patrick Cheney and Anne Lake Prescott. 2000.

Ellison's Invisible Man. Ed. Susan Resneck Parr and Pancho Savery. 1989.

English Renaissance Drama. Ed. Karen Bamford and Alexander Leggatt. 2002.

Works of Louise Erdrich. Ed. Gregg Sarris, Connie A. Jacobs, and James R. Giles. 2004.

Dramas of Euripides. Ed. Robin Mitchell-Boyask. 2002.

Faulkner's The Sound and the Fury. Ed. Stephen Hahn and Arthur F. Kinney. 1996.

Fitzgerald's The Great Gatsby. Ed. Jackson R. Bryer and Nancy P. VanArsdale. 2009.

Flaubert's Madame Bovary. Ed. Laurence M. Porter and Eugene F. Gray. 1995.

García Márquez's One Hundred Years of Solitude. Ed. María Elena de Valdés and Mario J. Valdés. 1990.

Gilman's "The Yellow Wall-Paper" and Herland. Ed. Denise D. Knight and Cynthia J. Davis. 2003.

Goethe's Faust. Ed. Douglas J. McMillan. 1987.

Gothic Fiction: The British and American Traditions. Ed. Diane Long Hoeveler and Tamar Heller. 2003.

Grass's The Tin Drum. Ed. Monika Shafi. 2008.

Hebrew Bible as Literature in Translation. Ed. Barry N. Olshen and Yael S. Feldman. 1989.

Homer's Iliad *and* Odyssey. Ed. Kostas Myrsiades. 1987.

Ibsen's A Doll House. Ed. Yvonne Shafer. 1985.

Henry James's Daisy Miller *and* The Turn of the Screw. Ed. Kimberly C. Reed and Peter G. Beidler. 2005.

Works of Samuel Johnson. Ed. David R. Anderson and Gwin J. Kolb. 1993.

Joyce's Ulysses. Ed. Kathleen McCormick and Erwin R. Steinberg. 1993.

Works of Sor Juana Inés de la Cruz. Ed. Emilie L. Bergmann and Stacey Schlau. 2007.

Kafka's Short Fiction. Ed. Richard T. Gray. 1995.

Keats's Poetry. Ed. Walter H. Evert and Jack W. Rhodes. 1991.

Kingston's The Woman Warrior. Ed. Shirley Geok-lin Lim. 1991.

Lafayette's The Princess of Clèves. Ed. Faith E. Beasley and Katharine Ann Jensen. 1998.

Works of D. H. Lawrence. Ed. M. Elizabeth Sargent and Garry Watson. 2001.

Lazarillo de Tormes *and the Picaresque Tradition*. Ed. Anne J. Cruz. 2009.

Lessing's The Golden Notebook. Ed. Carey Kaplan and Ellen Cronan Rose. 1989.

Mann's Death in Venice *and Other Short Fiction*. Ed. Jeffrey B. Berlin. 1992.

Marguerite de Navarre's Heptameron. Ed. Colette H. Winn. 2007.

Medieval English Drama. Ed. Richard K. Emmerson. 1990.

Melville's Moby-Dick. Ed. Martin Bickman. 1985.

Metaphysical Poets. Ed. Sidney Gottlieb. 1990.

Miller's Death of a Salesman. Ed. Matthew C. Roudané. 1995.

Milton's Paradise Lost. Ed. Galbraith M. Crump. 1986.

Milton's Shorter Poetry and Prose. Ed. Peter C. Herman. 2007.

Molière's Tartuffe *and Other Plays*. Ed. James F. Gaines and
    Michael S. Koppisch. 1995.

Momaday's The Way to Rainy Mountain. Ed. Kenneth M. Roemer. 1988.

Montaigne's Essays. Ed. Patrick Henry. 1994.

Novels of Toni Morrison. Ed. Nellie Y. McKay and Kathryn Earle. 1997.

Murasaki Shikibu's The Tale of Genji. Ed. Edward Kamens. 1993.

Nabokov's Lolita. Ed. Zoran Kuzmanovich and Galya Diment. 2008.

Poe's Prose and Poetry. Ed. Jeffrey Andrew Weinstock and Tony Magistrale. 2008.

Pope's Poetry. Ed. Wallace Jackson and R. Paul Yoder. 1993.

Proust's Fiction and Criticism. Ed. Elyane Dezon-Jones and
    Inge Crosman Wimmers. 2003.

Puig's Kiss of the Spider Woman. Ed. Daniel Balderston and Francine Masiello. 2007.

Pynchon's The Crying of Lot 49 *and Other Works*. Ed. Thomas H. Schaub. 2008.

Novels of Samuel Richardson. Ed. Lisa Zunshine and Jocelyn Harris. 2006.

Rousseau's Confessions *and* Reveries of the Solitary Walker. Ed. John C. O'Neal
    and Ourida Mostefai. 2003.

Shakespeare's Hamlet. Ed. Bernice W. Kliman. 2001.

Shakespeare's King Lear. Ed. Robert H. Ray. 1986.

Shakespeare's Othello. Ed. Peter Erickson and Maurice Hunt. 2005.

Shakespeare's Romeo and Juliet. Ed. Maurice Hunt. 2000.

Shakespeare's The Tempest *and Other Late Romances*. Ed. Maurice Hunt. 1992.

Shelley's Frankenstein. Ed. Stephen C. Behrendt. 1990.

Shelley's Poetry. Ed. Spencer Hall. 1990.

Sir Gawain and the Green Knight. Ed. Miriam Youngerman Miller and
    Jane Chance. 1986.

Song of Roland. Ed. William W. Kibler and Leslie Zarker Morgan. 2006.

Spenser's Faerie Queene. Ed. David Lee Miller and Alexander Dunlop. 1994.

Stendhal's The Red and the Black. Ed. Dean de la Motte and Stirling Haig. 1999.

Sterne's Tristram Shandy. Ed. Melvyn New. 1989.

Stowe's Uncle Tom's Cabin. Ed. Elizabeth Ammons and Susan Belasco. 2000.

Swift's Gulliver's Travels. Ed. Edward J. Rielly. 1988.

Teresa of Ávila and the Spanish Mystics. Ed. Alison Weber. 2009.

Thoreau's Walden *and Other Works*. Ed. Richard J. Schneider. 1996.

Tolstoy's Anna Karenina. Ed. Liza Knapp and Amy Mandelker. 2003.

Vergil's Aeneid. Ed. William S. Anderson and Lorina N. Quartarone. 2002.

Voltaire's Candide. Ed. Renée Waldinger. 1987.

Whitman's Leaves of Grass. Ed. Donald D. Kummings. 1990.

Wiesel's Night. Ed. Alan Rosen. 2007.

Works of Oscar Wilde. Ed. Philip E. Smith II. 2008.

Woolf's To the Lighthouse. Ed. Beth Rigel Daugherty and Mary Beth Pringle. 2001.

Wordsworth's Poetry. Ed. Spencer Hall, with Jonathan Ramsey. 1986.

Wright's Native Son. Ed. James A. Miller. 1997.